THE "VANITY OF THE PHILOSOPHER"

THE "VANITY OF THE PHILOSOPHER"
From Equality to Hierarchy in Postclassical Economics

Sandra J. Peart & David M. Levy

University of Michigan Press   Ann Arbor

2010   2009   2008   2007   5   4   3   2

A CIP catalog record for this book is available from the British Library.

Library of Congress Cataloging-in-Publication Data

Peart, Sandra.
The "vanity of the philosopher" : from equality to hierarchy in
postclassical economics / Sandra J. Peart, David M. Levy.
p.   cm.
Includes bibliographical references and index.
ISBN 0-472-11496-4 (cloth : alk. paper)
1. Economics—History—19th century.   2. Classical school of
economics.   3. Equality—Economic aspects.   4. Eugenics—Economic
aspects.   I. Levy, David M., 1944–   II. Title.
HB85.P43   2005
330.15'3—dc22   2004030730

ISBN 978-0-472-11496-2

CONTENTS

ACKNOWLEDGMENTS

This book began with a napkin—one of the coauthors would insist it was a serviette—and a couple of beers. The occasion was the *History of Political Economy* conference on measurement at Duke University in the spring of 2000. The word *homogeneity* was written on the napkin. *Eugenics* appeared soon after. A paper, which eventually became chapter 4 of this book, was soon sketched on the napkin.

Between the sketch of the homogeneity paper and the book, we have received much support. Perhaps most important, we have had many occasions to try out the research along the way. Beginning in the summer of 2000, the Earhart Foundation has generously supported the Summer Institute for the Preservation of the Study of the History of Economics. We like to assure ourselves that the Summer Institute is a place where people can say stupid things at zero marginal cost. What we mean by that is that new, and less than fully worked out, ideas can be shared and tested against good intellects and command of the texts at the Summer Institute. Most of the chapters in the book, in various states of finishedness, have been presented at the past five Summer Institutes, and we have benefited enormously from wonderful discussions and the suggestions of our colleagues there. Pete Boettke, Jim Buchanan, Bridget Butkevich, Tyler Cowen, Eric Crampton, Ross Emmett, Andrew Farrant, Sam Fleischaker, Samuel Hollander, Daniel Houser, Ali Khan, Robert Leonard, Tim Leonard, Kevin McCabe, Deirdre McCloskey, Edward McPhail, Phil Mirowski, David Mitch, Leonides Montes, Angelina Nikitenko, Neil Niman,

Maria Pia Paganelli, Warren Samuels, Eric Schliesser, Scott Sperling, Nicola Tynan, Anthony Waterman, and Marty Zelder all helped us clarify our thinking on these occasions.

We have also benefited greatly as we worked out new arguments in our articles for www.econlib.org. Much of the material in the "Secret History of Dismal Science" and in the articles that followed that series is in this book. The column has been a wonderful source of inspiration as we tried out many of the illustrations. We thank Liberty Fund for their support, Andy Ruttan for taking us on in the first place, and Andy, Lauren Landsburg, and Russ Roberts for help with subsequent columns.

Early on, the audience for eugenics-related papers was small. David Colander, of Middlebury College, gave us a much-needed venue as he organized the Christian A. Johnson Economics Conference "Race, Liberalism, and Economics" in April 2001. Coedited by David Colander, Falguni Sheth, and Robert Prasch, the conference proceedings, including an article that draws on our chapter 4, were published in April 2004, by the University of Michigan Press. At the conference, we received helpful comments from David Colander, Marcellus Andrews, Deirdre McCloskey, Falguni Sheth, and Susan Zlotnick.

Another early opportunity for discussion occurred when Wendy Motooka organized a symposium at Oberlin College in spring 2001, attended by members of the economics, history, English, and religion departments. We thank participants in that symposium, including Wendy Motooka and Hirschel Kasper. That presentation eventually became our chapter 3. We have been invited to summarize the transformational view of human nature for the Japanese Journal of the *History of Economic Thought*.

Larry Moss also deserves our thanks. From the outset, he encouraged us to pursue the work on eugenics, and he urged us to organize a session on eugenics at the History of Economics Society (2002), the Eastern Economics Association (2003), and the Allied Social Sciences Association (2004). The *American Journal of Economics and Sociology* will publish a resulting bundle of papers, including our chapter 10, along with comments by Malcolm Rutherford and Mark Smith.

We have benefited from conference presentations at the History of

Economics Society annual meetings in 2000, 2001, 2002, 2003, and 2004; the Allied Social Sciences Association annual meetings in 2001, 2002, and 2003; the Eastern Economics Association annual meetings in 2001, 2002, 2003, and 2004; the 2002 European Conference on the History of Economics annual meeting; the Society for the Study of Scientific Religion meeting in 2002; the Southern Economics Association annual meeting in 2001; and the Joint Statistical Meeting annual conference in 2002. Seminar presentations at the Public Choice Seminar at George Mason University and the York University–University of Toronto History of Economic Thought Workshop, the College of William and Mary, and Duke University were all wonderfully productive. On those occasions, the comments of David Banks, Gib Bassett, Gary Becker, James Buchanan, Charles Coleman, Roger Congleton, Annie Cot, Tyler Cowen, Robert Dimand, Evelyn Forget, Ira Gang, Marco Guido, Daniel Hammond, Arye Hillman, Kevin Hoover, Dan Houser, Allan Hynes, Larry Iannaccone, Roger Koenker, Robert Leonard, Tim Leonard, Deirdre McCloskey, Steve Medema, Mary Morgan, Joseph Persky, Robin Rowley, Malcolm Rutherford, Stephen Stigler, and Bart Wilson are gratefully acknowledged. Improved versions of these presentations resulted in publications in the *Journal of the History of Economic Thought* (chapter 4), *European Journal of Political Economy* (chapter 5), *European Journal of the History of Economic Thought* (chapter 7), *History of Political Economy* (chapter 8), and the *Journal of Economic Methodology* (chapter 11). Editors Kevin Hoover and Steve Medema deserve our thanks for their good advice as we revised our contributions.

We have also benefited along the way from a slew of proofreaders and quotation checkers: Andrew Farrant, Tim Fijalkovich, Nadine Jeserick, Angelina Nikitenko, Maria Paganelli, Beverley Peart, Steve Richards, and Tri Thai. Jo Ann Burgess read all carefully at the end and did a wonderful job on the index. We are grateful to her.

Thanks are due to Ken White for the customized beta release of *Shazam* 8 with which the first round of simulations were computed. We thank the University of Liverpool for permission to quote from its Fraser's Collection and reproduce the images by John Wallace.

Ellen McCarthy's continual encouragement from the time the book would almost fit on a napkin (serviette) is acknowledged with great thanks. We always knew that our book had a home. We have been fortunate to work with Marcia LaBrenz, Raphael Allen, and Pete Sickman-Garner at the Press.

Writing a book requires not only intellectual resources but also financial support. We could have done little with the wealth of intellectual help provided by our friends without some financial support, as well. David Levy is grateful to the Mercatus Center of George Mason University for providing him with summer support. The Dean of the College of Arts and Sciences and the Economics Department helped finance a trip to the University of Liverpool to talk about the *Cope's* images. Sandra Peart is grateful to Baldwin-Wallace College and the Gund Foundation for summer support.

Finally, a book takes time. For giving her the time to write, Sandra Peart thanks Craig, Nathan, and Matthew. David Levy thanks Nicholas for all the national parks given up.

PREFACE

This book attempts to explicate the transition from classical to postclassical economics.[1] Ours is a story that begins with the hegemony of egalitarian classical thinking and continues with attack, defense, and defeat. Between 1850 and 1890, classical economics came under fire from many directions: the literary community; the anthropological and biological sciences that produced eugenics and the law of natural selection; and within the social science community itself. By the end of the century, the transition to postclassical thinking was complete. Difference and hierarchy now figured prominently in economics.

We shall argue that the controversy surrounding classical economics occurred largely over the presumption of equal competence, or homogeneity. On the side of human homogeneity, we locate the great classical economists, who presumed that economic agents are all equipped with a capacity for language and trade, and that observed outcomes are explained by incentives, luck, and history.[2] In opposition,

---

1. For reasons that will become clear as we proceed, we prefer the broader term *postclassical* to the more familiar *neoclassical* terminology because we find the transition entailing the rise of hierarchical thinking, the loss of sympathy in economic analysis, and the endorsement of eugenical remaking infects a broad set of economists, not all of whom would be considered neoclassical.

2. The intellectual composition of classical economics is complex, and it is not our intention to minimize substantive differences among Adam Smith, Thomas Robert Malthus, David Ricardo, Robert Torrens, Harriet Martineau, Nassau William Senior, John Stuart Mill, or less well-known but nonetheless important contributors. Some of these will become apparent in what follows (see also Peart and Levy 2003). Yet, differences notwithstanding, by 1830 the analytics of classical growth, distribution, and value theories were well-developed, reflecting a preoccupation with land scarcity and diminishing returns, and formulated with the problem of population growth in mind. We choose to focus on what unites the economists of the time to help clarify

we find many "progressives,"[3] scientists in anthropology and biology, as well as social scientists late in the century, whose explanation of observed heterogeneity was race or hierarchy.

At midcentury, arguments about superiority and inferiority played out in terms of the Irish and the former slaves in Jamaica (Curtis 1997). In fact, notions of race and hierarchy are rather pliable in our period. Women and the "labouring classes" were frequently included in discussions of inherent incompetence. To name but a few additions considered later, Jews, Italians, and East Europeans all received special treatment as well. Most startling, perhaps, is the assertion that "race" is a choice. By choosing to leave behind the direction of one's betters, a person was said to turn into a lesser being. We will see many images from the time that show how choice was supposed to transform people. The collision with classical economics occurred then, almost by necessity, because for these economists such purported transformations made no sense.[4]

We have been told more than once that our outrage at the mid- to late-nineteenth-century notions of race and hierarchy we consider here is misplaced. Everyone, we have been told, "was a racist then." It will soon be clear that we reject this counterargument. We do so because we find it factually incorrect and analytically flawed. In point of fact, this book demonstrates that there was significant (though unsuccessful) resistance to those notions of hierarchy and race. From Smith to Mill, classical economists rejected racial explanations of observed behavior and were criticized for doing so. More than this, we find the counterargument embodies a form of not-so-subtle hierarchical thinking: the thought that we today are superior to those of the past; that we who are nonracist must excuse the racist writers of the past, because they simply reflect their times.

The classical economists' explanation for observed heterogeneity

---

what separated them from their critics. Therefore, the fact that Mill and Senior make almost interchangeable statements on racial differences (note 5) is of interest to us here, but we set aside their different views on the desirability of socialism.

3. Thomas Carlyle, John Ruskin, and Charles Dickens will figure prominently.

4. We will, however, argue that J. S. Mill allowed for the possibility of self-directed improvement.

was to appeal to the incentives associated with different institutions. So, for instance, classical economists such as John Stuart Mill argued that the Irish problem was largely a matter of institutions rather than one of inherent indolence.[5] Mill was strenuously opposed by those, such as W. R. Greg, who claimed the Irishman was "idiosyncratic" and would never be the hardworking Scot. The policy conclusion followed: special measures were required to look after the Irishman, whose inherent difference meant he lacked the capacity to rule himself. Mill struggled with the problem of transition from one set of institutions to another, how new habits are formed as institutions change. Economists who have become accustomed to institution-free analysis fail to appreciate how much of classical economics is designed to deal precisely with the problem of self-motivated human development in the context of institutional change.

In the period we study, economic analysis also supposed, as Mill put it in his essay "On the Definition of Political Economy; and on the Method of Investigation Proper to It" ([1836] 1967; hereafter, *Essays*), that it treats "man's nature as modified by the social state" (321). The classical tradition retained a key role for nonmaterial concerns, what Adam Smith had called "sympathy" and the desire for the approbation of other humans. Once human hierarchy was recognized, people were seen as unequally deserving of sympathy and approbation: those among us who were hardworking and frugal deserved more sympathy (and resources) than those among us who were inherently imprudent. So, as the attack on human homogeneity occurred, a related attack on (undirected) social sentiments began. If individuals extended sympathy (and charity) to the imprudent among us, then such social sentiments were not to be trusted. Biologists who wished to perfect the race argued that sympathy for the "feeble" and the "unfit" served to dilute what we might call the gene pool, and so it should be suppressed. As the transition to postclassical economics played out late in the century, sympathy disap-

---

5. Senior also attributed outcomes to institutions rather than inherent differences: "Almost all the differences between the different races of men, differences so great that we sometimes nearly forget that they all belong to the same species, may be traced to the degrees in which they enjoy the blessings of good government" ([1836] 1938, 76).

peared from economics never to return substantially. Material concerns became singularly important in postclassical analysis.[6]

For various reasons—not the least of which is the history that follows—we hold that the classical economists got it right: an analytical system in which everyone counts equally and is presumed equally capable of making decisions is the only system that seems morally defensible to us.[7] And, not surprisingly, we find analytical systems that presume hierarchy are indefensible. This book explains why.

First, we find the history compelling, and awful. In all the instances in which a group has been treated as "different," difference has turned into hierarchy, and hierarchy has sometimes led to terrible analytical and policy consequences.[8] We also find that systems in which hierarchy is invoked are extraordinarily pliable. The "inferior" becomes any group who is presently out of favor with the analyst.

Most compelling for us, the analysis that presumes difference is terribly tempting to analysts and policymakers. Once difference creeps into the analysis, the temptation is to presume that difference implies inferiority. It also seems often to imply that the writer, whether social commentator or scientist, somehow "knows better." And here we find that this is not simply a presumption that the analyst has better information. Instead, it extends to a presumption of inherent superiority. For whatever reason, the analyst presumes the subjects' choices aren't to be trusted but instead require looking after. Somehow, the analyst is privy to knowledge about what decisions "should" be made and what preferences individuals "should" have, if they only knew better. As a

---

6. It is widely accepted that the boundary of economic science was narrowed throughout the nineteenth century (Winch 1972; Peart 2001b). What has gone unrecognized is that this narrowing also entailed the removal of sympathy and rise in materialism late in the century. The following chapters explain why we find this removal to be an unfortunate development.

7. This is not to say that we agree in all respects with all classical economists, or that we disagree always with all their opponents. We find analysis that presumes homogeneity is compelling, and we object to treatments entailing hierarchy. And we find that, on balance, the classical economists fall on the side of homogeneity, while (again, on balance) their critics fall on the side of hierarchy.

8. Much of the material in the chapters that follow has in fact been difficult for us to read. We reproduce it, and examine the arguments made thereby, in order to set the record straight, to learn from the past, and to make our case in favor of analysis that presumes homogeneous competence.

society and as a community of academics, it is taken for granted that the scientist is somehow superior to—better motivated or more able than—the individuals under investigation, who are not trusted to make reasonable choices. We find such a presumption of superiority on the part of the analyst is the last, unrecognized and resisted, form of hierarchy in social science. It is, we shall argue, simply the "vanity of the philosopher."

Of course, a look around us at any moment suggests that people are, in fact, different. Inherent physical differences, for instance, abound. (One coauthor is under 5 feet 2 inches, the other is about 6 feet, and relative price changes are not likely to reduce this difference.) So, our argument has much in common with Lionel Robbins's, who in 1938 remembered the debates in economics over the differential capacity for happiness.

> . . . I have always felt that, as a first approximation in handling questions relating to the lives and actions of large masses of people, the approach which counts each man as one, and, on that assumption, asks which way lies the greatest happiness, is less likely to lead one astray than any of the absolute systems. I do not believe, and I never have believed, that in fact men are necessarily equal or should always be judged as such. But I do believe that, in most cases, political calculations which do not treat them *as if* they were equal are morally revolting. (1938, 635)

The point of what follows is that a presumption of *group* difference—when the definition of the group is pliable, and the analyst is presumed to be in the superior group—is dangerously tempting.

This book therefore attempts to show the consequences of hierarchy in social science. We show how the "vanity of the philosopher" has led to recommendations that range from the more benign but, in our view, still objectionable "looking-after," to paternalism, to overriding preferences, and, in the extreme, to eliminating purportedly bad preferences (and even those people who possess such preferences, and thus their future children). Our conclusion is that, at least as a first approximation, an analytical system that abstracts from difference and presumes equal competence (though unequal circumstances) is morally compelling. The difference between that and presuming unequal circumstances with unequal inherent abilities is, of course, crucial. If circumstances and abilities both differ, an equalizing transfer of resources (education and income) will not result in equality, and we are never warranted in fully trusting the inferior group to make the correct choices. If circumstances differ but abilities are the same, the same equalizing transfer of resources will lead to full equality of outcomes, and we can trust individuals to put the transfers to good uses. The test for egalitarianism in what follows, then, is whether the analyst sufficiently trusts the subject to make unimpeded economic and political choices, or instead insists on somehow coercing specific choices and overriding preferences.

FIGURES

TABLES

Part I

EQUALITY VERSUS HIERARCHY

I

ANALYTICAL EGALITARIANISM AND ITS OPPOSITION

> The difference of natural talents in different men is, in reality, much less than we are aware of; and the very different genius which appears to distinguish men of different professions, when grown up to maturity, is not upon many occasions so much the cause, as the effect of the division of labour. The difference between the most dissimilar characters, between a philosopher and a common street porter, for example, seems to arise not so much from nature, as from habit, custom, and education. When they came into the world, and for the first six or eight years of their existence, they were perhaps, very much alike, and neither their parents nor playfellows could perceive any remarkable difference. About that age, or soon after, they come to be employed in very different occupations. The difference of talents comes then to be taken notice of, and widens by degrees, till at last the vanity of the philosopher is willing to acknowledge scarce any resemblance.
> —Adam Smith, *Wealth of Nations*

INTRODUCTION

That political economy in the classical tradition *rightly* presupposed human homogeneity and consequently rejected hierarchical presuppositions of any sort is an underlying theme of this work. Starting with Adam Smith, classical economics is characterized by an analytical egalitarianism that presumes humans are the same in their capacity for language and trade; observed differences are then explained by incentives, luck, and history, and it is the "vanity of the philosopher" incorrectly to conclude that ordinary people are somehow different from the expert (Smith, *Wealth of Nations*, I.2.§4).

The questions at issue between analytical egalitarians and their critics are (1) whether everyone's preferences count equally and (2) whether everyone is equally capable of making economic decisions.[1] In Smith's account, all people, philosophers and subjects alike, are motivated by fame and fortune, and we are all equally capable of making decisions. We call this doctrine, which makes no distinction between the street porter and the philosopher, *analytical egalitarianism*. The oppositional view holds that some among us are different from others. Since difference implies superiority in the period we study, we call this doctrine *analytical hierarchicalism*. Our argument in what follows is that economics moved from a doctrine of analytical egalitarianism in the classical period to one of analytical hierarchy in the postclassical period.[2]

The notion of analytical hierarchy was expressed forcefully in economics by F. Y. Edgeworth, who argued that, post-Darwin, it was inappropriate to have a social norm in which everyone counted as one. Instead, Edgeworth held that economists needed to take evolutionary fitness—which mapped to the capacity for pleasure—into account. Since some preferences were "better" than others, these were to count more in the calculus of social happiness.

We argue in what follows that the "science" of eugenics is a consequence of analytical hierarchicalism. In eugenic science, "experts" presupposed its subjects to be inferior and proposed to remake the human herd more to the experts' liking, to obtain racial perfection or for the "general good," as Charles Darwin put it. It is no coincidence

---

1. The notion of "expert" is deliberately left broad here. The key feature of those we refer to as experts is that the expert is someone who makes recommendations about how others might achieve human happiness. Depending on the specific context involved in what follows, experts may be social commentators, biologists, or political economists. We provide a more restrictive, formal definition of an expert in chapter 11, so that we can distinguish between an expert's direction and the advice that flows from experience by way of proverbial wisdom. In Adam Smith's account, philosophy is a *social* enterprise that begins with universal experience. His proverbial wisdom confirms the advice of financial theorists not to "put all their eggs in one basket." When expert and proverb point in different directions, we need to be precise (chap. 11, this vol.).

2. As noted in the preface, we prefer the broader term *postclassical* to the more familiar *neoclassical*. On the origin of the term *neoclassical*, see Colander 2001, 154ff, and on the transition to early neoclassicism—the "Marginal Revolution"—see the collection in *History of Political Economy* (1972). We find that the transition entailing the rise of hierarchical thinking, the loss of sympathy, and the endorsement of eugenical remaking infects a broad set of economists, not all of whom would be considered neoclassical. In chapter 4 we argue that traditions within and outside of neoclassical economics—the Austrian school scattered by the coming of the Hitler era, as well as the London and Chicago schools—revived the presupposition of equal competence.

that in the period when eugenics acquired both its name and the analytical machinery purporting to locate "the unfit," its first and persistent target was classical economics and the early utilitarian presumption that all should count equally in the calculus of social good. The early eugenicists (W. R. Greg and Francis Galton) knew they were contending with the egalitarian doctrine of classical economics. The key point of contention was whether individuals could be trusted to regulate their numbers sufficiently, or whether individual preferences needed to be overridden in such decisions. One important instance of this contention occurred in the public debate concerning unregulated access to birth control. The contemporary report on this debate viewed the matter as a dispute between J. S. Mill's focus on human happiness, on the one hand, and Charles Darwin's pursuit of racial perfection, on the other (*Times* 20 June 1877, 11; chap. 10, this vol.).

Plato's *Republic* asked the eugenic question for the first time: why do we breed cattle but not people? Again it is no coincidence that when Galton's eugenic work was first reviewed, it was hailed as the first step beyond Plato (chap. 6, this vol.). The question supposes that *we*—the experts—are different from *them*—the human cattle, the subjects. In classical economics, by contrast, there is no Other because the philosopher, as Smith put it, is part of the analysis. The distinction (or lack thereof) is foundational and has enormous consequences: the classical view implies that, as a group, the subjects of a theory have the same moral standing and innate abilities as the experts who propose the theories. The hierarchical view places the subjects and experts on different moral and intellectual grounds.

For classical economists, the subject and the expert share moral standing, ability, and motivational structure. Following in the tradition of analytical egalitarianism, J. S. Mill developed his famous stance on homogeneity in his 1836 essay "On the Definition of Political Economy." Here, and in his *Principles of Political Economy* and *Logic*, Mill maintained that nonsystematical differences might be abstracted out when we use the device of "Abstract Economic Man."[3] For the politi-

---

3. We should note at the outset that, for Mill, principles of economics and morality apply equally well to men and women ([1869] 1970; chaps. 9, 11, this vol.) so that "Abstract Economic

cal economist, the common behavioral assumptions that matter are the hypotheses of competence as well as nonsatiation in the context of a social state.[4]

> [Political economy] does not treat of the whole of man's nature as modified by the social state, nor of the whole conduct of man in society. It is concerned with him solely as a being who desires to possess wealth, and who is capable of judging of the comparative efficacy of means for obtaining that end. . . . It makes entire abstraction of every other human passion or motive; except those which may be regarded as perpetually antagonizing principles to the desire of wealth, namely, aversion to labour, and desire of the present enjoyment of costly indulgences. (Mill, *Essays*, 321)

The wealth maximization axiom is selected because it is "the main and acknowledged end" in "certain departments of human affairs" (323).[5] Wealth maximizing and labor avoidance are *common* attributes of all humanity: those for whom institutions such as slavery or marriage prevent competent, self-directed decision making might nonetheless develop this competence if the barriers to doing so were removed.

Man" is a misnomer. We retain the phrase as it is the one most readily recognized by economists and noneconomists alike. The ungendering of Mill's language over his life is studied by J. M. Robson in the collation of editions of *Logic* (Mill [1843] 1973, *Logic*, xcii–xciii): "The fourth type of variant, that which is verbal, or gives semantic clarity, or reflects changing word usage, is the most common, and is not without importance, especially in cumulative effect. A few, of varying kinds, may be cited in illustration. A frequent change . . . is of 'men' to 'people' or 'mankind' (and a 'man' or 'he' to a 'person') in 1851, a change also found in the third edition of the *Principles* in the next year. [Note to text] One should remember, in this context, Mill's proposed amendment to the Second Reform Bill in 1867, to replace 'man' with 'person.'" See Peart 2005 for the visual representation of Mill in *Punch* that followed upon this occasion.

We have noted (Levy and Peart 2004) that Smith makes an important distinction between "humanity" and "generosity" on the basis of gender that in turn may express differences in circumstances. On this issue see Schliesser 2003.

4. We add the qualifying phrase on the social state to remind the reader that self-interested behavior, for the classical economists, entailed sympathy for others that, ideally, meant others would count in self-interested calculations, equally with the self (chap. 7, this vol.). In addition, in a social setting an individual might be able to obtain advice from others (chap. 11, this vol.).

5. Using this "approximation" (323), the political economist "shows mankind accumulating wealth, and employing that wealth in the production of other wealth; sanctioning by mutual agreement the institution of property; establishing laws to prevent individuals from encroaching upon the property of others by force or fraud; adopting various contrivances for increasing the productiveness of their labour; settling the division of the produce by agreement, under the influence of competition (competition itself being governed by certain laws, which laws are therefore the ultimate regulators of the division of the produce); and employing certain expedients (as money, credit, &c.) to facilitate the distribution" (Mill [1836] 1967, *Essays*, 322).

We pause to note that Mill's "hypothesis" of economic man does not imply that people are motivated *only* by material interests. Just as people are willing to trade material income for leisure so, too, if people are willing to trade material income for praise or praiseworthiness (or to avoid blame), then the economic calculus must take this desire for approbation into account. Smith explained the point in detail in his *Moral Sentiments* and *Wealth of Nations*. Individuals might willingly give up material income in return for the improved reciprocal standing of another group (such as slaves or women). In Smith's account, this depends upon the ability to imagine yourself in someone else's position. For Mill, human development is characterized by improved sympathetic judgments which provide the source of moral obligation. So understood, Mill's greatest-happiness utilitarianism is equivalent to the Golden Rule of Christianity (chaps. 7, 8, this vol.). We shall return later to the notion of sympathy and the consequences of its removal from economics on many occasions.

The foundational assumption that the street porter and the philosopher are essentially the same prompts us to ask whether we all have the same motivations when it comes to uncovering scientific "truth." In particular, are scholars motivated by the same self-interested desires for fame and fortune as the rest of the population? Since Smith supposes the philosopher is in all respects the same as the street porter, his answer must be yes. Since his time, however, many in the academy have come to presume that scholars are more public-spirited than the rest of the population; scholars are said to seek only (or at least mainly) the truth. We allow that prejudice infects the academy in the area of personal relationships, acknowledging, for instance, that a scholar might oppose hiring a talented colleague because of racial or religious prejudice. Yet we often cling to the belief that the same scholar would be unbiased in the evaluation of *ideas* or *intellectual output*—that he or she would never ignore or disparage ideas for racial or religious reasons. Such a presumption may be the final and most persistent form of hierarchical thinking. In chapters 5 and 6, we shall examine a case in which the presumption that experts seek only the truth was terribly wrong.

In the period we study, those who opposed the classical economists' presumption of homogeneity focused on two purported heterogeneities between the expert and his subject. First, the expert is presumed to be untainted by considerations of self-interest, while his subject is motivated by self-interest. Second, perhaps because of superior self-control or some other inherent difference, the expert is supposed to be "superior" to or smarter than the subject he studies. And it is important to note that this intellectual superiority is not merely a matter of better information: the expert with whom we are concerned is someone who simply doesn't trust all subjects, who holds that some will always be hopelessly prone to making persistent mistakes no matter how much we educate, train, and inculcate. F. Y. Edgeworth clearly captured the difference between the classical egalitarian framework in J. S. Mill and post-Darwinian ideas that implied that education and other institutional changes would fail to produce the desired social good. In 1881, he wrote that "the authority of Mill, conveying an impression of what other Benthamites have taught openly, that all men, if not equal, are at least *equipotential,* in virtue of equal educatability" would "probably result in the ruin of the race" because it failed to take into account "*difference of quality*" among men (132).[6] Ours is largely a story about how the category "inferior subjects" changes over time: from the Irish, to blacks, to Jews, and so on.

It is precisely this supposition of superiority that Smith opposed, as the "vanity of the philosopher": such vanity implies the subject is in need of guidance from the expert.[7] It also implies that the expert will be predisposed to disapprove of (and even disallow) the subject making unfettered choices in a marketplace or in the direction of her affections in the household and elsewhere. As long as the expert maintains that he possesses insight into the sorts of preferences people "should" possess—if they only knew better—he must also accept, and may perhaps even demand, responsibility for directing those preferences until the

---

6. Interestingly, in the light of our claims concerning prejudice, Edgeworth by 1881 can refer to the "equal educatability" argument in Mill as "pre-Darwinian prejudice" (1881, 132).

7. In chapter 11 we examine Smith on how proverbs might provide such guidance, and we develop a technical account of how ordinary people might obtain much of the advice they require from the experience of others.

subjects gain the sort of sophistication that he enjoys. The argument is as old as Plato's doctrine that the world will not be set right until the experts take charge. We shall argue that the "science" of eugenics operationalizes this doctrine. By contrast, the classical economists' egalitarian notion of homogeneity—motivational and otherwise—and choices unfettered by the direction of one's "betters" go hand in hand.

If we bring the expert and the subject of the theory, the ordinary person, to the same plane of existence in terms of motivation, we also need to consider *how* the ordinary person makes decisions. The attack on classical economics that we study here is a long-neglected example of the self-conscious expert's attack on the capacity of ordinary people to make decisions.

WHAT DOES EQUALITY LOOK LIKE?

It is straightforward to visualize difference—especially, perhaps, inferiority—among people: we all know of images of a beastlike being that are supposed to represent lower orders of humans. Since beasts participate in only a limited way in human rationality, images of human bestiality are powerful assertions of human difference. Images of bestiality can then be juxtaposed with choice to convey the claim of differential competence (see chaps. 2, 3, this vol.). How might we represent the economists' assumption of equal competence visually? How can the economists' egalitarian postulate of abstract economic man be represented in caricature? These questions initially startled us when they were put to us some time ago as we presented our work on images of hierarchy and transformation (the subject of chap. 3, this vol.).[8] The immediate response of supply and demand curves seemed only partly right, and also somewhat less interesting than some of the visual renderings of hierarchy, racial or otherwise, that we shall see in the chapters that follow.

Visualizing equality is difficult. But late in the nineteenth century,

---

8. We thank Dan Hammond for these questions that have long been on our minds. The response of supply and demand curves was both our own and also the response of members of the audience.

the engineer and political economist Fleeming Jenkin took great pains
to confront the critics of economics visually (1887, 2:150). He drew a
picture of exchange in which the participants are faceless: there is no
difference in competence to be inferred from physiognomical differences (fig. 1.1). Instead, in this delicate, dancelike drawing, the order is
circular, each actor in the drama of markets has his or her own goals,
and these private goals are revealed in the market order, the sponta-
neous order. Everyone dances and no one leads: Jenkin's drawing represents the economists' analytical tool of abstract economic man in the
context of exchange characterized by reciprocity and sympathy.
Because exchange is voluntary, it is mutually beneficial. There is no
hierarchy because no one is in charge and individuals are self-directed.

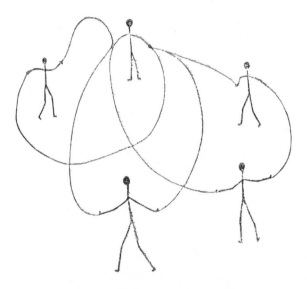

Fig. 1.1.   Fleeming Jenkin, "Exchange Diagram" (1887)

But the notions of equal competence, Abstract Economic Man, and
self-directed trade have always been contested. Early in our period, the
attack on homogeneity occurs in terms of racial difference and presupposes unequal economic and political competence. The attack on

unregulated sympathy concerned a woman's self-directed expenditure of household resources. As theories of racial heterogeneity were much discussed in British anthropological circles in the mid–nineteenth century, attacks on analytical egalitarianism also entered into economics itself and championed the anthropologists' claim that institutional reform would be a colossal failure because of inherent racial differences in the capacity to optimize. Without a "better" to specify what preferences the subject "should" have, reform would fail.

The failure is said to go beyond a simple disconnect between ends and means, something economists have always studied. If it were simply a matter of mistakes, competent people would learn and make corrections better to obtain their ends. But the failure at issue here is one of transformation. Left to their own devices, humans purportedly deteriorate, become lesser beings.

HOW THE DEBATES PLAY OUT

Those who held out for differences in competence relied on what we call *transformation theories*, the claim that incompetent economic man required remaking, directions for improvement, along with the claim that, left alone to make his own economic choices, economic man would *devolve* into something less-than-competent, so that remaking in line with the expert's recommendations was urgently required. Until such a transformation occurred, any appeal to changing conditions, incentives, or institutions was said to be infeasible. And to the extent that such groups as the Irish, women, or former slaves dared to place their own preferences on the same plane as those of the experts and to step outside the established institutional hierarchy, they were said to be incapable of economic or political self-rule. We examine this transformation argument in its literary and visual forms in chapter 3.

At the start of our period, economists vehemently opposed the worldview of Plato and Thomas Carlyle entailing hierarchy and transformation by one's betters, and presupposed homogeneity instead. By the early twentieth century, many (though not all) economists embraced a view of economic actors entailing (1) differential compe-

tence linked to race, gender, religion, or ethnicity; (2) calls for paternalistic intervention to look after systematically poor optimizers whose
preferences could not be trusted; and (3) eugenical remaking. In chapter 4, we examine the significance of the attacks on homogeneity in
anthropological circles and trace the influence of anthropologists such
as James Hunt on the cofounders of eugenics, Galton and Greg.
Eugenic thinking explicitly attacked the classical postulate of homogeneity that characterized the Malthusian recommendation of delayed
marriage. Early eugenicists argued, by contrast, that delay of marriage
would be dysgenic because the "foresightful" "improving element"
will be outbred by the "more reckless" lower orders (Greg 1875, 129). As
experiments in eugenics finally confronted the horror of the Holocaust, the classical tradition of equal competence (homogeneity) was
revived, at London, Chicago, and scattered throughout the Austrian
school. Not surprisingly, given the hierarchical characterization
focused on intertemporal decision making, time preference was central in the Chicago revival (Knight 1931; Stigler and Becker 1977). And
the antihierarchy argument was made even more emphatically, perhaps, by another admirer of classical economics, Ludwig von Mises
(1949). As the Chicago school revived the classical doctrine of homogeneity, it also (and by no coincidence) revived the presumption of
competence even in political activity.

The midcentury revival of the postulate of human homogeneity differed in one key respect from classical thinking, and this difference is a
major theme in what follows. In the classical system, the benefits associated with exchange—political or economic—accrue not only in
monetary terms, but also in terms of a second, incommensurate good,
"approbation," which is linked to sympathy.[9] But while equal competence and the presumption in favor of markets were revived at midcentury, the classical preoccupation with sympathy and the presumption
of reciprocity were not. We have already alluded to one result of the
removal of sympathy. Since the eugenics movement arose as a negative

---

9. Thus, we take issue with a reductionist representation of classical utilitarianism, such as
that found in Schumpeter (1954) regarding Mill. To assert that for Mill pleasure can be reduced
to material well-being is to read Mill through the postclassical commonplace.

result of A. R. Wallace's argument—early eugenicists such as Greg argued that "natural selection" ought to trump sympathy (Greg 1868, "Failure")—we have insight into the transition from classical to post-classical economics (chap. 4, this vol.). In the triumph of eugenics that accompanied the transition we see the "unfit" becoming "parasites," removed from sympathy. The enterprise of remaking economic man became a project of physical remaking, one in which, significantly, the expert was placed on a different plane from (that is, superior to) the subject.

This separation of expert and subject leads us also to examine the form of argumentation that governed these debates. How is it that visual and literary representations, apparently, so often fall on the side of transformation theories,[10] while the more analytical arguments are, in the main, nontransformational? This is the subject of chapter 11 where we examine the informational properties of proverbs or "stories," the anecdotes of ordinary people. There we find that centered stories, anecdotes, have desirable properties when there is reason to suspect that the theory (or the theorist) is systematically incorrect. Since a major characteristic of hierarchical theory is that the theorist is in some significant sense different from (better than) the subject, and is tempted by this assumption, there may be good reasons for such suspicion.

Is there any room for "remaking" in classical economics? If so, how might it occur? Chapter 9 addresses the question, Can individuals transform themselves in a context of nonpaternalistic, self-directed action? Mill tackled this hard problem in various contexts including the institution of marriage and the abolition of slavery. Today, when we neglect the problem of institutional reform in the context of a competitive democracy, we lose the context in which the analytical

---

10. Walt Whitman is an important exception, and reviews attacked his work on these grounds: "To Walt Whitman, all things are alike good—no thing is better than another, and thence there is no ideal, no aspiration, no progress to things better. It is not enough that all things are good, all things are *equally* good, and, therefore, there is no order in creation; no better, no worse—but all is a democratic level, from which can come no symmetry, in which there is no head, no subordination, no system, and, of course, no result" ("Studies among the Leaves" 1856, 17). We plan to address Whitman's role in the debate between Thomas Carlyle and J. S. Mill at a later date.

machinery of classical economics was developed. Looking at that context is also the subject of chapter 9. Mill's notorious statement of the difference between higher and lower pleasures in his 1861 *Utilitarianism* provides a case in point (211). But the same idea first appears in the 1848 *Principles* when Mill tackles the problem of how people make themselves into competent optimizers. To "civilize" a person, one immerses him in material desires ([1848] 1965, 104; quoted in chap. 8, this vol.). While these material desires might not be approved in Mill's society, they are critical steps in the development of the capacity for self-reliance ([1848] 1965, 104–5).

If people can move to self-government entailing farsighted concern for their own interest, can they also take the additional step toward concern for others? Materialism is only a step toward this end. Whether Mill succeeds or fails—authorities are divided—he points to a real difficulty in the transition between social states: habits that evolve for sensible reasons under one set of institutions, such as paternalism, marriage, or slavery, might be counterproductive in another.

CONCLUSION

Perhaps not surprisingly in the light of the rise of biological remaking that figures so prominently throughout this book, the possibility of Mill's self-directed sort of remaking was soon to be denied within economics. Mill envisaged an internal remaking that, in the context of experience, discussion, and the desire for approbation, resulted in the recognition of the desirability of political reform and the removal of institutional impediments to reciprocity. But the notion that individuals might change themselves was soon criticized and widely rejected. This denial forms a key part of our story, for it, too, followed as notions of biologically determined hierarchy entered economics. Coupled with an acceptance of hierarchical difference among individuals in their capacity for optimization, the denial of self-directed remaking implied that intervention in the form of biological and paternalistic experiments would become attractive to economists of the postclassical period.

II

PERCEIVING RACE
AND HIERARCHY

I have two sensations; we will suppose them to be simple ones; two sensations of white, or one sensation of white and another of black. I call
the first two sensations *like*; the last two *unlike*. What is the fact or phenomenon constituting the *fundamentum* of this relation? The two sensations first, and then what we call a feeling of resemblance, or of want of
resemblance. . . . these feelings of resemblance, and of its opposite dis-
similarity, are parts of our nature; and parts so far from being capable of
analysis, that they are presupposed in every attempt to analyse any of our
other feelings. Likeness and unlikeness, therefore, as well as
antecedence, sequence, and simultaneousness, must stand apart among
relations, as things *sui generis*. They are attributes grounded on facts,
that is, on states of consciousness, but on states which are peculiar,
unresolvable, and inexplicable.
—J. S. Mill, *Logic*

RACISM AS THE PRIMITIVE

It will soon be clear that notions of "race" and hierarchy are ill-defined,
indeed unstable, in the mid-nineteenth and well into the twentieth
century. Arguments about race and hierarchy frequently played out
both in terms of the Irish and the former slaves in Jamaica (Curtis 1968,
1997). The "labouring classes" were also included in racially charged
discussions of inherited incompetence. And as noted earlier, hierarchy
and competence were mapped to gender and religion, as well.

This instability of race and hierarchy invites us to take what we shall
call *racism* as primitive for our analysis and to consider what distinctions were made by those we study.[1] Taking racism as the foundation

---

1. We use the more familiar *racism* rather than the unwieldy *hierarchicalism* here, to signify
thinking in which groups are perceived as superior versus inferior. Glenn Loury's axiom "'Race'
is a socially constructed mode of human categorization" (2002, 5) is much to the point. We focus

for our analysis is very much akin to what Bishop Berkeley proposed by taking perception as the foundation for his work on vision. One learns, Berkeley said, to perceive distance (Levy 2001). As we see in our epigraph, Mill's work on resemblance is even more sharply focused on the perception of difference and similarity.

> Likeness and unlikeness, therefore, as well as antecedence, sequence, and simultaneousness, must stand apart among relations, as things *sui generis*. They are attributes grounded on facts, that is, on states of consciousness, but on states which are peculiar, unresolvable, and inexplicable. (Mill [1843] 1973, *Logic*, 70)

Following Mill, we suppose that one person perceives another directly through the immediate senses or indirectly through words and pictures of that other person. The judgment that results is "the same as me" or "different from me." "The same as me" affirms analytical egalitarianism; "different from me" affirms analytical hierarchicalism. In the debates we study, the step is always taken from "difference" to "inferiority" or "superiority."[2]

In line with Mill, we suggest that people learn to perceive "similarity" or "difference." Part of the learning process involves images and stories that insist upon human homogeneity—the Wedgewood image that accompanied the slogan supposing the truth of Genesis ("Am I not a man and a brother?") was central to the antislavery movement[3]—as well as images and stories that purport that some people are closer to beasts than they are to people (chaps. 9, 3, this vol.). Even as the perception of homogeneity widened to people across the globe and sympathy was extended to other races, the argument was put forward that some are more deserving of sympathy than others, that "charity begins at home." This slogan is central to nineteenth-century "paternalism" in

---

on the microfoundations of such a construction while attempting (by using Mill's constructions) to use the machinery found within the period we study.

2. The problem didn't end with our period. In 1963, Martin Luther King rightly urged that an "unjust" law was "*difference* made legal," while a "just law" was "*sameness* made legal."

3. The manacled African's nakedness emphasized *his* shared experience of human birth. When the opponents of the antislavery movement remade the image and changed the slave's gender, a message of another sort was conveyed. The painting, *Voyage of the Sable Venus, from Angola to the West Indies* (1793) by Thomas Stoddard, is reproduced in Wood 2000, 22.

that it recognizes that unregulated sympathy and choices can endanger hierarchy.

Taking racism as primitive lets us deal with the question of the Jewish "race" with the same facility with which we deal with the Irish "race." A "race" is what the people of the time perceive it to be. Francis Galton and Karl Pearson will tell us that Jews are a "race" because they can be distinguished visually from other people (chap. 5, this vol.). We will consider how Jews are thereby "proven" inferior, and how this reflects on our argument concerning the motivation of scholars, in chapter 6.

To provide a thumbnail sketch of the debates on human hierarchy, we use an index of humanity—or human hierarchy—which we denote α for the Greek *anthrop*, the human. We use this device to characterize four major positions in the period we study. We shall use α in what follows to *define* a "race" because we find that race is conflated in our period with religion, gender, and class.

Race is also conflated with *choice*. This conflation is perhaps best illustrated by the remarkable 1860 image by Charles Bennett that conveys the message that a woman who exits the household to engage in market activity changes race (fig. 2.1). The image, entitled "Slavey," captures the malleability of "race" unforgettably.[4] A woman who exits hierarchy through markets—by entering the labor force—devolves into "an enslaved African type of humanity." She is now perceived as different, and must be so.

The "progressive" doctrine—that hierarchy humanizes, while exiting hierarchy to make self-directed choices causes racial devolution—is central to Charles Kingsley's influential children's tale, *Water-Babies*, as well as the *Punch* images we study later (chap. 3, this vol.). *Water-Babies* contains the story of the Doasyoulikes—particularly fond of playing a Jew's harp—whose devolution to apes and con-

---

4. The accompanying text makes it clear that Bennett is on Carlyle's side in the debate over slavery with Mill: "It will be noticed that the eidolographic development of Miss Hipswidge is strikingly suggestive of the enslaved African type of humanity. The banjo, castanets, 'abundant pumpkin,' and other conventional solaces of that persecuted race are, however, wanting to make the resemblance perfect" (Bennett and Brough 1860, 33). The "abundant pumpkin" is a phrase from Carlyle's "Negro Question" discussed in Levy 2001 and Levy and Peart 2001–2.

Fig. 2.1.   Charles Bennett, "Slavey" (1860)

sequent extermination is a matter of no regret. As the last of the ape-men perishes at the hands of a European hunter, he tries to say that he was a "man and a brother" but, having lost the power of speech, fails in the attempt.

THEORIES OF HUMAN CAPABILITY

What is it that defines the human and measures human capability? By common consent it is "rationality." In the period we are discussing, the concept of rationality had a social aspect because it presupposed both common language as well as the capacity for individual choice. Adam Smith supposed a social foundation for political economy when he conjectured that humans trade because they reason and they speak a common language (Smith, *Wealth of Nations*, I.2.§2; Rubinstein 2000). While it is not quite the case that everyone in the eighteenth and nineteenth centuries defined the human in terms of an ability to use language, the exceptions were considered eccentric by their contemporaries.[5] Thus, in terms of our α, there will be a discontinuity of the relation between α and reason at the edge of the development of language.

Once human status is attained, human capability is related to the ability to make economic and political choices, including the decision to marry and have children. For classical economists, there are two key aspects of this capability: the ability to sympathize, that is, to take into account other people in the self-interested calculus; and what contemporary economists call "time preference."

The ability to reason involves the ability to abstract, on one's own, from surface differences. Those who opposed classical economics held that such judgments were not to be trusted unless they were directed. Unregulated sympathetic judgments might yield resources to the undeserving. In the debates we study, positive time preference was also viewed as a failing.[6] As the case was made that some among us fail to make decisions optimally, perceptions of hierarchy and race entered economics: early British postclassical writers maintained that lack of patience was a particularly Irish characteristic.

Here, we are interested in different specifications of the relationship between humanity and economic ability (entailing sympathetic and intertemporal judgments) in the great debates over hierarchy.[7] We focus on four foundational views of the relationship: the evangelical

---

5. The counterexample is Lord Monboddo (James Burnett) who defined humans as tool users and thus considered the great apes he knew about as instances of men without language.

6. W. S. Jevons, for instance, argued that in matters of intertemporal decisions, the laboring classes were inherently myopic and prone to making systematical mistakes. For a demonstration of such views in Jevons, Marshall, Pigou, and Fisher, see Peart 2000, Lipkes 1999, and Collard 1996.

7. Since we are more interested in racism than race, there are many aspects of the debates on race that will concern us very little. For example, we consider the doctrine of separate creation, "polygenesis," only briefly in Levy and Peart 2004 when we consider more closely differences between Hume's and Smith's views on human equality.

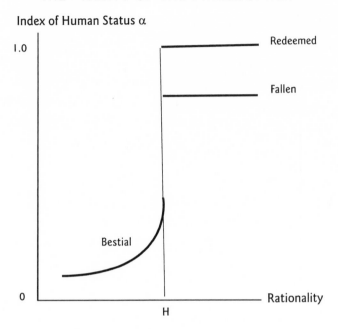

Fig. 2.2.   Evangelical view of human status

(fig. 2.2); Adam Smith's view; a developmental account; and a eugenic account.

Evangelicals

The evangelicals distinguished two—and only two—states of the human: the redeemed, or highest humanity, with $\alpha = 1$, and the fallen, with $\alpha < 1$. Since all of the fallen have the possibility of redemption open to them, they are above the beasts. Having achieved the status of the fallen or redeemed, all are equally human. We will see in what follows that the evangelicals and economists shared the same foundational conception of humanity.

Smith

Smith does not consider the redeemed, but he does discuss those who are regarded by their fellows as heroic. These "imagined" types are

Index of Human Status α

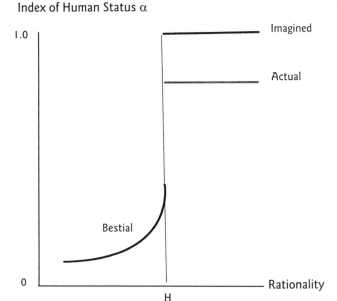

Fig. 2.3.   Adam Smith's view of human status

objects of approval and emulation. As we noted at the outset, Smith sees all "real" individuals as equally human (fig. 2.3).

The critical evangelical doctrine is that of original sin. What unites Smith and the evangelicals is the doctrine that all real men have the same potential. This suffices for them jointly to oppose slavery. Smith's *Theory of Moral Sentiments* describes the process by which people come to moral consciousness. We shall see at length that evangelicals approved of Smith's argument and relied on his intellectual authority in their own work (chap. 9, this vol.).

We have alluded to the significance of sympathy in Smith. The α construction represents our intuition that agents may be willing to pay more to make evils vanish for those whose α is "high" than for those who have a "low" α. If black slaves or British women are viewed as people just like us, then we must be willing to pay more to release them from bondage than if they are a lower order of humanity. On the other side of this, denigrating the humanity of distant people and those who sympathize with such people is part and parcel of the enterprise of hierarchy. When Charles Dickens expressed disapproval of a wife and mother who spent her time worrying about African slaves instead of being the person her husband and daughters wished her to be, he drew the only expletive—"that creature Dickens"—recorded in Mill's life and works.[8] We shall meet Dickens's character Mrs. Jellyby later (chap. 7, this vol.).

Developmental

The next graph presents two developmental views of human nature that are often confounded. First, there is the utilitarian developmental view associated with Mill and Herbert Spencer, which sees a positive monotonic relationship between α and economic ability. Second, there is the biological developmental view associated with Greg and Galton, where α attains a maximum at H^* and then bends down (fig. 2.4). The downward sloping portion reflects the biologists' criticism of utilitarians for paying insufficient attention to the deleterious consequence of undirected sympathy and ethics.[9]

Consider the solid line, which represents the utilitarian developmental view. The simple curvature does not tell us the direction of causation: do we become better humans as we gain ability to make sensible choices; or do more developed people make more sensible choices? Not surprisingly, there were different views on the matter. For Mill, improved ability to make choices, manifested in part as widened sympathy, improved one's human status (chap. 7, this vol.). Indeed, we

---

8. This occurs in a letter from John Stuart Mill to Harriet Mill of 20 March 1854. "That creature Dickens, whose last story, *Bleak House*, I found accidently at the London Library the other day and took home and read—much the worst of his things, and the only one of them I altogether dislike—has the vulgar impudence in this thing to ridicule rights of women. It is done in the very vulgarest way—just the style in which vulgar men used to ridicule 'learned ladies' as neglecting their children and household, etc." (quoted in Packe 1954, 311). This tells us that Mill had discovered only the book version and had not seen the public attack from Lord Denman on *Bleak House* in serial form.

9. Is it possible to be "too" rational? Thomas Carlyle judged his adversary, John Stuart Mill, to be a "logic-chopping machine." At the beginning of Mill's attempt to bring justice to murdered and mutilated Jamaicans (chap. 8, this vol.), he wrote that we must not let narrow self-interest distract us from the demands of impartial justice for our fellow creatures.

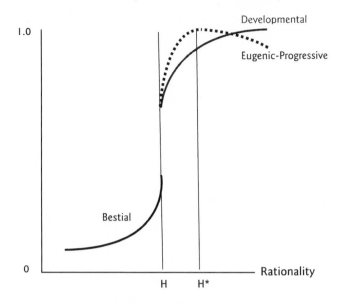

Fig. 2.4.   Developmental and eugenic views of human status

shall make the case that Mill's "higher pleasures" are simply those choices that reflect expanded sympathy. For Mill, the maximum α was attained by Socrates and Jesus Christ, who revealed a willingness to die for strangers. And although Mill was critical of crude American materialism, he believed that the highest national α was attained by Americans who were willing to die to abolish the slavery of their fellows.

Eugenic

In the second half of the century, biologists called for a reduction, or *at least a directing*, of human sympathy and ethics—critical considerations in the developmental view. A. R. Wallace had argued in 1864 that the principle of natural selection does not operate with humans because people possess sympathy for their fellow humans: we do not let the mentally infirm and the physically weak perish. Eugenicists responded that if this survival of the unfit were the result of sympathy in humans, sympathy should be suppressed. Thus, without suppression (via eugenic policy), beyond a certain point (H^*) an increase in ability entailing expanded sympathetic judgements actually *reduces* α. Such thinking led to the eugenicists' program of biological remaking in order to prevent the biological decay that was said to follow the undirected acquisition of sympathetic tendencies in humans, to keep the human race from moving to the right of H^*. In chapter 6, we consider the incentives facing the expert who purportedly possessed the ability to identify and sterilize "the unfit," those too simple to make reproductive choices.

There is a more subtle instance of eugenic theorists producing a downward sloping segment of the developmental index. Like most social scientists of the period who presupposed heterogeneity, eugenicists claimed that the impulsive behavior of "inferior" races revealed they lacked the ability to make reproductive choices and possessed high rates of time preference. However, when an evident "inferior" race—the Jews—seemed to reveal a *lower* rate of time preference than the British, the statistician Karl Pearson interpreted this finding as evidence of an inherent defect among the Jews. This is a result of the temptation confronting the expert that we have referred to earlier.

Eugenicists criticized classical economists and Jews, and for similar reasons. The downward sloping segment of the graph captures what unites these two groups in the imagination of eugenicists/progressives: both are supposedly characterized by abstraction, materialism, and lack of spiritualism. Eugenicists then reasoned that classical economists failed to see differences among people because of their tendency to abstract. The great divide upon which we focus in what follows is between those for whom the life of some people is worth more than the life of others and those for whom it is not.[10]

---

10. In opposition to Mill's equality proposition, Edgeworth responded, "Accordingly in the 'koomposh' of an unlimited pauper population, the most favourable disposition might seem to be (abstracted from practical considerations, and *if* the delineation of Wundt be verified within and beyond the region of sensation), might seem perhaps to be, that adhering *ex hypothesi* to the letter of the first problem, we should be guided by the spirit of the second problem, should wish to cut off the redundant numbers with an illusory portion, so as to transfer substantial (equal) portions to a few. There might be, as it were, a mulcting of many brothers to make a few eldest sons" (1877, 61). We shall return to Edgeworth's position in chapter 10.

WHO ARE THE PHARISEES?
HOW EVANGELICALS BECAME JEWS

In our account, *progressive* means a belief that human nature can and should be improved. This possibility is denied by Adam Smith, who held, as a modeling device, that human nature is fixed: human nature could not be transformed or remade. Christian evangelicals accepted the possibility of transformation, but only through the will of God. As a result of their shared doctrine of fixed human nature, evangelicals and economists were attacked together by Progressives as hypocritical "canters" (chap. 8, this vol.). If the economists appeared Jewish to their opponents, and economists share a set of beliefs about human nature with evangelicals, then we might expect the same Jewish label to be applied to the evangelicals. This three-way identification—economist, Jew, Evangelical—is a test of our approach, which takes perceptions as foundational.[11]

Throughout the nineteenth century, critics called the evangelicals "Pharisees." The ancient Pharisees were those with whom Jesus most disagreed and whom he accused of being hypocrites. Early-nineteenth-century use of the term signifies hypocrisy, or cant.[12]

"Pharisee" turns into more than an accusation of a personal disconnect between professions of belief and behavior, in the poem that serves as epigram to Kingsley's *Water-Babies*. Found in the magazine version but suppressed after the first 200 copies of the book were printed, the poem reads[13]

11. Taking *facts* as foundational, one might make the case that classical economists were Jews because David Ricardo's mother was a Jew and Ricardo was an important classical economist.

12. Here, the difference between the British *Oxford English Dictionary* and the American *Webster's Third International Dictionary* is worthy of note. The OED defines *pharisee* as hypocritical: "One of an ancient Jewish sect distinguished by their strict observance of the traditional and written law, and by their pretensions to superior sanctity." Compare the OED on *sadducee*: "A member of one of the three 'sects' (the others being the Pharisees and Essenes) into which the Jews were divided in the time of Christ. According to the New Testament and Josephus, they denied the resurrection of the dead, the existence of angels and spirits, and the obligation of the unwritten law alleged by the Pharisees to have been handed down by tradition from Moses." Only *Webster's* tells what the Pharisees actually professed, i.e., "immortality of the soul, the resurrection of the body, future retribution, and a coming Messiah . . . ."

13. Consequently, in the rare book market the poem is the marker of the two "states" of the first edition of *Water-Babies* (Macleod 1986, 40). Kingsley's anti-Semitism drew letters of protest to the *Times* (Harris 1981). The relationship of later editions to the suppressed "L'Envoi" is com-

L'ENVOI
Hence, unbelieving Sadducees,
And less-believing Pharisees,
With dull conventionalities;
And leave a country muse at ease
To play at leap-frog, if she please,
With children and realities. (August 1862, 273)

Although *Water-Babies* attacks those who do not believe in transformation by their betters, and it singles out economists for specific criticism, Kingsley does not explain why those who doubt transformation might be called Pharisees. For this insight, we turn to Werner Sombart, commentator on Marx and Engels and, later, admirer of National Socialism.[14] In Sombart's writings, Jewish law is identified with capitalism.[15] What has been less noticed is Sombart's next step, which speaks directly to our identification thesis:[16] his chapter "Judaism and Puritanism" identifies Puritans with Jews.[17]

---

plicated. The first of the one hundred illustrations drawn by Linley Sambourne, the visual epigraph, has children and frogs playing leapfrog. But a "new edition" of the original (illustrated by Noel Paton and Percival Skelton) printed in New York (Kingsley n.d.) contains "L'Envoi."

14. "The Jewish spirit is capitalistic. The English are said to possess the capitalist and, accordingly, the Jewish spirit. And Sombart thinks that the chief task of the German people and, above all, of National Socialism is the annihilation of the Jewish spirit" (Harris 1942, 813). "In identifying Judaism as a moral basis of capitalism Sombart closely follows the pattern set by such early pan-Germanists as his teacher, Adoph Wagner, who looked upon English free trade and laissez faire as 'Manchesterism' *as* Jewish" (832). Barkin traces Wagner's development from classical beginnings to exponent of hierarchy: "He had anticipated neither the predominance of Jews in Berlin's economic life nor the unrestrained profit motive at work in the stock exchange and in the dealings of real estate speculators. The working-class squalor that he observed had no parallel in his experience. His Manchester sympathies did not survive a year in this unrestrained boom-town atmosphere of Berlin" (1969, 147). "Industrialism fostered a society in which egotism was rewarded and a concern for the commonweal led to ruin. At times he pondered whether Christianity could long survive in an industrial age. In the recent rise to prominence of the Jews, with their reputed immorality and obsession with material acquisition, Wagner found conclusive evidence for the soundness of his observations" (155).

15. "Clearly, then, free trade and industrial freedom were in accordance with Jewish law, and therefore in accordance with God's will. What a mighty motive power in economic life!" (Sombart 1951, 248).

16. Harris (1942, 831) and Coleman (2002) catch the earlier, and related, identification "Scotchman and Jew are interchangeable terms" that follows from their trading nature.

17. Schumpeter tells us that Sombart was unique in the history of economics because he was the only economist for whom race is an analytic element: "In fact, so far as I know, Werner Sombart is the only economist of note that ever made significant use of the element of race" (1954, 792).

The Jews and Modern Capitalism begins to make the case:

> I have already mentioned that Max Weber's study of the importance of
> Puritanism for the capitalistic system was the impetus that sent me to
> consider the importance of the Jew, especially as I felt that the domi-
> nating ideas of Puritanism which were so powerful in capitalism were
> more perfectly developed in Judaism, and were also of course of much
> earlier date.

> . . . there is an almost unique identity of view between Judaism and Puri-
> tanism, at least, on those points which we have investigated. In both will
> be found the preponderance of religious interests, the idea of divine
> rewards and punishments, asceticism *within* the world, the close rela-
> tionship between religion and business, and above all, *the rationaliza-
> tion of life*. (1951, 248, 249; emphasis added)

After giving "an instance or two" of this identity, Sombart quotes poetic
authority.

> I would also recall the words of Heine, who had a clear insight into most
> things. "Are not," he asks in his *Confessions*, "Are not the Protestant
> Scots Hebrews, with their Biblical names, their Jerusalem, pharisaistic
> cant? And is not their religion a Judaism which allows you to eat pork?"
> (1951, 249)

From which it follows:

> Puritanism *is* Judaism. (1951, 249)

"Cant" is the hostile label for the nineteenth-century coalition of utilitarian economists and Evangelicals (chap. 8, this vol.). This three-way,
seemingly bizarre identification—economist, Jew, Evangelical—is
what our account predicts.

Part II

CLASSICAL ECONOMICS
AND THE CATTLE HERDERS

III

HIERARCHY AND TRANSFORMATION
"Chemical Political Economy"

Is it not, then, a bitter satire on the mode in which opinions are formed on the most important problems of human nature and life, to find public instructors of the greatest pretension, imputing the backwardness of Irish industry, and the want of energy of the Irish people in improving their condition, to a peculiar indolence and *insouciance* in the Celtic race? Of all vulgar modes of escaping from the consideration of the effect of social and moral influences on the human mind, the most vulgar is that of attributing the diversities of conduct and character to inherent natural differences.
—John Stuart Mill, *The Principles of Political Economy*

"Make them peasant-proprietors," says Mr. Mill. But Mr. Mill forgets that, till you change the character of the Irish cottier, peasant-proprietorship would work no miracle. He would fall behind in the instalments of his purchase-money, and would be called upon to surrender his farm. He would often neglect it in idleness, ignorance, jollity and drink, get into debt, and have to sell his property to the nearest owner of a great estate. . . . In two generations Ireland would again be England's difficulty, come back upon her in an aggravated form. Mr. Mill never deigns to consider that an Irishman is an Irishman, and not an average human being—an idiomatic and idiosyncratic, not an abstract, man.
—W. R. Greg, "Realities of Irish Life"

INTRODUCTION: THE USE OF HISTORY IN AN AXIOMATIC DISCIPLINE

Although there are important technical differences among contemporary schools of thought in economics, and between contemporary economic analysis and classical political economy, a common presumption underscores the analysis. A person who chooses one bundle (or life-style) in preference to another is presumed to be the same person were the choice reversed. In the simple, timeless economic theory of choice with certainty, two distinct points on an indifference curve relate to the same person. In more complicated formulations, of course, the choice itself may have irreversible elements as, for instance, when a person obtains information by the act of consumption. The consequences of the choice may also be irreversible.

The idea of consumer sovereignty has only occasionally been challenged in recent history. Two notable examples—by Maurice Dobb (1933) and J. K. Galbraith (1958)—were countered by Abba Lerner (1934) and F. A. Hayek (1961). But neither Dobb nor Galbraith challenged the doctrine of the stability of the agent's personal identity through choice. By contrast, this stability was precisely the contested ground in the debates we consider here. We examine this contested ground to shed light on the power of our axioms in economics. For while economists have a strong sense of what our axioms imply about consumer choice, we are sometimes less aware of what the axiomatic representation of consumer choice *prevents*. And few economists appreciate that what is prevented by our formulation was once up for grabs. The axiom at issue is the stability of personality through choice: we shall demonstrate that powerful intellects argued that choices irreversibly alter the agent.

Specifically, we demonstrate that race was conflated with choice in nineteenth-century popular culture and anthropology.[1] The contention that "bad" choices cause the human to deteriorate was a common theme in the nineteenth-century debates over human equality versus hierarchy. Classical economists, by contrast, held that human nature is fixed—it doesn't deteriorate—and humans are equal. In what follows, we focus primarily on the fallen or "devolved" human that figured heavily in these disputes: the Irish. The question at issue was whether, being human, the Irish were capable of self-government, or whether, being "inferior," they required direction instead.

---

1. It is important to reiterate that race is a rather ill-defined notion well into the twentieth century. At the mid–nineteenth century, the word *race* is sometimes used to indicate national or vaguely defined ethnic differences. Discussion in the Anthropological Society at this time focused on the Irish, and on whether a well-defined separate Irish "race" might be identified. Arguments about inferiority—and whether choices caused agents to devolve—were extended to religious groups (the Jews) and to women.

We begin by sketching John Ruskin's[2] criticism of the method of classical political economy. The classical political economists erred, Ruskin argued, in supposing that human nature was fixed, and that people simply respond to incentives. Instead, Ruskin held that humans were capable of being transformed—of deteriorating or being improved. The question is how. Therefore we examine this process in more detail and juxtapose Ruskin's position on the consequences of industrialization for the Irish with that of Mill. For Mill, the Irish would become productive so long as there were incentives to do so. For many critics of political economy, including the cofounder of eugenics, W. R. Greg, the Irish were inherently inferior and would not respond to incentives unless forced to do so.[3]

Next we outline the critics' paternalistic solution to such inferiority: those who were inferior might be prevented from the devolution attendant upon poor choices if their choices were directed by their betters. We then turn to an examination of how widespread such characterizations of the Irish were. We focus on how the argument was carried out in visual terms and in the popular press. In this context, we outline two main racial "theories" that were developed and applied to the Irish by the British anthropologist James Hunt and his followers at midcentury.[4] All of this was greatly reinforced by popular stories and images of the time, caricatures that represented the Irish as overly indolent, vio-

---

2. John Ruskin (1819–1900), British art critic, painter, and essayist, examined the religious, moral, economic, and political significance of art. He argued that art reached its zenith in the Middle Ages, when it reflected spiritual concerns.

3. William Rathbone Greg (1809–81) attacked the economics of Thomas Robert Malthus for ignoring the issue of the "quality"—as opposed to the quantity—of population. His essays were extensively quoted by contemporaries, including Charles Darwin (Peart and Levy 2003). For biographical details, see Levy and Peart 2004a. Toye (2000) calls this "the Greg problem" and considers how J. M. Keynes wrestled with these issues.

4. James Hunt was president of the Anthropological Society and the owner-editor of the *Anthropological Review*. All that has been written on Hunt pictures him with enormous vitality and energy. The obituary from *New York Weekly Day-Book* (6 November 1869), reprinted in the *Anthropology Review* under "Anthropological News" (1870, 97), gives some flavor of contemporary opinions: "We are pained to hear of the death of Dr. James Hunt . . . beyond doubt the best, or, at all events, the most useful man in England, if not, indeed, in Europe." Cf. Keith (1917, 19): "[Hunt] has the fire and enthusiasm of an evangelist and the methods of a popular political propagandist." Hunt is mentioned by all modern workers in "scientific" racism, e.g., Curtis (1968), Banton (1977), Rainger (1978), Lorimer (1978), Stepan (1982), Desmond (1994), Young (1995), and Levy (2001). Chapter 4 discusses Hunt's influence and links Hunt to Galton and eugenics.

lent, beastlike creatures. The mutual determination of such caricatures and the "science" of James Hunt are our final subjects.

Throughout this chapter, we explore the argument that, for the purportedly inferior group, a specific type of choice—obedience, or the surrendering of choice—supposedly prevents the devolution of the subject. Two sets of events provided the immediate context for this argument. First, the Fenian movement, which had been launched in 1858 in Ireland and America, became armed and dangerous by the 1860s in its agitation to promote the overthrow of the British government in Ireland. The movement instigated a rising in March 1867. Its leaders were arrested in Manchester on 11 September. A week later, they were rescued while being taken from court to jail. A police officer was killed, and three Fenians were hanged for his murder. They became known as the Manchester martyrs, and their execution for what was perceived as an accidental killing aroused great anger among Irish people at home and abroad. Equally, there was a growth of anti-Irish feeling in England, particularly in December 1867, when a number of Londoners were killed or severely injured after a Fenian bomb exploded during a rescue attempt at Clerkenwell Prison.

Second, what has become known as the Governor Eyre controversy occurred in 1865. The controversy was triggered by a seemingly trivial event in the British colony of Jamaica. Led by Paul Bogle—whose name lives on in Bob Marley's "So Much Things to Say"—former slaves resisted the serving of an arrest warrant. The island's governor, Edward Eyre, took command, imposed martial law, and called in the army to restore order. By the time the army was done, over four hundred Jamaicans were dead, and thousands were homeless. Britons were horrified by the methods of state terror, including flogging with wire whips and the use of military courts to deny civilians their rights. Among the dead was George Gordon, a Baptist minister and member of Jamaica's legislature. Although Gordon, a civilian, was nowhere near the original disturbances, he was arrested, tried in military court, convicted, and hanged. Upon his death, the Jamaica Committee was formed to protest the governor's actions and demand an investigation. The members of the Jamaica Committee included Herbert Spencer,

Charles Darwin and T. H. Huxley. As head, they unanimously chose John Stuart Mill. On the other side, the Eyre Defense Fund was led by Thomas Carlyle[5] and John Ruskin (Semmel 1962; Levy and Peart 2001–2, 2004a). Perhaps not surprisingly, given that these two events are part of the historical backdrop of the period, we find this period marks the high period of conflation of the Negro and the Irish "races."[6]

Though few commentators today hold that choices cause agents to deteriorate, residues of the perhaps more subtle versions of these arguments still color discussions about how choices are made, or ought to be: under the careful supervision of, or direction by, "experts" who know better. At stake is the issue of whether we can remake incentives and trust agents to respond, or whether we need instead to improve the choices—by remaking the agents—of those among us who are said to be fundamentally unable to make good self-directed choices. It is important to understand the historical context of the debate, how the characterizations of "inferior" and "superior" were constructed and used, historically, and how economic thinking, both then and now, ruled out such group characterizations as well as claims concerning the desirability of remaking human nature.

HUMAN NATURE: FIXED OR VARIABLE

For the critics of classical political economy, human nature was malleable, and classical economists erred in supposing that people simply respond to incentives. In 1860, John Ruskin contrasted his "chemical" view of political economy with the "mathematical" view of classical political economists such as J. S. Mill.[7] The mathematical approach supposed that the nature of man is fixed and people respond to incen-

---

5. Thomas Carlyle (1795–1881) was an essayist, a historian, and the greatest speaker for hierarchy of his era. A master stylist, he is quoted several thousand times in the *Oxford English Dictionary*.

6. The president of the Anthropological Society of London in 1870, John Beddoe, developed an "Index of Nigrescence" to apply to Celtic "types," and a racial category, "Africanoid Celts" (1870, 212–13).

7. Mill's statement is given later. We argue throughout this volume that classical political economy beginning with Adam Smith presupposed a deep form of human homogeneity in which all individuals were the same. See Smith, *Wealth of Nations*, quoted in chapter 1.

tives.[8] Social forces simply move the constant human from one point to another. By contrast, the chemical approach presupposes that such social forces change people.

> But the disturbing elements in the social problem are not of the same nature as the constant ones: they alter the essence of the creature under examination the moment they are added; they operate, not mathematically, but chemically, introducing conditions which render all our previous knowledge unavailable. (Ruskin [1860] 1905, 26)[9]

Before *Unto This Last*, Ruskin had explained that the most important subject of transformation was the human being.[10] This proposition made a considerable stir. We quote from an introduction to Ruskin's thoughts in Cope Tobacco's *Smoke Room Booklets* issued forty years later.

> This is Mr. Ruskin's condemnation of our modern social condition; that we manufacture every thing except men. "We blanch cotton, strengthen steel, and refine sugar, and shape pottery; but to brighten, to strengthen, to refine, or to form a single living spirit, never enters into our estimate of advantages." (Lewin in Ruskin 1893, 4)

For those who subscribed to the chemical view, the problem with classical economics was that it failed to contemplate how to improve the subject.

---

8. In fact, Mill takes something of an intermediate position between Smith and Ruskin: as noted previously (chap. 2), Mill is a developmentalist. What separates him from Ruskin and other "progressives" of the time is that for Mill, "improvement" was to be self- (rather than "expert"-) directed (chap. 8, this vol.).

9. Classical political economy also failed because it supposed that the exchange of untransformed goods was profitable. For exchange to generate net benefits, Ruskin held, there must be a transformation. "Profit, or material gain, is attainable only by construction or by discovery; not by exchange. Whenever material gain follows exchange, for every *plus* there is a precisely equal *minus*." "Thus, one man, by sowing and reaping, turns one measure of corn into two measures. That is Profit. Another, by digging and forging, turns one spade into two spades. That is Profit. But the man who has two measures of corn wants sometimes to dig; and the man who has two spades wants sometimes to eat: — They exchange the gained grain for the gained tool; and both are the better for the exchange; but though there is much advantage in the transactions, there is no profit. Nothing is constructed or produced" ([1860] 1905, 90–91).

10. See "Nature of the Gothic" in Ruskin's 1851–53 *Stones of Venice*. Ruskin (like other critics of Mill's political economy) sometimes writes as though one individual may be transformed into another (better or worse) individual. At the same time, the case was also made that there are group variations: that Irish or blacks as a whole need to be transformed (as detailed in this chapter).

Admirers of the transformative view often suppose that transformation works in the upward direction: exposure to the right sort of art can "improve" people, while exposure to market culture cannot.[11] The nineteenth-century view of transformation *also* focused on the possibility of transformation downward.[12] If direction and hierarchy improve the human, the question arises, what happens if such hierarchy were removed? In 1849, Thomas Carlyle asserted that the emancipation of the West Indian slaves reduced them to subhuman status (Levy 2001). But nineteenth-century arguments about institutions were more long-lasting than the attempt to preserve slavery by Carlyle and his followers. Other, less extreme, forms of hierarchy were offered up as transformative institutions that might improve not only the behavior but also the "essence" of individuals who operated within the hierarchy, while renunciation of hierarchy was said to degrade that essence.

This transformational argument was made both in literary and visual forms—in the popular children's tale by Charles Kingsley,[13] *Water-Babies*, and the caricatures of Irish Fenians published in the 1860s in *Punch*.[14] In both its literary and visual forms, the argument constituted an attack on classical political economy. In chemical political economy, the renunciation of hierarchy by those who need direction transforms a human into an ape-man of the Piltdown sort (Spencer 1990). The Irish who chose to achieve self-rule, like the

---

11. W. S. Jevons's "Amusements of the People" relied on this distinction when he called for the "deliberate cultivation of public amusement": "the well-conducted Concert-room *versus* the inane and vulgar Music-hall" ([1876] 1965, 7). The discussion within economics over the possibility of metapreferences (George 2001)—when an individual prefers one set of preferences to another—assumes that to the extent that an individual is remade, she is in charge of her own decisions. The problem of *adult* rehabituation as one moves from (say) slavery to markets was much on J. S. Mill's mind in his *Principles*. See Peart and Levy 2003.

12. Recent scholarship has examined the biological-statistical arguments of eugenicists who, beginning in the late 1860s, feared the possibility of racial degeneration (Carlson 2001). We examine the program of biological remaking later (chaps. 4, 5, 6, this vol.).

13. Charles Kingsley (1819–75) was a novelist and historian. With *Alton Locke*, Kingsley entered into controversy with economics as it contained a widely cited comparison of the black slaves of America with the white slaves (factory workers) of Britain. Kingsley is a key link between the scientific and literary communities who opposed classical political economy. See the biographical entry on Kingsley in Levy and Peart 2004a.

14. *Punch* was a popular magazine treating political, scientific, and literary subjects in a humorous fashion. Still published today, *Punch* was widely read in Victorian England.

woman who left the home to work (chap. 2, fig. 2.1, this vol.), devolved into a "lesser" race.[15]

While scholars have discussed the apelike quality of *Punch* carica-tures of the Irish (Curtis 1968, 1997),[16] we find no evidence that the devolution from human to ape in Kingsley's *Water-Babies* has been linked to this visual simianization. In line with our own argument, Curtis also links the process of "simianizing Paddy" that occurred on the pages of *Punch* to the political activism of the Fenian rebels and to developments in anthropological science during the 1860s (1997, 29). To this account we add two dimensions: the significance of hierarchy (or its renunciation to obtain self-government) in the predicted devo-lution of the subject; and an explanation for how the visual renderings proved oppositional to the economic theory (and policy) of classical economists.[17]

THE MOLECULES OF CHEMICAL POLITICAL ECONOMY

To illustrate the influence of Ruskin's chemical political economy, consider how *Appletons'* quotes Ruskin's analysis of the impact of rail-road travel on the lower orders.[18] Here is an English worker's trans-portation in the old days:

> "In old times, if a Coniston peasant had any business at Ulverstone, he walked to Ulverstone; spent nothing but shoe-leather on the road, drank

15. The drawing "Slavey" is by Charles H. Bennett, a lesser-known *Punch* illustrator who spe-cialized in transformational imagery. See Bennett and Brough 1860.

16. Curtis finds that caricatures of the Irish reflect four Irish types: Northern Irish Protestant; rustic male small farmer (Pat); prognathous and hairy plebeian Irishman (Paddy); and "simian Paddy." Like us, he sees a process by which caricatures became increasingly simian throughout the 1860s (1997, 20, 22, 29).

17. As a result, we are able to resolve a problem that remains unsolved in Curtis. Curtis acknowledges that "one of the most articulate" criticisms of *Apes and Angels* (by Roy Foster) held that "the writers and artists of *Punch* bore no special animus against Irish Catholics, least of all those who accepted the Act of Union" (1997, 116). Curtis runs into difficulty refuting this claim because he fails to see the significance of the variation among caricatures that we explain by oper-ation within or outside the hierarchy. Fenians become apish; loyal Irish remain human. In a sim-ilar vein, women who do not leave the household to work do not devolve (chap. 2, this vol.). In chapter 7 we consider how perception can alter sympathy and change behavior.

18. We quote from the nineteenth-century republication in an American periodical to emphasize the contemporary importance. The extracts by Walter Lewin in Ruskin 1893 are taken largely from *Fors Clavigera*.

at the streams, and if he spent a couple of batz when he got to Ulverstone, it was the end of the world." (*Appletons'* 1878, 61)

Now, in the market economy, postindustrialization, the worker has
devolved.

"But now he would never think of doing such a thing! He first walks
three miles in a contrary direction to a railroad-station, and then travels
by railroad twenty-four miles to Ulverstone, paying two shillings fare.
During the twenty-four miles transit, he is idle, dusty, stupid, and either
more hot or cold than is pleasant to him. In either case he drinks beer at
two or three of the stations, passes his time between them with anybody
he can find, in talking without having anything to talk of; and such talk
always becomes vicious. He arrives at Ulverstone, jaded, half-drunk, and
otherwise demoralized, and three shillings, at least, poorer than in the
morning. Of that sum a shilling has gone for beer, threepence to a railway shareholder, threepence in coals, and eighteen pence has been
spent in employing strong men in the vile mechanical work of making
and driving a machine, instead of his own legs to carry the drunken lout.
The results, absolute loss and demoralization to the poor on all sides,
and iniquitous gain to the rich. Fancy, if you saw the railway officials
actually employed in carrying the countryman bodily on their backs to
Ulverstone, what you would think of the business! and because they
waste ever so much iron and fuel besides to do it, you think it a
profitable one." (*Appletons'* 1878, 61)

An English worker got on the train. But who got off, "jaded, half-drunk,
and otherwise demoralized, and three shillings, at least, poorer than in
the morning"?

We have emphasized the importance of the doctrine of abstract economic man, of fixed human nature, in the opposition to racial
accounts of political economy. In his 1848 *Principles*, Mill outlined the
implication of such a method. He rejected racial "explanations" of outcomes, which he condemned specifically with reference to the Irish:

Is it not, then, a bitter satire on the mode in which opinions are formed
on the most important problems of human nature and life, to find public instructors of the greatest pretensions, imputing the backwardness of
Irish industry, and the want of energy of the Irish people in improving
their condition, to a peculiar indolence and *insouciance* in the Celtic
race? Of all vulgar modes of escaping from the consideration of the
effect of social and moral influences on the human mind, the most vul-

gar is that of attributing the diversities of conduct and character to inherent natural differences. (*Principles*, II.9.§9)

The doctrine of abstract economic man has always been contested, and in the Victorian period the criticism focused on abstraction from the "fact" of racial difference. As an important instance of this contestation we quote from an 1869 issue of the *Quarterly Review*, written by the cofounder of eugenics, W. R. Greg.

> "Make them peasant-proprietors," says Mr. Mill. But Mr. Mill forgets that, till you change the character of the Irish cottier, peasant-proprietorship would work no miracles. He would fall behind in the instalments of his purchase-money, and would be called upon to surrender his farm. He would often neglect it in idleness, ignorance, jollity and drink, get into debt, and have to sell his property to the nearest owner of a great estate. . . . In two generations Ireland would again be England's difficulty, come back upon her in an aggravated form. Mr. Mill never deigns to consider that an Irishman is an Irishman, and not an average human being—an idiomatic and idiosyncratic, not an abstract, man. (1869a)[19]

An Englishman got on Ruskin's train; Greg's Irishman got off. Chemical political economy allows the human to be transformed or devolved, to move from one race to another by institutional change or by making choices. In the images we present here, racial caricatures form the molecules of chemical political economy. For each α, we might expect a distinct caricature. In terms of our index of humanity, the unfettered choices that occur with industrialization and economic development serve to reduce human status, to lower α, because the improving influence of hierarchy is renounced. Guidance by the social commentator, embodied in paternalistic institutions, prevents a movement downward to a lower human status and may move the individual up in the hierarchy of human status.

TRANSFORMATION BY OBEDIENCE

If racial stereotypes form the molecules of chemical political economy, then we need to consider how Victorian perceptions of race changed

---

19. Greg (1869a, "Realities," 78). Curtis (1968, 47–48), who does not know the author—the *Victorian Index* was not yet published—emphasizes the importance of this review for its paradigmatic character.

in the latter half of the nineteenth century.[20] Scholars have long made a distinction between literary racists (Thomas Carlyle in the forefront) and the scientific racists who clustered around James Hunt and his *Anthropological Review*. These groups had at least one member in common: Charles Kingsley.[21] Kingsley is known for many contributions. He seems to have contributed one of the "facts" in Hunt's [September 1863] "Negro's Place in Nature."

> Many observers have noticed the fact that the Negro frequently uses the great toe as a thumb. (Hunt, "Negro's Place," 7)

The same claim appeared in Kingsley's *Water-Babies*, published in installments earlier that year in *Macmillan's Magazine*.

> They laid hold of the branches with their great toes, as if they had been thumbs, just as a Hindoo tailor uses his toes to thread his needle. (Kingsley 1862–63, 217)

First published in book form in 1863 and never thereafter out of print, Kingsley's story for children was arguably the most successful and long-lived disseminator of the chemical thesis. *Water-Babies* had the distinction of being reviewed by both the *Times* and Hunt's *Anthropological Review*. The story contains the doctrine of the transformation of matter by spirit:[22]

> [F]or you must know and believe that people's souls make their bodies, just as a snail makes its shell (I am not joking, my little man; I am in serious solemn earnest). (1863, 226)

---

20. As we noted earlier (chap. 2), we do not wish to imply that it is impossible to conceive of transformation possibilities independently of race. There may also be gender and religious transformations of the sort that make Evangelical Christians into political economists and then into Jews. There is a hint of simianization in a purely English context in a *Punch* cartoon of 4 August 1866, "No Rough-ianism," which carries the caption: "Working-Man: 'Look here, you vagabond! Right or wrong, we won't have *your* help!'" The *English* ruffian holds a rock and a broken branch.

21. Correspondence from Kingsley to Hunt is published in Levy 2001 answering an open question about the Hunt-Kingsley connection. Andrew Farrant and Nicola Tynan are thanked for bringing the importance of *Water-Babies* to our attention.

22. Clark: "The present writer very soon came to the opinion that the story had a deep, spiritual meaning, representing the inner life of man, in its various phases." "Tom is now the representative of the human soul brought into a right relation to God and man" (1901, 115, 116). Clark reports that his interpretation, when originally published, obtained Kingsley's approval.

One of Kingsley's explicit targets is the economics of his contemporaries that denies the possibility of transformation.[23]

One is transformed by following the recommendations of one's betters, by submitting to hierarchy. The telling episode in *Water-Babies* occurs in the tale of the now-extinct Doasyoulikes who exit hierarchy.

> And in the next five hundred years they were all dead and gone, by bad food and wild beasts and hunters; all except one tremendous old fellow with jaws like a jack, who stood full seven feet high; and M. Du Chaillu came up to him, and shot him, as he stood roaring and thumping his breast. And he remembered that his ancestors had once been men, and tried to say, "Am I not a man and a brother?" but had forgotten how to use his tongue; and then he had tried to call for a doctor, but he had forgotten the word for one. So all he said was "Ubbobboo!" and died. (1863, 247–48)

In the midst of the American Civil War, no one would miss the reference to the abolitionist question—"Am I not a man and a brother?"[24] And we have a loss of language that accompanies the devolution to bestial.

In this episode about how the absence of compulsion causes racial devolution, Kingsley makes an Irish reference to the jaw as a marker of the primitive:

> "Why," said Tom, "they are growing no better than savages."
> "And look how ugly they are all getting," said Ellie.
> "Yes; when people live on poor vegetables instead of roast beef and plum-pudding, their jaws grow large, and their lips grow coarse, like the poor Paddies who eat potatoes." (1863, 244)[25]

---

23. The agents of transformation in *Water-Babies* are fairies: "Some people think that there are no fairies. . . . And Aunt Agitate, in her Arguments on political economy, says there are none. Well, perhaps there are none—in her political economy" (1863, 60). Fairies also play a role in Kingsley's *Roman and Teuton*, his Regis Lectures of Modern History at Cambridge.

24. It was commented upon in the review in the *Anthropological Review* (Hunt 1863a, 472). The review adds to the information on the title page ("The Rev. Charles Kingsley") that the author is "Honorary Fellow of the Anthropological Society of London, and Professor of Modern History in the University of Cambridge" (Hunt 1863a, 472).

25. "Charles Kingsley's description of the poor peasants he saw in County Mayo and Connemara in 1860 as 'white chimpanzees'" (Curtis 1997, 100).

The conjunction of Darwinian science, Carlyle, and the devolution thesis in Kingsley is explicated by the review in the *Times*.

> And if we should have never heard of Tom and Ellie but for the development of Marine Zoology, we may add that Master Tom's education would have been impossible had not Mr. Darwin published his book on the Origin of Species. Mr Kingsley trips up the Darwinian theory, and asks us how we like its application when inverted. If an ascent in the order of life be possible, must not a degradation or movement downwards be equally possible? If beasts can be turned into men, must not men be liable to be turned into beasts? Here, indeed, Mr. Kingsley might have quoted the authority of one of his great masters, Mr Carlyle, who long ago warned us of the fate of the dwellers by the Dead Sea who refused to listen to the preaching of Moses. They became apes, poor wretches, and having once had souls they lost them. (26 January 1864, 6)

Those who exit hierarchy exit humanity.

IRISH CARICATURES

Long before Ruskin was born, the Irish served as the general-purpose English stereotype of "the primitive" to the extent that American colonists viewed the aboriginal peoples as "Irish."

> It was the "Wild Irish," fellow-Europeans, not the inhabitants of some far distant land, who provided the Englishman with his stereotype of primitive and barbarous society. When, therefore, the colonists came to deal with the Indians, they did so in the light of English experience in Ireland. (Muldoon 1975, 268–69)[26]

It may be natural to classify unknown native peoples in terms of what is only partially known. But the transformation of known Irish people into a type of brute goes beyond this.

> During the seventeenth century, Europeans who were creating the rudiments of anthropology were able to argue that many of the various primitive non-European societies existed "in a place in the hierarchical

---

26. We thank Gordon Schochet for the reference.

series of societies separate from and lower than European man but still higher than the animals." The nineteenth-century caricatures of the Irish with simian features illustrate how far the process could go. Even a people dwelling within the physical boundaries of Europe was not immune from being reduced to a subhuman status. (288–89)

Two types of racial theories, each with roots in nineteenth-century anthropological science, characterize the visual representations of the Irish at midcentury.[27] There was, first, what we call parametric racism—the visualization that portrays the Irish (or blacks) as different in some respects from Anglo-Saxons but with some variation. In the context of discussing T. H. Huxley's paper on the common racial heritage of Celts and Anglo-Saxons (cited in chap. 4, this vol.), L. Owen Pike argued that if only parametric differences distinguished the races (the parameter being the "creeping dulness" of the Saxon!), "there is nothing to prevent us from regarding an Irishman as 'a man and a brother'" (1870, 214).[28] Here the Irish is inferior, unable to control his impulses and save properly for the future, but human.

A second, and more devastating, caricature portrays one, and only one, Irish Fenian. This caricature was used to assert that outside the hierarchy, the Irishman devolves. Here, the Fenian is without personality, a nonhuman brute, Curtis's "simianized Paddy." This caricature is consistent with Hunt's view of the Other as a race without variation.[29] As the Irish in America grew in numbers the possibility of a disruption of British governance of Ireland became real, and the increasing brutality of the visual representations throughout the decade served to warn the British public of the danger ahead.[30]

This devolution of the Irish from (inferior) stereotype to subhuman

---

27. We provide a brief overview here to help explicate the images of transformation that follow. In chapter 4 we provide the details of the anthropological "science."

28. The context of the remarks is discussed in chapter 4, note 6.

29. Curtis recognizes the former of our arguments (that the visualizations of the earlier period are parametrically racist), but he does not stress the latter: "In [Cruikshank] one may find the Irish Celt portrayed as a creature with half-human and half-simian features. The wild eyes, the prognathous jaw, the ugly mouth and thick lips were designed to emphasize the Irishman's animal instincts and habits. It was not uncommon for English observers to compare Irishmen with the 'lowliest' of African tribes, the Hottentots, because they seemed to share so many attributes in common" (1968, 59).

30. A particularly revealing 20 August 1864 cartoon—"Something for Paddy"—has Death masqued as *Punch*'s Yankee recruiting Paddy. The paired poem (20 August 1864, 74) "Paddy

brute occurred in visual caricatures as well. To show this, we shall first consider an early image in which the Irish are apparently inferior but they have personality and the individuals differ. We turn next to two drawings from *Punch* in which the Irish are bereft of personality and are all the same. The first shows the Irish as people with human potential so long as they acquiesced to being looked after by the paternalist. By contrast, the second presents caricatures of those Irish who proposed self-government, the Fenians, and thereby revealed themselves as bereft of human potential. Launched in 1858 in Ireland and America, the Fenian movement became armed and dangerous as a result of Irish participation in the American Civil War.[31] British hierarchy was defended using the theory that those outside the beneficent hierarchy were subhuman.[32] We find an anthropological basis for this argument:

---

before Richmond" makes the role of the antislavery movement clear: "The Irish boy to the war is gone, / In the ranks of Grant you'll find him! / By Yankee bayonets goaded on, / With a frequent prod behind him. / 'Land of Crimps!' said the youth ill-starred, / 'Let BRIGHT and COBDEN praise thee / And ivery fool their words regard; / Och botheration saze thee!" Belatedly acknowledging that its American cause is lost with the two-page "The American Juggernaut" (3 September 1864)—one week earlier it was confidently predicting recognition of the Confederacy (27 August 1864, 85)—*Punch* worries about the Irish in the American army (5 November 1864, 184).

   31. Kiernan (1864, 14): "The allegation has been made that Irishmen are incapable of self government; this allegation is one of the calumnies spread abroad by England and believed by many. When we see Irishmen in the councils, leading the armies and moulding immense influence in some of the greatest nations of the world, even when recreant to their own country, in that of England, it is certainly fair to infer that when concentrating their talents at home, they can not only govern themselves but give Ireland a glorious future." The judgment of one of the authorities on the Fenian literature (D'Arcy 1947, 421)—"A repetition of the ancient grievances against England. Nothing of value in it"—pays insufficient attention to what Kiernan's title "Brig. Gen." would convey in a world in which warfare was mechanized and the feudal ideology of chivalry first came upon the breech-loading, repeating rifle and the industrial age. Perhaps the only *Punch* cartoons in the mid–nineteenth century that approve of American policy are those that comment upon the suppression of the Fenian raids into the Dominion of Canada.

   32. A Fenian polemic during the American Civil War would have dehumanization an official imperial policy: "But the slave trade was carried on with such atrocious cruelty that other nations of Europe, for the sake of our common humanity, murmured and to silence such murmurings the Imperial Parliament of Great Britain passed an Act that, 'The black man was not a son of Adam nor redeemed by Christ and consequently not entitled to human sympathy.' This horrible blasphemy met at the time with a rebuke from the Pope, who issued a bull excommunicating any Catholic who dared reiterate so inhuman an edict" (Kiernan 1864, 7). Compare with Kingsley (1863, 193): "Did you never hear of the blessed St. Brandan, how he preached to the wild Irish, on the wild wild Kerry coast; he and five other hermits, till they were weary, and longed to rest? For the wild Irish would not listen to them, or come to confession and to mass, but liked better to brew potheen, and dance the pater o'pee, and knock each other over the head with shillelaghs, and shoot each other from behind turf-dykes, and steal each other's cattle, and burn each other's homes; till St. Brandan and his friends were weary of them, for they would not learn to be peaceable Christians at all."

Fig. 3.1.   George Cruikshank, "Plunder at the Palace of the Bishop of Ferns" (1845)

such visual representations of the Irish Fenians were informed by the racial theorizing of James Hunt and the Anthropological Society.[33]

We start with an example from George Cruikshank's dramatic series of illustrations in W. H. Maxwell's *History of the Irish Rebellion in 1798* (1845). These illustrations bring to light all sorts of characteristics of the Irish generally associated with "inferior" races, but they also show variation among Irish folk. Consider figure 3.1, the rousing portrayal entitled "Plunder at the Palace of the Bishop of Ferns" (1845, 82).

---

33. Hunt made the case for the Negro; the images are Irish. Contemporaries recognized that the argument transferred "Negro characteristics" to the Irish. "In the year 1880 Gustave de Molinari (1819–1912), the Belgian political economist and radical essayist, published a series of epistolary articles on the condition of Ireland. . . . England's largest newspapers, he wrote, 'allow no occasion to escape them of treating the Irish as an inferior race—as a kind of white negroes [*sic*]—and a glance at *Punch*'" (Curtis 1997, 1).

Here we find the jolly Irish rebels celebrating, overly enjoying food and drink. Music and dance figure prominently. The typical Irish rebel is impulsive, at the mercy of his senses, and has a tenuous control over his passions.[34]

In Cruikshank's illustrations, some of the Irish are drawn with ape-like qualities, the ape-jaw, wild eyes, bulging forehead, and thick lips. Most of the figures are human, though inferior. But as we move to the foreground, the figures move from excessive joviality to increasing brutality, and at the same time they acquire the apelike jaw and protruding forehead.

Until 1865, *Punch* followed Cruikshank in its characterization of the Irish as racially inferior but with variation. Then, sometime in the mid-1860s, *Punch* was taken with the racial theory of James Hunt and the Anthropological Society that saw inferior races as without variation.[35] That theory turned the editor and illustrators of *Punch* to what might be called racial brutalization, the visual representation of the Irish Fenian as a brute without variation. At the same time, *Punch* began to champion a racialized version of the chemical political economy theme (devolution) in Ruskin and Kingsley's *Water-Babies*. Increasingly after 1865, we find what is the same visual representation of the Fenian who rebels against hierarchy.

By 1865, *Punch's* caricatures of the Irish Fenians, mostly by John Tenniel,[36] take on a strange uniformity. Tenniel's characterization of the Fenians is now informed by a theory that Fenians who rejected the hierarchical order were condemned to devolve into apelike brutes

---

34. Chapter 4 shows how widespread these characteristics are for the inferior race. Peart 2000 shows how early neoclassical economists linked them to the purported inability to theorize intertemporally.

35. *Punch* followed the Anthropological Society debates carefully, noticed with enthusiasm Hunt's paper "Negro's Place in Nature," and took the same extremist position in the Eyre controversy as Hunt. Prasch (1989) documents Hunt's influence on the explorers R. F. Burton and W. W. Reade.

36. Tenniel joined *Punch* at the invitation of its editor, Mark Lemon, in December 1850. Initially, his contributions were limited to the decorative borders and initials of the journal, but he became *Punch's* principal artist upon the death of John Leech in 1864. The *Dictionary of National Biography* article on Tenniel refers to his "delightful humour which never degenerated into coarseness nor was lacking in dignity." Curtis (1997) remarks that, more than any other artist of the time, Tenniel was responsible for turning Paddy into apes (37).

PUNCH, OR THE LONDON CHARIVARI.—September 30, 1865.

ERIN'S LITTLE DIFFICULTY.

Britannia. "YES, MY DEAR! THAT'S THE SORT OF DRILLING TO DO *HIM* MOST GOOD!"

Fig. 3.2.   John Tenniel, "Erin's Little Difficulty" (1865)

without any variation. The Fenians have Cruikshank-style faces, with misshapen jaws, and they sport distinctive feathered caps.[37] An example of "simianized Paddy" appears in September in "Erin's Little Difficulty" (30 September 1865), where a diminutive Fenian rebel is receiving a whipping from his (female) master (fig. 3.2). And in "Rebellion Had Bad Luck" (10 December 1865), John Bull again appears with the *same* apelike Fenian (fig. 3.3). Now, however, a week after *Punch* reports the Fenian support for the hanged and brutalized "cannibalistic" Jamaicans, the caricature shows Bull holding a pamphlet entitled

---

37. The feathered cap is layered with meaning—the feather signifying a decoration or mark of honor, as well as the badge of a fool (*Oxford English Dictionary*).

Fig. 3.3. John Tenniel, "Rebellion Had Bad Luck" (1865)

"Jamaica," and the rebel is presumably being warned about the possibility of similar treatment in store for the Irish rebels.

The Fenians were attempting to escape from the British hierarchical order and achieve Irish self-government. Not surprisingly, however, some Irish sided with the British in this controversy. Here from 4 January 1868 we find a cartoon in *Punch* showing "A Hint to the Loyal Irish" (fig. 3.4). The Irishmen are clearly different and, perhaps, drawn less as caricatures than the English constable who looks a little unqualified for the severe labor of running down a miscreant.[38] But they are

___

38. Commenting on "A Hint to the Loyal Irish," Curtis writes: "The faces of these Irishmen reveal the equation in Tenniel's mind between loyalty to the Queen and high facial angles" (1997, 40). We should add that these men are individuals with personality.

PUNCH, OR THE LONDON CHARIVARI.—January 4, 1868.

FENIANISM
SPECIAL
CONSTABLES

A HINT TO THE LOYAL IRISH.

"AH, THIN, MISTHER BULL! GIVE US THE OATH AN' SOME O' THIM STICKS. SURE, THERE'S
HUNDHREDS O' THE BOYS AS IS READY TO HELP YE, SOR."

Fig. 3.4. John Tenniel, "Hint to the Loyal Irish" (1868)

human. The caricature shows that the Irish can *escape* devolution into Fenian ape-men by following the direction of their betters, desiring to Doasyouaretold. Hierarchy humanizes.

We have not reproduced images of women and children among *Punch*'s Irish caricatures. Indeed, women and children in some *Punch* cartoons are so apparently unsimianized that we have puzzled about whether they are supposed to be Irish.[39] The solution, we conjecture, follows from the identification of acceptance of hierarchy with normal

---

39. Judging from his comments on the "Loyal Irish" image, Curtis might have been as puzzled as we were: "Tenniel increases the degree of prognathism in this stereotype of a Fenian dynamiter, while playing on old anti-Catholic prejudices in his new version of the gunpowder plot" (1997, 39).

human status in the chemical view. As long as people Doastheyaretold, they remain human. Women and children who accept their assigned role in society are, on this reading, fully human. Obedience humanizes.

CARICATURES "MAKING HISTORY"

The visual representation of the Fenian in *Punch* was taken as fact in the wider community. Evidence for this claim exists in more than one venue, in several disciplines. Consider first this discussion of caricature in *Punch* in the *Southern Literary Messenger* in December 1863. The hypothesis is that caricature is an antiabstraction device, and one that both is and makes history.

> In the very nature of caricature there is a substance which cannot be extinguished, apart from the realities of which it is the mockery and the burlesque. In a relative sense, caricature is the *reductio ad absurdum* of our gravest acts and imaginings; it is the average sense taking stock of our would-be pretensions, stripping our majesty of its externals, and reducing them to jest. But to accomplish its ends it employs a positive amount of invention, and it leaves, as a residuum, a creation of its own. Such creations, if felicitous in the conception and handling, are as permanent as the fabrications of the poet or romancer; they are substantive existence . . . Caricatures help to make history—and they are history also—in the matter of costume, fashions, and social usages, the only history which is clear, entertaining, and to the point. (*Southern Literary Messenger*, 1863, 711–12)

Both Tenniel's "big cartoon" and *Punch*'s characterization of the Irish were invoked in this context (*Southern Literary Messenger*, 1863, 714).[40] *Punch* is given credit for having articulated what we might call the Irish α, and so for altering perceptions of the Celtic rebels:

> It is in no slight degree the work of *Punch*, that the vapour of Milesian sentiment and false pretence has been dissipated from our political atmosphere, and that while we remain alive to Ireland's real grievances,

---

40. "Punch has owed more of his power in politics to the pencils of Doyle and Tenniel than to the pens of his most famous writers" (*Appletons'* 1873, 750). *Appletons'* also focused on the "thoroughly English" nature of caricature in *Punch* (*Appletons'* 1879, 513).

we are so completely sickened of the Irish view of them. From *Punch's* pictures of the burly impudence of O'Connell, of the little vitriol throwing imp Young Ireland, of the Yahoos, whose only arguments are brickbats and shillelaghs, England has obtained a vivid impression of Celtic types which it will take many years to induce her to forget, and an unusual display of candour, equity, and good sense on the part of the Celt himself, to modify or mitigate. (*Southern Literary Messenger*, 1863, 714)[41]

Just as vivid, perhaps, is the evidence that *Punch's* characterization of the Irish Fenian was accepted as "fact" within the Anthropological Society. Here we have in mind an 1870 discussion of John Beddoe's paper presented to the Anthropological Society, "On the Kelts of Ireland." In the discussion of the paper from the floor, Carter Blake referred specifically to John Tenniel's drawings of the Fenians as representative of an Irish "type."

But the other Irishman, the "Connaught man," who was perhaps also found in Kerry, as shown by Dr. Beddoe's "Arran" photographs, was another being altogether. Mongoloid in aspect, with the *orbicularis oris* muscle strongly marked, we see in Mr. Tenniel's caricatures in *Punch* examples of this type. Surely there was no race affinity between these two forms of Irish countenance, and it was wrong to take the "Arran" type as an example of the true Irishman. (Blake 1870, clxxxiii)

The drawings of the Irish ape in *Punch* were regarded as drawings of real anthropological types and therefore constituted "evidence" against the classical political economists' doctrine of human homogeneity and abstract economic man.

RUSKIN ON THE *PUNCH* ILLUSTRATIONS AS A MAP TO HIERARCHY

We opened this chapter with the claim that the *Punch* caricatures of the Irish Fenian illustrate Ruskin's "chemical" political economy. In *Punch's* view, some choices—choices that the social commentator or

---

41. Caricatures "indicate the passions and illusions of the hour, but they contribute materially to the conclusions of the hour about to follow" (1863, 711).

policymaker dictates,[42] such as the acceptance of hierarchy—can transform an individual upward. On the other hand, unfettered choices, choices that are not approved of by the expert, can cause racial devolution. It is therefore not surprising that Ruskin has important things to say in his November 1883 lecture on *Punch* and its artists, "The Fireside: John Leech and John Tenniel."

What makes the *Punch* illustrators so interesting, Ruskin suggests here, is that unlike the artists he discussed in previous lectures, their subjects include a "class entirely beneath" the usual sophisticated subjects of art ([1883] 1908, 350). He pauses to explicate his transformation thesis with respect to material.

> To my own mind, there is no more beautiful proof of benevolent design in the creation of the earth, than the exact adaptation of its materials to the art-power of man. The plasticity and constancy under fire of clay; the ductility and fusibility of gold and iron; the consistent softness of marble; and the fibrous toughness of wood, are in each material carried to the exact degree which renders them provocative of skill by their resistance, and full of reward for it by their compliance: so that the delight . . . enjoyment of the workman in managing a substance so pliable to his will . . . ([1883] 1908, 351)

The thesis of the transformability of the natural world resonated with those who endorsed Ruskin's criticism of market economies in which people are taken as fixed ends and not as material to be remade (see Walter Lewin in Ruskin 1893).

Ruskin turns to the topic of the lecture and considers what the *Punch* artists drew.

> Gradually the kind and vivid genius of John Leech, capable in its brightness of finding pretty . . . jest in everything, but capable in its tenderness also of rejoicing in the beauty of everything, softened and illumined with its loving wit the entire scope of English social scene; the graver power of Tenniel brought a steady tone and law of morality into the licence of political contention . . . ([1883] 1908, 359)

---

42. The *Punch* cartoons do not always make it clear whether the choice is to be made by policymaker or social commentator, but the key is that the individual subject cannot be trusted to choose without direction.

He describes how art represents *Punch*'s politics:

> He is a polite Whig, with a sentimental respect for the Crown, and a practical respect for property . . . from his heart adores Mr. Gladstone; steadily, but not virulently, caricatures Mr. D'Israeli; violently and virulently, castigates assault upon property, in any kind, and holds up for the general ideal of perfection, to be aimed at by all the children of heaven and earth, the British Hunting Squire, the British Colonel, and the British sailor. ([1883] 1908, 360)

Ruskin discusses the illustrations of daily life by Töpffer.

> His power is never so marvellously exerted as in depicting a group of roguish guides, shameless beggars, or hopeless cretins.

> Nevertheless, with these and such other materials as our European masters of physiognomy have furnished in the portraiture of their nations, I can see my way to the arrangement of a very curious series of illustrations of character, if only I could also see my way to some place wherein to exhibit them. ([1883] 1908, 363)

Then he proposes that the study of the masters' drawings of people's faces can supplement, and perhaps even replace, physical anthropology in the search for the primitive among us:

> I find myself grievously in want of such a grammar of the laws of harmony in the human form and face as may be consistent with whatever accurate knowledge of the elder races may have been obtained by recent anthropology, and at the same time authoritative in its statement of the effect on human expression, of the various mental states and passions. And it seems to me that by arranging in groups capable of easy comparison, the examples of similar expression given by the masters whose work we have been reviewing, we may advance further such a science of physiognomy as will be morally useful than by any quantity of measuring savage crania. ([1883] 1908, 364)

Since such a gallery is a long way off, for the moment we can employ collections of heads from *Punch*.

> [I]f, therefore, among the rudimentary series in the art schools you find, before I can get the new explanatory catalogues printed, some more or less systematic groups of heads collected out of *Punch*, you must not

think that I am doing this merely for your amusement, or that such examples are beneath the dignity of academical instruction. ([1883], 1908, 364)

The point of such a collection of heads from *Punch* is to inform us as to whether a subject is in need of transformation, or not.

My own belief is that the difference between the features of a good and a bad servant, of a churl and a gentleman, is a much more useful and interesting subject of inquiry than the gradations of snub nose or flat forehead which became extinct with the Dodo, or the insertions of muscle and articulations of joint which are common to the flesh of all humanity. ([1883] 1908, 364–65)

For Ruskin, therefore, the *Punch* caricatures serve as a guide to human hierarchy. This is the reading for which we have argued here.[43]

WHAT ARE *PUNCH*'S SIMIANIZED FENIANS?

An elegant description of the nature of caricature is offered by the art historian E. H. Gombrich, who writes that artists "mythologize the world by physiognomizing it" (Curtis 1997, 28). The artist's rendition of the human face is supposed to convey the character of the subject's soul, its place in the natural hierarchy. We suggest that the images of the Irish Fenians in *Punch* are the visual equivalents of models, in the sense that they operationalize a theory. Like economists' models, they serve as intermediaries between theory and policy; they represent or render a theory in a particular setting or context (Morgan and Morrison 1999).[44] The theory that they represent visually is a version of Ruskin's chemical political economy combined with mid-nineteenth-century anthropology, whereby individuals who step outside the hierarchical structure devolve to the lowest of the humans, to what Hunt

---

43. It comes as no surprise to us that eugenicists—who wished to transform the human—also sought information concerning the need for transformation in physiognomy. Galton's composite photography was an attempt to identify inheritable traits in the subjects' faces (chap. 5, this vol.).

44. "[A] representation is seen as a kind of rendering—a partial representation that either abstracts from, or translates into another form, the real nature of the system or theory, or one that is capable of embodying only a portion of the theory" (Morgan and Morrison 1999, 27).

called a race which has "no history" (Hunt 1863b, 13, quoted in chap. 4, this vol.) characterized by complete lack of differentiation and thus personality. Indeed, as visual caricatures, these images function like the economic models that are described as caricatures by Gibbard and Varian (1978).[45] Like the narrative in *Water-Babies*, the *Punch* caricatures focus exclusively on one issue: how the rejection of hierarchy devolves a race.

If we accept that caricature involves exaggeration and distortion, then the simianized Fenian is not something to be believed as a "realistic" rendering of economic agents (Gibbard and Varian 1978, 676). On the other hand, this begs the question of how the model—in this case, the caricature—is used. In line with our argument concerning perception (chap. 2, this vol.), our sense is that it was used to create and reinforce a perception of inferiority and as "fact" to support science. It remains an open question whether the model was used by scientists who believed that it illuminated some aspect of economic reality or by scientists who had reason to distort the representation of that reality. We shall return to this question in chapter 11.

In fact, "Mr. Punch" believed that his simianized Fenian was real. It is no coincidence, we believe, that while *Water-Babies* was appearing in serial form in *Macmillan's Magazine*, in the 22 November 1862 *Punch* there appears a "letter" to Mr. Punch headed "Our Ancestry" which contains a sentence from Darwin's *Origin of Species*.

> I can, indeed, hardly doubt that all vertebrate animals having true lungs have ascended by ordinary generation from an ancient prototype, of which we know nothing, furnished with a float-apparatus or swim-bladder. (209)

The "letter" closes by explicating *Punch's* contribution:

> You, yourself, Sir, did good service, the other week, to the cause of this scientific investigation in its more advanced stage, by pointing out that the missing link between man and the Gorilla is undeniably found in

---

45. Caricatures as models "seek to 'give an impression' of some aspect of economic reality not by describing it directly, but rather by emphasizing—even to the point of distorting—certain selected aspects of the economic situation" (Gibbard and Varian 1978, 665).

A REAL NATIVE.

Fig. 3.5. *Punch*, artist unknown, "A Real Native" (1862)

the Irish Yahoo. And it is to be hoped that, as ray after ray of light thus dawns upon us, we shall in due time be able to complete the family registery. (209)

The "letter" is signed "Natural Selection," from "Struggle for Life Place" (see fig. 3.5).

IV

DENYING HUMAN HOMOGENEITY

Eugenics and the Making of
Postclassical Economics

I believe that now and always the conscious selection of the best for
reproduction will be impossible; that to propose it is to display a fundamental misunderstanding of what individuality implies. The way of
nature has always been to slay the hindmost, and there is still no other
way, unless we can prevent those who would become the hindmost
being born. It is in the sterilization of failures, and not in the selection
of successes for breeding, that the possibility of an improvement
of the human stock lies.
—H. G. Wells on Galton's "Eugenics"

INTRODUCTION: ANTHROPOLOGY AND "RACE" AT MIDCENTURY

How did peace come to the conflict between economics and hierarchy? How did economics move from the classical period characterized
by the hardest possible doctrine of initial human homogeneity—that
all the observed differences among people arise from incentives, luck,
and history[1]—to become comfortable with accounts of human behavior that alleged foundational differences among and within races of
people (Darity 1995)? We argue that early British eugenics thinkers
racialized economics in the postclassical period. We do not wish to
suggest that the transition was the same in Britain and America. One
difference may be noted at the outset: the statistical theorists who
founded the "science" of eugenics were British. But there is this com-

---

1. Smith (*Wealth of Nations*, 1.2§4), quoted in chapter 1 as epigraph.

monality: ideas of race and hierarchy became central in both Britain and America during this period.[2]

Given their stature as mathematical statisticians, we find it odd that the importance of the eugenic writing of Francis Galton and Karl Pearson has been neglected in the secondary literature on postclassical economics.[3] We contend that early eugenics thinking emerged in direct opposition to the classical account of economic decision making entailing homogeneity, and that, temporarily, eugenicists succeeded in moving economics to accounts of competency involving racial difference. To make our case, we trace the opposition to race-blind accounts from Thomas Carlyle to the cofounder (with Francis Galton) of eugenics, W. R. Greg, by way of James Hunt and the Anthropological Society of the 1860s. Hunt is important in our account for his new—and devastating—theory of race entailing lack of differentiation within the race, which, we argue, influenced the other cofounder of eugenics, Galton. Next, we examine how the early eugenicists' characterization of race influenced economic analysis in the postclassical period: both in terms of Hunt's zero-variation theory and also in terms of the anthropologists' parametric claims about the features of "lower" races. We also show that postclassical economists endorsed each of the three major policy recommendations of the eugenicists. Finally, we note how L. von Mises and the Chicago school revived the classical econo-

---

2. See Leonard 2003a, 2003b, and Bateman 2003 for details on how ideas of race entered into and influenced American thinking in social science at the turn of the century.

3. The silence in the commentary on Fisher is noted in the first sentence of Aldrich 1975, 33: "Irving Fisher's long and enthusiastic support for the American eugenics movement receives nary a word of mention in most standard histories of economic thought." Electronic searches allow a systematic, albeit limited, exploration of the scholarship on the subject. Using JSTOR we find no use of the word *eugenics* in any of the literally hundreds of articles and reviews written by Joseph Schumpeter, George Stigler, or A. W. Coats. The search results conducted on 23 May 2002 are available in HTML form upon request. While recognizing the limitations associated with such a search, we suggest the outcome indicates the emphasis (or lack thereof) in the literature on this topic. (The case of Schumpeter's *History of Economic Analysis*, which, as Aldrich notes, pays attention to racist doctrines, and as a book is not accessible in JSTOR, is discussed later.) Among the past generation of historians of economics, as far as we can determine only Spengler systematically paid attention to eugenics (Spengler 1955, 1966). Mirowski 1989 discusses energetics at length with a slight glance at eugenics. The papers in Mirowski 1994 mention eugenics once, in connection with Marshall. The eugenic involvement of the neoclassical economists is apparent in specialist accounts of eugenics, such as that by Soloway (1995). Toye 2000 reports resistance to publishing Keynes's views on eugenics.

mists' doctrine of human homogeneity.[4] Perhaps not surprisingly, the Chicago revival began with skepticism about the common link, supposed in early neoclassical economics, between time preference and race.

Well into the twentieth century, "race" remained a rather ill-defined notion. In this period, "race" is sometimes used to indicate national or vaguely defined ethnic differences.[5] Nonetheless, by 1870 two theories of racial hierarchy can be identified as coexisting in the scientific community and the popular press. The more devastating view, that of the owner of the *Anthropological Review*, James Hunt, held that there were races whose physical development was arrested prematurely, dead races incapable of elevation.

> We now know it to be a patent fact that there are races existing which have no history, and that the Negro is one of these races. From the most remote antiquity the Negro race seems to have been what they are now. We may be pretty sure that the Negro race have been without a progressive history; and that they have been for thousands of years the uncivilized race they are at this moment. (Hunt 1863b, "Negro's Place," 13)

The second theory, which we call *parametric racism*, held that the inferior race differed from the superior (Anglo-Saxons) along some parameter(s). W. R. Greg (discussed later for cofounding the eugenics movement with Galton) persistently attacked classical political economy for its assumption that the Irishman is an "average human being," rather than an "idiomatic" and an "idiosyncratic" man, prone to "idleness, ignorance, jollity, and drink" (Greg 1869a, "Realities," 78; quoted as epigraph to chap. 3).

That both types of racial accounts coexisted and were applied to the

---

4. Max Weber, whose influence on von Mises is common knowledge, severely criticized the racialization of the social sciences (Proctor 1991, 182). The antiracist connections among Weber, von Mises, and Eric Voegelin need specialist attention. As noted below, Weber does not make Schumpeter's list of the "three greatest sociologists," but Galton joins Vico and Marx (Schumpeter 1954, 791).

5. Discussion in the Anthropological Society at this time focused on the Irish and on whether a well-defined separate Irish race might be identified. Allen notes that eugenicists were also unclear on the meaning of race (1993, 150).

Irish is evident from these remarks by Thomas Huxley in an 1870 address to the Anthropological Society.

> If the writer means to be civil, the Celt is taken to be a charming person, full of wit and vivacity and kindliness, but, unfortunately, thoughtless, impetuous, and unstable, and having standards of right and wrong so different from those of the Anglo-Saxon that it would be absurd, not to say cruel, to treat him in the same way; or if the instructor of the public is angry, he talks of the Celt as if he were a kind of savage, out of whom no good ever has come or ever will come, and whose proper fate is to be kept as a hewer of wood and a drawer of water for his Anglo-Saxon master. This is the picture of the lion by the man. (Huxley 1870, 197)[6]

EARLY EUGENICS AND THE OPPOSITION
TO CLASSICAL ECONOMICS

Darwin's theory of natural selection profoundly influenced early eugenicists, and the admiration was mutual. But there was a key difference between Darwinism and the "theory" put forward by early eugenicists. To the extent that Darwinism was undirected evolution, applied to humans, the argument predicted the fit would survive, *without intervention*, naturally.[7] Yet A. R. Wallace made the case early on that the doctrine of natural selection did not apply to humans. Recognizing that humans could not count on such a tendency, eugenicists recommended that human (state) action should be used to obtain it.

In 1864, Wallace argued that the doctrine of natural selection did not apply to humans because of ethical concerns generated by human sympathy. Our morals do not allow us to let the infirm perish. Wallace described nonhuman animals and then turns to people.

---

6. The context of the remarks is a debate over differences between the Celts and the Anglo-Saxons, which, Huxley asserted, amounted only to linguistic differences. That position was opposed by the president of the Anthropological Society of London, John Beddoe (Beddoe 1870, 212–13).

7. The role of Herbert Spencer is considered in chapter 8. Spencer's theory of evolution is pre-Darwinian, without systematic reliance on the natural selection mechanism that eugenics proposed to emulate. Sympathy is the driving force in Spencer's account and, as Wallace pointed out, sympathy blocks natural selection. Spencer suggested that control of births would turn off "the struggle for existence" so that sympathy might flourish. For Edgeworth's criticism of Spencer, see chapter 10.

> But in man, as we now behold him, this is different. He is social and sympathetic. In the rudest tribes the sick are assisted at least with food; less robust health and vigour than the average does not entail death. . . . Some division of labour takes place. . . . The action of natural selection is therefore checked. (clxii)

W. R. Greg responded that sympathy blocked the "salutary" effects of the survival of the fittest, and therefore such sentiments should be suppressed.

> My thesis is this: that the indisputable effect of the state of social progress and culture we have reached, of our high civilization in its present stage and actual form, is to *counteract and suspend* the operation of that righteous and salutary law of "natural selection" in virtue of which the best specimens of the race—the strongest, the finest, the worthiest—are those which survive . . . and propagate an ever improving and perfecting type of humanity. (1875, 119)

To testify to the importance of Greg and his 1868 *Fraser's* "On the Failure of 'Natural Selection' in the Case of Man," what better authority can there be than Darwin himself?

> *Natural Selection as affecting civilized nations.* I have hitherto only considered the advancement of man from a semi-human condition to that of the modern savage. But some remarks on the action of Natural Selection in civilized nations may be worth adding. This subject has been ably discussed by Mr W. R. Greg, and previously by Mr Wallace and Mr Galton. Most of my remarks are taken from these three authors.[8]

Darwin was taken by the following passage in Greg.

> The careless, squalid, unaspiring Irishman, fed on potatoes, living in a pig-stye, doting on a superstition, multiply like rabbits or ephemera:—the frugal, foreseeing, self-respecting, ambitious Scot, stern in his morality, spiritual in his faith, sagacious and disciplined in his intelligence, passes his best years in struggle and in celibacy, marries

---

8. Charles Darwin (1871, 138–39). In the later *Enigmas of Life*, Greg seems rightly pleased to report this endorsement: "Mr. Darwin, who has done me the honor to quote a monograph which I wrote four or five years ago on this subject . . ." (1875, 137). Galton writes: "The verdict which I most eagerly waited for was that of Charles Darwin, whom I ranked far above all other authorities on such a matter. His letter, given below, made me most happy" (1908, 290).

late, and leaves few behind. (Greg 1868, "Failure," 361; quoted with omissions in Darwin *Descent*, 143)

In his *Enigmas of Life*—now informed by Galton's "Hereditary Genius"—Greg focused his attack on the homogeneity doctrine implicit in T. R. Malthus's recommendation of delay of marriage. Malthus cared only about the quantity of births. Early eugenicists worried instead about the *quality*. Greg argued that the "improving element" would soon be outbred by the "more reckless":

> Malthus's "prudential check" rarely operates upon the lowest classes; the poorer they are, usually, the faster do they multiply; certainly the more reckless they are in reference to multiplication. It is the middle classes, those who form the energetic, reliable, improving element of the population, those who wish to rise and do not choose to sink, those in a word who constitute the true strength and wealth and dignity of nations,—it is these who abstain from marriage or postpone it. (Greg 1875, 129)[9]

In a chapter entitled "Malthus Notwithstanding," Greg emphasizes a new law in opposition to Malthus's.

> Possibly the danger *ultimately* to be apprehended may be the very reverse of that which Malthus dreaded; that, in fact, when we have reached that point of universal plenty and universal cultivation to which human progress ought to bring us, the race will multiply too slowly rather than too fast. One such influence may be specified with considerable confidence,—namely, THE TENDENCY OF CEREBRAL DEVELOPMENT TO LESSEN FECUNDITY. (Greg 1875, 103; emphasis in original)

To see how the eugenics movement was influenced by the racist views in Carlyle's "Negro Question," we begin with the two cofounders

---

9. Galton argued similarly: "The check to over-population mainly advocated by Malthus is a prudential delay in the time of marriage; but the practice of such a doctrine would assuredly be limited, and if limited it would be most prejudicial to the race, as I have pointed out in *Hereditary Genius*, but may be permitted to do so again. The doctrine would only be followed by the prudent and self-denying; . . . Those whose race we especially want to have, would leave few descendants, while those whose race we especially want to be quit of, would crowd the vacant space with their progeny. . . . The practical application of the doctrine of deferred marriage would therefore lead indirectly to most mischievous results, that were overlooked owing to the neglect [of] considerations bearing on race" (1907c, *Human Faculty*, 207).

of eugenics: Galton and Greg. Here is the passage of Galton's 1865 "Hereditary Talent and Character" in which he announces his adherence to the doctrine of national characters:

> Still more strongly marked than these are the typical features and characters of different races of men. The Mongolians, Jews, Negroes, Gipsies, and American Indians severally propagate their kinds; and *each kind differs in character and intellect,* as well as in colour and shape, from the other four. They, and a vast number of races form a class of instances worthy of close investigation, in which peculiarities of character are invariably transmitted from the parents to the offspring. (1865, 320; emphasis added)

Galton's explanation for racial hierarchy conjoins Thomas Carlyle's argument that labor makes us fully human with the principle of natural selection.

> The most notable quality that the requirements of civilization have hitherto bred in us, living as we do in a rigorous climate and on a naturally barren soil, is the instinct of continuous steady labour. This is alone possessed by civilized races, and it is possessed in a far greater degree by the feeblest individuals among them than by the most able-bodied savages. . . . men who are born with wild and irregular dispositions, even though they contain much that is truly noble, are alien to the spirit of a civilized country, and they and their breed are eliminated from it by the law of selection. (1865, 325)

Next, we juxtapose Carlyle's *Shooting Niagara*—his defense of Governor Eyre and attack on democracy in America and Britain—with Greg on the survival of native races:

CARLYLE

One always rather likes the Nigger; evidently a poor blockhead with good dispositions, with affections, attachments,—with a turn for Nigger Melodies, and the like:—he is the only Savage of all the coloured races that doesn't die out on sight of the White Man; but can actually live beside him, and work and increase and be

GREG

The Indians of the Antilles, the Red man of North America, the South Sea Islanders, the Australians, even the New Zealanders (the finest and most pliable and teachable of savages), are all alike dying out with rapidity—in consequence of the harshness, or in spite of the forbearance and protection, of the stronger and more

merry. The Almighty Maker has appointed him to be a Servant. (1867, 5)

capable European. The negro alone survives—and, but for the observation of what is now going on in our sugar islands and in the United States we should say, seems likely to survive. He only has been able to hold his own in a fashion, and to live and flourish, side by side with masterful and mightier races. (1868, 357)

There is a difference of course in style between Carlyle and Greg. The connection between Carlyle and the eugenics movement can be appreciated by considering Carlyle's claims about "swarmery" in *Shooting Niagara* alongside Galton's 1872 "Gregariousness in Cattle and in Men."

CARLYLE

[T]here soon comes that singular phenomenon . . . "*Swarmery*," or the "Gathering of Men in Swarms," and what prodigies they are in the habit of doing and believing, when thrown into that miraculous condition. Some big Queen Bee is in the centre of the swarm; but any commonplace stupidest *bee* . . . whatever of palpable incredibility and delirious absurdity, universally believed, can be uttered or imagined on these points, "the equality of men," any man equal to any other; Quashee Nigger to Socrates or Shakspeare; Judas Iscariot to Jesus Christ;— and Bedlam and Gehenna equal to the New Jerusalem, shall we say? If these things are taken up, not only as axioms of Euclid, but as articles of religion burning to be put in practice for the salvation of

GALTON

I propose, in these pages, to discuss a curious and apparently anomalous group of base moral instincts and intellectual deficiencies, to trace their analogies in the world of brutes, and to examine the conditions, through which they have been evolved. I speak of the slavish aptitudes, from which the leaders of men, and the heroes and the prophets, are exempt, but which are irrepressible elements in the disposition of average men. I refer to the natural tendency of the vast majority of our race to shrink from the responsibility of standing and acting alone, to their exaltation of the *vox populi*, even when they know it to be the utterance of a mob of nobodies, into the *vox Dei*, to their willing servitude to tradition, authority, and custom.[10] (Quoted in Pearson 1924, 72)

---

10. The phrase *vox populi, vox dei* will be revisited in appendix 1 and in our study of Galton's use of the median (chap. 5, this vol.).

the world,—I think you will admit
that *Swarmery* plays a wonderful
part in the heads of poor
Mankind. (1867, 4–5)

Here is the judgment of Galton's disciple, Karl Pearson, on this article.

Wonderful, is it not, how Darwinism had already gripped Galton? How he thought in terms of heredity and natural selection and was ready to apply them to the past history of man in order to explain its present and suggest its future! The notion that it is necessary for human progress to breed out the men of slavish morals and intelligence—the essential foundation of eugenics—is already a truth to him. (Pearson 1924, 74)

The link to Carlyle's teaching is obvious. With eugenics we can breed the Hero.

Galton had an immense veneration for genius as he defines it; not only like Carlyle would he have made his heroes rulers of the mediocre, but unlike Carlyle he would have had his heroes steadily and surely replace the latter.[11]

JAMES HUNT CONVERTS FRANCIS GALTON

Galton's 1876 criticism of economics as practiced in Section F of the British Association has been widely discussed.[12] Earlier testimony from Nassau Senior demonstrates that the criticism was not new.[13] But what was the feasible alternative to economics as practiced in the 1870s? Gal-

---

11. Pearson (1924, 94). Cf. chapter 5, note 7.

12. See Peart 2001b; Stone 1980; Henderson 1994; Porter 1986, 135–36.

13. Nassau Senior (1860, 357): "In 1856 the General Committee of the British Association decided that the Section over which I have the honour to preside, should be entitled 'The Section of Economic Science and Statistics.'

"I have looked through the papers which since that time have been communicated to us, and I have been struck by the unscientific character of many of them.

"I use that word not dyslogistically, but merely distinctively, merely as expressing that the writers have wandered from the domain of science into that of art."

Henderson (1994, 499): "Any number of the early arguments defending the continued existence of Section F are curious and fail to confront directly Galton's primary argument that the section dealt with unscientific matters."

ton evidently approved of the alternative offered in anthropology by Dr. James Hunt.[14] When he defended anthropology in the British Association from the type of charges leveled against economics, Galton focused on the quality of the anthropologist, not their procedures.[15]

How could Hunt have had anything in common with Galton? No one has ever called Galton a quack. Two claims that Hunt made in public at the London Anthropological Society, then had printed, helped him earn this label:

> Many observers have noticed the fact that the Negro frequently uses the great toe as a thumb. (1863b, "Negro's Place," 7)

> [T]he typical woolly-haired races have never invented a reasoned theological system, discovered an alphabet, framed a grammatical language, nor made the least step in science or art.[16]

The assertions that toes are used as thumbs and that a people exist without the capacity for a human language prepare one for the truly bizarre.[17]

The modern theory of statistical racism as first explained by Arrow (1972) and Phelps (1972) supposes that groups will be divided on the basis of sample means. One race differs from another on the basis of an estimate of some central tendency. In nineteenth-century Britain, this dimension might have been willingness to work, or the ability to save.[18]

---

14. Another theme common to Hunt and Galton is their disdain for the presence of women at academic meetings. This aspect of Galton's attack on Section F is discussed by Henderson (1994). Hunt separated himself from the Ethnological Society over its admission of women. On the disparagement Mill received for his attempt to extend the franchise to women, see Peart 2005.

15. In "Economic Science" (1877, 471–72), Galton remarked: "This Section [F] therefore occupies a peculiar position of isolation, being neither sufficiently scientific in itself, nor receiving help from other Sections. In the first respect it may be alleged that the Anthropology Department and the Geographical Section are open to the same charges; but in the latter respect the case is very different. The leading anthropologists are physiologists, geologists, or geographers, and the proceedings of the department are largely indebted to their special knowledge." Stepan (1982, 127) explains Galton's reference to anthropologist as geographer.

16. Hunt (1863b, "Negro's Place," 19). The language slur resurfaced early in the twentieth century, when Commons (1916, 94) asserted that the Yiddish spoken by Russian Jews "is scarcely a language—it is a jargon without syntax, conjugation, or declension." We return to the claim concerning spiritual incapacity in chapter 5.

17. As noted earlier (chap. 3), however, similar claims were also made by Charles Kingsley.

18. See Peart 2000. The table provides evidence concerning both of these characteristics.

But as noted previously (chap. 3), we have argued that, at least as an approximation, the racists we consider also distinguish one race from another on the basis of an estimate of the dispersion around the center. "Inferior" was a judgment about the race that is said to be a dead race, as Hunt put it, "incapable of elevation," a race with zero variance. In this case, the sample mean of the race, its stereotype in Arrow-Phelps terminology, *is* the "inferior race." The images from *Punch* we reprinted in chapter 3, in which all Fenians look alike, illustrate Hunt's race-without-variation theory. Not surprisingly, Hunt's argument concerning the Negro was countered, in his time, by "cases of intelligent Negros." Hunt's response was that such instances were evidence of "impostures" rather than examples of variation.[19]

In Hunt's theory of racial development, both the mean and variance of intelligence and other moral characteristics are said to be functions of the length of time one's mind develops. Development of the "lesser" races stops sooner. If this notion spread no further than Hunt's claim that blacks used the big toe as a thumb, it would be without consequence. But this was not the case; Hunt's theory was widely influential.[20]

The first issue of Hunt's *Anthropological Review* contains abstracts of anthropological papers presented at Section E of the British Association along with reports of the floor discussion. The third paper is Hunt's "On the Physical and Mental Characters of the Negro." This occasion generated considerable discussion when an escaped slave and abolitionist writer, William Craft, rose to challenge Hunt.[21] But before

---

19. The details are provided in Desmond 1994, 353; Young 1995; and Levy 2001. Hunt provides an example of how this "imposture" argument works: "The exhibitions of cases of intelligent Negroes in the saloons of the fashionable world by so-called 'philanthropists,' have frequently been nothing but mere impostures. In nearly every case in which the history of these cases has been investigated, it has been found that these so-called Negroes are the offspring of European and African parents" (1863b, "Negro's Place," 16).

20. Reade (1864, 399): "The growth of the brain in the negro, as in the ape, is sooner arrested than in those of our race." We quote Reade when we consider the discussion of whether Africans were suited to Christianity (chap. 9). We hope to examine the role of Richard Burton, Hunt's associate in the Anthropological Society, at a later date. Burton's important translations of the *Arabian Nights* began with his discussions with Hunt. See Desmond 1994.

21. Lorimer (1978, 47–48) discusses Craft and the confrontation with Hunt. Levy (2001) transcribes Charles Kingsley's letter to Hunt about the event. It is illuminating that Mill's disciple,

Craft spoke, Galton pointed out the stupidity of the zero variance assertion, based on his own experience in Africa.

> MR. GALTON said that the case was briefly this:—Among the Negroes of
> Africa there were more frequent instances of an abject and superstitious
> character, combined with brutal behavior, than could be paralleled
> elsewhere in the world. It was a wonder that people like those of
> Dahomey could mould themselves into any form of society at all, and it
> was actually found that when the chief of such a tribe died it disinte-
> grated and rapidly disappeared. In short, the tribes of Africa were
> remarkable for their rapid formation and short continuance. Many of
> their chiefs were of alien descent, and it was remarkable how their great-
> est kingdoms had been ruled by Tawareks—men with Arab blood—or,
> as Captain Speke now informed us, by straight-haired Wahumas. How
> did it happen, then, that so degraded a people could furnish men capa-
> ble of constructing nations out of the loosest materials? The question
> once stated was almost its own reply. The Negro, though on average
> extremely base, was by no means a member of a race lying at a dead
> level. On the contrary, it had the capacity of frequently producing able
> men capable of taking an equal position with Europeans. The fact of a
> race being distinguished by the diversity of its members was well known
> to ethnologists. There were black and red sub-divisions of many North
> African races, and the contrast between the well-fed and ill-fed classes of
> the same tribe of Negroes was often such as amount apparently to a
> specific difference.[22]

How did Galton's ideas "evolve" from a recognition of the diversity
of African peoples to his 1865 *Macmillan's* articles?[23] Before his
encounter with Hunt, Galton's views represent his African experience
viewed through the lens of a theory not-too-distant from that held by
the classical economists. After his encounter with Hunt, he reads, in

---

J. E. Cairnes (1865, 336), cites "William Crafts [*sic*], the African explorer, the eloquent defender
of the humanity of his race, and now the leading merchant and reformer in the kingdom of
Dahomey" along with Frederick Douglass and others as counterexamples to the zero-variance
claim. The confrontation between the judgment of science versus that of ordinary people is examined in chapter 11.

22. Galton in "Anthropology at the British Association" (1863, 387–88). We find no discussion
of this in any report in any of the secondary literature even though Pearson's *Life* (1924) devotes
an extensive section to Galton's anthropological writings.

23. Stepan (1982, 127): "Galton clearly recognized the variety in physical character, language,
and social organization of the various African tribes he encountered; once home, however, the
tribal distinctions became merged in a single Negro race."

the passages from the articles that we quote later, as if he were seeing the world through Hunt's racial theory.

How is this possible? By contemporary judgment, Hunt was a quack. Galton's integrity is beyond reproach.[24] But Galton had a weakness: he seems to have wanted to believe that the physicality of a man was positively correlated with his intellect. Many years after Hunt's death he candidly stated that he really wanted to believe in the uniformity of Negro fingerprints.[25] Here is Pearson's report where he first quotes Galton:

> I think most of my readers would be surprised at the statures and physical frames of the heroes of history, who fill my pages, if they could be assembled together in a hall. I would undertake to pick out of any group of them, even out of that of the Divines, an "eleven" who should compete in any physical feats whatever, against similar selections from groups of twice or thrice their number, taken at haphazard from equally well-fed classes. (Pearson 1924, 94)

Then Pearson comments.

> Perhaps Galton laid too great stress on the high wranglers and classics of his own day who had been "varsity blues"; or again on the big-headed men on the front benches at the Royal Society meetings in the early 'seventies. (1924, 94)[26]

---

24. At age eighty-five he found technical reasons to believe that majoritarian decision making had desirable properties. And he called attention to this "unexpected" result with great clarity, choosing to title the second of a pair of articles "*Vox Populi*," explicitly challenging his Carlylean assertions quoted previously. See Galton 1907a and 1907b. These articles are sufficiently important that they were reprinted by us in a 2002 issue of *Public Choice* where we call attention to Pearson's judgment that Galton chose to publish these results in *Nature* to maximize their contemporary (policy?) impact. Porter (1986, 130) notes Galton's antiegalitarianism in the years before these papers were published. Our *Public Choice* reprint is included at the end of this book as an appendix.

25. Galton (1892a, 195–96); cited in table 4.1.

26. Pearson himself was not immune to this sort of argument, e.g., Pearson (1924, 94): "Galton illustrates this by a case in which trained Highlanders challenged all England to compete with them in their games of strength. They were beaten in the foot-race by a youth, a pure Cockney, and clerk to a London banker. Perhaps I may be permitted to cite another illustration from an occurrence at 'varsity sports over 40 years ago. The high jump had been won by a highly trained athlete, and the rod had been replaced at the last half inch he had failed to surmount; a non-combatant, a somewhat sedentary mathematician in every day costume, stepped again from among the spectators, leapt the rod to the astonishment of the onlookers, and disappeared again into the crowd."

He adds the following note.

> He was very unhappy about the low correlations I found between intelligence and size of head, and would cite against me those "front benches"; it was one of the few instances I noticed when impressions seemed to have more weight with him than measurements. It is possible, however, that between his day and mine science changed its recruiting fields, and "eminence" became less common. (94)

All that has been written on Hunt pictures him with enormous vitality and energy.[27] Galton would not be the first intellectual to have been seduced by charisma. Nor would he be the only African explorer to learn to see the world through Hunt's eyes.[28] By 1865 Galton on savages in general reads just like Hunt on the Negro.

It is important to notice that Galton never—as far as we know—employed the "mixed race" immunization strategy described earlier. Thus he lacks Hunt's device for dealing with the difference between the hypothetical "Negro" and observed people of color. Hunt

---

27. The obituary from *New York Weekly Day-Book* (6 November 1869), reprinted in the *Anthropology Review* under "Anthropological News" (1870, 97) gives some flavor of contemporary opinions: "We are pained to hear of the death of Dr. James Hunt . . . beyond doubt the best, or, at all events, the most useful man in England, if not, indeed, in Europe. . . . Dr. Hunt, in his own clear knowledge and brave enthusiasm, was doing more for humanity, for the welfare of mankind, and for the glory of God, than all the philosophers, humanitarians, philanthropists, statesmen, and, we may say, bishops and clergy of England together. He was teaching them what they are in *fact*—what God has made them, what their relations to other *species* of human kind, Mongols, Malays, Negroes, etc., and thus preparing them for the fulfilment of their duties to each other, and to the dependent races that were, or might be, in juxtaposition with them." Cf. Keith (1917, 19): "We must now turn back to the year 1863 to witness one of the most remarkable and instructive of all the episodes which chequer the history of our Institute. We have seen how young Hunt became Secretary of the Ethnological Society in 1859, under the Presidency of Crawfurd. He has the fire and enthusiasm of an evangelist and the methods of a popular political propagandist." Stocking (1971, 377) explains the growth of the Anthropological Society by appeal to "a leader of Hunt's evident dynamism." Banton (1977, 77) describes Hunt as "England's brashest exponent of the theory of permanent racial types." Desmond (1994, 320) writes: "The coarsest attacks on *Man's Place* were closest to home. As the American Civil War raged the doom-mongering about racial conflict inspired a charismatic reactionary with a PhD., James Hunt, to found the Anthropological Society."

28. Reade (1864, 399): "Thus it has been proved by measurements, by microscopes, by analyses, that the typical negro is something between a child, a dotard, and a beast. I can not struggle against these sacred facts of science.* [*At the last meeting of the British Association, in the Section E, the president of the Anthropological Society [Hunt] ventured to quote them. His audience felt insulted when informed that they were more intellectual than the negro, and endeavored to prove the contrary by hisses!] . . . But I contend that it is only degradation; that it is the result of disease."

never denied that observed people of color had considerable variation. Instead, he insisted that all the variation was the result of their white ancestors. Without this quackery to distinguish between the hypothetical "Negro" and actual people of color, Galton later assumes that variance is a constant across observed races.[29] Nonetheless, in 1865 his words give warrant to Hunt's claim that the "savage" is without variation.

HUNT

M. Gratiolet[30] has also observed that in the anterior races the sutures of the cranium do not close so early as in the occipital or inferior races. From these researches it appears that in the Negro the growth of the brain is sooner arrested than in the European. The premature union of the bones of the skull may give a clue to much of the mental inferiority which is seen in the Negro race. There can be no doubt that in puberty a great change takes place in relation to physical development; but in the Negro there appears to be an arrested development of the brain, exactly harmonizing with the physical formation. Young Negro children are

GALTON

Another difference, which may either be due to natural selection or to original difference of race, is the fact that savages seem incapable of progress after the first few years of their life. The average children of all races are much on a par. Occasionally, those of the lower races are more precocious than the Anglo-Saxon; as a brute beast of a few weeks old is certainly more apt and forward than a child of the same age. But, as the years go by, the higher races continue to progress, while the lower ones gradually stop. They remain children in mind, with the passions of grown men. Eminent genius commonly asserts itself in tender years, but it continues long

29. In the book version of *Hereditary Genius*, Galton assumes for exposition that races have the same variance: "In comparing the worth of different races, I shall make frequent use of the law of deviation from an average, to which I have already been much beholden; and, to save the reader's time and patience, I propose to act upon an assumption that would require a good deal of discussion to the limit, and to which the reader may at first demur, but which cannot lead to any error of importance in a rough provisional inquiry. I shall assume that the *intervals* between the grades of ability are the *same* in all the races" (1892b, 337). More pointedly he asserted that there was considerable overlap in the abilities of blacks and whites: "First, the negro race has occasionally, but very rarely, produced such men as Toussaint l'Ouverture. . . . Secondly, the negro race is by no means wholly deficient in men capable of becoming good factors, thriving merchants, and otherwise considerably raised above the average of whites" (1892b, 338). We thank Bryan Caplan for the reference.

30. Louis Pierre Gratiolet was a French anatomist and anthropologist. His work was cited by Darwin, and he worked with Paul Broca on brain localization.

nearly as intelligent as European children; but the older they grow the less intelligent they become. They exhibit, when young, an animal liveliness for play and tricks, far surpassing the European child.

With the Negro, as with some other races of man, it has been found that the children are precocious, but that no advance in education can be made after they arrive at the age of maturity. (1863b, "Negro's Place," 8, 12)

to develop. The highest minds in the highest races seem to have been those who had the longest boyhood. (1865, 326)

"CHARACTERISTICS" OF "LOWER" RACES

If the writings of a thinker like Galton seem to reflect the views of Hunt, perhaps the influence of Hunt and the anthropologists extends to the economics community as it was reshaped toward the end of the century. To this end, we summarize how the anthropologists and eugenicists characterized "inferiority," and we consider how those characteristics carry over to the postclassical economics literature.[31] Our intention is not to argue that the treatment of race is uniform across or within our groups of analysts. Within Britain, differences persisted within the anthropological treatments (Duff 1881), and among British postclassical economists the discussion was by no means uniform. And differences characterized the British and the American experiences.[32] The analysis and reform-minded zeal of the Progressive era in America were not significant features of the British experience.[33] Yet the common language and themes evident in table 4.1 suggest that

---

31. We confine our study to the period in which the influence of eugenics is strongest, roughly from 1870 through 1920. A number of well-known economists who were prominent in the Eugenics Society remain outside our scope, notably J. M. Keynes and James Meade. Keynes's Galton Lecture (Keynes 1937) reveals a deep concern with population growth, but it confines itself to the effect of an overall slowing in population growth without mention of racial or income-related variations in reproductive rates. See Toye 2000 on Keynes's treatment of population and the "Greg problem."

32. Compare Leonard 2003a and Rutherford 2003 with Peart 2000 and Collard 1996.

33. See Leonard 2003b and Bateman 2003.

TABLE 4.1. Anthropologists, Eugenicists, and Postclassical Economists on the "Lower" Races

	Homogeneity of "Lower" Race	"Characteristics" of "Lower" Races
Hunt 1863, 1866	In the negro race there is a great uniformity of temperament. In every people of Europe all temperaments exist; but in the Negro race we can only discover analogies for the choleric and phlegmatic temperaments. (1863b, 11) We now know it to be a patent fact that there are races existing which have no history, and that the Negro is one of these races. From the most remote antiquity the Negro race seems to have been what they are now. We may be pretty sure that the Negro race have been without a progressive history; and that they have been for thousands of years the uncivilized race they are at this moment. (1863b, 13)	Susceptible to impulse, lack willpower, improvident; cannot resist temptation (1866b, 117); ungovernable appetite (1866b, 125); lack foresight
Galton 1865	The race [of American Indians] is divided into many varieties, but it has fundamentally the same character throughout the whole of America. (1865, 321) Here, then, is a well-marked type of character, that formerly prevailed over a large part of the globe, with which other equally marked types of character in other regions are strongly contrasted . . . the typical West African Negro. (1865, 321)	The Red man has great patience, great reticence, great dignity; the Negro has strong impulsive passions, and neither patience, reticence, nor dignity. He is warm-hearted, loving towards his master's children, and idolised by the children in return. He is eminently gregarious, for he is always jabbering, quarrelling, tom-tom-ing, or dancing. He is remarkably domestic, and he is endowed with such constitutional vigour, and is so prolific, that his race is irrepressible. (1865, 321)
1892	The impressions from Negroes betray the general clumsiness of their fingers, but their patterns are not, so far as I can find, different from those of others, they are not simpler as judged either by their contours or by the number of origins, embranchments, islands, and enclosures contained in them. Still, whether it be from pure fancy on my part, or from the way in which they were printed, or from some real peculiarity, the general aspect of the Negro print strikes me as characteristic. The width of the ridges seems more uniform, their intervals more regular, and their courses more parallel than with us. In short, they give an idea of ~~greater simplicity, due to causes that I have not yet succeeded in~~	Savages lack instinct of continuous steady labor, possess wild untameable restlessness, wild impulsive nature of negro (1865, 325, 327)

Pearson 1924 Pearson and Moul 1925	Servile, gregarious, herdlike; undifferentiated; remain the Red Man and Negro despite environmental differences (1924, 73–74); oppression reduces differentiation (weeds out physically and mentally fit individuals) (Pearson and Moul 1925, 8)	Want of self-reliance; sexual passion; imprudent; feckless; feeble minded; high birth rates (1924, 73, 80, 111)	
Jevons* 1869, 1870, 1871		Intemperate, improvident, lacking foresight (1869, 186–87); ignorant, careless, unsubdued, vicious, want of self-reliance (1870, 196, 200).	Questions of this kind [work effort] depend greatly upon the character of the race. Persons of an energetic disposition feel labour less painfully than their fellow-men, and, if they happen to be endowed with various and acute sensibilities, their desire of further acquisition never ceases. A man of lower race, a negro for instance, enjoys possession less, and loathes labour more; his exertions, therefore soon stop. A poor savage would be content to gather the almost gratuitous fruits of nature, if they were sufficient to give sustenance; it is only physical want which drives him to exertion. (1871, 182-83)
Marshall 1890	strange uniformity of general character among savages (723)		Savage life ruled by custom and impulse; never forecasting the distant future; seldom providing for near future; servitude to custom; fitful; governed by the fancy of the moment; incapable of steady work (723); Anglo-Saxon are steadfast (581); 'great mass of humanity' lack patience, self control, self discipline (581); England peopled by the strongest members of the strongest races of northern Europe (740); capital-labour division of labour characterizes English race/ modern civilization (745); race of undertakers develops in England (749)

TABLE 4.1.—*Continued*

	Homogeneity of "Lower" Race	"Characteristics" of "Lower" Races
Pigou§ 1907, 1920		"Feckless"; high birth rates; (1907, 364–65); "faulty telescopic faculty"; "propagation untrammelled by economic considerations" (1920, 123); "lack initiative and understanding" (326); over-estimate chances of success (493)
Fisher¶ 1909, 1930		Lack foresight and self-control; improvident; impatience; weak wills, weak intellect; susceptible to alcohol (1930, 73; 1909, 94, 376)
Webb‡ 1910	American blacks less differentiated than whites (236–37)	Maximum birth rates; thriftless; idle; drunken; profligate; feeble-minded; unfit; lacking in self-respect and foresight
Fetter 1916	Can master a limited range of occupations (367)	Defective mentally and physically; high birth rates (369, 375).
Commons 1916	Can perform a limited range of tasks. Unmechanical and unintelligent. Slavery reduced differentiation.	Impulsive, strong sexual passion, debauchery; high birth rate; lack self-control, foresight, self-reliance, willpower, ingenuity; ignorant; unstable; indolent; adverse to solitude; improvident; superstitious; contented (39, 40, 49, 60, 212–13)

Notes
Jevons* 1869: laboring classes; 1870: Irish explanation for mortality rates (208ff)
Pigou§ Lower classes; non-race.
Fisher¶ Characteristics are specified in terms of lower classes with (Irish) racial components
Webb‡ The fecundity characteristic applies both to the lower classes and American blacks (237, 240), while the other characteristics are specified in terms of class alone (233, 239, 240).

the influence of early racial theorizing was persistent and wide, and took on the two forms outlined at the outset: the "inferior" race differed in terms of some parameter(s) such as work effort, time preference, or family size; and the other—more devastating—model that held that the Other was a dead race incapable of progress.

Table 4.1 documents claims by postclassical economists concerning the lack of differentiation among the "inferior" or "lower races." It also provides evidence from postclassical economists of parametric racism, the presumption that inferior races are characterized by lower work effort,[34] improvidence, alcoholism, inability to control sexual passion, and overall carelessness.[35] Throughout, some imprecision exists as to whether the economist has in mind the lower classes or a racial or ethnic type. British economists typically focused on the lower classes and argued that the working classes are creatures of passion, unable to plan for the future and unusually susceptible to alcoholism (Peart 2000). Yet when the Irish were involved, class signifies race (as Jevons 1870 reveals; Peart 2001a). For Marshall, the "industrial" classes are racially inferior: as conquest and the intermixture of races occurred, the inferior (yet still white) races sort themselves into the lower ranks of industrial society (1890, 195). The legacy of slavery looms large in the work of early-twentieth-century American writers. Finally, for both British and American postclassical economics, an overriding fear of the dysgenic effects of immigration is present.

---

34. As in Carlyle's "Negro Question," climate is often offered as an explanation for reduced work effort among the "lower races" (and, since lack of work effort implies that simple and then more complex tasks are neither attempted nor mastered, climate is also associated with lack of differentiation within the race). See Marshall 1890, 195, 205, 528. Commons contends that a tropical climate is associated with ignorance and debauchery, while a temperate climate requires work effort and develops self-reliance, self-control, and ingenuity (1916, 212–13). Jevons is also struck by the relationship between climate and race (1869). For an application of Jevons's argument to the American context, see F. Walker (1881) in Darity 1995. Thus, an economic explanation is provided for "facts" of anthropology.

35. While we find no discussion of lack of variation in the secondary literature, there are several good discussions of parametric racism in postclassical thinking. See Collard 1996 for an examination that links Pigou's "faulty telescopic tendency" to the distribution of resources over time. White 1994 discusses issues of race and gender in Jevons. Peart 2000 discusses racial determinants of rationality in Jevons, Marshall, Pigou, and Fisher; Levitt 1976 mentions Marshall on eugenics; Aldrich 1975 discusses Fisher's economic analysis and eugenics.

BREEDING AND IMMIGRATION POLICY

Eugenicists urged that a policy of selective breeding and immigration be used to improve racial composition of the nation. Without intervention, they argued, the quality of the population would decline over time. What was required, then, was a wide-ranging program to counteract eugenic tendencies, what Sidney Webb referred to as the "social machinery" of eugenic intervention (1910, 237). The common thread in eugenic policies is coercion, overriding reproductive choices of individuals. The implication for national greatness was stressed repeatedly.[36] Eugenicists—biologists and social scientists alike—made their case in explicit opposition to utilitarian economists of the nineteenth century for whom the happiness of one counts as that of another (Hankins 1923, 398),[37] and in opposition to democratic theory.

> Democracy is still the fundamental religion of the nation, but grave doubts begin to appear as to the speedy realization of the happy day-dreams of our fathers. The land is full of strangers of alien race and tradition; in spite of popular education and heroic efforts at social betterment objective inequality has increased so that the wilful unbeliever must now admit it. Class lines are appearing even in the democratic west; even class war stalks through the land in which our cant-mongering political orators and purblind newspaper editors say there are no classes. (Hankins 1923, 395)[38]

Among economists, as among the anthropologists, the argument was often that the Irish overbreed, while Anglo-Saxons reproduce at relatively low rates. In America, the Irish are frequently offered as an example of an "inferior" race, but the "Negro" and "immigration problems" formed the central backdrop to discussions of eugenics policies. Waves of immigration drawn predominantly from "inferior races" are

---

36. Leonard Darwin claims the limitation of family size by those who can afford children is both "immoral" and "unpatriotic" (1916a, 173). Macbride, discussing Darwin, "regrets" to admit that eugenics is taking greater hold in the United States than England, a fact that leads him to the conclusion that America "would beat them [England] in the race for commercial supremacy" (in L. Darwin 1919, 31). Pearson also linked eugenics with national welfare, arguing in 1925 that Galton's phrase "national eugenics" was well chosen (Pearson and Elderton 1925, 3–4).

37. We take up this point in detail in chapters 7 and 10.

38. We examine the use of the word *cant* (and *cant-mongering*) in chapter 8.

said to have reduced the quality of the nation (Commons 1916, 200ff). Since such immigrants multiply at high rates, the deterioration would be ongoing.[39]

Among the British postclassical economists, Marshall most strenuously endorsed the differential fertility rate argument. He wrote about a "cause for anxiety," "some partial arrest of that selective influence of struggle and competition which in the earliest stages of civilization caused those who were strongest and most vigorous to leave the largest progeny behind them; and to which, more than any other single cause, the progress of the human race is due" ([1890] 1930, 201).[40] Advances in public health that saved the "feeble" and "unfit" served to reduce the quality of the population.

> Thus there are increasing reasons for fearing, that while the progress of medical science and sanitation is saving from death a continually increasing number of the children of those who are feeble physically and mentally; many of those who are most thoughtful and best endowed with energy, enterprise, and self-control are tending to defer their marriages and in other ways to limit the number of children whom they leave behind them. (Marshall [1890] 1930, 201)[41]

Pigou also accepted that the lower classes reproduce at relatively high rates, while the "higher classes" delay marriage and have few chil-

---

39. In England, economists such as Marshall feared that such deterioration would occur within cities (Marshall 1884). Here the argument is that the Irish form a relatively large and (due to high birthrates) growing constituency in cities (Jevons 1870; Peart 2001a). Cf. "The slums and courts of our large cities are chiefly inhabited by the unfit, who are recruited by the failures in the industrial struggle; and among these early marriages and illegitimate intercourse is more common than among the saner and more intelligent class" (Ashby, comments on Reid 1906, 38).

40. The argument was specified in the common terminology of low fertility rates among the "upper classes" and high birthrates among the poor. At least in Marshall's case, however, the racial element is quite clear. Historically, the intermixture of races that followed conquests led him to speculate that the lower races selected into the industrial classes ([1890] 1930, 195). Elsewhere he used the more obvious eugenic phrase, referring to the tendency of the "higher strains of the population to marry later and to have fewer children than the lower" ([1890] 1930, 203).

41. "Again, on the Pacific Slope, there were at one time just grounds for fearing that all but highly skilled work would be left to the Chinese; and that the white men would live in an artificial way in which a family became a great expense. In this case Chinese lives would have been substituted for American, and the average quality of the human race would have been lowered" (Marshall [1890] 1930, 201 n. 1). Galton's argument concerning the inheritance of traits of genius is endorsed in this context, as well (202, 206). The contention that, without sterilization or segregation, saving the "feeble" entails a reduction in genetic quality is common; see Fisher 1909; L. Darwin 1916a; Webb 1910.

dren (1907, 364–65).[42] The "injurious" effects of such relatively high reproductive rates among the poor might be counteracted by policies designed to improve the well-being of low-income people (cf. Webb 1910). But the biological question remained: "Is there reason to believe that bad original properties and poverty are closely related?" Pigou answers affirmatively.

> For, if we consider the matter, it is apparent that among the relatively rich are many persons who have risen from a poor environment, which their fellows, who have remained poor, shared with them in childhood. Among the original properties of these relatively rich presumably there are qualities which account for their rise. A relatively high reproductive rate *among those who have remained poor* implies, in a measure, the breeding out of these qualities. It implies, in fact, a form of selection that discriminates against the original properties that promote economic success. (1907, 365)

In America, the argument regarding relatively low fertility rates among the highly civilized becomes known as "race treason," a phrase that elicited no small amount of resentment among the educated and well-to-do. For economists, eugenics provided at least a partial solution to two related problems, the "relative decrease of the successful strains of the population," as well as the racial mix of the existing population that resulted from slavery and ongoing immigration (Fetter 1916, 366).[43] For Fetter the "most grave" population problem, the Negro problem, was "insoluble." The alternatives of intermixture of races, existence in separate geographical regions, and extinction are said to be "repugnant," "impractical," and unrealistic. Fetter concludes with

---

42. Pigou is singled out by Leonard Darwin (1916b, 311): "[A]s far as I know, [Pigou] is almost the only economist who has paid serious attention to eugenics in connection with economics." Indeed, a JSTOR search for *eugenics* in the economics list finds Pigou 1907 and Fetter et al. 1907 as the earliest. Schumpeter writes: "Economists entirely failed to bestow on these problems [the quality of the human stock] the amount of attention they deserve: flippant phrases pro or con form the bulk of their contribution; the only one of the leading men to take more trouble was Pigou" (1954, 790).

43. Black population growth was low relative to that of whites. But there was still cause for alarm. Commons (1916, 60) argued that the difference resulted from high mortality rates among blacks (attributed in large measure to the effects of "sexual immorality and debauchery"), differences that could be eliminated and even reversed in the event of improved public health standards.

"futile expressions of regret" (1916, 366–68). Perhaps Fetter is an instance of that oddity whose existence Sandy Darity conjectured: the laissez-faire eugenicist.[44] His unwillingness to countenance state action leaves nothing but despair on racial matters.

Why the pessimism regarding the intermixture of race? There is an obvious implication of the doctrine that "lower races" were characterized by lack of variation. Eugenics policy, as is well known (Soloway 1995), proposed to encourage reproduction from the desirable part of the distribution of abilities and discourage reproduction from the undesirable part. But if the "lower race" is without variation, there is no "desirable part," and a eugenic policy of differential intraracial breeding makes no sense.[45]

Three sets of eugenics policies were endorsed by economists to improve what we might call the genetic makeup of the economic unit (generally, in this context, the nation):[46] (1) positive measures, to

---

44. Darity wondered about this possibility in his comments at our 2000 History of Economics Society presentation. The predictable answer, from Sidney Webb, is: "The policy of 'Laisser faire' is, necessarily, to a eugenist the worst of all policies, because it implies the definite abandonment of intelligently purposeful selection. . . . No consistent eugenist can be a 'Laisser Faire' individualist unless he throws up the game in despair. He must interfere, interfere, interfere!" (1910, 234, 237). We thank Ed McPhail for reminding us of this passage in Webb. Even earlier Fetter had made this same point: "Unless effective means are found to check the degeneration of the race, the noontide of humanity's greatness is nigh, if not already passed. Our optimism must be based, not upon laissez faire, but upon the vigorous application of science, humanity, and the legislative art to the solution of the problem. Great changes of thought are impending, and these will include the elimination of the unfit, the establishment of qualifications for marriage, the education of parents, and the conscious improvement of the race. Under the touch of the new science of eugenics, many of the most perplexing social problems will disappear" (Fetter et al. 1907, 92–93).

A laissez-faire advocate might well propose a repeal of government policies that, in his view, have a dysgenic impact. The question would remain whether the eugenic argument added anything to motivate the advocacy of repeal.

45. Soloway (1995, 60): "In the case of the United States, tortured race relations and extensive alien immigration were the principal sources of eugenic worry; in Britain, where long-established ethnic and racial homogeneity prevailed the relative contribution of indigenous classes to the population was the predominant concern."

46. As Collard (1996) has noted regarding Pigou, economists typically favored a combination of eugenics and environmental policy. See Pigou 1907; 1920, 120–25. The purported relative efficacy of eugenics proposals is made clear in a series of papers presented to the School of Economics and Political Science at the University of London in 1904, 1905, and 1906. One by Archdall Reid is particularly representative for its nationalistic overtones and the concern with alcoholism (1906, 22): "We should bear in mind, however, that, were eugenic breeding possible, we could improve the race to an unlimited extent; whereas our power of improving the individual by

encourage fertility among the "superior" genetic stock; (2) negative policies, to reduce fertility among those of "inferior" natural abilities; and (3) immigration restrictions, which increasingly became central to these discussions. Irving Fisher, Frank Fetter, and J. R. Commons each argued that without such restrictions on immigration, the "race treason" problem in America would only worsen.[47]

While Pigou finds a "heavy burden of proof" for advocates of genetic selection (1907, 366), he nevertheless favored policies to alter the incentives for family formation. Accepting that the evidence on the heredity of defects is strong, Pigou also favored a policy of "permanent segregation" or sterilization to improve "the general economic welfare of the community" (1920, 112, cf. 110; 1907, 269).[48]

Economists also focused on the need to select immigrants in order to reduce the numbers from "inferior," "defective," and "undesirable" classes of immigrants (Commons 1916, 230).[49] In their study of Jewish immigration in the first several issues of the *Annals of Eugenics*, Pearson and Moul explained in detail why immigration is the central matter in eugenics policy. They asked, "What purpose would there be in endeavouring to legislate for a superior breed of men, if at any moment it could be swamped by the influx of immigrants of an inferior race, hastening to profit by the higher civilisation of an improved humanity?" (1925, 7). The practical measure seized upon by Commons in this context was the simple device of a literacy test, which would "raise the average standard" of immigrants (235). Fetter argued for an overall reduction in immigration, as well as the eugenic selection of immi-

---

placing him under better conditions is strictly limited. We should remember, moreover, that an improved environment tends ultimately to degrade the race by causing an increased survival of the unfit. If then, we wish to improve the nation physically, it must be mainly by selective breeding. . . . certain types of men are unfit for existence under civilised conditions of life; for example, people susceptible to consumption or the charm of alcohol."

47. See Cherry 1976 and Commons 1916, 198ff.

48. Fisher 1909 also endorsed government "bounties" to encourage births among the "vital" classes (673). Proposals ranged from sterilization, to German-style marriage tests, to developing social prejudice against such reproduction, as well as a fuller appreciation of women's rights (Thomson 1906, 179).

49. Pearson favored restrictions of immigration, arguing that immigration should be restricted to those who are at least 25 percent above the mean for natives in intelligence and physical characteristics (Pearson and Moul 1925, 127; chap. 5, this vol.).

grants in order to "improve the racial quality of the nation by checking the multiplication of the strains defective in respect to mentality, nervous organization, and physical health, and by encouraging the more capable elements of the population to contribute in due proportion to the maintenance of a healthy, moral, and efficient population" (1916, 378).

An image from *Punch* at the time also made the case for immigration control (fig. 4.1). The unwanted immigrants, "untaxed imports," then came from Italy, and they reveal a remarkable uniformity. Perhaps the *Punch* artist feared that his readers, so accustomed to the ape-like features of Fenians, would be slow to catch the point in an Italian context without the addition of pictures of two real monkeys.

THE RETURN TO FIXED HUMAN NATURE

Whatever disputes remain about how economic theory changed with the transition to neoclassicism, it is widely accepted that the boundary of economic science was narrowed throughout the late nineteenth century (Winch 1972). The 1870s in particular were characterized by often intense disputes over the nature and scope of economic "science." By the turn of the century it became clear that the historical school would not prevail, and the profession would follow the lead of W. S. Jevons in his calls for narrowing economic science, for subdivision and specialization (Jevons [1871] 1911; Peart 2001b). Jevons's subdivision rendered economic *theory* unassailable, but severely incomplete: he recognized all sorts of cases where the theory required modification—and these, he argued, should be taken into account in *applications* (Peart 2001b). This chapter has examined one example of such narrowing, in terms of the "race" to which economics might be applied: late in the century economists began to argue that the intertemporal decision making of a "higher race" might not be applicable to a "lower race."

Though today we sometimes fail to appreciate the racial context of nineteenth-century disputes about economic methodology, anthropologists and evolutionary scientists of the late nineteenth century fully

Fig. 4.1.   Edward Tennyson Reed, "Some Untaxed Imports from Italy" (1903)

recognized that their theory directly opposed the classical political economists' doctrine of human homogeneity (chaps. 1, 2, this vol.). This chapter has demonstrated that, for a time at least, the classical economists' postulate of homogeneity was overthrown, and racial theories prevailed in economics. Hierarchical, often racial, accounts won the day well into the twentieth century.[50] Perhaps the last, albeit unrecognized, statement of this position occurred in Schumpeter's *History of Economic Analysis* when he describes the role of Galton.

---

50. The new translation by Becker and Knudsen of omitted material from Schumpeter's *Theory of Economic Development* (2002) makes it clear that Schumpeter's entrepreneur is Carlyle's Hero.

Of his many exploits, the following are relevant for us: he was the man who may be said to have independently discovered correlation as an effective tool of analysis; the man who set eugenics on its feet (in 1905 he founded the Eugenics Laboratory); the man who realized the importance of, and initiated, a new branch of psychology, the psychology of individual differences; . . . all of which makes him in my humble opinion one of the three greatest sociologists, the other two being Vico and Marx. (1954, 790–91)

Near the middle of the century the classical tradition of equal competence (homogeneity) was revived at Chicago, at the London School of Economics, and by the Austrians.[51] Not surprisingly, given that racial characterizations focused on intertemporal decision making, time preference was central in the Chicago revival. In his 1931 review of Irving Fisher's *Theory of Interest*, Frank Knight voiced his skepticism about the common link supposed in economists' accounts between time preference and race. Knight, and after him George Stigler and Gary Becker, questioned myopic accounts of intertemporal decision making. As the Chicago school revived the classical doctrine of homogeneity it also (and by no coincidence) revived the presumption of competence in economic and political activity.

When Knight reviewed Fisher's theory of interest, he saw no difference in the motivation of different sorts of people.

It seems to me indisputable in fact that people desire wealth for many reasons, of which the guaranty of the future delivery of groceries or other consumable services is sometimes the main and sometimes a quite minor consideration. It is desired for the same reasons a head-hunting hero desires a goodly collection of skulls; it is power, a source of prestige, a counter in the game, an article of fashion, and perhaps a mere something to be "collected." It is wanted to use, but also just to have, to get more, in order to get still more. (Knight 1931, 177)[52]

---

51. The role of Lionel Robbins is considered in chapter 10.

52. Knight objected to how "this discussion has been cluttered up and the issue beclouded by theorizing (mostly quite bad) regarding the ultimate motivations involved in the choice between present and future ('spending' and 'saving'—or 'investing,' which is not the same thing), on the one hand, and, on the other hand (not nearly so bad), regarding the technological nature and implications of the investing progress" (1931, 198).

There is nothing here about the "curious lack of variation" of savages, but instead an illustration of economic problems across time, culture, and race. And the antiracial argument was made even more emphatically, perhaps, by Ludwig von Mises.

> [The ethnologists] are utterly mistaken in contending that these other races have been guided in their activities by motives other than those which have actuated the white race. The Asiatics and the Africans no less than the peoples of European descent have been eager to struggle successfully for survival and to use reason as the foremost weapon in these endeavors. (1949, 85)

The Stigler and Becker attack on the postulate of positive time-preference (Stigler and Becker 1977) continued the argument that Stigler made in his dissertation: positive time-preference has no role in the making of abstract economic man.[53] In this, Stigler remained a faithful student of Frank Knight.

Was the Chicago revival in some sense motivated by the racial attacks on classical economics and the widespread acceptance of racial accounts of human behavior that we have demonstrated here? Here one must be cautious, but it is surely no coincidence that the reading list for Stigler's history of economics classes in the 1960s included Walter Bagehot's *Postulates of English Political Economy*. In this work, which impressed Marshall enough that he introduced a student edition (Bagehot 1885), Bagehot "explained" the classical doctrines by appealing to the "race" of classical theorists. Individuals were optimizers because Adam Smith was a Scot; they were careful with money because David Ricardo was a Jew. Marshall was of course not the only one taken by Bagehot: Bagehot seems to have obtained his editorship of the *Economist* through the intervention of that close friend of the *Economist's* owner (James Wilson)—none other than W. R. Greg (Barrington 1933).

---

53. Stigler (1941, 213): "The second ground for valuing present goods more highly is that '. . . to goods which are destined to meet the wants of the future, we ascribe a value which is really less than the true intensity of their future marginal utility.' This is a failure of perspective, an irrationality in human behavior—the only irrationality, it may be noted, that Böhm-Bawerk introduces into his 'economic man.'" From this, Stigler concludes that positive time-preference plays no role in economic theory.

V

STATISTICAL PREJUDICE

From Eugenics to Immigration

Let us bear in mind the words of Galton written almost in the last years
of his life, words not of despair, but of wise caution: "When the desired
fullness of information shall have been acquired, then and not till then,
will be the fit moment to proclaim a 'Jehad' or Holy War against
customs and prejudices that impair the physical and
moral qualities of our race."
—Karl Pearson and Ethel M. Elderton,
"Foreword," *Annals of Eugenics*

PREJUDICE AND RESEMBLANCE

The foundational assumption that the street porter and the philosopher are essentially the same prompts us to ask whether we all have the
same motivations or whether there is something special about uncovering scientific "truth." In particular, are scholars motivated by the
same self-interested desires for fame and fortune as the rest of the population? Today, we are often ready to presume that scholars are more
public-spirited than the rest of the population; they are said to seek only
(or at least mainly) the truth. We allow that prejudice infects the academy in the area of personal relationships, acknowledging, for instance,
that a scholar might oppose hiring a talented colleague because of
racial or religious prejudice. Yet we often cling to the belief that the
same scholar would be unbiased in the evaluation of *ideas* or *intellectual output*—that he or she would never ignore or disparage ideas for
racial or religious reasons. Such a presumption—that the expert has
more public motivation than ordinary people—may be the final and
most persistent form of hierarchical thinking.

In this chapter, we examine a case in which the presumption that
experts seek only the truth was terribly wrong. We demonstrate that

prejudice infected the (public) "science" of the prejudiced and was then passed on to other scientists.[1] The historical record reveals that prejudice afflicted powerful intellects, namely, Karl Pearson and Francis Galton.[2] Galton and Pearson supposed at the outset of their statistical study that Jews are inferior. Although Galton was candid about his presuppositions and warned the reader to beware of them,[3] Pearson presented himself as a disinterested truth-seeker uncontaminated by such vulgar motives as might taint ordinary people. He interpreted his statistical results of "difference" to obtain the conclusion "inferior," even though the eugenics doctrine and the statistical procedures he favored ought to have led him to the opposite conclusion. Eugenic doctrine held that a feature of the "inferior" stocks of people was "imprudence," "intemperance," or high time-preference.[4] Yet when Pearson found empirical evidence suggesting the Jew might be prudent and patient, he interpreted his results as evidence of Jewish inferiority, while maintaining silence as to the issue of time preference.[5]

Our contention is that scholars, like other people, are motivated by fame and fortune, as well as the desire to obtain the truth. For statisticians, one value of an estimate may be preferred to another (Feigenbaum and Levy 1996). The trade-offs we consider here are (1) the per-

---

1. The argument of Arrow (1972) and Phelps (1972) characterizes prejudice as an intellectual shortcut. In such cases, information about a group is a means to another end, e.g., an input to profit-maximizing employment decisions. Here, we consider the characterization of the group itself in Galton and Pearson. We do not intend to assert that all scientists who accepted eugenicists' results were either unprejudiced or prejudiced. But it does seem clear to us that at least some of the postclassical economists (such as Pigou) were reluctant to accept eugenic claims about genetic variation by class and were convinced by the "scientific" status of such claims (Pigou 1907; chap. 4, this vol.).

2. Stephen Stigler summarizes the importance of Galton and Pearson for economists (Stigler 1986, 265–66).

3. We discuss Galton's candor in footnote 24 of chapter 4 and in the appendix at the end of the book.

Galton presented both his presuppositions and his results in the analysis of fingerprints. He was predisposed to believe that the fingerprints of black people were more uniform than those of white people but confessed an inability to find this result in the data (1892a, 195–96, quoted in table 4.1, this vol.).

4. Although there was some variation at the time, the words *imprudence* and *intemperance* are frequently used interchangeably to signify high time-preference. Peart 2000 gives details on time preference in postclassical economic thought. See table 4.1, this volume.

5. Pearson thus provided an unexpected instance of the eugenic case of declining human status as ability improved, described in our diagram of human capacity (chap. 2, this vol.).

ception that Jews are different; (2) eugenic theory concerning time preference; and (3) the statistical philosophy enunciated by Galton and Pearson. The fact that Pearson's findings ought to have led him to reject the hypothesis of inferiority suggests how incorrect and dangerous the assumption of motivation by truth-seeking can be.

The first "racial" hierarchy discussed by the British eugenic thinkers was the difference between the Irish and Scots "races." The following episode concerns Jews and Gentiles. By examining the statistical work in service of eugenics, we may learn something about how prejudice interacts with statistical procedures and economic theory to become public "science." That eugenic doctrine came to dominate economics as scientific "truth," supported by the biometric research of Francis Galton and Karl Pearson, is clear from the testimony of postclassical economists such as Pigou (1907), Fisher (1909), and Schumpeter (1954, 791). The statistical case having been made by Galton and more fully by Pearson, postclassical economists came to accept their claim that Jews were inferior. Such statistical research helped to move economics from the classical period characterized by the hardest possible doctrine of initial human homogeneity—that observed differences among people arise from incentives, luck, and history—to a period in which economics alleged foundational differences among and within races of people (Darity 1995). As a consequence, economists in the postclassical period came to recommend restrictions on Jewish immigration alongside other eugenic policies (chap. 4, this vol.).

GALTON AND THE JEWS

Galton's project of composite photography was an early exercise in his agenda of racial improvement.[6] He was convinced that the results would show physiognomic differences of the criminal or Jewish "type" and could then be employed for the principle of human selection.

> This face and the qualities [the composite] connotes probably gives a
> clue to the direction in which the stock of the English race might most

---

6. Composite photography was featured in the exhibition "Perfecting Mankind" (Squiers 2001).

easily be improved. It is the essential notion of a race that there should be some ideal typical form from which the individuals may deviate in all directions, but about which they chiefly cluster. . . . The easiest direction in which a race can be improved is towards that central type, because nothing new has to be sought out. It is only necessary to encourage as far as practicable the breed of those who conform most nearly to the central type, and to restrain as far as may be the breed of those who deviate widely from it. Now there can hardly be a more appropriate method of discovering the central physiognomical type of any race or group than that of composite portraiture. (1907c, *Human Faculty*, 10)

Galton goes on to explain his failure to recognize criminals using composites.

I have made numerous composites of various groups of convicts, which are interesting negatively rather than positively. They produce faces of a mean description, with no villainy written on them. The individual faces are villainous enough, but they are villainous in different ways, and when they are combined, the individual peculiarities disappear, and the common humanity of a low type is all that is left. (1907c, *Human Faculty*, 11)

But the composite photography had one purported success, identifying the "Jewish type." Here is Pearson's retrospective judgment on the Jewish composites (figs. 5.1 and 5.2), likened to "a great work of art."

There is little doubt that Galton's Jewish type formed a landmark in composite photography, and its success was, I think, almost entirely due to (a) increased facility in the process, and (b) to the fact that his composites were based on physiognomically like constituents. In the case of criminality and phthisis he has based his composites on mentally and pathologically differentiated components, and had expected to find mental and pathological characters highly correlated with the facial. His negative results were undoubtedly of value, but they cannot appeal to the man in the street like his positive success with the Jewish type. We all know the Jewish boy, and Galton's portraiture brings him before us in a way that only a great work of art could equal—scarcely excel, for the artist would only idealise from *one* model. (1924, 293)

The Jewish composite photographs were discussed in two 1885 articles by Galton and his coexperimentalist, Joseph Jacobs. Galton wrote that the composites captured the Jewish acquisitive soul.

Fig. 5.1.   Francis Galton, "Illustrations of Composite Portraiture" (1885)

They were children of poor parents, dirty little fellows individually, but wonderfully beautiful, as I think, in these composites. The feature that struck me the most, as I drove through the adjacent Jewish quarter, was the cold scanning gaze of man, woman, and child, and this was no less conspicuous among the schoolboys. There was no sign of diffidence in any of their looks, nor of surprise at the unwonted intrusion. I felt, rightly or wrongly, that every one of them was coolly appraising me at market value, without the slightest interest of any other kind. (1885, 243)

Jacobs, to whom Galton (1885) had referred the reader, disagreed.

I fail to see any of the cold calculation which Mr. Galton seems to have noticed in the boys at any of the composites A, B, and C. There is something more like the dreamer and thinker than the merchant in A. In

Fig. 5.2.   Francis Galton, "The Jewish Type" (1885)

fact, on my showing this to an eminent painter of my acquaintance, he exclaimed, "I imagine that is how Spinoza looked when a lad," a piece of artistic insight which is remarkably confirmed by the portraits of the philosopher, though the artist had never seen one. The cold and somewhat hard look in composite D, however, is more confirmatory of Mr. Galton's impression. It is note-worthy that this is seen in a composite of young fellows between 17 and 20, who have had to fight a hard battle of life even by that early age. (1885, 268)

For Jacobs, the portraits simply showed the Jewish boys had lived a hard life. Pearson dissented from Jacobs, warning that "many will criticise, and I think rightly criticise the analysis Mr. Jacobs gives of the 'Jewishness' in these portraits" (1924, 293).

PEARSON AND THE JEWS

For Galton and Pearson, breeding the Carlylean hero was the goal of eugenics.[7] Like many eugenicists, Pearson feared that Britain would increasingly fail to produce such "heroes" as it became more affluent.

> Where are the younger civil servants to replace our dying pro-consuls, and to whom the nation can commit with a feeling of security and confidence the future problems of South Africa? Where are the new writers to whom the nation listens as it did to Carlyle, Ruskin, and Browning? or for whose books it eagerly waits as for those of Thackeray and George Eliot? Where are the leaders of science who will make the epoch that Darwin and Huxley made in biology, or Faraday and Clerk Maxwell in physics? (1901, 56)

Here is Pearson's distinction between the average and the exceptional.

> There may be a steady average ability, but where is the fire of genius, the spirit of enthusiasm, which creates the leader of men either in thought or action? Alas! it is difficult to see any light on the horizon predicting the dawn of an intellectual renaissance, or heralding social and political reforms such as carried the nation through the difficult fifty years of the middle of this century. Possibly our strong men may have got into the wrong places . . . but I must confess to feeling sometimes that an actual dearth is upon us. And if this should be so, then the unchangeable law of heredity shows us only too clearly the source: we have multiplied from the inferior, and not from the superior stocks. (1901, 56–57)

It will soon become clear that what Pearson says about exceptional Jews—the Spinozas and Einsteins—and the policy response to Jewish immigration runs counter to his position here.

The first article in the *Annals of Eugenics* of which Pearson was the founding editor is part 1 of "The Problem of Alien Immigration into

---

7. "Here was Galton fifty years ago calling out for the 'superman,' much as the younger men of to-day are doing. But he differed from them in that he saw a reasoned way of producing the superman, while they do not seem to get further than devoutly hoping that either by a lucky 'sport' or an adequate exercise of will power he will one day appear!" (Pearson 1924, 78).

Great Britain, Illustrated by an Examination of Russian and Polish Jewish Children" by Pearson and Margaret Moul. Since their procedure violates Pearson's commitment to the method of moments, we shall argue that the article suggests how eugenic presuppositions colored the statistical results.

Pearson and Moul motivate the exercise with a concern over racial quality in densely settled countries. They begin by telling a story of climate and race suitability.[8] The inherent inferiority of the Negro — unsuitable even for Africa! — was said to be obvious.

> It is perfectly idle to talk in these matters either of pride of race or of the common humanity of all mankind. The reasons that can be given for admitting orientals as permanent immigrants into a densely populated occidental country apply equally to the admission of occidentals into oriental countries. When it comes to settling or resettling a sparsely peopled country, then it is possible to find out whether the individual is a real humanitarian or not, according as he thinks only of his own race, or of the actual suitability of other races, as judged by their culture and their adaption for the proposed environment. From this standpoint it is probable that the Japanese would be far more valuable than men of Nordic race in many of the Pacific islands, and that the Hindoo and still more the Chinaman might, to the great advantage of the general world progress, replace the negro in many districts of Africa. (1925, 6–7)[9]

Pearson and Moul then review contending views of the results of immigration. On the one hand, there is the human homogeneity story, while on the other hand, immigrants might overly compete for jobs and resources.

> In the years preceding the Great War the question of indiscriminate immigration — especially that of the Polish and Russian Jews into the East End of London, and the poorer quarters of other large towns in Great Britain — had become a very vital one. It was asserted on the one hand that the immigrants were a useful class of hard workers fully up to

---

8. This was a common argument at the time. Jevons (1869) was also struck by the relationship between climate and race; for the American context, see also F. Walker 1881, in Darity 1995.

9. We consider discussions of immigration by economists in chapter 4 and in this chapter in the section "Eugenics and the Economists." See also Commons 1916; Fetter et al. 1907; Fetter 1916.

the level of the English workman in physique and intelligence, and on the other hand these immigrants were painted in lurid colours as weaklings, persons with a low standard of life and of cleanliness, *under-bidding native workers in sweated trades and spreading anarchic doctrines,* so that the continued inflow of this population was leading not only to economic distress, but to a spread of doctrines incompatible with the stability of our social and political systems. (1925, 7; emphasis added)[10]

In the face of these competing predictions, Pearson and Moul call for disinterested scientific study.

It was very obvious to the onlooker that whatever might be the real facts of the situation, those facts were not available for the calm discussion of the case. The partizans of cheap labour and the partizans of monopolistic trades-unionism were both undoubtedly acting from personal and party inspirations, and there was no one whose business it really was to find the true answer to the question of whether Great Britain could assimilate to its national profit this mass of new and untested material. (1925, 7)

They then explain why immigration is the central matter in eugenics policy, and they remind the reader that "special cases" do not support general conclusions.

The whole problem of immigration is fundamental for the rational teaching of national eugenics. What purpose would there be in endeavouring to legislate for a superior breed of men, if at any moment it could be swamped by the influx of immigrants of an inferior race, hastening to profit by the higher civilisation of an improved humanity? To the eugenist permission for indiscriminate immigration is and must be destructive of all true progress. . . . No sane man, however, doubts that at various periods of English history our nation has been markedly strengthened by foreign immigration. The Huguenots . . . the Dutch . . . that of the Germans of 1848—the "Achtundvierziger"—many of whom were indeed of Jewish extraction. But these special cases do not prove the general desirability of free immigration. (1925, 7)

---

10. "The effect is noticeable and disastrous in the case of the Irish-Americans. Displaced by Italians and Slavs, many of the young men have fallen into the hoodlum and criminal element. Here moral causes produce physical causes of race destruction, for the vicious elements of the population disappear throughout the diseases bequeathed to their progeny, and are recruited only from the classes forced down from above" (Commons 1916, 204).

Pearson and Moul begin the serious work by testing whether Jewish children were as clean or as well-dressed as Gentile children. They conclude that Jewish children were poorly dressed compared to their Gentile counterparts, a result that gives "some ground" for the argument that Jews "undersell natives in the labour market."

> It is clear that the alien Jewish children are far below the average of the Gentile children, being indeed below the Gentiles of the poorer districts. They are only in excess of the "Ragged School," although well in excess of this. There seems some ground for the statement frequently made that they undersell natives in the labour market because they have a lower standard of life. (1925, 49)

The result was challenged in the *Journal of the Royal Statistical Society* in an article that claimed that Pearson and Moul contradicted the "common view" of those who dealt with Jewish children—"does not accord with the common view held by social workers and school teachers who labour among Jewish children" ([F. S.] 1926, 148–49).[11]

Assuming that they held income constant across groups—which they attempted to do[12]—Pearson and Moul detected a difference in cultural expenditure patterns, evidence that Jewish parents were spending less on their children's clothing than non-Jewish parents. If Jewish parents were saving the rest of their income, or spending it on education, then the results suggest that Jews in their sample have a *lower* rate of time preference than their Christian neighbors. As noted in chapter 4, eugenicists identified lower time-preference with racial superiority.

But Pearson and Moul were silent on where the income went.[13] Instead, they concluded that lower expenditure on clothing was evi-

---

11. In chapter 11, we defend the use of centralized anecdotal evidence when the theory is suspect.

12. This attempt was criticized ([F. S.] 1926, 149).

13. It has been suggested to us that Pearson and Moul inappropriately pool Christian judgment of Christian clothing with Christian judgment of Jewish clothing. If the Jewish children are observant, then their clothing might appear odd to those outside the religion. As the Pearson and Moul data come from Polish-Russian children, this is a serious possibility. These considerations were raised by Maria Pia Paganelli of Yeshiva University at the GMU Summer Institute.

dence of a racial failing, for which intelligence might compensate. They used the result to argue that Jews should prove they are *superior* in intelligence to make up for their poor physical traits and habits.

> The Americans have learnt from experience how unwise it is to admit an untested and motley stream of immigrants even into a land of vacant spaces; it is far more urgent to restrict immigration in the case of a crowded country. There should always be room in a country for the highest type of immigrants, for men who, with superior intelligence or with superior physique, will readily mingle with its stock and strengthen its vitality. But for men with no special ability—above all for such men as religion, social habits, or language keep as a caste apart, there should be no place. They will not be absorbed by, and at the same time strengthen the existing population, they will develop into a parasitic race*, [*A striking instance of such a race is that of the gypsies, who without any thought were allowed to enter this country, and who being there serve no useful and profitable national purpose.] a position neither tending to the welfare of their host, nor wholesome for themselves.
>
> We hold therefore that the problem of admission of an alien Jewish population into Great Britain turns essentially on the answer that may be given to the question: Is their average intelligence so markedly superior to that of the native Gentile, that it compensates for their physique and habits certainly not being above (probably a good deal below) the average of those characters here? (1925, 124–25)

Pearson and Moul proceed to compare the intelligence of Jewish and Christian children. They find little difference between the intelligence of Jewish boys and their Christian peers, but a significant difference between Jewish boys and girls. Since Jewish boys are not more intelligent than non-Jews, and girls are inferior, Pearson and Moul conclude that Jewish immigration should be curtailed.

> An examination of this table shows us once that the Jewish girls have less intelligence than the Gentile girls in any type of Council school. The comparison of the Gentile and the Jewish boys is less clear cut. . . . What is definitely clear, however, is that our own Jewish boys do not form from the standpoint of intelligence a group markedly superior to our natives. But that is the sole condition under which we are prepared to admit that immigration should be allowed. . . . Taken on the average, and regarding both sexes, this alien Jewish population is somewhat inferior physically and mentally to the native population. (1925, 126)

In short, Pearson and Moul first impute a racial failing on the basis of expenditure patterns. They allow that Jewish intellectual superiority might overcome this failing, and they attempt to measure intelligence. They find no difference in the intelligence of Jewish and Christian boys but a difference between the girls. They then pool by gender and impute a racial difference in intelligence.

Not surprisingly, the Pearson and Moul study made its case in terms of average intelligence, the first moment of the distribution. The study turned next to the question of the occasional extremely capable Jew, a Spinoza or an Einstein.[14]

> We know and admit that some of the children of these alien Jews from the academic standpoint have done brilliantly, whether they have the staying powers of the native race is another question.* [*A member of an eastern race said to the senior author of this paper recently: "It puzzles me when I see how late in life you English can work; all I have to do, must be done before I am fifty."] No breeder of cattle, however, would purchase an entire herd because he anticipated finding one or two fine specimens included in it; still less would he do it, if his byres and pastures were already full. (1925, 127)

Acknowledging that the occasional immigrant will have exceptional talent, Pearson and Moul dismiss the need to consider such outliers.

As is well known, elsewhere Pearson strenuously defended method-of-moments estimation procedures against both maximum likelihood methods as well as the subjective discarding of outliers.[15] To

---

14. See Holmes 1926, 233.

15. Here is how Pearson begins his blistering attack on maximum likelihood estimation in principle, and Fisher in particular. Pearson quotes Fisher (first) giving a personal insult and (second) explicating the methods of moments in opposition to maximum likelihood estimation: "'Wasting your time fitting curves by moments, eh?

"'Perhaps the most extended use of the criterion of consistency has been developed by Pearson in the "Method of Moments." In this method, which is without question of great practical utility, different forms of frequency curves are fitted by calculating as many moments of the sample as there are parameters to be evaluated. The parameters chosen are those of an infinite population of the specified type having the same moments as those calculated from the sample. . . . Moreover for that class of distribution to which the method can be applied, it has not been shown except in the case of the normal curve, that the best [sic! KP] values will be obtained by the method of moments'" (Pearson 1936, 34).

Stigler (1986, 338) notes that Pearson "would not budge on the matter of excluding extreme values from his analysis."

ascertain the reliability of the estimate of the first moment (the mean), the procedure entails estimating the second moment (the variance). To ascertain the reliability of the estimate of the second moment, one estimates higher moments.[16] But when Pearson and Moul claim that information about characteristics of exceptional Jews is not important, they have thrown out information that is critical to the estimation of the third and fourth moment of the distribution. The Pearson and Moul study therefore violated Pearson's own statistical principles. Discarding the exceptional asymmetrically is particularly striking in this context, when Pearson had clearly remarked on the dearth of exceptional talent in Britain. All of this suggests that prior judgments about Jews, rather than statistical principles, drove the results.[17]

EUGENICS AND THE ECONOMISTS

By the turn of the century economists in Britain and America came to accept the eugenicists' claim that "inferior" races overbreed, while

---

16. "Before Student's time [and the *t*-test], every analysis of data that considered 'what might have been' resembled a long staircase from the near foreground to the misty heights. One began by calculating a primary statistic, a number that indicated quite directly what the data seemed to say about the point at issue. The primary statistic might, for instance, have been a sample mean. Then one faced the question of 'How different might its value have been?' and calculated a secondary statistic, a number that indicated quite directly how variable (or perhaps how stable and invariable) the primary statistic seemed to be. The secondary statistic might have been an estimate of the standard deviation of such a sample mean. After this step, one again needed to face the question of 'How much different?' . . . In principle, one should have gone on to a tertiary statistic . . . then to a quaternary statistic" (Mosteller and Tukey 1977, 2).

17. We know, too, that Karl Pearson's attack on the use of the sample median was central to his disagreement with Galton. "It is well-known that the median is subject to a larger probable error than the mean and this has discouraged its use in statistical inquiries dealing with carefully recorded observations. But Galton realized that while its chief value in such cases was the rapidity with which it could be ascertained, [KP note: That Galton used median and quartiles so frequently even on careful records must, I think, be attributed to his great love of brief analysis. He found arithmetic in itself irksome; he would prefer to interpolate by a graph rather than by a formula, and while his rough approximations were as a rule justified, this was not invariably the case.] yet there existed certain cases in which the median may be said to be far more reliable than the mean" (1924, 34). Pearson cites Galton (1907a, 1907b) in which Galton proposes the sample median as a model for democratic decision making and works an example by computing the median guess in an ox-judging contest (see the appendix at the end of this book). Pearson then computes the mean and finds it closer to the true weight of the ox than Galton's median. So even in a case where there is theoretical reason to prefer the sample median, Pearson finds the mean superior.

Anglo-Saxons reproduce at relatively low rates, as well as the statistical case concerning the "immigration problem": waves of immigration drawn predominantly from "inferior" races are said to have reduced the quality of the nation's population (Commons 1916, 200ff). Since such immigrants multiply at high rates, the deterioration would be ongoing.

For economists, eugenics provided at least a partial solution to two related problems, the "relative decrease of the successful strains of the population," as well as the racial mix of the existing population that resulted from slavery and ongoing immigration drawn predominantly from the "vicious strains of humanity" (Fetter 1916, 366, 369).[18] Irving Fisher, Frank Fetter, and J. R. Commons each argued that without such restrictions on immigration, the "race treason" problem in America would only worsen.[19] Commons pointed to the "shifting of the sources" of immigrants toward Eastern Europe, which resulted in an increased proportion of Jews in the immigrant pool (1916, 217).

CONCLUSION: DISMISSING IDEAS USING RACE

Making the foundational assumption that the street porter and the philosopher are essentially the same has prompted us to ask whether we all have the same motivations when it comes to uncovering scientific "truth."[20] Those who deal with ideas frequently presume that scholars are more public-spirited than the rest of the population; scholars are said to seek only (or at least mainly) the truth. We have sug-

---

18. Fetter points to the heritage of bad immigration policy, "which survives in many defective and vicious strains of humanity, some of them notorious, such as the Jukes, the Kallikak family, and the Tribe of Ishmael" (1916, 369). The "evidence" of the "Jukes family" is discussed in detail in Carlson 2001. The role of the "Jukes family," as well as an unremarked exposé (published in 1931) of the empirical shortcomings of eugenicists' claims concerning the Jukes, are detailed in chapter 6.

19. "On the whole it seems that immigration and the competition of inferior races tends to dry up the older and superior races" (Commons 1916, 208). For a wide-ranging discussion of immigration, see Commons 1916, 198ff. On "race suicide" and American economics see Leonard 2003b.

20. Rubinstein (2000) shows what remarkable results can be obtained by supposing only that the motivation of the theorist and the ordinary language user is the same and so brings the theorist and the theorized to the same plane of existence.

gested, by contrast, that a presumption of homogeneity, a presumption that scholars are motivated by the same self-interested desires as the rest of the population, leads us to a skeptical view of scientific practice. In the context of the "science" of eugenics and the statistical work that supported eugenic recommendations, this chapter suggests such skepticism is well-placed.

While we might reluctantly acknowledge that scholars on occasion are led to manipulate data or statistical techniques to obtain desired results, we may still wish to believe that scholars are unbiased in the evaluation of *ideas* or *intellectual output*, that they would never ignore or disparage ideas for racial or religious reasons. This presumption may be the final and most persistent form of hierarchical thinking. Perhaps the most subtle form of prejudice is the claim that an idea that is true and useful for one group may be neither for another. We close with a historical example of such a presumption.

In 1885, the same year Galton published his Jewish composite photographs, Alfred Marshall delivered his inaugural lecture at Cambridge. Here, Marshall repeated Walter Bagehot's explanation for the ("excessive") abstraction in classical economics by appeal to Ricardo's Jewish heritage.[21]

The context of the adjective *excessive* is important. As is well known, the classical economists' method of abstraction was strenuously resisted in the 1870s by British historicists, notably John Kells Ingram and T. E. Cliffe Leslie.[22] Contemporary critics of economic method feared that the deductive method, abstracting as it did from the full array of causes that influenced economic phenomena, would lead to unjustifiable neglect of relevant causes. Instead, Ingram and Leslie called for empirical studies, upon which they envisaged the theory of

---

21. Walter Bagehot's position at the *Economist* came through his friendship with Greg whose opinion of classical economics we have seen earlier. Bagehot played a role in creating the illusion that Mill's economics were unoriginal. When Stigler attacked Bagehot's claim (Stigler 1965, 1–15) it was so widespread that he did not find it useful to ask how it came to be.

22. A leading proponent of the Historical school, the Irish political economist Thomas Edward Cliffe Leslie (1825–82) was Professor of Political Economy and Jurisprudence in Queen's College, Belfast, from 1853 until his death. A second major proponent, whose work proved to be of significant popular appeal, was John Kells Ingram. Ingram's (1888) *History of Political Economy* went through numerous printings and was translated into nine languages.

economics (and the broader sociological study they favored) could be constructed.[23] Walter Bagehot, conservative editor of the *Economist* and author of *Lombard Street*, also figured in debates about the generality of the axioms of political economy. Bagehot argued that the conclusions of political economy were of limited relevance, applicable only to countries with institutional structures similar to those of England at the time (1876). His racial explanation for this limited relevance has been neglected in the secondary accounts.[24]

We provide the relevant passages to compare Marshall with Bagehot here.

BAGEHOT

For this trade Ricardo had the best of all preparations—the preparation of race. He was a Jew by descent (his father was one by religion), and for ages the Jews have shown a marked excellence in what may be called the "commerce of imperceptibles."... The fact remains that the Jews have now an inborn facility in applying figures to pure money matters.... The writings of Ricardo are unique in literature, so far as I know, as a representative on paper of the special faculties by which the Jews have grown rich for ages. ... I know none but Ricardo's which can awaken a book-student to a sense of the Jewish genius for the mathematics of money-dealing. His mastery over the abstractions of Political Economy is of a kind almost exactly identical. (1880, 152–53)

MARSHALL

And as to their tendency to indulge in excessively abstract reasonings, that, in so far as the charge is true at all, is chiefly due to the influence of one masterful genius, who was not an Englishman, and had very little in common with the English tone of thought. The faults and the virtues of Ricardo's mind are traceable to his Semitic origin; no English economist has had a mind similar to his. (1925, 153)

They [Ricardo and his followers] regarded man as, so to speak, a constant quantity, and gave themselves little trouble to study his variations....

This did little harm so long as they treated of money and foreign trade, but great harm when they treated of the relations between the different industrial classes. (1925, 154–55)

---

23. For an overview of the Historical school, see Hutchison 1953. A detailed review of Leslie's ideas is contained in Koot 1975. The prominent economic historian J. E. T. Rogers is also considered an important influence in the Historical school.

24. The issue turns on whether the explanation was one of innate differences or different circumstances. The material that follows on Bagehot suggests that he falls in the former camp. Leslie and Ingram, as well as Mill, seem more accurately placed in the latter category.

In his 1890 presidential address before Section F (Economics and Statistics) of the British Association, Marshall used a racial explanation for the difference between English and German economists' ideas concerning state regulation. Economists in Germany (and to a lesser extent in America) are more apt than Anglo-Saxon ones to favor bureaucracy. We can therefore think of economists as spokespersons for the race and work backward.

> The advantages of a bureaucratic government appeal strongly to some classes of minds, among whom are to be included many German economists and a few of the younger American economists who have been much under German influence. But those in whom the Anglo-Saxon spirit is strongest would prefer that such undertakings, though always under public control, and sometimes even in public ownership, should whenever possible be worked and managed by private corporations. We (for I would here include myself) believe that bureaucratic management is less suitable for Anglo-Saxons than for other races who are more patient and more easily contented, more submissive and less full of initiative, who like to take things easily and to spread their work out rather thinly over long hours. (1925, 274–75)

Ideas that are true and useful for one "race" are therefore not necessarily useful for another.[25] And if the economist is different from us, his ideas can be dismissed as meaningful for his race, but not for ours. Later economists might dismiss Bagehot's and Marshall's opinions as private and inconsequential prejudice, but Galton and Pearson turned such opinions into public science.

---

25. The malleability of "race" in this context is important: as noted in chapter 3, "race" signifies perceived difference and may be identified with national boundaries as it is here or some similarly imprecise notion.

VI

PICKING LOSERS FOR STERILIZATION
Eugenics as Demographic
Central Planning

> I think we must face the fact that behind the sovereignty of the philoso-
> pher king stands the quest for power. The beautiful portrait of
> the sovereign is a self-portrait.
> —Karl Popper, *The Open Society and Its Enemies*

INTRODUCTION

We can now situate eugenics policy within the economics debate over central planning versus market alternatives. After a substantial period of neglect, the involvement of postclassical economics in the eugenics movement is now becoming clear (chap. 4, this vol.; Toye 2000; Cot 2003; Dimand 2003; Leonard 2003b). Postclassical economists supported sterilization and race-based immigration restrictions, practices that have become a source of embarrassment to their successors in professional roles.[1]

The neglect of the role of social scientists in the eugenics movement was unfortunate for two reasons. First, there is a historical issue. We are led to misunderstand the relationship between classical and postclassical economics if we do not realize that early eugenics thinkers (W. R. Greg and Francis Galton) attacked the classical economists' presuppo-

---

1. The embarrassment may explain the silence of the commentators. A JSTOR search of the official history of the American Economic Association by A. W. Coats fails to locate the word *eugenics*. Irving Fisher's collected works were supported by the American Economic Association with the proviso that the AEA funding not be acknowledged (Cot 2003; Dimand 2003). On a personal note, a panel organized by the authors at the Allied Social Science Association's 2004 annual meeting was approved with the suggestion that *eugenics* be removed from the session title.

sitions of human homogeneity (chap. 4, this vol.). We also fail to appreciate that F. Y. Edgeworth's attack on the early utilitarianism of Mill and Spencer was influenced by eugenic suppositions (chap. 10, this vol.). Second, once we appreciate the strong incentives to obtain specific answers in eugenic "science," we may question the community's conclusions.

We will argue in what follows that eugenics was a program that entailed wide-ranging intervention by the state, intervention purportedly designed to obtain the appropriate "quality" of the population. As such, it was a demographic form of central planning. We usually think of central planning as it relates to material things, setting prices and outputs of goods and services. And we know that *this* form of planning was vigorously opposed within the economics community, notably by Ludwig von Mises and F. A. Hayek. We begin this chapter by asking the natural follow-up question: were the opponents of material forms of central planning also opposed to planning for the quality of human beings?[2]

At first glance, the opposition to eugenics as demographic planning seems to have had little to do with the opposition to central planning in economics. The intellectual case against eugenics was largely contained in a noneconomist's work—Karl Popper's attack on Plato's doctrine, the first volume of *The Open Society and Its Enemies*.[3] But economics was not always separate from the philosophy of science and the history of ideas. Popper tells us, in fact, that Hayek's "interest and support" were instrumental to the publication of *Open Society*.[4] He explic-

---

2. Initially, it puzzled us that there seemed to be no credible intellectual opposition to eugenic arguments either before or after the Holocaust.

3. "Inherent in Plato's programme there is a certain approach towards politics which, I believe, is most dangerous. Its analysis is of great practical importance from the point of view of rational social engineering. The Platonic approach I have in mind can be described as that of *Utopian engineering*, as opposed to another kind of social engineering which I consider as the only rational one, and which may be described by the name of *piecemeal engineering*" (Popper, *Open Society* 1:157).

4. "I am deeply indebted to Professor F. A. von Hayek. Without his interest and support the book would not have been published" (Popper, *Open Society*,1:x). This is from the acknowledgments in the first edition. The point was not lost on Popper's critics. "So those who approve of limited or 'piece-meal' planning are suspicious of radical planning, which they regard as the 'road to serfdom.' It is to von Hayek, whose phrase I have just used, that Popper says he is 'deeply indebted.' And Popper bitterly criticizes the 'radical planning' of Plato's *Republic*" (Greene 1953, 47). Popper (1974, 95) adds details.

itly linked his argument to Hayek's work: "what I call 'Utopian engineering' corresponds largely, I believe, to what Hayek would call 'centralized' or 'collectivist' planning" (1962, *Open Society*, 1:285).[5] The
opposition to eugenics among the anti–central planners is further evident when we read in archives that the American edition of *Open Society* was published by Princeton University Press through the efforts of
the great historian of economics and trade theorist Jacob Viner.[6]

Splendidly effective as a polemic, Popper's *Open Society* did not
have to confront eugenics seriously in the midst of the horrors of the
Holocaust. It contains no discussion of the work of Galton or Pearson.
Instead, Popper needed only to point to the racial politics of the Hitler
era (Carlson 2001 contains an overview) and to observe that eugenic
theorizing begins with Plato.[7]

There were important differences between the debates over demographic planning and central planning more generally construed. For
instance, Popper questioned the *motives* of the proponents of eugenics.
Here is one of his many attacks on Plato.

> I think we must face the fact that behind the sovereignty of the philoso-
> pher king stands the quest for power. The beautiful portrait of the sov-
> ereign is a self-portrait. (*Open Society*, 1:155)[8]

---

5. In later editions, Popper pointed out that *Open Society* was written before *Road to Serfdom*
and Hayek's papers on scientism that clarified Hayek's attitudes: "Readers of Hayek's *The Road to
Serfdom* (1944) may feel puzzled by this note; for Hayek's attitude in this book is so explicit that no
room is left for the somewhat vague comments of my note" (Popper, *Open Society* 1:285).

6. Quoting from correspondence with Jeremy Shearmur (2003): "There is some correspondence between Viner and Popper. Viner seems to have been responsible for placing the American rights of *Open Society* with Princeton (Popper was unable to get a U.S. publisher). In that
connection, he sent Popper a list of points about the book, via Princeton; it was not in the file
under Viner, though there is just a chance that it might be held under Princeton U.P." It is worthy of note that Jacob Viner shares responsibility for reintroducing the Pareto criterion into
English-language economics (Robbins 1981). Later we argue that the Pareto principle would prevent the start of eugenic planning (chap. 10, this vol.).

7. "The one great figure in ancient eugenics is really Plato, who alone can be said to have perceived the spiritual significance and potentialities of the crude methods of social selection which
were practised in the Greek world" (Schiller 1914, 63). The texts cited by Schiller and Paul Shorey
were known to Charles Darwin. In chapter 7, we review his discussion in *Descent of Man* of the
Greek proponents of human breeding.

8. "He suggests that what Plato recommended is what might have been expected from a polit-
ically thwarted member of a 'laconising' aristocratic family. He even suggests that the prescription
of philosopher-kings was intended to point to Plato himself as the Fuehrer by whom society could
be saved; the 'Republic' was not only Plato's 'Das Kapital', it was also his 'Mein Kampf.' I think

In response to Popper, the most systematical defense of Plato insisted that the discussion remain at the level of logic and analysis, rather than motives or "imputations."[9] We question whether one can neatly dichotomize the "science" from the incentives of the scientists. We shall argue that eugenics overly tempts the researcher to separate himself from the "herd." There can be no veil of ignorance that clouds the identity of expert and subject when the expert begins with the supposition that he is superior to some or all of the subjects. Additional temptations follow from such a violation of reciprocity between expert and the expert's subjects. We shall see that this very case was made in the nineteenth century by those in the utilitarian tradition, George Grote and then John Stuart Mill.

---

myself that there are limits within which the interpretation of alogical motives should be kept and that Dr. Popper is inclined to overstep them. But it would be silly to pretend that interpretation can dispense with such imputations. If a thinker uses bad arguments or uses no arguments at all, if his exposition is obscure, his analogies false and his illustrations bad, the interpreter must offer some explanation for these defects. The official commentators have always done so, though the alogical motives which they have chosen to impute have tended to be respectable, if not noble, motives. So it is legitimate for Dr. Popper to pit against these reverent imputations his own more scathing diagnoses, so long as he can show that they give a better explanation of the logical failings in the dialogues" (Ryle 1947, 169).

9. The burden of Popper's attack (*Open Society*, 1:242–44) involves Plato's interpretation of the mysterious nuptial number, *Republic* 546B. Popper finds Plato contradicts himself here: "The crucial statement on which I base my interpretation is (A) that the guardians work by '*calculation aided by perception*'. . . . Regarding (A), it should be clear to every careful reader of Plato that such a reference to perception is intended to express a criticism of the method in question" (243). (Shorey translates what Popper italicized as "*reasoning combined with sensation.*")

Here is an alternative account quoted in the full-scale *Defense of Plato* (Levinson 1953, 616): "It thus appears that Brumbaugh agrees with Popper in taking Plato's genetic program as Pythagorean in origin and serious in intent; Brumbaugh also takes Plato's announcement of the number through the speech of the Muses as an indication that Plato had an operationally significant number to communicate. But here the resemblance ends. Brumbaugh finds Plato's genetics inspired by a sober and scientific spirit of research capable of recognizing its own limitations and honest enough to qualify its results when these conflicted with knowledge derived from other sources. . . . In fine, Brumbaugh sees in these inquiries not what Popper sees, the replacement of the philosopher's function by that of the shaman-breeder, but rather the attempt within the limits of human possibility to integrate a theory of value—philosophy—with a program for its realization through the rational control of every possible agency of human betterment." There is no disagreement about the purpose of the genetics: "Plato was inspired by Pythagorean and Hippocratic science with the hope of finding reliable principles according to which the higher human types required for preserving his ideal city could be bred" (616).

INCENTIVES AND EUGENIC "SCIENCE"

We focus here on the incentives facing eugenicists, as opposed to their motives. This allows us to presume those who favored eugenics were no better (nor worse) than those who opposed it. Such motivational homogeneity is in line with our human homogeneity story that runs throughout this book. But even if everyone has the same motivation, different incentives will generate different behavior.

In contrast to our focus on incentives here, little attention was paid during the central planning debates to the incentives facing planners (Levy 1990). The von Mises–Hayek criticism of central planning made the case in terms of the difficulty of aggregating information.[10] Economists did not question why there was so much "scientific" support for planning among would-be planners even as the planned economies disintegrated. Nor did they ask why scholars of the stature of von Mises and Hayek could not obtain paid employment as teachers in American universities. Both were supported by business-funded foundations (Vaughn 1994, 62–64).

The eugenic question that "Socrates" asks in Plato's Republic—why is it that "we" breed animals but "we" do not breed people?—offers the expert different rewards for different answers.[11] One answer, that it is desirable and possible to remake people, offers the expert satisfaction for creatively exercising his craft, as well as power and plenty. The other answer, that it is neither desirable nor possible to remake the subjects, offers the theorist only satisfaction.

The asymmetric incentives resulting from different answers to the eugenic question are a result of a violation of equality of stand-

---

10. Farrant (2004) establishes that Frank Knight understood perfectly well that the substantial problem with central planning, as it was then proposed, was monopoly politics. This created the temptation to the planner to price for private interest (see Levy 1990). Farrant also shows that Knight viewed this consideration as outside the purview of economics. The one systematic discussion of the motivation of planners centered around Hayek's Road to Serfdom. See Levy, Peart, and Farrant (2005).

11. "'The race of the guardians must be kept pure,' says Plato (in defence of infanticide), when developing the racialist argument that we breed animals with great care while neglecting our own race, an argument which has been repeated ever since" (Popper, Open Society, 1:51). The parenthetical remark drew the criticism.

ing—between the expert and the subject.[12] Such analytical egalitarianism was a presupposition of classical economics (chap. 1, this vol.).[13]
Two developments in eugenic "science" changed the incentives
regarding the answer to the eugenics question. The first was that it
apparently became possible to identify "the unfit" (using methods
described in chap. 5, this vol.). Economists sometimes characterize
proposals for the government direction of investment as an attempt to
"pick winners." Ex post, picking winning investments is easy; the trick
is doing it ex ante. The "unfit" were groups of demographic "losers"
whom would-be eugenic central planners proposed to identify ex ante
as targets for sterilization or immigration restrictions. The purported
ability to identify these targets changed demographic central planning
from a vague possibility to a straightforward application of laws
directed at such losers.

The subtitle of Elof Carlson's book *The Unfit* is *A History of a Bad
Idea*. We see the purported identification of "the unfit" as an idea that
changed the incentives open to theorists answering Plato's very old
question about breeding. Galton used the "unfit" as evidence of inherited criminality. In the early twentieth century, postclassical economists and sociologists seized upon the now purportedly identified
"unfit" to propose sterilization laws. This history makes for sobering
reading, as economists and their colleagues in sociology, statistics, and
biology thrust themselves forward as race purifiers. We conclude with
a rare contemporary assessment of just what "junk" their evidence was.

When the eugenic practices of the Hitler era became common
knowledge, the incentives to make eugenic claims changed again, and

---

12. The unhappiness of the subject at being treated like animals is much on "Socrates's" mind
in Plato's telling: "'Thus,' said I: 'it seems likely that our rulers will have to make considerable use
of falsehoods and deception for the benefit of their subjects. We said, I believe, that the use of that
sort of thing was in the category of medicine.' 'And that was right,' he [Glaucon] said. 'In our marriages, then, and the procreation of children, it seems there will be no slight need of this kind of
'right'" (*Republic* 459d). For reasons that will be made clear, we use Paul Shorey's translation.

13. Specialists (Popper, *Open Society* 1:88, 216, 328) noted that Popper revived the interpretation of Plato presented by John Stuart Mill's friend George Grote, who found the later Platonic
dialogues disturbing. We examine Grote's account of Plato's method later, in the section called
"Plato and Classical Economics."

now in the opposite direction. The involvement of postclassical economists in eugenics simply vanished from the secondary literature at midcentury (chap. 5, this vol.; Toye 2000; Cot 2003; Dimand 2003;
Leonard 2003b). As eugenic proposals vanished from the literature, the
memory of such discussions was also erased. We have, in fact, been
asked whether World War II constitutes a "firewall" against the return
of such ideas.[14] We return to this question in our conclusion.

"WE" BREED ANIMALS SO WHY NOT PEOPLE?

Perhaps the most effective way to locate both sides of the debate over
eugenics in the scholarly literature is to conduct two literature searches
using JSTOR. The first search, for texts containing the three words
eugenics Plato Galton, finds the first phase of the debate. Here, Plato is
discussed as forerunner to Galton's eugenic theories. The search for
texts containing the words *eugenics Plato Popper* finds the second
phase of the debate, in which Plato is now discussed as forerunner to
Hitler's eugenic practice. The search for *eugenics Plato Galton Popper*
turns up nothing.

To see why the debate has this structure, consider the following passage from Paul Shorey's once-standard translation of Plato's *Republic*
459 where "Socrates" recounts a conversation with Plato's brother,
"Glaucon," about the desirability of breeding "indiscriminately" or
"from the best." We quote from the Loeb edition in which the reader
is instructed by Shorey on both Greek and eugenics.

> "Obviously, then, we must arrange marriages, sacramental so far as may
> be. And the most sacred marriages would be those that were most
> beneficial." "By all means." "How, then, would the greatest benefit
> result? Tell me this, Glaucon. I see that you have in your house hunt-
> ing-dogs and a number of pedigree cocks. Have you ever considered
> something about their unions and procreations?" "What?" he said. "In
> the first place," I said, "among these themselves, although they are a

---

14. Deirdre McCloskey put the question to us at the Conference on Race and Liberalism in
Economics, organized by David Colander at Middlebury College in 2001. For the papers that
emerged from the conference, see Colander et al. 2004. We return to McCloskey's question in
the conclusion to this chapter.

select breed, do not some prove better than the rest?" "They do." "Do you then breed from all indiscriminately, or are you careful to breed from the best?" [Shorey notes: This commonplace of stirpiculture or eugenics, as it is now called, begins with Theognis 184, and has thus far got no further.] "From the best." . . . ". . . And if they are not thus bred, you expect, do you not, that your birds' breed and hounds will greatly degenerate?" "I do," he said. "And what of horses and other animals?" I said; "is it otherwise with them?" "It would be strange if it were," said he. "Gracious," said I, "dear friend, how imperative, then, is our need of the highest skill in our rulers, if the principle holds also for mankind." . . . "It follows from our former admissions," I said, "that the best men must cohabit with the best women in as many cases as possible and the worst with the worst in the fewest, and that the offspring of the one must be reared and that of the other not, if the flock [Shorey notes "αὖ below merely marks the second consideration, harmony, the first being eugenics."] is to be as perfect as possible." (459–61)[15]

To testify as to whether Shorey's command of the "commonplace" of eugenics is adequate to explain Plato for the Greekless world of the 1930s, consider a 16 March 1908 letter from Francis Galton (then aged 86) to Karl Pearson about a planned exhibit on eugenics.

MY DEAR KARL PEARSON, In reply to your card asking me for something to exhibit at the U.C. soirée, I have thought of an effective, yet somewhat absurd thing. But I have failed to get it. It is a *Punch* cartoon, pub-

---

15. Here is Shorey in 1903: "As implied in the *Meno* and *Euthydemus*, and stated in the *Republic*, he is to teach virtue and inculcate right opinion. And that his teaching may be effective and the seed fall in good ground, he is, like the rulers of the *Republic* and the *Laws*, to control marriages and the propagation of the race — especially with a view to harmonizing and blending the oppositions of the energetic and sedate temperaments" (62).

Between then and 1933 he has found a word to describe the practice Plato recommends: "As implied in the *Meno* and *Euthydemus* and stated in the *Republic*, he is to teach virtue and inculcate right opinion. And that his teaching may be effective and the seed fall on good ground, he is, like the rulers of the *Republic* and the *Laws*, to control marriages and the propagation of the race — especially with a view to blending by both eugenics and education the oppositions of the energetic and sedate temperaments" (1933, 314).

Shorey's interpretation of Plato's doctrine as *of course* eugenic and the translation that follows from this interpretation raise an obvious question. Why didn't Popper avoid the controversy over *his* amateur translation instead of using Shorey's? No one who gave three Sather Lectures as Shorey did would be exposed to the abuse that was heaped upon Popper. Indeed, in response to Levinson, Popper (*Open Society* 1:328–32) defends his translations by appeal to Shorey's. Popper (1974, 94) tells us, with evident regret, that in wartime New Zealand, he did not have access to the Loeb editions. Popper here identifies his interpretation with Shorey's, except that he disagrees with Shorey's endorsement of Plato.

lished I fancy in the early '70s, of a weedy nobleman addressing his prize bull:

> *Nobleman*—By Jove, you are a fine fellow!
> *Bull*—So you would have been, my Lord, if they had taken as much pains about your ancestors, as you did about mine.

I wrote to *Punch* to make inquiries, but they have not succeeded in identifying the picture. It would have been a capital thing to frame and to let lie among other exhibits. I should have been much disposed towards utilising it in some way farther on my own account. I cannot think of anything else suitable. Your Tables of the Coefficients of Hereditary Resemblance ought to be shown somewhere. (Pearson 1930, 3A:335)

A year later Galton reported that he located the cartoon, with the help of a Miss Burnand—"half-sister of the caricaturist."

It was drawn by *Punch*'s principal caricature artist of the 1880s, George du Maurier, and appeared in *Punch* on 20 March 1880 (Pearson 1936, 3:375). The cartoon, with the dialogue that Galton misremembered, is reproduced in figure 6.1. We return to the misremembering in our conclusion. The Platonic question—"Why do 'we' breed animals but not people?"—flatters the "scientist's" vanity, supposing eugenicists are a species apart from the subjects they hope to breed.[16]

GALTON AND "THE UNFIT"

Thanks to Carlson's 2001 *The Unfit* we now know the importance of "degenerate families" in the debates over eugenics. The Jukes family and the "Tribe of Ishmael" are the most famous of the colorful families of "degenerates" that served as "facts" in the calculations over the potential benefit of "negative" eugenics.[17] Carlson tells us how these "degenerates" were identified and how the hereditary nature of their

---

16. "Now we can understand why Plato drops his first hint that a more than ordinary excellence is needed in his rulers in the same place where he first claims that the principles of animal breeding must be applied to the race of men. . . . it thus prepares us for the demand that they ought to be philosophers" (Popper, *Open Society*, 1:150).

17. The "Jukes family" is a Library of Congress subject classification. Christianson (2003) reports on the recent unmasking of the "Jukes" and the demonstration of how the eugenic conclusions were drawn from these "data."

Fig. 6.1.   George du Maurier, "Happy Thought! Let Us All Have a Voice in the Matter" (1880)

criminality was asserted. "Degenerate" families were located by visiting prison after prison and then reporting the maximal family criminality.

One of the "degenerate" families—the Jukes—figured into Galton's *Human Faculty*.[18] The Jukes passage is a page and a half so we quote only extracts. He begins with the claim that criminal behavior is inherited.

> It is, however, easy to show that the criminal nature tends to be inherited; while, on the other hand, it is impossible that women who spend a large portion of the best years of their life in prison can contribute many

18. Although the first paragraph of *The Unfit* discusses Galton's coinage of *eugenics* and the next two pages of the chapter contain handsome reproductions of the title pages of *Human Faculty* (2001, 10) and *Essays in Eugenics* (2001, 11), Carlson does not discuss the importance of the Jukes family in Galton's *Human Faculty*. Carlson rightly stresses Galton's support for "positive eugenics" (234, 244–45). Carlson's view that Galton was not all that capable—"He also made some significant, but not brilliant, contributions to many fields" (144)—may have led him to overlook the possibility that Galton could both defend positive eugenics and point to information that could be used to justify negative eugenics. We have found this to be characteristic of Galton (chap. 4 and app. 1, this vol.). Stigler (1986, 1999) gives details on Galton's contributions.

children to the population. The true state of the case appears to be that the criminal population receives steady accessions from those who, without having strongly-marked criminal natures, do nevertheless belong to a type of humanity that is exceedingly ill suited to play a respectable part in our modern civilisation, though it is well suited to flourish under half-savage conditions, being naturally both healthy and prolific. These persons are apt to go to the bad; their daughters consort with criminals and become the parents of criminals. (1907c, *Human Faculty*, 44)

The Jukes are seen as a fine illustration of that claim.

An extraordinary example of this is afforded by the history of the infamous Jukes family in America, whose pedigree has been made out, with extraordinary care, during no less than seven generations, and is the subject of an elaborate memoir. . . . It includes no less than 540 individuals of Jukes blood, of whom a frightful number degraded into criminality, pauperism, or disease. (*Human Faculty*, 43–44)

The genetic success of such families needs to be explained.

Now the ancestor of all this mischief, who was born about the year 1730, is described as having been a jolly companionable man, a hunter, and a fisher, averse to steady labour, but working hard and idling by turns, and who had numerous illegitimate children, whose issue has not been traced. He was, in fact, a somewhat good specimen of a half-savage without any seriously criminal instincts. The girls were apparently attractive, marrying early and sometimes not badly; but the gipsy-like character of the race was unsuited to success in a civilised country. So the descendants went to the bad, and such hereditary moral weaknesses as they may have had, rose to the surface and worked their mischief without check. (*Human Faculty*, 44)

There was no suggestion in Galton that the problem of hereditary criminality can be solved by sterilizing criminals. For other commentators, the answer was self-evident. Irving Fisher put the case plainly in his 1909 *National Vitality*.

From the one man who founded the "Juke" family [*sic*] came 1,200 descendants in seventy-five years; out of these, 310 were professional paupers, who spent an aggregate of two thousand three hundred years in poorhouses, 50 were prostitutes, 7 murderers, 60 habitual thieves, and 130 common criminals.

Dugdale has estimated that the "Juke" family was an economic loss to the State, measured in terms of potential usefulness wasted, costs of prosecution, expenses of maintenance in jail, hospital, and asylums, and of private loss through thefts and robberies of $1,300,000 in seventy-five years, or over $1,000 for each member of the family. . . .

Had the original criminals in the "Juke" family and the "Tribe of Ishmael" been sterilized under some law like that of Indiana, this country would not only have been spared a widely disseminated criminal, epileptic, and immoral strain, but would have saved hundreds of thousands of dollars paid out for criminal suits. (1909, 675)

Fisher then proceeds to discuss the *benefits* to society from families such as the Hohenzollern family and the Darwin family (1909, 675–76). The Darwin family includes Francis Galton, whose eugenic work is cited by Fisher.

The existence of such "degenerate families" soon became grist for various mills among economists. Here is Frank Fetter's 1916 "explanation" of the consequences of immigration.

It led to the fateful introduction of slavery from Africa, and it encouraged much defective immigration from Europe, the heritage of which survives in many defective and vicious strains of humanity, some of them notorious, such as the Jukes, the Kallikak family, and the Tribe of Ishmael. (1916, 368–69)

That the possibility of identifying "degenerate familes" enabled eugenicists to take a step beyond Plato is also clear from the study of eugenics in the Danish experience. The great Danish geneticist, Wilhelm Johannsen, strenuously objected to Platonic utopian eugenics (Hansen 1993, 23).[19] But at least in the case of readily identified degen-

---

19. "In his book . . . (*Heredity in Historical and Experimental Light*), published in 1917, Johannsen devoted a full chapter, forty pages, to the subject of eugenics. In the historical introduction, he mentioned Plato and his utopian eugenics, and he did not hide his distaste for the idea of 'human stockbreeding plans with systematic control, fraudulently organized marriage lottery, abortion and exposure as eugenic measures—dreamers and fanatics from the prohibition and eugenics movements of our own period can see themselves as in a mirror'" (Hansen 1993, 23).

erate families, "negative eugenics" was another matter.[20] The role of degenerate families evidently helped shape the debate among "moderate" eugenicists in Denmark.

> Steincke and most of the Danish followers of eugenics can be regarded as moderate or "reform" eugenicists, since they openly stated that they disapproved of the more violent eugenics propaganda and of the early American practice of sterilization, particularly as it was done in California. But when we take a closer look at their views—the belief in horror stories about the "Jukes" and the "Kallikaks," the acceptance of the dangers of differential reproduction, and their uncritical hereditarianism—they do not appear particularly moderate. (Hansen 1993, 29)

GALTON AND PLATO

We suggested earlier that there was a divide in the debate over eugenics that is visible before and after World War II. Before World War II, Galton is regarded as taking a step beyond Plato; after the war, eugenic science is dismissed. Here, we provide some examples of the earlier assessments that credit Galton with moving eugenics beyond Plato.

Science was in its second volume when it published a review of the first edition of Galton's *Human Faculty* in 1883. The issue of eugenics occupies the bulk of the first paragraph.

> Mr. Galton means to introduce to our notice new aspects of the study of human character. He wishes to make this study more exact and scientific by founding it upon detailed investigations of facts previously neglected; and he proposes to offer the results as useful for a future science or art of eugenics, which shall teach the human race how to breed so that its best stock shall be preserved and improved, and its worst stock gradually eliminated. (1883, 80)

---

20. "This was what he called positive eugenics. He was more inclined to accept negative eugenics, where the procreation of individuals with strongly flawed genotypes was inhibited. But he emphasized that it would be very difficult and complicated to carry this out in a responsible fashion. He certainly did not approve of 'the haphazard surgical sterilization methods' applied in the United States" (Hansen 1993, 25). "In Johannsen's writings on eugenics in the 1920s he hardly appears as a zealot for the cause. He toned down his criticism of the biometrical school. . . . He still rejected what he called positive eugenics but found negative eugenics acceptable, when it was applied with caution. The same attitude is apparent in his contributions to the negotiations of the commission on castration and sterilization" (26).

The second paragraph credits Galton with improving upon the Greek discussion.

> That Mr. Galton's researches will be of much immediate use to young people about to marry, no truthful reviewer can promise; but to the psychologist, at least, they are in their present condition both attractive and useful; and, for the rest, it is much for Mr. Galton merely to have suggested, more definitely than Plato was able to do, that there ought to be, and some day may be, a real art of eugenics, which may be of practical importance for mankind. (1883, 80)

Close to forty years later, Leonard Darwin advocated demographic controls in *Science*. He dismissed changing circumstances ("improvement of environment") as a reform measure.

> Do we not blush to talk of peace on earth and good-will towards men whilst remembering what has happened during the last seven years? And, in view of all this, have we any right to assume that improvement of environment will do more for mankind during the next two thousand years than it has done since the days of Plato? Reformers who look only to surroundings should consider well the foundations on which their projects are based before pointing the finger of scorn at the believers in heredity. Eugenics has been called a dismal science, but it should rather be described as an untried policy. (Darwin 1921, 315)

In 1939, on the eve of World War II, *Science* published S. J. Holmes's presidential address before the American Eugenics Society, "The Opposition to Eugenics." Here, Professor Holmes (1939, 352) confronted the fact that there was growing opposition to eugenics. To explain this, he reminded his listeners that eugenic policy became feasible only recently.

> In seeking for the reasons for the opposition to eugenics it is important to bear in mind that the idea of improving the inborn qualities of man is, for the great mass of humanity, of relatively recent origin. To be sure, race improvement through selective breeding had been advocated by Theognis, Plato, Campanella and a few other lonely voices, but their doctrines were regarded more in the light of curiosities of philosophical speculation than as feasible measures for practical application. It was only after the doctrine of evolution came to be finally accepted in the scientific world that eugenics was brought clearly before the reading public as a subject to be seriously reckoned with. (1939, 352)

Holmes recognized that eugenics depends upon the doctrine of the "natural inequality of man" (1939, 352). He then asked who might oppose eugenics on the basis of egalitarian presuppositions. In response to his own query, Holmes pointed to some social reformers (such as Edwin Markham) who presupposed equality. He also singled out Libertarians (such as Clarence Darrow) who opposed interference with marriage choices (Holmes 1939, 354). He mentioned Catholics such as G. K. Chesterton as well (354).[21] And then he included J. S. Mill, who claimed that the appeal to natural inequality is the height of vulgarity (355). The list comprised: a poet, a libertarian lawyer, a Catholic literary figure, and a dead classical economist. As noted at the outset of this chapter, early opposition to eugenic "science" was remarkably thin.[22]

Moving to the other side of the divide, we find Edward Sisson's 1939 presidential address to the Pacific division of the American Philosophical Association, "Human Nature and the Present Crisis." Sisson raised the question of the survival of philosophy itself. In his judgment Plato becomes "one of the most dangerous items in the education of the western world."

> Consequently in preparing for this discussion I have paid attention mostly to the opposition. I have earnestly reconsidered that original philosophical charter of fascism—a noble and austere doctrine indeed, but fascism—Plato's *Republic*, the beauty and surpassing genius of which has made it, I think, one of most dangerous items in the education of the western world. (Sisson 1940, 143)

Sisson then recommends Walt Whitman's *Democratic Vistas* for its argument against Plato's vision of the masses (144–46). Whitman's

---

21. On Chesterton and eugenics, see McPhail 2003.

22. Eggen (1926, 104) notes the infrequent opposition before proceeding with his criticism: "There seem to be few adequate criticisms of the eugenicist's standpoint. Here and there a lone environmentalist raises his voice in heresy, but definite presentations of the controversy, examining the arguments on both sides, are lamentably few or even non-existent." Eggen confronts the Jukes evidence directly. "For Estabrook to assume (and Dugdale before him) that, because *idleness* (shades of the Faculty psychologists!) or something resembling it is to be found in successive generations of the Jukes family, that idleness is a Mendelian character inheritable through the germ-plasm, is as laughable an error as any to be found in all contemporary (pseudo) science. The same thing is true of all the eugenicist's 'characters': pauperism, harlotry, crime, insanity, blindness, syphilis, et cetera" (107).

Democratic Vistas began with an opening tribute to Mill's *On Liberty*, and it attacked Thomas Carlyle's *Shooting Niagara*.[23] We have also seen that Galton's work in the 1860s reads like *Shooting Niagara* (chap. 4, this vol.).

Hitler-era eugenic practice destroyed the basis for continued popular support of eugenics, and the debate thereafter became a debate over Plato.[24]

PLATO AND CLASSICAL ECONOMICS

Despite their political differences, both Holmes and Sisson saw that Mill was an opponent of hierarchy and eugenics. Mill wrote extensively on Plato when he reviewed George Grote's history of Greek philosophy. Consequently, we examine Grote's discussion of the *Republic* in *Plato* (1865) and Mill's 1866 review.

Grote wrote *Plato* before eugenics had a name, but he clearly saw that eugenic teaching in the *Republic* was wrapped up in racial fictions.

> What he seeks as lawgiver is, to keep the numbers of the Guardians nearly stationary, with no diminution and scarcely any increase: and to maintain the breed pure, so that the children born shall be as highly endowed by nature as possible. To these two objects the liberty of sexual intercourse is made subservient. The breeding is regulated, like that of noble horses or dogs by an intelligent proprietor. (1865, 3:203)[25]

23. "As the greatest lessons of Nature through the universe are perhaps the lessons of variety and freedom, the same present the greatest lessons also in New World politics and progress. If a man were ask'd, for instance, the distinctive points contrasting modern European and American political and other life with the old Asiatic cultus, as lingering-bequeath'd yet in China and Turkey, he might find the amount of them in John Stuart Mill's profound essay on Liberty in the future, where he demands two main constituents, or sub-strata, for a truly grand nationality—1st, a large variety of character—and 2d, full play for human nature to expand itself in numberless and even conflicting directions . . ." (Whitman 1982, 929). The document mentioned in chapter 8, note 27 suggests an unexpected linkage between Carlyle and Whitman.

24. Sterilization continued in America, however, through the 1970s. It was not until 2002 that a governor of a state (Mark R. Warner, Virginia) apologized to the victims of eugenic practice.

25. "Yet unless certain fundamental fictions can be accredited among his citizens, the scheme of his commonwealth must fail. They must be made to believe that they are all earthborn and all brethren; that the earth which they inhabit is also their mother: but that there is this difference among them—the Rulers have gold mingled with their constitution, the other Guardians have silver, the remaining citizens have brass or iron. This bold fiction must be planted as a fundamental dogma" (Grote 1865, 3:185). "What Plato here understands by marriage, is a special,

He also recognized that the eugenic question tempts the theorist. He finds that Plato abandoned his own philosophical principles in the face of this temptation.

Grote notes, first, that the *Republic* attacks the classical economists' idea of reciprocity. Instead of reciprocal relations based on equality of moral standing, Plato denies the "onerous duty" of justice.

> It is clear that Plato—in thus laying down the principle of reciprocity, or interchange of service, as the ground-work of the social union—recognises the antithesis, and at the same time the correlation, between obligation and right. The service which each man renders to supply the wants of others is in the nature of an onerous duty; the requital for which is furnished to him in the services rendered by others to supply his wants. (1865, 3:139)
>
> We see therefore that Plato contradicts his own fundamental principle, when he denies the doing of justice to be an onerous duty, and when he maintains that it is in itself happiness—giving to the just agent, whether other men account him just and do justice to him in return—or not. By this latter doctrine he sets aside that reciprocity of want and service, upon which he had affirmed the social union to rest. (1865, 3:139)

Grote continues, adding that Plato attacks the proverbial wisdom to "do unto others as they would be done by."[26]

> The fathers, whom he blames, gave advice in full conformity with his own principle of reciprocity—when they exhorted their sons to the practice of justice, not as self-inviting, but as an onerous service toward others, to be requited by corresponding services and goodwill from others towards them. (1865, 3:139–40)

Earlier, Grote had explained that the dialectic method consisted of a method of exchange where reciprocity is central. Yet to protect his eugenic thinking, Plato gives up the dialectic method.

---

solemn, consecrated, coupling for the occasion, with a view to breed for the public. . . . The case resembles that of a breeding stud of horses and mares, to which Plato compares it" (Grote 1865, 3:205).

26. "Glaukon (as I have already observed) announces the doctrine against which Sokrates contends, not as a recent corruption broached by the Sophists, but as the generally received view of Justice: held by most persons, repeated by the poets from ancient times downwards, and embodied by fathers in lessons to their children" (Grote 1865, 3:145). We discuss the significance of this proverb in detail in chapters 7, 8, and 11.

Though Sokrates, and Plato so far forth as a follower of Sokrates, employed a colloquial method based on the fundamental assumption of the Protagorean formula—autonomy of each individual mind—whether they accepted the formula in terms, or not—yet we shall find Plato at the end of his career, in his Treatise De Legibus, constructing an imaginary city upon the attempted deliberate exclusion of this formula. We shall find him there monopolising all teaching and culture of his citizens . . . when he constitutes himself as lawgiver, the measure of truth or falsehood for all his citizens—has at the same time discontinued his early commerce with the Sokratic Dialectics. (1865, 2:357–58)

Mill focused on this preferential treatment in his review of Grote's *Plato*.

It is singular that Plato himself did not fully profit by the principal lesson of his own teaching. This is one of the inconsistencies by which he is such a puzzle to posterity. No one can read many of the works of Plato, and doubt that he had positive opinions. But he does not bring his own opinions to the test which he applies to others. "It depends on the actual argumentative purpose which Plato has in hand, whether he chooses to multiply objections and give them effect, or to ignore them altogether." "The affirmative Sokrates only stands his ground because no negative Sokrates is allowed to attack him." Or, what is worse, Plato applies the test, and disregards its indications; states clearly and strongly the objections to the opinion he favours, and goes on his way as if they did not exist. (Mill 1866, 412)

He agreed with Grote, that "[t]here are thus, independently of minor discrepancies, two complete Platos in Plato—the Sokratist and the Dogmatist" (415).[27] Eugenics was one of the doctrines of the "dogmatic" Plato for which there was no "Sokratic" challenge.

---

27. "But as he advanced in life, and acquired a persuasion of knowledge of his own; when, to use a metaphor of Mr. Grote's, he ceased to be leader of opposition, and passed over to the ministerial benches, he came to think that the Sokratic cross-examination is a dangerous edge-tool. Already in the *Republic* we find him dwelling on the mischiefs of a purely negative state of mind. . . . he came to think that the doctrines which had the best ethical tendency should be taught, with little or no regard to whether they could be proved true, and even at the risk of their being false" (Mill 1866, 414–15).

THE JUNK SCIENCE JUDGMENT FROM 1931

We have noted that two economists, Hayek and Viner, played critical roles in questioning eugenics as central planning. We conclude by reviewing a rare attack on the "evidence" of "degenerate families" published by Lancelot Hogben[28] in an 1931 issue of *Economica*, the journal in which Popper's "Poverty of Historicism" later appeared.[29] In his article, Hogben made the case that the "evidence" of degenerate families in eugenic studies was biased and unscientific, that it would not be "legally admissible."

Hogben starts this section of his paper by posing the question as one between Galton and Watson (the environmentalist). While the legal system might ensure that the evaluation of evidence is impartial, Hogben claimed that there is great pressure to choose the evidence selectively in science.

> In English law there is an estimable provision which forbids the public discussion of evidence until the case is closed. In science unhappily there is none. I have presented for your reflection some of the difficulties of biological inquiry into social problems. One of the greatest dangers is an undue haste prompted by enthusiasm for legislative applications of half-assimilated knowledge. The discussion of the genetic foundations of racial and occupational stratification in human society calls for discipline, for restraint and for detachment. Nothing could make the exercise of these wholesome virtues more difficult than to force the issues into the political arena in the present state of inquiry. The disposition to do so has already encumbered social biology with a vocabulary of terms which have no status in an ethically neutral science. . . . Of these shortcomings anecdotalism is the most prevalent. Every experimental biologist recognises the disastrous consequences of constructing evolutionary hypotheses on the testimony of the pigeon fancier and the stock breeder. Only an undue haste to establish conclusions which can be made the basis of legislation has arrested the development of social biology in its anecdotage. (1931, 18–19)

---

28. In 1930, Lancelot Hogben was appointed to the new research professorship of social biology at the London School of Economics.

29. Hogben (1998) criticized Lionel Robbins's nonmathematical economics. This is unfortunate; as chapter 10 suggests, they might have had much to say to each other. Their shared view of Carlyle would have been a beginning (Hogben 1998, 20).

The case in point is the degenerate family "evidence." Hogben continues:

> Two quotations will exempt me from the charge of overstating the dan-
> ger to which I allude, when I speak of the anecdotal method. One prob-
> lem which engages the attention of the social biologist is the contribu-
> tion of heredity to feeblemindedness. Goddard's familial studies on this
> subject will be known to many of my audience. . . . The method which
> Goddard adopted to identify feeblemindedness in the ancestors of his
> cases is thus stated in his own words:
> "The ease with which it is sometimes possible to get satisfactory evi-
> dence on the fifth generation is illustrated in the Kallikak family. The
> field worker accosts an old farmer—'Do you remember an old man
> Martin Kallikak (Jr.) who lived on the mountain edge yonder?' 'Do I?
> Well I guess. Nobody'd forget him. Simple, not quite right here (tap-
> ping his head), but inoffensive and kind. All the family was that. . . . they
> would drink. Poverty was their best friend in this respect, or they would
> have been drunk all the time. . . .'"
> At the conclusion of this recital Goddard asks, "Is there any doubt
> that Martin was feebleminded?" I am tempted to imagine what the
> same old farmer would say to his crony. "Seemed a decent sort of fellow.
> Asked a lot of fool questions and wrote down the answers in a book. Sim-
> ple, I'd say. Not quite right here." (1931, 19–20)

He then considers the "evidence" concerning the Jukes.

> In his monograph *The Jukes in 1915*, Estabrook ventures to proffer only
> one definite statement concerning hereditary transmission in the Jukes
> family. It is that "there is an hereditary factor in licentiousness." I have
> searched through his memoir for a single indication of the way in which
> he defines licentiousness and its allelomorphic opposite chastity. (1931,
> 20)

> The attitude of the experimental biologist to those who accept as sci-
> entific evidence data which would not even be regarded as legally
> admissible is well expressed by Thomas Hunt Morgan, the leading
> geneticist of our time. "The numerous pedigrees," . . . "are open to the
> same criticism from a genetic point of view, for it is obvious that these
> groups of individuals have lived under demoralising social conditions
> . . . It is not surprising that, once begun from whatever cause, the effects
> may be to a large extent communicated rather than inherited. . . ." (1931,
> 21)

And finally, Hogben suggests we put the expert himself in Estabrook's calculations.

> I confess I am sceptical about the cogency of Dr. Estabrook's arithmetic. How damaging a case against higher education could be made, if we included all the port consumed in the fellows' common rooms during the last century and a half. Other curious items are included in the two million dollar bill. *Inter alia* we note the following:
>
> > "Aggregate of children who died prematurely, cash cost $50 each child $18,900
> > Number of lives sacrificed by murder (ten) valued $1,200 .... $12,000
> > Capital in brothels $60,000, compound interest twenty-six years at 6 per cent .... $18,000"
>
> One is left to wonder why this felicitous blend of biological and economic science is not rounded off by adding to the financial loss incurred by the State on account of the Jukes family, the cost of printing Carnegie Institute Publication No. 240, together with Dr. Estabrook's salary and that of his staff. (1931, 21–22)

Presumably, the answer to Hogben's rhetorical question is that from the point of view of the eugenic researcher, eugenic research is a benefit and not a cost. This is another way of making our point. Answers of one sort, but not of another, provide power and plenty.

If Hogben's argument had an impact, it escaped Carlson (2001) even though Hogben's lecture was introduced by none other than H. G. Wells, who called attention to the importance of "some peculiar strain of human being, known as the *Unfit* (and not otherwise defined)" (Wells 1931, 4).[30]

CONCLUSION

Eugenics is based on a presumption of inherited human heterogeneity. We have argued here that this eugenic presumption tempts the expert

---

30. We find a solitary paper in JSTOR with the search *Hogben eugenics Jukes:* MacKenzie 1975.

to presume he is in the favored group. This temptation, coupled with the fact that intellects as great as Pearson and Plato have apparently succumbed, is a major reason for our contention that only a hard doctrine of homogeneity is compatible with research and policy prescription by "experts." We have been asked on more than one occasion, what if Plato were right about inherent differences among peoples?[31] Alternatively put, what if Adam Smith were incorrect about the porter and the philosopher? In response to such questions, we have come to answer that the dangers of presuming difference or hierarchy are great enough to outweigh whatever failings result from lack of empirical realism. One instance in which surface differences are supposed to reveal underlying differences is discussed in the Postscript to this volume. We suggest that such an explicit recognition of reciprocity and homogeneity—in all dimensions, including the expert and the subject—erects a firewall against eugenic practice and theory directed by the expert-guided state. Firewalls do not maintain themselves. One purpose of our book is to help maintain a firewall in the space of ideas by discussing the consequences that have followed from the assumption that surface differences among people reveal underlying differences among persons.[32]

Does the relationship between the expert—here, the scientist—and the subject include the requirement of reciprocity?[33] In other words, is the expert to be treated as he treats the subject? The *Punch* cartoon was remembered by Galton as a simple illustration of eugenics, but perhaps it is something more. Perhaps the caption "Let us all have a voice in the matter" questions whether there is such a justifiable divide between expert and the subjects.[34] And several of the humorous objec-

---

31. James Buchanan was the first. Buchanan's own analytical egalitarianism makes his challenge particularly memorable.

32. Deirdre McCloskey's question posed in footnote 14—"Does the Holocaust provide a firewall to eugenics?"—can be answered with "Only if we remember."

33. At least on an informal basis, this presumption guides experimental procedures in economics and constrains the experimentalist from deceiving the subject. See Houser 2004.

34. We thank Ira Gang for making this point when discussing our paper at the Eastern Economic Association in New York.

tions of Hogben seem to be suggestions that if we apply the experts' standards of "unfit" to the experts themselves, they might not pass the examination. Finally, if experts rely on different standards than their subjects, then perhaps we have an explanation for why the post–World War II literature maintains a rational silence on the involvement of the economists in the eugenics movement.

Part III

DEBATING SYMPATHY

VII

SYMPATHY AND ITS DISCONTENTS
"Greatest Happiness" versus
the "General Good"

Human beings, on this point, only differ from other animals in two par-
ticulars. First, in being capable of sympathizing, not solely with their offspring, or, like some of the more noble animals, with some superior animal who is kind to them, but with all human, and even with all
sentient, beings. Secondly, in having a more developed intelligence . . .
any conduct which threatens the security of the society generally, is
threatening to his own, and calls forth his instinct (if instinct it be) of
self-defence. The same superiority of intelligence joined to the power of
sympathizing with human beings generally, enables him to attach himself to the collective idea of his tribe, his country, or mankind, in such
a manner that any act hurtful to them, raises his instinct of
sympathy and urges him to resistance.
—J. S. Mill, *Utilitarianism*

COMPETING VIEWS OF THE SCIENTIST

Early utilitarians held that the scientist is akin to the philosopher in
book V of Adam Smith's *Wealth of Nations*, someone who arranges
and makes systematical sense of ordinary wisdom.[1] This systematiza-
tion begins with a judgment, founded on our common sense of sympathy, about the character and actions of other people (*Wealth of
Nations*, V.1.§153).[2] The scientist makes models that summarize infor-

---

1. In this chapter, as in the study of eugenics (esp. see chaps. 5, 6, this vol.), we consider the
characterization of the "scientist"—as opposed to the broader notion of the "expert"—by the scientist himself.

2. "As soon as writing came into fashion, wise men, or those who fancied themselves such,
would naturally endeavour to increase the number of those established and respected maxims,
and to express their own sense of what was either proper or improper conduct, sometimes in the
more artificial form of apologues, like what are called the fables of Æsop; and sometimes in the

mation and help other ordinary people see their way, but there is little beyond this division of labor among equals that separates him from those he studies.[3] And, significantly in our view, the scientist is included in the phenomena under study. In the latter half of the nineteenth century, by contrast, the scientist became a self-proclaimed expert who can distinguish between superior and inferior humans, and who consequently knows how best to direct sympathy.[4]

We argue here that Charles Darwin's *Descent of Man* was a critical text in the transition. Darwin proposed to replace the early utilitarians' "greatest happiness" principle with a goal of the "general good" entailing biological perfection. He stressed the evolutionary role of sympathy in developing moral sense among humans. At the same time, he asked whether undirected sympathetic tendencies served to interfere with biological perfection.

Between Darwin's 1859 *Origin of Species* and the 1871 *Descent of Man*, many social commentators considered whether and how the principle of natural selection applied to humans. We focus on a popularizer we have seen before (chap. 3), Charles Kingsley. Kingsley con-

---

more simple one of apophthegms, or wise sayings, like the Proverbs of Solomon, the verses of Theognis and Phocyllides, and some part of the works of Hesiod. They might continue in this manner for a long time merely to multiply the number of those maxims of prudence and morality, without even attempting to arrange them in any very distinct or methodical order, much less to connect them together by one or more general principles from which they were all deducible, like effects from their natural causes. The beauty of a systematical arrangement of different observations connected by a few common principles was first seen in the rude essays of those ancient times towards a system of natural philosophy. Something of the same kind was afterwards attempted in morals. The maxims of common life were arranged in some methodical order, and connected together by a few common principles, in the same manner as they had attempted to arrange and connect the phenomena of nature. The science which pretends to investigate and explain those connecting principles is what is properly called moral philosophy" (Smith, *Wealth of Nations*, V.1§153).

3. See Smith's famous example of the street porter and the philosopher, quoted earlier as epigraph to chapter 1 (*Wealth of Nations*, I.2§4).

4. David Hume's problem of the fate of "another rational species" strictly inferior to ours is much to the point (Levy and Peart 2004). Hume's analysis distinguishes between the thought experiment of actual inferiority and belief in the inferiority of non-Europeans confronted with European military technology. Unlike his more famous "sensible knave" problem, Hume sees no way out of his conclusion that the other rational race will be exterminated or enslaved. We have argued that Smith's sympathetic approach offers a different conclusion. The difference between equals who sympathize with each other, as Hume has it, or sympathy that equalizes people, as Smith has it, is critical.

nected the Carlylean belief that "charity begins at home" with the racial anthropology of James Hunt (chap. 4) to argue that sympathy required direction toward the truly deserving.

We begin by examining the notion of sympathy in Hume and Smith. Hume's sympathetic principle moves from *equality in fact* to sympathy. This we juxtapose to Adam Smith's reversal of the causation, which goes from sympathy to *judgment of equality*.[5] Second, we explicate the utilitarian principle of sympathy in terms of concern for those nearby and afar. We consider the challenges to the early utilitarian impartial weighting scheme that emerged in the literary community and from evolutionary biology. As sympathy came to be seen as an impediment to evolutionary perfection, more voices urged that sympathy be suppressed. Darwin's *Descent of Man* explicitly countenanced the suppression of sympathy in a trade-off of happiness for the perfection of the race.

SYMPATHY IN HUME AND SMITH

For Hume, sympathy is an empathy we feel for those like us.[6] We are motivated to obtain the praise or approbation of those with whom we

---

5. If, as Smith insists, we start with sympathy, then we can appeal to Edgeworth's demonstration that sympathetic traders will share more equally than unsympathetic ones (1881, 45–46).

6. For detail on sympathy in Hume and Smith, see Levy and Peart 2004. There is a recent history of attempts to incorporate sympathy and/or empathy into economic models, e.g., Arrow 1977 and the literature discussed in Sugden 2002. The nineteenth-century controversy over the concern for family relative to strangers has received less attention.

It should be noted that we attend only to Smith's discussion of experience in which rules of justice have emerged and function well. Smith worries a great deal in both *Theory of Moral Sentiments* and *Wealth of Nations* about how religious instruction, which he thinks inculcates these rules, gets twisted for private ends. In *Wealth of Nations* Smith develops the argument that religious competition without state intervention would bring forth a pure, rational religion. These texts are discussed in Levy 1978. Smith is aware that morality can be ignored by a minority. Although Smith begins his *Theory of Moral Sentiments* with a clarion denial of selfishness— "How selfish soever man may be supposed, there are evidently some principles in his nature, which interest him in the fortune of others, and render their happiness necessary to him" (I.1§1)—this is how he describes the rich and powerful in *Wealth of Nations*: "All for ourselves and nothing for other people, seems, in every age of the world, to have been the vile maxim of the masters of mankind" (III.4§10) The passages in *Theory of Moral Sentiments* that suggest we ought to discard minority experience often come in the post–*Wealth of Nations* edition (Levy 1995). See also the account of proverbial wisdom offered in chapter 11 that "paired proverbs" come from the difference between majority and minority experience.

sympathize. By contrast, Smith holds that we feel sympathy for and earn the approbation (or disapprobation) of those unlike as well as those like us. We obtain approbation as we step outside ourselves and regard our own actions dispassionately. Hume and Smith agree that approbation applies only in conditions of existential equality, but for Smith this condition embodies all of humankind, whereas in Hume it extends only to those who are not "strictly inferior" to us. For this reason, the analysis that follows is a result of Smith's deep analytical egalitarianism considered throughout this book.

For Hume, sympathy requires entering into the sentiments of others, something we can do only if the other is similar to us. In book II, chapter 11 ("Love of Fame") of the *Treatise*, Hume holds that the ability to sympathize requires physical and intellectual similarity among people.

> Now 'tis obvious, that nature has preserv'd a great resemblance among all human creatures, and that we never remark any passion or principle in others, of which, in some degree or other, we may not find a parallel in ourselves. The case is the same with the fabric of the mind, as with that of the body. However the parts may differ in shape or size, their structure and composition are in general the same. There is a very remarkable resemblance, which preserves itself amidst all their variety; and *this resemblance must very much contribute to make us enter into the sentiments of others, and embrace them with facility and pleasure.* (1739–40, 318; emphasis added)

The sentence we emphasize is at the foundation of the difference between Hume and Smith on sympathy, approbation, and moral obligation. Hume pointed to this difference himself in a famous letter to Smith.[7] Sympathy for Hume is akin to what we might call empathy

---

7. Hume's letter of 28 July 1759 in Smith 1977, 43: "I am told that you are preparing a new Edition, and propose to make some Additions and Alternations, in order to obviate Objections. I shall use the Freedom to propose one, which, if it appears to be of any Weight, you may have in your Eye. I wish you had more particularly and fully prov'd, that all kinds of Sympathy are necessarily Agreeable. This is the Hinge of your System . . . And indeed, as the Sympathetical Passion is a reflex Image of the principal, it must partake of its Qualities, and be painful where that is so." Lindgren (1973, 21–22): "The doctrine of sympathy is typically thought to be simple and straightforward. The most popular interpretation is that sympathy is the same as empathy. . . . This view, first suggested by David Hume (letter to Smith, July 28, 1759), was rejected in a note added by

today: we enter in the passions of others, and we can do so because these people think and look like us.[8]

For Hume, human beings are made moral because they are motivated by the approbation that they receive from others with whom they sympathize (1739–40, 316). Hume infers that the amount of approbation (or disapprobation) we obtain from those with whom we sympathize "depends on the relation of the object to ourselves."

> [W]e are most uneasy under the contempt of persons, who are both related to us by blood, and contiguous in place. Hence we seek to diminish this sympathy and uneasiness by separating these relations, and placing ourselves in a contiguity to strangers, and at a distance from relations. (1739–40, 322)[9]

By contrast, Smith holds that sympathy is something akin to an estimation procedure, a projection, in which we imaginatively exchange positions while preserving our consciousness. Sympathy is Smith's device to connect our concerns with those of others by imagining how others see us.[10] In his construction, sympathy differs from "fellow feel-

---

Smith to the third [second] edition of the *Moral Sentiments*." Haakonssen (2002, xiv) highlights how the discussion helped Smith formulate his position: "This pleasure [of understanding another's sentiments] is distinct from whatever sentiments we may have about the object of our sympathetic understanding, sentiments which may be either pleasing or displeasing. It seems that Smith himself only came to complete clarity about this matter in the light of David Hume's criticism of his handling of it in the first edition."

8. Schochet (2001) argues that the difference between Hume's and Smith's use of the word *sympathy* marks the transition from an older to a new use. *Sympathy* had traditionally been associated with musical vibrations where physical similarity was important for generating mutual vibration. Musical theory and Renaissance magic are connected in Walker 1975. A glance at the indexes in Thorndike 1923–58 reveals hundreds of references to *sympathetic magic* and *sympathy*.

9. Approbation (and disapprobation) from those unlike us is less powerful as a motivating force: "[W]e receive a much greater satisfaction from the approbation of those, whom we ourselves esteem and approve of, than of those, whom we hate and despise. In like manner we are principally mortify'd with the contempt of persons, upon whose judgment we set some value, and are, in a great measure, indifferent about the opinions of the rest of mankind" (Hume 1739–40, 321). Since approbation is external to the individual receiving it, people may escape disapprobation by leaving kin and kith behind (322).

10. Harman (1986, 14): "There is an interesting irony in the way in which Hume's use of the term 'sympathy' leads Smith to his own very different theory, a theory that in my view is much better than Hume's at accounting for moral phenomenology. Smith's criticism of Hume's use of the term 'sympathy' is not a serious one. It is of no importance whatsoever whether the meaning that Hume gives to the term 'sympathy' is the ordinary one. . . . The irony is that taking Hume's term seriously leads Smith to a more accurate account of morality. A purely verbal point yields a powerful substantive theory."

ing" or some self-motivating experience of what is in another's mind. Without reflection and education, we may very well get bizarre results—in Smith's example, we think the problem of death is the cold, lonely grave and the gnawing vermin—but we sympathize nonetheless. With education and reflection, we learn that the problem of death is really the "awful futurity."

Because sympathetic judgments are predictable, albeit often biased, sympathy is similar instead to what we would today call an estimate.[11]

> Every man, as the Stoics used to say, is first and principally recommended to his own care; and every man is certainly, in every respect, fitter and abler to take care of himself than of any other person. Every man feels his own pleasures and his own pains more sensibly than those of other people. The former are the original sensations; the latter the reflected or sympathetic images of those sensations. The former may be said to be the substance; the latter the shadow. (*Theory of Moral Sentiments*, VI.2§4)

Smith continues to describe how sympathy is felt most readily for those we know best.

> After himself, the members of his own family, those who usually live in the same house with him, his parents, his children, his brothers and sisters, are naturally the objects of his warmest affections. They are naturally and usually the persons upon whose happiness or misery his conduct must have the greatest influence. He is more habituated to sympathize with them. He knows better how every thing is likely to affect them, and his sympathy with them is more precise and determinate, than it can be with the greater part of other people. It approaches nearer, in short, to what he feels for himself. (*Theory of Moral Sentiments*, VI.2§5)

---

11. Levy 1995 defends this reading in part by noting that early in *Theory of Moral Sentiments* Smith considers how individuals sympathize with the dead and the insane. They erroneously impute unhappiness to the insane. Sugden (2002, 76) quotes the insanity evidence against Fontaine's (1997) account of the sympathetic individual "becoming" the other person. The estimation interpretation allows one to apply such considerations as robustness to other aspects of the utilitarian discussions. See Levy 2001. As a result of discussions at the 2004 Summer Institute, we have come to prefer the term *projection* to describe the process at work. We thank Sam Fleischaker and Ali Khan for helping us to see this.

Then, Smith makes the leap from habituated imagination to affection: "What is called affection, is in reality nothing but habitual sympathy" (*Theory of Moral Sentiments*, VI.2§10).

Sympathy is the foundation of rules of justice (i.e., reciprocity), which become internalized as conscience. We are motivated by what we imagine—"reason, principle, conscience, the inhabitant of the breast, the man within, the great judge"—to perform what Smith describes as "generous" acts.

> When our passive feelings are almost always so sordid and so selfish, how comes it that our active principles should often be so generous and so noble? When we are always so much more deeply affected by whatever concerns ourselves, than by whatever concerns other men; what is it which prompts the generous, upon all occasions, and the mean upon many, to sacrifice their own interests to the greater interests of others? It is not the soft power of humanity, it is not that feeble spark of benevolence which Nature has lighted up in the human heart, that is thus capable of counteracting the strongest impulses of self-love. It is a stronger power, a more forcible motive, which exerts itself upon such occasions. It is reason, principle, conscience, the inhabitant of the breast, the man within, the great judge and arbiter of our conduct. (*Theory of Moral Sentiments*, III.1§46)

Generosity is founded on the same principles as justice, but it has a wider scope because it extends beyond contractual relationships (Smith, *Theory of Moral Sentiments*, IV.1§21; Levy and Peart 2004). It establishes "noble" feelings of connection even among strangers, those unlike us (*Theory of Moral Sentiments*, III.1§46). Smith considers how individuals evaluate the well-being of others. He poses the issue as one consequent to a disaster far away.

> Let us suppose that the great empire of China, with all its myriads of inhabitants, was suddenly swallowed up by an earthquake . . . . (*Theory of Moral Sentiments*, I.3§46)

An individual does not directly experience the pain of others, but only his own.

If he was to lose his little finger to-morrow, he would not sleep to-night; but, provided he never saw them, he will snore with the most profound security over the ruin of a hundred millions of his brethren, and the destruction of that immense multitude seems plainly an object less interesting to him, than this paltry misfortune of his own. . . .

How would this "man of humanity" choose?

To prevent, therefore, this paltry misfortune to himself, would a man of humanity be willing to sacrifice the lives of a hundred millions of his brethren, provided he had never seen them? Human nature startles with horror at the thought, and the world, in its greatest depravity and corruption, never produced such a villain as could be capable of entertaining it.

Smith asks why we cannot infer choice from *direct* feelings.

But what makes this difference? When our passive feelings are almost always so sordid and so selfish, how comes it that our active principles should often be so generous and so noble?

He answers by appealing to the importance of imagination.

It is reason, principle, conscience, the inhabitant of the breast, the man within, the great judge and arbiter of our conduct. It is he who, whenever we are about to act so as to affect the happiness of others, calls to us, with a voice capable of astonishing the most presumptuous of our passions, that we are but one of the multitude, in no respect better than any other in it; and that when we prefer ourselves so shamefully and so blindly to others, we become the proper objects of resentment, abhorrence, and execration. It is from him only that we learn the real littleness of ourselves, and of whatever relates to ourselves, and the natural misrepresentations of self-love can be corrected only by the eye of this impartial spectator. It is he who shows us the propriety of generosity and the deformity of injustice; the propriety of resigning the greatest interests of our own, for the yet greater interests of others, and the deformity of doing the smallest injury to another, in order to obtain the greatest benefit to ourselves. It is not the love of our neighbour, it is not the love of mankind, which upon many occasions prompts us to the practice of those divine virtues. It is a stronger love, a more powerful affection, which generally takes place upon such occasions; the love of what is honourable and noble, of the grandeur, and dignity, and superiority of our own characters. (*Theory of Moral Sentiments*, I.3§46)

For Smith, man becomes a moral agent by earning the approbation that comes from recognizing we are all equally deserving of sympathy. The question of whether perceived inferiority removes a person from sympathy is central to the debates we study here.

HABITUAL SYMPATHY FOR THOSE ABROAD AND AT HOME

The phrase "habitual sympathy" is taken from the discussion in which Smith lays out the idea that habituated sympathy, one's affection for others, varies inversely with their social distance from us.[12] Economists and social commentators alike in the mid–nineteenth century were preoccupied with the weight of one's obligation to strangers relative to those of family. The utilitarian ideal was one of strict impartiality between self and other.[13] Writing in the *Edinburgh Review* on James Mill's theory of government, T. B. Macaulay identified the Utilitarian Greatest Happiness Principle with the Golden Rule of Christianity.

> The "greatest happiness principle" of Mr Bentham is included in the Christian morality; and, to our thinking, it is there exhibited in an infinitely more sound and philosophical form, than in the Utilitarian speculations. . . . "Do as you would be done by: Love your neighbour as yourself," these are the precepts of Jesus Christ. Understood in an enlarged sense, these precepts are, in fact, a direction to every man to promote the greatest happiness of the greatest number. (Macaulay in Lively and Rees 1978, 175)

In his most considered statement on utilitarianism, John Stuart Mill also identified the spirit of utilitarian philosophy with the Golden Rule.

> [T]he happiness which forms the utilitarian standard of what is right in conduct, is not the agent's own happiness, but that of all concerned. As between his own happiness and that of others, utilitarianism requires him to be as strictly impartial as a disinterested and benevolent specta-

---

12. This is sometimes referred to as the shape of the "sympathetic gradient."

13. In chapter 9 we provide detailed evidence and examine the policy implications of this claim.

tor. In the golden rule of Jesus of Nazareth, we read the complete spirit of the ethics of utility. To do as you would be done by, and to love your neighbour as yourself, constitute the ideal perfection of utilitarian morality. (Mill, *Utilitarianism*, 218)

Darwin ended chapter IV of the first part of the second edition of *Descent*—"Comparison of the Mental Powers of Man and the Lower Animals—*continued*"—with an allusion to how the Golden Rule of Christianity forms "the foundation of morality."

The moral sense perhaps affords the best and highest distinction between man and the lower animals; but I need say nothing on this head, as I have so lately endeavoured to show that the social instincts—the prime principle of man's moral constitution—with the aid of active intellectual powers and the effects of habit, naturally lead to the golden rule, "As ye would that men should do to you, do ye to them likewise;" and this lies at the foundation of morality. (*Descent*, 131)

He then announced the topic of the next chapter.

In the next chapter I shall make some few remarks on the probable steps and means by which the several mental and moral faculties of man have been gradually evolved. That such evolution is at least possible, ought not to be denied, for we daily see these faculties developing in every infant; and we may trace a perfect gradation from the mind of an utter idiot, lower than that of an animal low in the scale to the mind of a Newton. (*Descent*, 131)

The question he addressed next was whether we can retain our current moral sense—entailing sympathy for the weak—and continue to advance.

If humans evolve, they are not homogeneous, and the question arises as to whether they are all equally deserving of sympathy or the resources that flow to them from sympathetic agents. Between Smith and Darwin, social commentators challenged the notion of unregulated sympathy in the service of hierarchy.[14] The doctrine that sympathy required direction—by an expert of some sort who was able best to

---

14. As we have seen (chaps. 3, 4, 5, 6, this vol.), such challenges were often specifically directed at the Irish, Africans, former West Indian slaves, women, and Jews.

distinguish the deserving from the undeserving—was embodied in the Carlylean phrase "charity begins at home." The phrase found its way into attacks on human homogeneity, such as Kingsley's 1850 *Alton Locke* (Levy and Peart 2001–2). Maintenance of hierarchy within the *household* also requires that sympathy be extended first to those who "deserve" it most, that is, to those at home, and only thereafter to those elsewhere. This is one lesson in Charles Dickens's 1852 *Bleak House* in which the character of Mrs. Jellyby is criticized for neglecting her family for the benefit of African slaves.

Here is how Mrs. Jellyby is introduced.

> . . . a lady of very remarkable strength of character, who devotes herself entirely to the public. She has devoted herself to an extensive variety of public subjects, at various times, and is at present (until something else attracts her) devoted to the subject of Africa; with a view to the general cultivation of the coffee berry—*and* the natives . . . (1977, 35)

Mr. Jellyby has, in some sense, lost personality, inverting the usual hierarchy.

> "And Mr. Jellyby, sir?" suggested Richard.
> "Ah! Mr. Jellyby," said Mr. Kenge, "is—a—I don't know that I can describe him to you better than by saying that he is the husband of Mrs. Jellyby."
> "A nonentity, sir?" said Richard, with a droll look.
> "I don't say that," returned Mr. Kenge, gravely. "I can't say that, indeed, for I know nothing whatever *of* Mr. Jellyby. . . . he is, so to speak, merged—Merged—in the more shining qualities of his wife." (1977, 35)

If Mrs. Jellyby's affections were refashioned so that she sympathized more with those close to her, her services could be freely available to her husband and daughters. As it is, she neglects them while she is distracted by the supposedly nondeserving.

A cartoon from *Punch* published 4 March 1865, just months before the Eyre controversy,[15] conveys the same theme (fig. 7.1). The caption,

---

15. We discuss the Eyre controversy briefly in chapter 3 and chapter 8. See Levy and Peart 2001–2, article 3. Even after forty years, the standard work on the British debates remains Semmel 1962.

TELESCOPIC PHILANTHROPY.

LITTLE LONDON ARAB. "PLEASE 'M, AIN'T WE BLACK ENOUGH TO BE CARED FOR?"

(With MR. PUNCH's Compliments to LORD STANLEY.)

Fig. 7.1.   John Tenniel, "Telescopic Philanthropy" (1865)

"Telescopic Philanthropy," is the title of the chapter from *Bleak House* in which Mrs. Jellyby is introduced. The message here is that while resources are being diverted to help the undeserving in Jamaica, English children go hungry. To solve the problem of the poor of England, one needs to convince people like Mrs. Jellyby to sympathize less with distant folks and more with those within her household.

The issue of the "appropriate" level of weighting of the well-being of strangers and kin suggests that there is a good deal at stake in how (and whether) we sympathize with others. As strangers are believed to be more like family, we sympathize with them more, and resources will be diverted from the household to strangers. Belief is important here because Smith's European has actually never seen a person from

China; he has read about them, and he may have seen them in pictures. The stories and pictures in *Punch* and elsewhere contain representations that tell people that the undeserving are unlike their family and more akin to beasts.[16]

Given the difficulty of following through on the utilitarian moral imperative,[17] it is perhaps not surprising that the equal-weighting ideal of early utilitarians would soon be overthrown. Evolutionary biology provided the "scientific" rationale for the criticism of impartiality that had first been launched in literary criticism of the evangelical-economic antislavery movement.[18]

SYMPATHY IN NINETEENTH-CENTURY BIOLOGY

Sympathy played a key role in nineteenth-century evolutionary biology, as the means by which individual self-interest is connected to group interests in matters of justice and beneficence, and thus as a means of protecting the weak from the strong.[19] As such, sympathy was also seen as the key impediment to natural selection. Even as the suggestion was made that humans are creatures motivated by sympathy, early eugenicists responded that such sympathetic tendencies should be suppressed. As eugenics triumphed in the late nineteenth century, the "unfit" became "parasites" removed from sympathy.

---

16. We have touched upon an example from Charles Kingsley's *Water-Babies* in chapter 3. Later we provide the text and image in which characters who are undeserving of sympathy are represented as beastlike.

17. That difficulty left early utilitarian economists open to the charge of hypocrisy or "cant." See chapter 8.

18. In his study of the British debates over emancipation, Drescher finds that racism played no interesting role but that it entered British discussion in an important way with Thomas Carlyle's 1849 "Negro Question" (Drescher 2002, 79–81, 219).

19. Scholars who think about the "Adam Smith Problem" (Peters-Fransen 2001) have puzzled over where Smith's sympathetic principle goes in the nineteenth century. To our knowledge, the link between sympathy and evolutionary biology has escaped attention. Haakonssen (2002, xxiii) notes: "*The Theory of Moral Sentiments* did, however, have an independent legacy, though one that is ill charted. Together with the work of Hume, it had established sympathy as a central moral concept for any attempt at a naturalistic ethics, and we find this reflected—though with few explicit acknowledgments— . . . by the utilitarians of the nineteenth century." In the utilitarian-influenced evolutionary ethical discussions, citations to Smith or *Moral Sentiments* are explicit (e.g., Erasmus Darwin 1803, 122–23; Herbert Spencer 1851, 96; T. H. Huxley [1894] 1934, 88).

The earliest instance we know of the principle of sympathy in evolutionary biology is found in Erasmus Darwin's 1803 *Temple of Nature*.

> How Love and Sympathy the bosom warm,
> Allure with pleasure, and with pain alarm,
> With soft affections weave the social plan,
> And charm the listening Savage into Man. (1803, canto I:219–23)

In a note to canto III:466 Darwin adds:

> From our aptitude to imitation arises what is generally understood by the word sympathy, so well explained by Dr. Smith of Glasgow. (1803, 122–23)

A detailed discussion of the role of sympathy in evolution begins with the work of Herbert Spencer.[20] Relying explicitly on Smith, Spencer argued in his 1851 *Social Statics* that sympathy is the foundation for our perception that others possess rights. Thus it forms the basis for moral action.

> Seeing, however, that this instinct of personal rights is a purely selfish instinct, leading each man to assert and defend his own liberty of action, there remains the question—Whence comes our perception of the rights of others?
>   The way to a solution of this difficulty has been opened by Adam Smith in his "Theory of Moral Sentiments." It is the aim of that work to show that the proper regulation of our conduct to one another, is secured by means of a faculty whose function it is to excite in each being the emotions displayed by surrounding ones . . . the faculty, in short, which we commonly call Sympathy. (1851, 96)

After a two-page discussion extending Smith's account, Spencer explains that justice and beneficence are both rooted in sympathy.

> It was elsewhere hinted . . . that though we must keep up the distinction between them, it is nevertheless true that *justice* and *beneficence* have a common root, and the reader will now at once perceive that the common root is—Sympathy. (1851, 98)

---

20. In chapters 8 and 10 we consider the question of who directs evolution for Spencer and Darwin. We also consider Spencer and Mill on utilitarianism, as well as Edgeworth's criticisms of both for assuming humans to be homogeneous.

It soon became clear that as sympathy was extended to the weak among us, the principle of natural selection would not apply to humans. In 1864, A. R. Wallace made the case precisely.

> If a herbivorous animal is a little sick and has not fed well for a day or two, and the herd is then pursued by a beast of prey, our poor invalid inevitably falls a victim. So in a carnivorous animal the least deficiency of vigour prevents its capturing food, and it soon dies of starvation. There is, as a general rule, no mutual assistance between adults, which enables them to tide over a period of sickness. Neither is there any division of labour; each must fulfill *all* the conditions of its existence, and, therefore, "natural selection" keeps all up to a pretty uniform standard.
>
> But in man, as we now behold him, this is different. He is social and sympathetic. In the rudest tribes the sick are assisted at least with food; less robust health and vigour than the average does not entail death. . . . Some division of labour takes place. . . . The action of natural selection is therefore checked. (1864, clxii)

The question was whether this result was to be greeted with enthusiasm, or not. The cofounder (with Francis Galton) of eugenics, W. R. Greg, responded that, since sympathy blocked the "salutary" effects of natural selection, it should be suppressed (Greg 1875, 119). Eugenicists used Hume's dimensions of inferiority—physical and intellectual— and the debate that followed focused largely on what it was to be undeserving, "feeble and unfit" (Carlson 2001). Much of the eugenics rhetoric attempted to show that the "unfit" were a *breed* apart, and therefore *undeserving* of sympathy. Greg described the Irish, who for all intents and purposes were subhuman relative to their human counterpart, the Scot: "careless, squalid, unaspiring Irishman, fed on potatoes, living in a pig-stye, doting on a superstition, multiply like rabbits or ephemera" (Greg 1868, 360; chap. 4, this vol.). In later years, the eugenics movement focused on families of criminals such as the Jukes to make the case that sympathy stops at the door of the unfit (chap. 6, this vol.).

Between the *Punch* cartoons of Fenians as subhuman and the eugenics movement, we find a justification of biological improvement in Charles Kingsley's 1862–63 *Water-Babies*. Although *Water-Babies* is regarded today as a "charming" children's story, it was reviewed by both the *Times* and James Hunt's *Anthropological Review* in all due seriousness as a popularization of Darwin that applied the doctrine of natural selection to humans (Levy and Peart 2001–2).

We reprint the ape image drawn by Linley Sambourne that accompanied the 1885 edition (fig. 7.2), and we quote in full the passage excerpted in chapter 3.

> And in the next five hundred years they were all dead and gone, by bad food and wild beasts and hunters; all except one tremendous old fellow with jaws like a jack, who stood full seven feet high; and M. Du Chaillu came up to him, and shot him, as he stood roaring and thumping his breast. And he remembered that his ancestors had once been men, and tried to say, "Am I not a man and a brother?" but had forgotten how to use his tongue; and then he had tried to call for a doctor, but he had forgotten the word for one. So all he said was "Ubbobboo!" and died.
>
> And that was the end of the great and jolly nation of the Doasyoulikes. And, when Tom and Ellie came to the end of the book, they looked very sad and solemn; and they had good reason so to do, for they really fancied that the men were apes . . . though they were more apish than the apes of all aperies.
>
> "But could you not have saved them from becoming apes?" said little Ellie, at last.
>
> "At first, my dear; if only they would have behaved like men, and set to work to do what they did not like. But the longer they waited, and behaved like the dumb beasts, who only do what they like, the stupider and clumsier they grew; till at last they were past all cure, for they had thrown their own wits away. It is such things as this that help to make me so ugly, that I know not when I shall grow fair."
>
> "And where are they all now?" asked Ellie.
>
> "Exactly where they ought to be, my dear." (Kingsley 1863, 236–37)

The *Times* recognized that *Water-Babies* turned the possibility of Darwinian devolution into a Carlylean trope (see "Transformation by Obedience," chap. 3, this vol.).

When Darwin's son, Leonard Darwin, reflected upon how shocking it would have been for Gregor Mendel, a Catholic priest, to visit his father, he recalled the name of only one famous religious visitor, Kingsley (Keynes 1943). There is perhaps no better testimony to Kingsley's role in adding a theological element to the idea of natural selection. As early as 1855, Kingsley rejected the factual claims associated with the

Fig. 7.2.   Linley Sambourne, untitled (1885)

Bible in favor of science—"Geology has disproved the old popular belief that the universe was brought into being as it now exists, by a single fiat" (71). In his 1871 "The Natural Theology of the Future," Kingsley rejected the ethical claims of sympathy by appeal to physical science.

> Physical science is proving more and more the immense importance of Race; the importance of hereditary powers, hereditary organs, hereditary habits, in all organized beings, from the lowest plant to the highest animal. She is proving more and more the omnipresent action of the differences between races; how the more favoured race (she cannot avoid using the epithet) exterminates the less favoured, or at least expels

it, and forces it, under penalty of death, to adapt itself to new circumstances; and, in a word, that competition between every race and every individual of that race, and reward according to deserts, is (as far as we can see) an universal law of living things. (373)[21]

The second pillar of eugenic thinking was that the unfit lacked the capacity for reason and the ability to control their impulses (chap. 4, this vol.). Thus, the unfit were unable to participate in the reciprocal relationships associated with markets. At best, they *might* deserve help; they would never achieve equality. Here again the cofounder of the movement, Greg, held that the Irish were incapable of being peasant proprietors (1869a, 78). The counterargument was of course made by Mill.[22]

In the disagreement between Hume and Smith on sympathy and approbation, we can see how the later eugenics argument played out. The "unfit" were held to be undeserving of sympathy, human "parasites" whose removal was needed if the human was to save himself (Carlson 2001, 188–89).[23]

These discussions of biological science and the unfit culminated in Darwin's *Descent of Man*. Here, Darwin put forward a new goal, the "general good," to replace the greatest happiness goal of utilitarianism. The general good signified biological perfection, as opposed to human happiness.

In the case of the lower animals it seems much more appropriate to speak of their social instincts, as having been developed for the general

---

21. "At some future period, not very distant as measured by centuries, the civilized races of man will almost certainly exterminate, and replace, the savage races throughout the world. At the same time the anthropomorphous apes, as Professor Schaaffhausen has remarked, will no doubt be exterminated. The break between man and his nearest allies will then be wider, for it will intervene between man in a more civilized state, as we may hope, even than the Caucasian, and some ape as low as a baboon, instead of as now between the negro or Australian and the gorilla" (Darwin, *Descent*, 160).

22. The passages in Greg and Mill are quoted in full, as epigraphs to chapter 3. In chapter 8, we present a *Punch* cartoon of simpleminded Irish folk, incapable of making trades with John Bright. We find this contrast unsurprising in the light of the view by Greg that sympathy must be blocked and Mill's position that undirected sympathy extends to those across the globe.

23. The "parasite" under many guises—the "Jew harpy," the Irish/Jamaican "cannibal," the economic/evangelical "canter"—plays a much-neglected role in paternalistic theorizing. See Levy and Peart 2001–2 and chapter 9, this volume.

good rather than for the general happiness of the species. The term, general good, may be defined as the rearing of the greatest number of individuals in full vigour and health, *with all their faculties perfect,* under the conditions to which they are subjected. As the social instincts both of man and the lower animals have no doubt been developed by nearly the same steps, it would be advisable, if found practicable, to use the same definition in both cases, and to take as the standard of morality, the general good or welfare of the community, rather than the general happiness; but this definition would perhaps require some limitation on account of political ethics. (*Descent,* 125; emphasis added)

The emphasized passage gives warrant to the "scientist" to decide what is or is not "perfect."

Darwin provides a classical gloss on how self-interested calculations interfere with biological improvement.

The Grecian poet, Theognis, who lived 550 B.C., clearly saw how important selection, if carefully applied, would be for the improvement of mankind. He saw, likewise, that wealth often checks the proper action of sexual selection. He thus writes:

"With kine and horses, Kurnus! we proceed
By reasonable rules, and choose a breed
For profit and increase, at any price;
Of a sound stock, without defect or vice.
But, in the daily matches that we make,
The price is everything: for money's sake,
Men marry: women are in marriage given;
The churl or ruffian, that in wealth has thriven,
May match his offspring with the proudest race:
Thus everything is mix'd, noble and base!
If then in outward manner, form, and mind,
You find us a degraded, motley kind.
Wonder no more, my friend! The cause is plain,
And to lament the consequence is vain." (*Descent,* 33)

Sympathy is vital in Darwin's account of human development. In chapter IV of part I he uses the sympathetic principle to move from individual to group interests.[24] But Darwin questioned whether sympa-

24. Darwin (*Descent,* 110): "The all-important emotion of sympathy is distinct from that of love. . . . Adam Smith formerly argued, as has Mr. Bain recently, that the basis of sympathy lies in

thy has survival value in the next chapter, which opens with a discussion of Wallace (1864).

> It is extremely doubtful whether the offspring of the more sympathetic and benevolent parents, or of those who were the most faithful to their comrades, would be reared in greater numbers than the children of selfish and treacherous parents belonging to the same tribe. He who was ready to sacrifice his life, as many a savage has been, rather than betray his comrades, would often leave no offspring to inherit his noble nature. The bravest men, who were always willing to come to the front in war, and who freely risked their lives for others, would on an average perish in larger numbers than other men. Therefore it hardly seems probable, that the number of men gifted with such virtues, or that the standard of their excellence, could be increased through Natural Selection, that is, by the survival of the fittest. (*Descent*, 135)

Here, interestingly enough, Darwin appeals to a Lamarckian process.

> As the reasoning powers and foresight of the members became improved, each man would soon learn that if he aided his fellow-men, he would commonly receive aid in return. From this low motive he might acquire the habit of aiding his fellows; and the habit of performing benevolent actions certainly strengthens the feeling of sympathy which gives the first impulse to benevolent actions. Habits, moreover, followed during many generations probably tend to be inherited. (*Descent*, 136)

Thus, we have no really good reason from the principle of natural selection to believe that traits that tend to produce biological perfection will be inherited.

It is important to recognize that biological perfection is the new goal. Darwin clarified this when he asked whether sympathy ought to be checked (in the section entitled "Natural Selection as Affecting Civilized Nations," *Descent*, 138–46). The context entails a policy of vacci-

---

our strong retentiveness of former states of pain or pleasure. . . . In a like manner we are led to participate in the pleasures of others." [Darwin's note to text: "See the first and striking chapter in Adam Smith's *Theory of Moral Sentiments*."] Thomas Huxley was also explicit in his use of Smith's sympathetic principle for evolutionary explanations that require moving from individual to group interests: "An artificial personality, the 'man within,' as Adam Smith calls conscience, is built up beside the natural personality. He is the watchman of society, charged to restrain the anti-social tendencies of the natural man within the limits required by social welfare" ([1894] 1934, 88).

nation. For a utilitarian, the policy of vaccination is justified because, on balance, it saves lives. But for Darwin, vaccination serves to preserve the weak, and it is consequently "injurious to the race of man."

> There is reason to believe that vaccination has preserved thousands, who from a weak constitution would formerly have succumbed to small-pox. Thus the weak members of civilized societies propagate their kind. No one who has attended to the breeding of domestic animals will doubt that this must be highly injurious to the race of man. It is surprising how soon a want of care, or care wrongly directed, leads to the degeneration of a domestic race; but excepting in the case of man himself, hardly any one is so ignorant as to allow his worst animals to breed. (*Descent*, 136)

Darwin explicitly attributes this misdirection of effort to the "instinct of sympathy." Although he finds that sympathy leads to such dilatory effects, he nonetheless concludes that it is mainly a positive attribute. But he worries about the effects of unregulated sympathy in the case of the "weak and inferior," and he hopes that marriage among this group will be checked.

> The aid which we feel impelled to give to the helpless is mainly an incidental result of the instinct of sympathy, which was originally acquired as part of the social instincts, but subsequently rendered, in the manner previously indicated, more tender and more widely diffused. Nor could we check our sympathy, even at the urging of hard reason, without deterioration in the noblest part of our nature. . . . We must therefore bear the undoubtedly bad effects of the weak surviving and propagating their kind; but there appears to be at least one check in steady action, namely the weaker and inferior members of society do not marry so freely as the sound; and this check might be indefinitely increased by the weak in body or mind refraining from marriage, though this is more to be hoped for than expected. (*Descent*, 139)[25]

As the chapter continues, Darwin cites the arguments of Greg and Galton, against the Malthusian recommendation to increase human hap-

---

25. He had informed the reader earlier about his worry over the uncontrolled breeding of humans: "In another and much more important respect, man differs widely from any strictly domesticated animal; for his breeding has never been long controlled, either by methodical or unconscious selection" (Darwin, *Descent*, 33).

piness by delaying marriage. The problem with Malthus is that the "poor and reckless" cannot be trusted to restrain from marriage (chap. 4, this vol.).

> A most important obstacle in civilized countries to an increase in the number of men of a superior class has been strongly insisted on by Mr. Greg and Mr. Galton, namely, the fact that the very poor and reckless, who are often degraded by vice, almost invariably marry early, whilst the careful and frugal, who are generally otherwise virtuous, marry late in life. (*Descent*, 143)

Darwin returns to this contention when the book concludes. The attraction of breeding a better race is again clear, and he suggests a "plan" is needed to regulate marriages.

> Man scans with scrupulous care the character and pedigree of his horses, cattle, and dogs before he matches them; but when he comes to his own marriage he rarely, or never, takes any such care. . . . When the principles of breeding and inheritance are better understood, we shall not hear ignorant members of our legislature rejecting with scorn a plan for ascertaining whether or not consanguineous marriages are injurious to man. (*Descent*, 642–43)

He adds that there is a trade-off between the struggle for survival and happiness that results from overpopulation.

> The advancement of the welfare of mankind is a most intricate problem: all ought to refrain from marriage who cannot avoid abject poverty for their children; for poverty is not only a great evil, but tends to its own increase by leading to recklessness in marriage. On the other hand, as Mr. Galton has remarked, if the prudent avoid marriage, whilst the reckless marry, the inferior members tend to supplant the better members of society. Man, like every other animal, has no doubt advanced to his present high condition through a struggle for existence consequent on his rapid multiplication; and if he is to advance still higher, it is to be feared that he must remain subject to a severe struggle. Otherwise he would sink into indolence, and the more gifted men would not be more successful in the battle of life than the less gifted. Hence our natural rate of increase, though leading to many and obvious evils, must not be greatly diminished by any means. (*Descent*, 643)

This paragraph featured prominently in a trial over the distribution of contraceptive information in which the contending parties were seen by the *Times* as Darwin and Mill (chap. 10, this vol.).

Thus, evolutionary biology was used to provide a rationale for suppressing sympathy toward the undeserving. At the same time, evolutionary theory was used to oppose the utilitarian ideal of strict impartiality. In both cases, hierarchy and control of sympathy were at issue.

SELF-DIRECTED SYMPATHY AND MILL'S "URGE TO RESIST"

Mill had envisioned a process by which sympathy would be extended to persons who formerly enjoyed a less-than-fully-human status as such persons were increasingly given the means to participate fully in political and economic decision making.[26] But the analytical machinery required for this process of self-directed improvement was soon to be denied. Post-Darwin, individuals came to be regarded as governed inexorably by the same natural laws that govern the nonhuman. The notion that sympathetic individuals might change themselves was criticized in 1879 by W. S. Jevons who held that humans were essentially unimprovable.

> Human nature is one of the last things which can be called "pliable." Granite rocks can be more easily moulded than the poor savages that hide among them. We are all of us full of deep springs of unconquer-

---

26. Society "improves" because a growing number of individuals acquire "social feelings of mankind": "[T]he desire to be in unity with our fellow creatures, which is already a powerful principle in human nature, and happily one of those which tend to become stronger, even without express inculcation, from the influences of advancing civilization" (*Utilitarianism*, 231). They do so without direction. While "the old theory" held that individuals were unable to recognize what was best for them, experience had shown the contrary: "The old theory was, that the least possible should be left to the choice of the individual agent; that all he had to do should, as far as practicable, be laid down for him by superior wisdom. Left to himself he was sure to go wrong. The modern conviction, the fruit of a thousand years of experience, is, that things in which the individual is the person directly interested, never go right but as they are left to his own discretion; and that any regulation of them by authority, except to protect the rights of others, is sure to be mischievious" (1869, 18).

able character, which education may in some degree soften or develop, but can neither create nor destroy. The mind can be shaped about as much as the body; it may be starved into feebleness, or fed and exercised into vigour and fulness; but we start always with inherent hereditary powers of growth. (1879, 536)

Once individuals came to be regarded as "granite," self-directed improvement came to be regarded as a pipe dream, and the dimension of sympathy became analytically irrelevant in economics.

The later utilitarian economist F. Y. Edgeworth was instrumental in the removal of sympathy from economic and utilitarian analysis near the end of the century.[27] Edgeworth likened the utilitarian problem of maximizing well-being to that of lamps generating light.

Up to this, sentients being regarded as so many lamps of different lighting power, the questions have been what lamps shall be lit, and how much material shall be supplied to each lamp, in order to produce the greatest quantity of light. And the answers, neither unexpected, nor yet distinctly foreseen by common sense, are, that a limited number of the best burners are to be lit, and that most material is to be given to the best lamp. (1877, 74)

In Edgeworth's account, individuals differ in approaching perfection; evolutionary fitness maps to the capacity for pleasure. The scientist can see into the minds of other humans to measure their subjective states, just as he might measure luminescence.

The scientist must question Mill's doctrine of equality.

Pending a scientific hedonimetry, the principle "Every man, and every woman, to count for one," should be very cautiously applied. (1881, 81)[28]

In Edgeworth's eugenic exercise, agents receive orders to remove their lesser associates to unprogressive lands or to celibate monaster-

---

27. See chapter 10 for the details of Edgeworth's criticisms, in particular the limited context in which sympathy matters.

28. Mill "take[s] for granted that there is no *material* difference (no difference of kind, as Mill says in his 'Logic') between human creatures. If, however, utilitarians were really convinced that there existed either now, or (what is more conceivable) in a past stage of the world's evolution, a broad distinction . . . , presumably the establishment of a privileged class would commend itself to utilitarian sense" (Edgeworth 1877, 55).

ies.[29] And the agents obey the decrees. Let us reflect again upon what Mill has told us about human nature in *Utilitarianism*.

> Human beings, on this point, only differ from other animals in two particulars. First, in being capable of sympathizing, not solely with their offspring, or, like some of the more noble animals, with some superior animal who is kind to them, but with all human, and even with all sentient, beings. Secondly, in having a more developed intelligence. . . . any conduct which threatens the security of the society generally, is threatening to his own, and calls forth his instinct (if instinct it be) of self-defence. The same superiority of intelligence joined to the power of sympathizing with human beings generally, enables him to attach himself to the collective idea of his tribe, his country, or mankind, in such a manner that any act hurtful to them, raises his instinct of sympathy, and urges him to resistance. (Mill, *Utilitarianism*, 248)

Sympathetic beings would resist Edgeworth's decrees.[30] But late in the century the hedonic calculus, supported by evolutionary theory, purportedly enabled the scientist to dismiss the bounds of sympathy which otherwise link him to the concerns of ordinary people, and to turn off the heartbreak that accompanies their concerns.

---

29. For people with an inferior capacity for pleasure, Galton had offered a solution: "What approach is useful in such cases is to be determined by Mr. Todhunter's principle. [Note to text: *Researches*; below, p. 93] Again, mitigations might be provided for the classes not selected. [Note to text: Cf. Galton, 'The weak could find a welcome and a refuge in celibate monasteries,' &c. also Sully, *Pessimism*, 392.] . . . Again, *emigration* might supplement total selection; emigration from Utopia to some unprogressive country where the prospect of happiness might be comparatively zero" (1881, 72). We return to this passage when we consider the technical argument in the section "Edgeworth Reconciles Darwin and Utilitarianism" of chapter 10.

30. Martin Luther King made the case, more than half a century later: "Moreover, I am cognizant of the interrelatedness of all communities and states. I cannot sit idly by in Atlanta and not be concerned about what happens in Birmingham. Injustice anywhere is a threat to justice everywhere. We are caught in an inescapable network of mutuality, tied in a single garment of destiny. Whatever affects one directly, affects all indirectly" (1963, 1–2). In chapter 10 we show that the Pareto principle blocks Edgeworth's proposal. This suggests that commitment to the Pareto principle is the expression of a minimal amount of sympathy.

VIII

"WHO ARE THE CANTERS?"
The Coalition of Evangelical-
Economic Egalitarians

Truly, my philanthropic friends, Exeter Hall Philanthropy is wonderful;
and the Social Science—not a "gay science," but a rueful—which finds
the secret of this universe in "supply-and-demand," and reduces the
duty of human governors to that of letting men alone, is also wonderful.
Not a "gay science," I should say, like some we have heard of; no, a
dreary, desolate, and indeed quite abject and distressing one; what we
might call, by way of eminence, the *dismal science*. These two, Exeter
Hall Philanthropy and the Dismal Science, led by any sacred cause of
Black Emancipation, or the like, to fall in love and make a wedding of
it,—will give birth to progenies and prodigies; dark extensive
moon-calves, unnameable abortions, wide-coiled monstrosities,
such as the world has not seen hitherto!
—Thomas Carlyle, "Negro Question"

INTRODUCTION

In our period, evangelicals and political economists functioned as a
coalition in support of the presumption of human equality. They were
opposed by literary and scientific racists who made the case for
inequality and who blamed the coalition for what became known as
the Governor Eyre controversy (discussed in the conclusion of this
chapter). Opponents of the coalition were deeply prejudiced, and their
arguments passed for "quackery" according to the scientific standards
of the day.[1] In this chapter we explore how Mill was singled out and
explicitly attacked by anthropologists for his inability to discriminate

---

1. In chapter 4 we showed that James Hunt earned the judgment "quack." Chapter 5 showed
how Karl Pearson violated his own statistical principles to get a desired result. Chapter 6 pointed
to the judgment of George Grote and J. S. Mill that Plato gave up his greatest contribution to philosophy to preserve hierarchy.

purported inherent differences of capacity. Having established the violent nature of the attacks, we explicate the nature of the coalition between Evangelicals and economists. We focus briefly on the connection between utilitarian economics and the Golden Rule of Christianity as well as the antislavery roots of the coalition. Then, we turn to the analytical details of how the presupposition of human homogeneity united the Evangelicals and economists who followed in the tradition of Adam Smith. Here, we suggest that Adam Smith's doctrine became a useful tool for the theological writings of William Wilberforce and Hannah More.

"AN AGE OF CANT"

Perhaps the most explicit challenge to the economists' inability to see difference was offered by the influential anthropologist James Hunt, then president of the Anthropological Society. Mill, he said, "will not admit that the Australian, the Andaman islander, and the Hottentot labour under any inherent incapacity for attaining the highest culture of ancient Greece or modern Europe!" (1866b, 122).[2] Those who sought to make the case of racial inferiority used the label *cant*, along with images of violence against the canters, in a campaign to discredit the coalition of classical economists and Evangelicals.

The assertion of hierarchy took a visual form (chap. 3, this vol.), and so we begin with images from the time that portray the contest between hierarchy and equality. One dramatic example is reproduced next from a series of tobacco public relations posters produced by Cope's Tobacco in Liverpool in the late 1870s (Wallace 1878b).[3]

The trampled figure is an Evangelical—the broad-brimmed hat and the collar signify that (fig. 8.1). The paper he carries says "Political

---

2. The alternative view offered by Hunt is discussed later. In chapters 3 and 4 we review the literature on Hunt's importance and argue for a connection between Hunt and eugenic theorizing.

3. A large black-and-white version is available in Levy and Peart 2001–2. Cope's pioneered the use of sporting imagery in tobacco advertising. Its golf posters are perhaps the most famous of these. The Evangelical also makes an appearance in these.

Fig. 8.1.   John Wallace, "Ruskin Trampling," detail from *Peerless Pilgrimage* (1878)

Economy."[4] The tag on the Evangelical reads "Cant." He is trampled by John Ruskin who rides next to Thomas Carlyle (*Cope's Key* 1878). Elsewhere in the painting/poster, friends of political economy who seek to escape from hierarchy have evidently devolved and are drawn as parasites, the noxious Colorado beetle (fig. 8.2).[5] In an Irish context, the nonhuman skull is suggestive of the simianized Fenians who were a common target of *Punch* (chap. 3, this vol.). Cope's artist, John Wallace, signed these productions "George Pipeshank," paying tribute to his employer's products and to George Cruikshank, who drew earlier

4. In the original painting, the paper says "Anti-Tobac" (Wallace 1878a). For a broad examination of antieconomics arguments, see Coleman 2002.

5. The Irish "insects" in Wallace 1878a and 1878b, as *Cope's Key* 1878 makes clear, are associated with the Home Rule movement (Levy 2001).

Fig. 8.2.   John Wallace, "Colorado Beetles," detail from *Peerless Pilgrimage* (1878)

versions of simianized Irishmen (see chap. 3, this vol., section entitled "Irish Caricatures" and fig. 3.1).

In 1879, Cope's produced another Wallace poster, *In Pursuit of Diva Nicotina* (fig. 8.3), modeled after Delacroix's *Liberty Guiding the People*. Here, Diva Nicotina leads the crowd in an attack on the Evangelical-Utilitarian coalition. The Evangelical in the sky with "Cant" on the umbrella is easy enough to read.

These images were designed both to amuse and puzzle. They were often accompanied by an explanation and a poem by the accomplished poet John Thomson.[6] To find out who is being tram-

---

6. The joke in *Cope's Key* (1878, 29), November 30: "Cope's Poet refuses Laureateship," reflects his contemporaries' judgment of his abilities, as one learns from the *Dictionary of National Biography* or Schiller 1934. Thomson's death seems to have brought an end to the Cope's posters.

Fig. 8.3.   John Wallace, *In Pursuit of Diva Nicotina* (1879)

pled in *Diva Nicotina*, we quote from the unpublished decoding key:

> Under their hurrying & unheeding feet are trampled (9) the innocent girl [how the deuce does the painting make clear her innocence?] that dear innocent Anti, the Rev. John Kirk: (10) the unwedded mother [no wedding ring on the improper left third finger!] with the dead offspring of her shame. Dr. C. R. Drysdale, Anti-Tobacconist, Anti-Alcoholist, Anti-Progenist, nursing tenderly a retort of Nicotine Poison, & the Fruits of that Philosophy which prides itself on having no fruits: and (unnumbered) Profr. F. W. Newman, who is not only all these Antis, like Mrs. Malaprop's Cerberus "three single gentlemen rolled into one," but likewise Anti-Carnivorist & a mort of other Antis, in brief, Anti-Everything. (Fraser Collection 1516 (1–2), 6)[7]

---

7. The *Oxford English Dictionary* defines *mort* as "a dead body, corpse," possibly obsolete when Thomson wrote. In Figure 10.1 we take a closer look at one of the figures on the ground.

C. R. Drysdale was the head of the Malthusian League, as the neo-Malthusian (birth control) movement called itself. F. W. Newman, brother of the cardinal, was an important enough writer on economics to be discussed by J. S. Mill (Mill 1851). John Kirk was an evangelical who in 1867 entered the service of the Ragged School Union, housed in Exeter Hall. Newman was not a neo-Malthusian; Christians of that period were not. But Christians and Utilitarians functioned as a coalition when the Jamaica Committee Evangelicals unanimously elected the most famous neo-Malthusian of their time, J. S. Mill, to speak for them in the matter of justice for people of color. And in January 1879, Newman denounced nostalgia for slavery and the actions of Governor Eyre in *Fraser's*.[8] The Cope's poster sees the coalition between economists and Evangelicals. And it seems to propose death to canters.

The text that describes the Wallace poster is also vitriolic. The manuscript version—but not the published text—contains the following description of "Cant," armed with a useless umbrella, carrying the book of the Anti-Tobacco Society,[9] and "livid with impotent wrath; darkened by equally impotent envy."

> . . . & come finally to (31) "Over all,
> with uplifted Sword, & open book, hovers the minister of
> Doom"; & truly by his attire he appears a minister, & of
> such as roar out doom against the World in general to the
> intense exaltation of a few bilious fanatics; but when
> have the lightnings of Doom authenticated their theatrical
> thunderings? The world rightly passes them by with
> contempt, not untempered with compassion, but it
> knows their case is hopeless. The sword of our minister is

---

8. "Space does not permit to detail the deeds of Governor Eyre. Suffice it to say in outline, that in 1865 an alarming outbreak of some hundreds of coloured men took place; that martial law was proclaimed in a limited district; that Governor Eyre arrested a coloured member of the Legislature, his political opponent, Mr. G. W. Gordon, the advocate of justice for the blacks; carried him by force into the district where civil law was suspended, had him tried by martial law by two young officers, and hanged. Many besides were hanged; men and women were flogged with piano-wire, houses of black men were burnt, and after all semblance of insurgency of resistance was put down, violent horrors continued" (Newman 1879, 106).

9. In this, the unpublished manuscript, the Cant personification carries the book of the Anti-Tobacco Society; as noted earlier, such a slip was changed in the published version of the *Pilgrimage* to "Political Economy" (the entire set of notes accompanying the painting remained unpublished).

but a gingham umbrella whose name is Cant, & his book is the
book of the Anti-Tobacco Society; & he looms livid with
idiotic & impotent wrath, darkened by equally impotent envy,
beholding the rapturous ardour of the countless millions
in pursuit of our most gracious & glorious <u>Diva Nicotina</u>. (Fraser Collection 1516 (1–2), 10)

In the typeset manuscript, as well, Cope's attacked the "patron Demon of all dismal Anti's," emphasizing his connection to political economy, as well as his dissentors' garb, "loose brown-seedy black and limp white chokers." Here is the full description of the "Life-in-Death" canter.

But what of *Him*, our Minister of Doom,
Whom spite and envy steep in livid gloom?
He is not Death, as Patron's motto saith,
"The end of these things [yea, of all] is Death;"
And yet he is a sort of Death-in-Life
Or living death, essentially at strife
With all the good that Nature has unfurled,
With all the joyance of the vital World:
He the embodied Puritanic Cant is;
The patron Demon of all dismal Anti's,
Of all those murky soulless souls of DANTE'S
Adust, with verjuice for their only juice;
Scrofulous, atrabilious, lank, uncouth,
Dry-rotted doubtless in their greenest youth;
Blatant and latrant, every-streperous croakers
In loose brown-seedy black and limp white chokers;
Blotched with bad blood, unwholesome to the core,
Wolf-gaunt and grim and hunger-bitten, or
Pallid flat-flabby as a skin of lard,
With rancid unctuous speech, furtive regard,
And prurient pawing benedictive hands
Toad-pleasant in their touch: these are the bands
Of holy ones who would reform the earth
From all its damning sins of harmless mirth
And innocent joy and healthy human love,
And make a lively set of saints above! (Fraser Collection 1516 (8–9), 9–10)

Apostles of the Anti, we learn, are "canters and ranters."

The drama is most damnable, but hear
The fluent claptrap gross and insincere,
The grosser mutual flatteries and greetings,
The grossest pious fictions, at their meetings;
Dancing's lascivious and to be abhorred,
But catch them with dear sisters in the Lord.—
Pah! let us leave this howling congregation,
Apostles of the Gospel of Damnation,
Canters and ranters symboled in this feller
Whose only sword's a bloated umbereller;
This Minister of Dooms as false as dire,
This Sulphurous Prophet of the Nether Fire,
This croaking frog of Stygian waters dark,
This ominous raven of the holy ark:
What can our Diva of the glorious mien,
What can the fervent followers of our Queen,
Care for such rancous carrion fowl obscene?
   Behold our Diva beautiful and bright!
   (Fraser Collection 1516 (8–9), 10–11)

What is the connection between *cant*—a term meaning the secret language of thieves and religious fraud[10]—and the coalition of evangelicals and political economists late in the nineteenth century? Near the end of the classical period of economics Mill's follower, J. E. Cairnes, wrote a pamphlet with the unlikely sounding title "Who Are the Canters?" Cairnes begins the pamphlet:

> "England hates slavery much, but she hates cant more"—so say the friends of the South—she prefers, that is to say, the reality of evil to the affectation of good. (1863, 3)

Three years later, another friend of Mill spoke about the "abuse" directed at the antislavery philanthropists in his "Cant and Counter-Cant."

> Only the other week we had a brilliant field-day about the Jamaica business. We exhausted all our vocabulary of abuse against the philan-

---

10. *Oxford English Dictionary* (CD): "The peculiar language or jargon of a class: a. The secret language or jargon used by gipsies, thieves, professional beggars, etc.; transf. any jargon used for the purpose of secrecy."

thropists who were foolish enough to wish to do good to Quashee. With an air of lofty superiority, we told the negrophilists that they had better look to the London Arabs, to the labouring poor of Dorsetshire, before they troubled themselves about a lot of black rascals, with whom they had no concern or connexion. We ridiculed the notion that any good had ever come of treating negroes with justice and kindness; we gloried in the assertion that the men who went out to labour in foreign lands for the absurd idea of saving black souls were in reality the chief instigators of blood thirsty massacres; we held up Exeter Hall to derision. (Morley 1866, 78)

Cope's Tobacco Plant, whose images we featured earlier, shortly thereafter declared the Victorian age an "Age of Cant."[11]

Why is the word *cant* used to stigmatize the coalition of evangelicals and political economists? The basic dictionary definition of a canter is a hypocrite. In the stigmatized "cant language," Evangelicals are found among the canters.[12] The cant that so offended those who argued for hierarchy was the doctrine shared by Evangelicals and political economists that all people's behavior fell short of the moral law, the Golden Rule. As a consequence, there was no one capable of leading by example. There were no mortal heroes whom one could follow in worshipful obedience. Nor were there groups of people systematically better than other groups. The egalitarianism of the "canters" explains why we find Carlyle in the center of the anti-cant camp (Froude 1885, 2:10).[13]

---

11. *Smoke Room Booklets* 2 (1889, iv): "The Elizabethans represent an Age of Tobacco, Queen Anne's men an Age of Coffee, George III.'s men an Age of Revolutions, and the Victorians an Age of Cant." The *Smoke Room Booklets* were published in Liverpool by *Cope's Tobacco Plant.*

12. The *New Canting Dictionary* (1725) contains these definitions: "CANT, an Hypocrite, a Dissembler, a double-tongu'd, whining Person; usually apply'd to *Presbyterians* and other *Dissenters,* from one *Cant,* a *Cameronian* Preacher in *Scotland,* who was wont to harangue his Audience, in a whining and hypocritical Tone, and through the Nose.

CANTING-CREW. Beggars, Gypsies; also Dissenters in Conventicles, who affect a disguised Speech, and disguised Modes of speaking, and distinguish themselves from others by a peculiar Snuffle and Tone, as the *Shibboleth* of their Party; as Gypsies and Beggars have their peculiar Jargon; so they are known no less by their several Tones in praying, than Beggars are by their whining Note in Begging."

And from Humphry Potter's dictionary ([1800?], 21): "CANT, an hypocrite, a dissembler, a double dealer, a cheat, a clergyman. CANTER GLOCK, a parson, a liar. CANTICLE, a parish clerk. CANTING, the mischievous language of thieves, rogues, gipsies, beggers, &c.—Crew, dissenters, clergymen, conventiclers, gipsies and other impostores, under the pretence of religion."

13. "His objection was to the cant of Radicalism; the philosophy of it, 'bred of philanthropy and the Dismal Science,' the purport of which was to cast the atoms of human society adrift,

THE EVANGELICAL–POLITICAL ECONOMY COALITION

There are four pieces of the coalition between Evangelicals and political economists. We discuss the first and second briefly, because we have written on them at length elsewhere.

Connection 1: Utilitarianism and the Golden Rule

The first connection was the agreement by Evangelicals and utilitarians that the Golden Rule of Christianity is formally equivalent to the Greatest Happiness Principle of utilitarianism (Levy 2001). In chapter 7, we showed that T. B. Macaulay identified the utilitarian Greatest Happiness Principle with the Golden Rule of Christianity (in Lively and Rees 1978, 175). John Stuart Mill also identified the true spirit of this philosophy with the Golden Rule (Mill, *Utilitarianism*, 218).[14]

The agreed-upon equivalence of the Greatest Happiness Principle and the Golden Rule of Christianity explains how the great Christian utilitarian Edward W. Blyden could defend free trade for Liberia early in the twentieth century with a *direct* application of the Golden Rule. Free trade is a principle of reciprocity: it is doing as we would be done by.[15] Thus, for Blyden and other Christian utilitarians, the laws of political economy are the laws of God, which ought to be applied in an unprejudiced manner. Nowhere was this clearer than in the port-of-entry law, an act that Blyden blamed for a decline in Liberia's commercial prosperity.[16]

---

mocked with the name of liberty, to sink or swim as they could. Negro emancipation had been the special boast and glory of the new theory of universal happiness" (Froude 1885, 2:14–15).

14. In chapter 10 we provide additional support for this claim and consider the policy implications that follow from it.

15. Blyden is famous in the world of ideas (Lynch 1965), but few have appreciated his Christian utilitarian defense of free trade: "With our sad experience in the house of bondage, and all we could hear and read of the treatment accorded to descendants of Africa by the white race, the first thing that naturally claimed our attention was the necessity for self-defense and self-preservation. We rightly assumed that the safety of the people was the supreme law, and to secure this we erected walls to fence ourselves off from the rest of mankind—laws which we supposed were adapted to our peculiar condition, but which were a violation of the principles of political economy and of natural growth. We were confronted with a serious dilemma. In shutting out what we considered the evils of unrestricted intercourse with foreigners we also shut out the advantages of such intercourse. We did not understand the solidarity of humanity" (Blyden 1976, 42).

16. We thank Gary Becker for pressing us to develop the equivalence in this direction.

Whereas before the passage of the act we had a large fleet of Liberian craft, every settlement having its sloops and schooners and two settlements having vessels large enough to trade with Europe and America, after the law came into effect our Liberian craft disappeared one after another, until now the Liberian flag on a trading vessel is scarcely ever seen along the coast. We violated the golden rule and we are reaping the penalty. We did unto others what we should not like others do unto us, and we behold the result.

We shall never be again financially independent of the foreigner until we unshackle the wings of commerce and cease to violate the laws of political economy, which are the laws of God. (Blyden 1976, 43)

Connection 2: Black Emancipation

The coalition nature of the antislavery movement was first pointed out by Carlyle (1849) when he juxtaposed the "dismal science" of political economy with philanthropic Evangelicals of Exeter Hall in alliance for the cause of black emancipation (Levy 2001). When the *Anti-Slavery Reporter* reprinted Carlyle's unsigned "Negro Question" in January 1850, they had no doubt who wrote it.[17]

Here are Carlyle's words. We italicize the portion quoted in the *Oxford English Dictionary*, which contains nothing to suggest that "dismal science" equals "antislavery," to highlight the cost economists have paid for giving up research in the history of economics.[18]

Truly, my philanthropic friends, Exeter Hall Philanthropy is wonderful; and *the Social Science—not a "gay science," but a rueful—which finds the secret of this universe in "supply-and-demand,"* and reduces the duty of human governors to that of letting men alone, is also wonderful. Not a "gay science," I should say, like some we have heard of; no, a dreary, desolate, and indeed quite abject and distressing one; *what we might call, by way of eminence, the dismal science.* These two, Exeter Hall Philanthropy and the Dismal Science, led by any sacred cause of Black

---

17. But they failed to perceive that the January 1850 *Fraser's* response to Carlyle they reprinted in February 1850 was by John Stuart Mill. *The Anti-Slavery Reporter* was published in London under the full title of *The Anti-Slavery Reporter under the Sanction of the British and Foreign Anti-Slavery Society.*

18. We make the case that knowledge of the past is a public good in the conclusion (chap. 12, this vol.) and, in more detail, in Peart and Levy 2005. In chapter 10 (note 33) we note that Lord Robbins, who knew these texts, declined to discuss them on the basis that they were beneath contempt. This was doubtless the best decision on private grounds, since the texts are loathsome. But we question whether it was a socially optimal decision.

Emancipation, or the like, to fall in love and make a wedding of it, — will give birth to progenies and prodigies; dark extensive moon-calves, unnameable abortions, wide-coiled monstrosities, such as the world has not seen hitherto! (Carlyle 1849, 672–73)

Fifteen years later, the Evangelicals of the Jamaica Committee— formed to protest the murder and mutilation of the freed Jamaican slaves under the governorship of Edward Eyre—elected Mill to speak for them. This public political undertaking made the coalition transparent to both its friends and its foes. As this visibility helps explain the words and images of violence directed at economists following Eyre's tenure as governor of Jamaica (1864–66), it is appropriate to conclude this chapter with evidence of this transparency.

Connection 3: Adam Smith and William Wilberforce

Connection 3 was made when the antislavery spokesperson, William Wilberforce, translated Adam Smith into Christian terms. When *Cope's Tobacco Plant* published Carlyle's "Table Talk" late in the nineteenth century, they reported Carlyle's characterization of Wilberforce as the "famous nigger philanthropist."[19] In the next section we explore how Smith and Wilberforce shared common views of human potential, as suggested by our images of human status (chap. 2, this vol.).

Wilberforce's motives were denigrated in an attempt to prevent the sort of extension of sympathy to people in foreign lands that his (and Smith's) view of human status implied. A virulent example is contained in James Gilray's 1796 etching "Philanthropic Consolations after the Loss of the Slave Bill" (fig. 8.4).

Connection 4: Africans and Christianity

The economics-evangelical view of human potential was challenged during the American Civil War by the newly developed "science" of anthropology. Later, in the section "Anthropological 'Science' versus

---

19. *Smoke Room Booklets* 5 (1890, 30): "Wilberforce, the famous nigger-philanthropist, drawing-room Christian and busy man and politician."

Fig. 8.4. James Gilray, "Philanthropic Consolations" (1796)

Evangelical Economics," we juxtapose Mill's view of human development with the anthropological view expressed in Hunt's paper "The
Negro's Place in Nature." The anthropologists quickly came to dominate one side of the debate over the capacity of Africans for Christianity in which the African was said to lack a capacity for sophisticated religion.

ECONOMIC THEORY AND EVANGELICAL RELIGION

Calvinism, the theological system most closely identified in the Protestant community with the doctrine of original sin, held that humankind
was equally unable to act in accord with the Word of God. Two prominent antislavery spokespersons, Hannah More and William Wilber-

force, relied on this argument. Their position was criticized by Richard Fellowes.[20]

The different views of Christianity are apparent in the confrontation with the imperative to love one's neighbor as one's self. For the Evangelicals, the fact that people are motivated by self-love instead of universal love implied that we live in a fallen world. For Fellowes, our motivation by self-love implied that Christ's imperative ought not be followed. Fellowes disagreed first with Wilberforce and then with Christ. Wilberforce answered criticisms of the doctrine of original sin and human equality, and in so doing, he relied heavily upon the non-theological writings of Adam Smith.

To draw out the connection between Wilberforce and Smith—and hence between the Evangelicals and political economists—we begin with Fellowes's 1801 *Religion without Cant*, where he targets the theological reflections of More and Wilberforce (64–72). "Mr. Wilberforce," he writes there (1801, 64), "seems to suppose, that the moral part of human nature is a mass of putrefaction." He continues on More: "I am surprised, and not more surprised than concerned, that Miss Hannah More, in her very sensible, lively, and highly polished work on education, should have allotted a chapter to the defence of the innate corruption of human nature" (1801, 72). Fellowes's attack on Calvinism and the doctrine of original sin centers on the Evangelical claim that no person is capable of living up to God's commands and so meriting his own redemption. As a consequence, no person is a perfect guide for any other person.

For the Evangelicals, original sin means self-love. Thus, the economists who explained the operation of the earthly world by considerations of self-love were making an evangelical case. To use the terms of an older Christian community, for Wilberforce Adam Smith is an inspired guide to a world without God, a Doctor of the Fallen World.[21]

---

20. Fellowes is discussed in Brown 1961, 156, 176–79.

21. Smith is cited as authority on moral issues at Wilberforce 1797, 81, 197–98. "'There is indeed no surer mark of a false and hollow heart, than a disposition thus to quibble away the clear injunctions of duty and consciences.' [Vide Smith's theory of moral sentiments.] It is the wretched resource of a disingenuous mind, endeavouring to escape from convictions before which it cannot stand, and to evade obligations which it dares to disavow. The arguments which

Smith has himself fallen,[22] but this would not distinguish him from the evangelicals in their own telling (More 1840, 416–17). For Smith, there is no essential difference between the philosopher and the porter, the philosopher's belief to the contrary being evidence only of his "vanity." The philosopher can at best summarize and condense ordinary experience. He has no warrant to guide the porter in his life. Evangelicals express this thought by demanding unmediated confrontation with the Word of God.

Here are More's words testifying to the role of self-love.

> We are apt of speak of self-love as if it were only a symptom, whereas it is the distemper itself, a malignant distemper which has possession of the moral constitution, of which malady every part of the system participates. . . .
> Self-love is the center of the unrenewed heart. (1840, 461)

Wilberforce used Smith's argument to explain why religion is local in the fallen world. There are lower-class and upper-class religions that follow social and personal interests.

> Indeed, several of the above-mentioned vices ["idolatry, to general irreligion, to swearing, drinking, fornication, lasciviousness, sensuality, excessive dissipation; and, in particular circumstances, to pride, wrath, malice, and revenge!"] are held to be grossly criminal in the lower ranks, because manifestly ruinous to their temporal interests: but in the higher, they are represented as "losing half their evils by losing all their grossness," as flowing naturally from great prosperity, from the excess of

---

have been adduced would surely be sufficient to disprove the extravagant pretensions of the qualities under consideration, though those qualities were *perfect* in their *nature*. But they are not perfect. On the contrary, they are radically defective and corrupt; they are body without a soul; they want the vital actuating principle, or rather they are animated and actuated by a false one. Christianity, let me avail myself of the words of a friend [The writer hopes that the work to which he is referring is so well known, that he needs scarcely name Mrs H. More.] in maintaining her argument, is 'a religion of motives'" (Wilberforce 1797, 197).

22. "Can it then occasion surprise, that, under all these circumstances, one of the most acute and forward of the professed unbelievers [Mr. Hume] should appear to anticipate, as at no great distance the complete triumph of his sceptical principles; and that another author of distinguished name [Vide Dr. A. Smith's Letter to W. Straham, Esq.] not so openly professing those infidel opinions, should declare of the writer above alluded to, whose great abilities had been systematically prostituted to the open attack of every principle of religion, both natural and revealed, 'that he had always considered him, both in his life-time and since his death, as approaching as nearly to the idea of a perfectly wise and virtuous man, as perhaps the nature of human frailty will permit'?" (Wilberforce 1797, 288–89).

gaiety and good humour; and they are accordingly "regarded with but a small degree of disapprobation, and censured very slightly, or not at all." [Vide Smith on the *Wealth of Nations*, vol. iii] (1797, 214–15)[23]

The moral issue is whether "ought" implies "can." If belief is primary, there is no reason to expect that we can do what we ought to do. Then as a matter of course articulated belief will deviate from observed behavior. Thus, the believer leaves himself open to the charge of being a hypocrite, his professions of belief, fraudulent. Because there is no mortal to whom an Evangelical can point as exemplar, there are no examples of moral law to follow. We are all, all of us, miserable sinners.[24]

The great imperative of Christianity—to which we have seen the utilitarians assented—was the greatest happiness of all people. And what does the opponent of the Evangelicals, Richard Fellowes, say? In his commentary on the Sermon on the Mount, in which Christ says "Love your enemies," Fellowes responds:

> Our Lord does not mean that we should love our enemies as well as our friends; for this is impossible. (1804, 214)

Thus, if there is no one who can follow an imperative, it is an imperative we *need not* follow. To make the law binding, we need to point to an exemplar.

Fellowes's *Body of Theology* (1807) reveals the social and political consequences of this argument. Here he considers whether Christianity is accessible to all or must wait until the nature of man improved. To this, Fellowes gives a clear and distinct answer: wait.

---

23. One notes how useful Smith is to Wilberforce. *Smith's* argument cannot be dismissed as that of a religious fanatic. Perhaps Wilberforce's coreligionists were not slow to appreciate this point.

24. On this point, Fellowes made these remarks in his *Religion without Cant*: "Thus they are predisposed to lend a willing ear to the instructions of any religious juggler who endeavours to persuade them, that faith without holiness, grace without exertion, or righteousness by imputation will supersede the necessity of personal goodness, and exempt the favoured convert from the painful toils of practical morality. Such admonitions, coloured over with a great deal of cant, in order to disguise the rottenness of the ingredients and the unwholesomeness of the mixture, have been called '*Evangelical Preaching;*' and, at the other times, emphatically '*Preaching the Gospel;*' and the great and everlasting principles of moral duty have been shamelessly libelled, and most industriously lowered in the public estimation, by men professing to teach the holy doctrine of the holy Jesus" (1801, xii–xiii).

Christianity was not promulgated, till mankind had made a considerable progress in civilization, and it was first preached, in those countries
which formed the centre of civilized life; whence its rays were diffused
over the other regions of the globe. For though christianity is fitted to
soften the ferocity of barbarians, if they could be brought to listen to its
precepts, yet it seems better adapted and received and more likely to be
practiced by those who have made some advances in civilization and in
the arts of social intercourse. And indeed, it will I believe generally be
found of little avail to inculcate a religion of pure benevolence among
savages, who derive a scanty and precarious subsistence from fishing
and the chace, and in whom of course the suffering of their fellow creatures must be overlooked, and the precepts of beneficence forgotten
amid the more pressing solicitudes of self-preservation. (1807, 1:126–27)

God's omnipotence would allow him to bring Grace as he wished.
However, Fellowes claims that God operates by the law of progressive
human development.

For God has decreed, that all nations shall pass from a rude to a more
polished state of being; and that this gradual improvement in their condition should be proportioned to the vigour and constancy of their natural exertions. God does not infuse the habit, but he communicates the
power of industry.—Barbarians could not be converted into christians
without a total alteration being made, not only to their inward sentiments, but in their external circumstances, not only in the principles of
their conduct, but in their habits of industry. (1:126–27)

Fellowes has adopted a developmental view of human nature of the
sort outlined in chapter 2 (this vol.). By contrast, the Christian doctrine
of original sin implies that human nature is *not* developmental: no
man or woman has changed in deep structure since Adam or Eve. Fellowes is particularly interesting because his developmentalism and the
consequent antimissionary position are not driven by racism. Instead,
they are inspired by theology. He edited the *Critical Review* over the
period 1804 through 1808. The *Dictionary of National Biography*
reports that the *Critical Review* opposed racial slavery and any idea of
fundamental racial difference.[25]

---

25. Consider these remarks from his *Critical Review* (1806, 520): "We trust that no further
remarks on analogies are necessary to show that the different colour of the human animal in different climates, is an accidental and not an essential difference, and that our readers are fully con-

ANTHROPOLOGICAL "SCIENCE" VERSUS
EVANGELICAL ECONOMICS

The fourth and final connection between Evangelicals and political economists concerned human development. John Stuart Mill contended that human beings could develop, reaching greater and greater levels of sophistication and material comfort. Anthropologists such as James Hunt and Winwood Reade argued that humans of some races—among them the Negro—could not. In the course of making statements on that point, Hunt and Reade disavowed the capacity of Africans to understand and respond to Christianity. Mill, by implication, would argue the opposite and would thereby become linked with the Evangelicals.

One of Mill's major contributions to economic theory was integrating the notion of human development for competent agents in the context of institutional change (Peart and Levy 2003; chaps. 7, 9, this vol.). Material desires may be helpful for educational purposes in the transition to freedom.

> To civilize a savage, he must be inspired with new wants and desires, even if not of a very elevated kind, provided that their gratification can be a motive to steady and regular bodily and mental exertion. If the negroes of Jamaica and Demerara, after their emancipation, had contented themselves, as it was predicted they would do, with the necessaries of life, and abandoned all labour beyond the little which in a tropical climate, with a thin population and abundance of the richest land, is sufficient to support existence, they would have sunk into a condition more barbarous, though less unhappy, than their previous state of slavery. (*Principles*, I.7§7)

If the freed slaves, being competent agents, were to choose leisure over material income the outside observer would have no basis for intervention.[26] In Mill's account, development is measured by concern for others (chap. 7, this vol.).

---

vinced of this scriptural truth, that God made of one body and produced from one pair all the individuals of every nation under heaven." Cf. *Critical Review* 1808, 130. Fellowes asks Why Ceylon is such a mess even though "their minds [are] not deficient in sagacity"? His answer is "the institution of castes" (1817, 231).

26. Mill's statement against Carlyle (Mill 1850) is clear on this.

> In an improving state of the human mind, the influences are constantly on the increase, which tend to generate in each individual a feeling of unity with all the rest; which feeling, if perfect, would make him never think of, or desire, any beneficial condition for himself, in the benefits of which they are not included. (*Utilitarianism*, 232)

The high point of human development is found in the "loud roughs" of America who were willing to die so that another race might choose happiness as they saw it.[27]

> I confess I am not charmed with the ideal of life held out by those who think that the normal state of human beings is that of struggling to get on; that the trampling, crushing, elbowing, and treading on each other's heels, which form the existing type of social life, are the most desirable lot of human kind, or anything but the disagreeable symptoms of one of the phases of industrial progress. It may be a necessary stage in the progress of civilization, and those European nations which have hitherto been so fortunate as to be preserved from it, may have it yet to undergo. It is an incident of growth, not a mark of decline, for it is not necessarily destructive of the higher aspirations and the heroic virtues; as America, in her great civil war, has proved to the world, both by her conduct as a people and by numerous splendid individual examples, and as England, it is to be hoped, would also prove, on an equally trying and exciting occasion. (*Principles*, IV.6§5)

If crude, materialistic Americans are capable of human development, then so are we all.

But the egalitarian theory of human potential received a "scientific" jolt in Hunt's influential anthropological classic, "The Negro's Place in Nature" (see chap. 4, this vol.). Hunt's views of human potential were critical in the debate over whether Africans were capable of Christianity, a variation on Fellowes's challenge to Wilberforce sixty years before.[28]

---

27. The phrase "loud roughs" is common to Walt Whitman's democratic poem *Leaves of Grass* and Carlyle's antidemocratic tract *Shooting Niagara*. Whitman's marked copy of *Shooting Niagara* in the Rare Book Room of the Library of Congress suggests a connection.

28. From the poem that was originally meant to accompany the *Diva Nicotina* image, we find that consequently Quakers who fail to recognize this message are (barely) tolerated at home, but "harmful" out of place.

(So Quakers flourish in a martial State;
But what would be a Quaker-people's fate?

The African explorer Winwoode Reade emphasized the "scientific" authority of Hunt.[29]

> Thus it has been proved by measurements, by microscopes, by analyses, that the typical negro is something between a child, a dotard, and a beast. I can not struggle against these sacred facts of science. (1864, 399)

Here is Reade's account of the difference between antislavery and paternalism.

> Such are the "men and brothers" for whom their friends claim, not protection, but equality!
> They do not merit to be called our brothers, but let us call them our children. Let us educate them carefully, and in time we may elevate them, not to our own level—that, I fear, can never be. (1864, 430)

Following Hunt, Reade asserted that Africans are incapable of grasping Christianity.

> The negroes are not yet able to grasp the doctrine of the Trinity, of the Immaculate Conception, and of Everlasting Punishment; but they have a taste for music, an aptness for language, and perfect talent for mechanics. I think that their bodies ought to be trained before their minds. . . .
> Much has been said of the early arrestation of brain-growth in the negro. . . . Now, as a rule, as soon as a negro boy has finished his education with the missionary, he returns to his savage relations and becomes a savage. His brain no longer makes progress. (1864, 444–45, 445)

Affronted, harried, put to fire and sword
Or slavery by the nearest fighting horde:)
Say this, they are most harmless in their place,
Most harmful out of it, when evil case
Sets them in posts of peril or great trust,
Demanding royal minds and wills robust
And hearts full-charged with the imperious flood
Of Nature's passionate dauntless hot red blood:
Say this, they are unto themselves a law,
But not to others; let them learn with awe
That goodness weak is evil very strong
When called to sway in realms where Right and Wrong
Wage their Titanic warfare. (Fraser Collection 1516 (8–9), 5)

29. Hunt's influence on the explorers Winwood Reade and Richard Burton is emphasized in Prasch 1989.

This undeveloped race is suited only to Islam and slavery.

> Slavery, or rather servitude, is a necessity in Africa. . . .
> Finally, we say that the Mohammedan religion is one of the fire and the sword; that converts to it are made by butchery; that their mosques are raised on the ashes of cities and of men.
> But the fire and sword are those two methods of reasoning by which alone the savage mind is influenced. (1864, 449, 450)

Edward Blyden, the Christian utilitarian mentioned earlier, offered an extraordinary response to the anthropological claim concerning the incapacity of Africans for Christianity. He noted that the Islamic missionaries treated Africans in a less condescending manner than the Christian missionaries. To explain this difference, he pointed to Carlyle's malevolent influence and the fact that those who defended human equality—and hence were more likely to treat Africans with respect—were not Christians (Blyden 1876, 567; 1888, 50). Mill was one of the powers behind the *Westminster Review*, which spoke for the radical utilitarianism associated with Jeremy Bentham. To Blyden, as he told Gladstone, Mill's unbelief was patently obvious.[30]

CONCLUSION: THE COALITION VISIBLE AND THE GOVERNOR EYRE CONTROVERSY

Ultimately, the coalition became obvious and was blamed for racial unrest by those who opposed them, during what historians call the Governor Eyre controversy (see chap. 3). In November 1865, news of the revolt in Jamaica hit Britain. Governor Eyre blamed the Exeter Hall philanthropists for the massacre. The members of the Anti-Slavery Society felt that Governor Eyre and his supporters had stigmatized them for supporting the Jamaican former slaves and the rule of law.[31]

---

30. Blyden referred to Mill's unbelief in the course of commenting on the reaction to Gladstone's valedictory address at the University of Edinburgh: "But why all this fear and anxiety? Will it do a question any harm to 'sift it,' as Lord Macaulay in one of his essays suggests? But from the gloomy forebodings of some periodicals one would suppose that you had adopted the religious creed—if creed he has—of J. Stuart Mill" (1978, 71). Carlyle ("Negro Question") ridiculed the capacity of people of African descent for self-government; hence his "malevolent influence."

31. *The Anti-Slavery Reporter* 13 (1 December 1865), 306. Later, Carlyle (1867, 14) likened Eyre's opponents to rabid dogs: "Truly one knows not whether less to venerate the Majesty's Mini-

And the Anti-Slavery Society's secretary, L. A. Chamerovzow, was parodied in this poem, which appeared in *Punch* on 13 January 1866.

CHAMEROBZOW
(A Negro Melody)

De niggers, when dey kick up row,
No hang, no shoot, say, CHAMEROBZOW.
CHAMEROBZOW de friend ob nigger,
In all de world dar arn't a bigger.
    Gollywolly, gorraworra, bow-wow-wow!
    De nigger lub him CHAMEROBZOW.

De buckra try, de buckra swing;
Yoh! CHAMEROBZOW, dat ar's de ting.
De nigger am your man and brudder:
You tell de debble take de udder.
    Gollywolly, gorrawarra, bow-wow-wow!
    De nigger's friend Ole CHAMEROBZOW.[32]

The treasurer of the Anti-Slavery Society, G. W. Alexander, reacted against Eyre's stigmatization of the coalition of political economists and evangelicals.

> I am sorry to perceive the terms which the Governor of Jamaica has thought fit to use with regard to certain religious bodies in the country, and those whom he calls pseudo-philanthropists. I think it is exceedingly unbecoming in the Governor of a Colony thus to stigmatize persons who had been, it was true, instrumental in procuring the abolition of slavery in the British West-India colonies; and, I hope, in leading to the abolition of slavery throughout the world.[33]

On 12 December, the antislavery forces held their first public meeting at Exeter Hall. We read from the 15 January 1866 *Anti-Slavery Reporter.* The first statement is by Samuel Gurney, M.P.

> Ladies and gentlemen, I was not at all aware until I came into this room, that I should be called upon to take the chair; but I have great pleasure

---

sters, who, instead of rewarding their Governor Eyre, throw him out the window to a small loud group, small as now appears, and nothing but a group or knot of rabid Nigger-Philanthropists, barking furiously in the gutter."

32. *Punch* 51 (13 January 1866), 16.
33. *Anti-Slavery Reporter* 13 (1 December 1865), 306.

in responding to the call, as affording me an opportunity to entering my practical protest against the character of the proceedings in Jamaica, and as an indication of my desire that justice should be done. I have seen in the *Pall-Mall Gazette*, an article referring to the deputation which waited upon Mr. Cardwell[34] on Saturday last, and stating that it was noisy and ill-behaved. I desire to say, having introduced that deputation to Mr. Cardwell, that that statement is not correct. I wish also to contradict the assertion, that on that occasion it was said that Governor Eyre should be hanged by the neck. That expression, so far as I know, was not used. (1)

The pro-Eyre forces apparently suggested that Eyre's opponents—utilitarian economists and Evangelicals—wished to hang him without benefit of a trial. The fact that such was the fate of G. W. Gordon at the hands of Eyre himself might have prompted such an interpretation.

We continue reading.

The Secretary then came forward, and read the following letter.

S. Véron, Avignon, Dec. 8, 1865

Dear Sir,—I highly applaud the course which your Society has taken on the horrors committed in Jamaica, and if I were in England I should attend the meeting on Tuesday.

There is little danger that a Government, containing such men as some of the present ministers, will defend or uphold the savage deeds which have been perpetrated, or absolutely screen the perpetrators. But there is always danger from human weakness, there is danger lest the sympathies of a Government, with its agents, should enable the guilty to get off with mere disavowal and rebuke, or some almost nominal punishment. I earnestly hope that the nation will not allow justice to be thus trifled with, but will insist on a solemn judicial trial of the Governor of Jamaica, and of all under his orders who have been guilty of hanging or flogging alleged rebels without trial. . . .

To those who object that men ought not to be judged without a hearing, I answer, that we do not judge them; we demand that they should be judged.

I am, Dear Sir,

Yours very sincerely,

(Signed) J. S. Mill (1)

---

34. Viscount Edward Cardwell (1813–86). In 1864 he was made secretary of the colonies. For this reason it was Cardwell who dealt with the Governor Eyre controversy. He sent a commission of inquiry and appointed Sir Peter Grant as governor to arbitrate between the conflicting races.

In spite of his grumbling about evangelicalism in *On Liberty*, the spirit of J. S. Mill was at Exeter Hall speaking on behalf of impartial justice.[35] He would later head the Jamaica Committee.

In the same issue of the *Anti-Slavery Reporter*, to ensure the Evangelicals recognized the usefulness of political economists, a column headed "A Suggestion Concerning Jamaica" begins:

> A letter has been addressed to us, throwing out a suggestion which strikes us as quite worthy of serious attention. We do not hold ourselves responsible for the whole of the writer's program . . . (19)

The letter from J. A. Franklin of the London Institution begins with a call for explicit coalition:

> Sir—Unless philanthropists take counsel with economists for immediate action—not waiting until the Commission of Inquiry shall have enabled one of the conflicting parties to convict the other—then a golden opportunity may be lost for engaging both parties in co-operating with advantage to both, although each be prompted only by the instincts of self-preservation. (2)

Thereafter, blame for the violence would be shared by the Evangelicals' coalition partners, the political economists.

The pro-Eyre forces mobilized quickly too. In January 1866, Hunt launched the *Popular Journal of Anthropology* to capitalize on the Eyre controversy. A few months later, he explained the political facts of life to the readers of the established *Anthropological Review*. He begins by quoting Mill's "vulgarity" doctrine[36] and then explicates the antiracial coalition and its opposition to anthropological "science."

> [T]wo great schools are, on principle, decidedly opposed to our pretensions. These two influential parties, while differing widely from each other on many other points, at least cordially agree in discarding and even denouncing the truths of Anthropology. They do so because these truths are directly opposed to their cardinal principle of absolute and original equality among mankind. The parties to which we refer are the orthodox, and more especially the evangelical body, in religion, and the

---

35. Mill is also making a case here for impartial sympathy—for sympathy extended to those far away as well as those at home. We will explore this aspect of the controversy in chapter 9.

36. See the passage from Mill's *Principles of Political Economy*, cited in chapter 3 as epigraph.

Fig. 8.5.   John Tenniel, "The Fenian-Pest" (1865)

ultra-liberal and democratic party in politics. The former proceed on
the traditions of Eden and the Flood . . . the latter base their notions on
certain metaphysical assumptions and abstract ideas of political right
and social justice, as innocent of scientific data, that is, of the fact as it is
in nature, as the wildest of the theological figments which set Exeter
Hall in periodic commotion. (1866b, 114)

He explains that he has been late in worrying about the economists
(1866, 115).

Hunt's message was widely appreciated and applied. An image of
John Bright appeared soon after in the London magazine *Punch*. The
Quaker member of Parliament John Bright, who was known for his
free-market, antiracist views, attempts to hawk "Radical reform" to the

Irish, who are caricatured as lacking the capacity for self-rule (chap. 9, fig. 9.2, this vol.).[37] *Punch* identified "murderous" former slaves in Jamaica with Irish Fenians (fig. 8.5).

The Fenian violence of 1867 (chap. 3, this vol.) was also blamed on those such as Mill, who had defended the actions of the former Jamaican slaves and who criticized Eyre's response to the violence. Mill and the Unitarian radical P. A. Taylor were given special attention in the *Punch* poem "A Fenian and his Friends."

A Fenian and His Friends

To bring a loyal subject to
The gallows was their aim,
And oh may they exert themselves
To save us from the same!
Success to P. A. TAYLOR,
JOHN STUART MILL, and those
That seek the life of England's friends,
And side with England's foes.
The House of Commons won't expel
The friends that all find who rebel. (7 March 1868, 107)

---

37. This marks the high period of conflation of "Irish" and "Negro"; the president of the Anthropological Society of London, John Beddoe, developed an "Index of Nigrescence" to apply to Celtic "types," and a racial category, "Africanoid Celts" (1870, 212–13).

IX

A DISCIPLINE
WITHOUT SYMPATHY
The Happiness of the Majority
and Its Demise

Bentham's followers . . . may have been led by Bentham's incautious
use of the phrase ["Greatest Happiness of the Greatest Number"]
into exaggerating the democratic or isocratic tendencies implicit
in *Utilitarianism* . . .
—F. Y. Edgeworth, *Mathematical Psychics*

INTRODUCTION

This chapter examines some neglected implications of the deeply egalitarian nature of classical political economy. It is well-known that classical economics was part of a utilitarian tradition characterized by the
imperative to find "the greatest happiness for the greatest number."[1] It
is less well-known, however, that key utilitarian economists at the time
interpreted the formula to mean the greatest happiness of the *majority*.
From this identification of the general interest with the interest of the
majority, the next step was the identification of democracy with the
public interest (James Mill [1820] 1978). We highlight a classical
insight: sympathetic agents may be willing to effect political and eco-

---

1. As a guiding principle for classical economic policy, utilitarianism has been much studied.
See Hollander 1985, 602f, for a review of the literature and Robbins 1952 for an overview on classical economic policy. See also Stephen 1900, 1:235f. In his *History of Economic Analysis*, Schumpeter claimed that utilitarianism is "boisterous and vulgar" (1954, 66). Like late-nineteenth-century critics of utilitarianism, Schumpeter objected to the egalitarian nature—the "equal
weighting"—associated with the classical economists' system (131). Schumpeter's distaste for classical economics is well known. Less well known is his distaste for the egalitarian nature of classical analysis. As noted earlier, Schumpeter much admired advocates of human hierarchy and
eugenics.

nomic reforms that are not self-financing, that is, in which the benefits from the action accrue to someone who is not part of the "exchange."

In a tradition that identifies public interest with majority well-being, the problem of the tyranny of the majority emerges.[2] Since utilitarianism was a system designed to provide the basis for moral motivation, the question utilitarians faced was how to ensure that majority-rule politics and the policies that ensued would pass the test of morality. We have argued that classical economists used the device of sympathy as a source of moral obligation (chap. 7, this vol.). For classical economists, the majority—like all others—are bound by sympathy so that policies that benefit the majority are also "just" actions, rather than a form of taking.[3] We call this tradition of classical economics "utilitarianism by counting," and we trace the implications of such a policy norm in appendix 9.1.

As a norm for self-directed agents, classical utilitarianism requires a motivation principle that leads individuals to take other persons' interests into account.[4] Sympathy does just that, placing individuals to whom sympathy extends on the same moral and analytical plane. Beyond that, classical economists also foresaw the extension of sympathy to persons distant from the family. We consider an important consequence of this extension: using the device of sympathy, classical economists conceptualized political and economic reform in a democratic context as exchange, and not simply taking.

We begin by demonstrating that classical economists analyzed the effect of growth or reform on the basis of its wide (majoritarian) impact on well-being. The outcome was to be assessed in terms of the number

---

2. "It has been seen, that the dangers incident to a representative democracy are of two kinds: danger of a low grade of intelligence in the representative body, and in the popular opinion which controls it; and danger of class legislation on the part of the numerical majority, these being all composed of the same class" (Mill [1861] 1977, 448). Bentham's concern with a majority enslaving a minority is noted in Levy 1995.

3. "The injustice and violation of principle are not less flagrant because those who suffer by them are a minority; for there is not equal suffrage where every single individual does not count for as much as any other single individual in the community" (Mill [1861] 1977, 449).

4. "[Bentham and James Mill] believed themselves to have found a common-sense philosophy, by which ordinary selfish men could be convinced that the interest of each invariably coincided with the interests, if not of all, at any rate, of the majority. . . . Every man, therefore, if he were reasonably well educated in his youth, would throughout the rest of his life aim at 'the greatest happiness of the greatest number'" (Wallas 1898, 89–90).

of people whose lot in life was improved as a consequence of the reform. Recognizing that benefits to reform might accrue to agents in the dimension of sympathy, classical political economists advocated a broad set of reforms to improve the well-being of the majority of subjects. In particular, a reform that cost agents in terms of taxes might be overcompensated by benefits that accrue from improved moral standing. Agents might willingly vote to tax themselves in order to effect such a reform. In contemporary parlance, we might say that people agree a policy is the "right thing to do" even though it "costs" the taxpayer higher taxes. If a majority of people agree on the "right thing to do," this can motivate a majority vote in favor of the policy. In classical utilitarianism, the device of sympathy creates the moral obligation that ensures such policies are forthcoming.

The classical political economist foresaw a flattening of the sympathetic gradient over time, reflecting a widened perception of those deserving sympathy. As a result of the extension of sympathy to those farther from the family, taxpayers would be more likely to enact economic and political reforms yielding benefits to those in distant lands ("savages") or at home (women).

This analysis was strenuously resisted and partly overcome by critics of classical political economy who attempted to direct sympathy in order to preserve hierarchy. In particular, critics countered the extension of sympathy to those "far" from home. We show that visual representations of "savages" opposed the classical economists' egalitarianism by rendering those far from home subhuman, unworthy of sympathy.

As the transition to postclassical economics occurred and the dimension of sympathy disappeared from economic analysis, economists focused on only those reforms that served to improve total (and thus average) well-being measured in a single dimension. As a consequence, we see a shift of concern from the majority to the average. In the transition, two features of the classical analysis almost disappeared, never again to be an important part of mainstream economic analysis.[5]

---

5. The qualification is necessary because Edgeworth (1881, 54–56) considered how sympathy might shrink the contract curve. Fontaine (1997, 276–77) examines this episode in context. We return to sympathy and *Mathematical Psychics* when we examine how Edgeworth modeled eugenic operations (chap. 10, this vol.).

First, the underlying conceptual framework entailing a dimension of sympathy was overthrown. In the context of reform, sympathy enabled the classical economist to hold that political or economic reform that placed other human beings on a footing more closely approximating equality yielded benefits to both parties in the transaction. Those in the majority benefited from having their view of the world, and of their standing within the world, improved, and for this they were willing to contribute something. When sympathy vanished from economics, this source of financing reforms vanished with it. Thereafter, only reforms that entailed a net increase in total output were considered. Similarly, in the postclassical period compensation no longer ensured that utilitarian transfers would also be just acts.

THE HAPPINESS OF THE MAJORITY

The policy analysis of classical economists is, perhaps, most clearly illustrated by Adam Smith's statement about why economic growth and the attendant high wages are to be desired. Growth benefits "the circumstances of the greater part."

> Is this improvement in the circumstances of the lower ranks of the people to be regarded as an advantage or as an inconveniency to the society? The answer seems at first sight abundantly plain. Servants, labourers, and workmen of different kinds, make up the far greater part of every great political society. *But what improves the circumstances of the greater part can never be regarded as an inconveniency to the whole.* No society can surely be flourishing and happy, of which the far greater part of the members are poor and miserable. ([1776] 1976, I.8§35; emphasis added)

Growth is good because it increases the well-being of the majority, in their own judgment of well-being. The qualifying phrase is important: observing former slaves freely choosing leisure over market activity, critics of classical political economy retorted that such a choice and the corresponding judgment on well-being were simply mistaken (Carlyle 1849, "Negro Question").

Here is T. R. Malthus's reading of Smith, which clarifies that his contemporaries regarded Smith as a majoritarian.

The professed object of Dr Adam Smith's inquiry is the nature and causes of the wealth of nations. There is another inquiry, however, perhaps still more interesting, which he occasionally mixes with it, I mean an inquiry into the causes which affect the happiness of nations, or the happiness and comfort of the lower orders of society, which is the most numerous class in every nation.[6]

We find this emphasis on the well-being of the majority in Harriet Martineau's writings as well. Martineau, the most gifted popularizer of the Smith and Malthus tradition, contrasted the well-being associated with nineteenth-century markets with that of a feudal past.

> It is interesting to observe by what regulations all are temperately fed with wholesome food, instead of some being pampered above-stairs while others are starving below; how all are clad as becomes their several stations, instead of some being brilliant in jewels and purple and fine linen, while others are shivering in nakedness; how all have something, be it much or little, in their purses. . . . Such extremes as these are seldom or never to be met with under the same roof in the present day, when domestic economy is so much better understood than in the times when such sights were actually seen in rich men's castles: but in the larger family,—the nation,—every one of these abuses still exists, and many more. (1834, 1:v–vi)

J. S. Mill was also much preoccupied with the well-being of the majority.[7] In a footnote added to the last edition of his *Logic*, he provided this explanation for the familiar term *mean*.

---

6. Malthus (1798, 16§1). Smith's median-based utilitarianism is considered in Levy 1995. Malthus's own concern for the well-being of the majority is discussed by Samuel Hollander (1997, 830–31).

7. Mill, *Principles*, IV.6§7: "On the other hand, we may suppose this better distribution of property attained, by the joint effect of the prudence and frugality of individuals, and of a system of legislation favouring equality of fortunes, so far as is consistent with the just claim of the individual to the fruits, whether great or small, of his or her own industry. We may suppose, for instance (according to the suggestion thrown out in a former chapter), a limitation of the sum which any one person may acquire by gift or inheritance to the amount sufficient to constitute a moderate independence. Under this twofold influence society would exhibit these leading features: a well-paid and affluent body of labourers; no enormous fortunes, except what were earned and accumulated during a single lifetime; but a much larger body of persons than at present, not only exempt from the coarser toils, but with sufficient leisure, both physical and mental, from mechanical details, to cultivate freely the graces of life, and afford examples of them to the classes less favourably circumstanced for their growth. This condition of society, so greatly preferable to the present . . ."

In the preceding discussion, the *mean* is spoken of as if it were exactly the same thing with the *average*. But the mean for purposes of inductive inquiry, is not the average, or arithmetical mean, though in a familiar illustration of the theory the difference may be disregarded. If the deviations on one side of an average are much more numerous than those on the other (these last being fewer but greater), the effect due to the invariable cause, as distinct from the variable ones, will not coincide with the average, but will be either below or above the average, the deviation being towards the side on which the *greatest number of the instances* are found. (emphasis added)[8]

Thus, for scientific purposes Mill proposed to use something akin to what we would call the sample median.

We emphasize Mill's intuition that there is something attractive about counting occurrences, although he had no name to give the procedure, to further emphasize that the classical economists used the condition of the majority as the norm for well-being.[9]

HIERARCHY, RECIPROCITY, AND "HABITUAL SYMPATHY"

Adam Smith was troubled by hierarchical systems for moral equals because they fail the test of reciprocity.[10] He insisted that everyone

---

8. Mill (*Logic*, 531). Two unfortunate events then occurred that are related to Jevons's methodological disagreements with Mill (Peart 1995a). Mill continued in the passage to claim that the use of what Francis Galton would call the median was justified by the principle of least squares and Quetelet's work on probability. When Jevons took issue with Mill's statement (Jevons 1879) he truncated Mill's quotation so that his readers could not recover Mill's intuition behind the faulty statement of principle that the sample mean is the one-dimensional least squares estimator.

9. Carlyle's *Shooting Niagara* (1867) is perhaps the most emphatic contemporary identification of utilitarian economics with majority-rule democracy. In chapter 4 we considered how this text influenced Francis Galton and others. The linkage between the properties of majoritarian democracy and those of the *sample* median was considered in a pair of papers by Galton in 1907 in which he came to question his Carlylean presuppositions. Until very recently, workers in statistical politics have focused on the identification of democracy with the *population* median (Black 1958; Downs 1957). Our 2002 *Public Choice* reprint of these papers is contained in the appendix at the back of this book. Galton's machinery is extended in chapter 11 from location estimation to regression.

10. Mill, who was convinced that much progress had already occurred, judged that bad institutional arrangements resulted in a failure of reciprocity for some "nineteen-twentieths" of the population (*Utilitarianism*, 217).

ought to own something be it as humble as his time, as long as he subjects himself to the constraint of reciprocity.

> The property which every man has in his own labour, as it is the original foundation of all other property, so it is the most sacred and inviolable. The patrimony of a poor man lies in the strength and dexterity of his hands; and to hinder him from employing this strength and dexterity in what manner he thinks proper *without injury to his neighbour*, is a plain violation of this most sacred property. It is a manifest encroachment upon the just liberty both of the workman, and of those who might be disposed to employ him. As it hinders the one from working at what he thinks proper, so it hinders the others from employing whom they think proper. To judge whether he is fit to be employed, may surely be trusted to the discretion of the employers whose interest it so much concerns. The affected anxiety of the law-giver lest they should employ an improper person, is evidently as impertinent as it is oppressive. (*Wealth of Nations*, I.10§67; emphasis added)[11]

The "habitual sympathy" phrase is taken from an extended discussion in Smith's *Theory of Moral Sentiments* (1759) in which he lays out the idea that our affection for other persons varies inversely with their social distance from us. Here, we consider the allocative implications of Smith's argument. Suppose that affection and the allocation of resources that results follow a sympathetic gradient described by the positive half of a t-distribution with ν degrees of freedom (Evans, Hastings, and Peacock 1993). A t-distribution has the familiar normal distribution at one extreme and a distribution without moments, the Cauchy, at the other. Simple integration (Macsyma 1998) produces

---

11. Mill found that a failure of reciprocity was in large measure responsible for the lack of prudence among the labouring classes, agreeing in the main that "there can be no healthful state of society, and no social or even physical welfare for the poor, where there is no relation between them and the rich except the payment of wages, and (we may add) the receipt of charity; no sense of co-operation and common interest between them and those natural associates who are now called the employers and the employed. . . . the need of greater fellow-feeling and community of interest between the mass of the people and those who are by courtesy considered to guide and govern them, does not require the aid of exaggeration." While he agreed also that "'cash payment' should be no longer the 'universal *nexus* between man and man;'" a return to feudalism was unfeasible as well as undesirable ([1845] 1967, 379).

table 9.1, showing the allocations that result for various shapes of the
t-distribution.[12]

TABLE 9.1.   Percent Allocation by Interval

Gradient	[0,1]	[1,2]	[2,∞)
Normal	.68	.27	.05
t with 5df	.64	.26	.10
t with 2df	.58	.24	.18
Cauchy	.50	.20	.30

The sympathetic approach suggests that household allocation
occurs in terms of *shares*.[13] It should be noted immediately that household allocation by means of integration over intervals does not tell us
what interval corresponds to what person.[14] We suppose that in fact this
is something that develops over one's life. Young and without family, a
person may perceive his $[0, \tau]$ differently than when older with a family to care about.[15] We also avoid consideration of differences in sympathy—and allocative differences that result—within families. These
are substantive issues that would doubtless arise if one were to employ
such devices to estimate household allocations.

Our main concern here, however, preoccupied economists and

---

12. The traditional imperative of 10 percent to extrafamily charity corresponds quite neatly to
the [2,∞] area of a t with 5 df. We defend the proverbial wisdom from which this follows in chapter 11.

13. This is consistent with the thirty-year-old insight of Becker and Lewis, that a child of a rich
family is more expensive than a child of a poor family: "This price effect, however, does offer a
correction to the argument advanced by Becker (1960), and followed by many others, that the
price of children is the same for rich as for the poor (aside from the cost-of-time argument), even
though the rich choose more expensive children. The relevant price of children with respect to
their number *is* higher for the rich precisely because they choose more expensive children"
(Becker and Lewis 1973, s281).

14. Arrow closes his paper on sympathy with a kindred thought: "In a way that I cannot articulate well and am none too sure about defending, the autonomy of individuals, an element of
mutual incommensurability among people seems denied by the possibility of interpersonal comparisons. No doubt it is some such feeling as this that has made me so reluctant to shift from pure
ordinalism, despite my desire to seek a basis for a theory of justice" (1977, 225). This is related to
Reid's earlier worries about intrapersonal allocations within the family: "Failure to differentiate
explicitly nonmarket activities of personal utility or enjoyment from those that provide products
for another person, or for oneself that might be provided by someone else, is, in my opinion, a
source of confusion in a general model of household production functions" (1973, S165).

15. The parallel with intertemporal theorizing is clear. Irving Fisher insisted that one's view
of the future changed over the life cycle ([1910] 1913, 387–88; Peart 2000).

social commentators alike in the mid–nineteenth century, the controversy over the weight of one's obligation to strangers relative to those of family. Charles Dickens's *Bleak House*, and the choice made by his character, Mrs. Jellyby, to spend time helping African slaves rather than her husband and daughters, played a critical role in the debate (chap. 7, this vol.)

The selection of gradient suggests different weighting of the well-being of strangers and kin, and the numbers in our table suggest that there is a good deal at stake in the matter of gradient selected. The gradient will be flattened as strangers are believed to be more like family. Belief is important here because Smith's European has actually never seen a person from China (1759, III.1§46); he has read about them, and he may have seen them in pictures. These stories and pictures contain representations that tell him whether they are like his family or more akin to beasts.

Our formulation of the sympathetic gradient reflects one aspect of nineteenth-century utilitarianism: the ideal distribution is uniform, with no distinction between stranger, family, and self. J. S. Mill put this clearly.

> I must again repeat, what the assailants of utilitarianism seldom have the justice to acknowledge, that the happiness which forms the utilitarian standard of what is right in conduct, is not the agent's own happiness, but that of all concerned. As between his own happiness and that of others, utilitarianism requires him to be as strictly impartial as a disinterested and benevolent spectator. In the golden rule of Jesus of Nazareth, we read the complete spirit of the ethics of utility. To do as you would be done by, and to love your neighbour as oneself, constitute the ideal perfection of utilitarian morality. (*Utilitarianism*, 218)

We shall see in chapter 10 that F. Y. Edgeworth objected to Mill's argument on the grounds that people were inherently unequal in their capacity for happiness.

Economists have had little to say about why the most effective aspect of many political campaigns is visual. By all accounts, the British anti-slavery movement was greatly assisted by the image of the bound slave who asked, "Am I Not a Man and a Brother?" (fig. 9.1) The slave is clearly someone with whom we sympathize, someone *like us*. We sug-

Fig. 9.1.   Josiah Wedgewood, "Am I Not a Man and a Brother?" (1787)

gest that if political controversy has a sympathetic dimension, the question of whether we are taxing ourselves for the benefit of someone like us or for someone different from (and, in these debates, *inferior to*) us becomes important. And representations of "like" and "unlike" are carried visually.[16]

Just as images assert likeness, they also assert difference or (in all the cases we consider) inferiority, distance from the self that removes the subject from deserving sympathy. Caricatures of the apish Irish Fenian in *Punch* have been presented (chap. 3, this vol.; Curtis 1968, 1997). Two additional examples speak to our purpose here. In figure 9.2, the great economist-democrat John Bright attempts to introduce democracy into Ireland. He is portrayed as a medicine man hawking wares to fundamentally subhuman dupes.[17] In figure 9.3, also from *Punch*, we

16. We shall return to why J. S. Mill considered the Act of Emancipation as paradigm for government policies of reform later in this chapter, in the section entitled "The Classical Paradigm of Reform as Exchange."

DR. DULCAMARA IN DUBLIN.

Fig. 9.2.   John Tenniel, "Dr. Dulcamara in Dublin" (1866)

see a visualization of how the British worker, clearly human, is bur-
dened to benefit the simianized Irishman.

THE CLASSICAL PARADIGM OF REFORM AS EXCHANGE

Classical economists favored economic and political reforms that
improved the well-being of the majority, the laboring classes.[18] The
question that remains is how reform was to be financed.

J. S. Mill made it clear that compensation was a condition of eco-

17. Dr. Dulcamara is the quack doctor in Donizetti's *L'Elisir d'Amore*. We thank David Laid-
ler for the reference.

18. We find the explicit recognition that government is part of the process of exchange only
when Richard Whately adds a footnote to the second edition of his *Introductory Lectures* clarify-
ing his proposal to rename "political economy" as the "Science of Exchange," "Catallactics"
(1832, Lecture II, footnote 5). Whately's 1833 *Money Matters* devotes a chapter to the theme of taxation as an exchange for protection. See Peart and Levy 2003.

THE ENGLISH LABOURER'S BURDEN;
Or, THE IRISH OLD MAN OF THE MOUNTAIN.

Fig. 9.3. John Tenniel, "The English Labourer's Burden" (1849)

nomic or political reform.[19] This raises the question of how the winners were supposed to compensate the losers if there are no monetary gains in the total. Here we must consider one aspect of classical economics that did not survive the transition to neoclassicism: the sympathetic principle. If agents are motivated by sympathy in addition to monetary gain, then taxpayers may be willing to pay for reform because they are willing to give something up to make a perceived evil go away. In this case, the benefits of reform need not be restricted to a resulting material gain.[20] Instead, benefits might occur in terms of sympathy, as indi-

---

19. By contrast, a generation later W. S. Jevons's examination of questions of reform neglects entirely the issue of compensation (see *Methods of Social Reform*, 1883). The only mention of compensation occurs in *Investigations in Currency and Finance* (Jevons [1884] 1964); see Peart 1995a.

viduals recognize that there are mutual benefits associated with improved reciprocal standing. In contemporary parlance, we might say that people agree a policy is the "right thing to do" even though it "costs" the taxpayer higher taxes. If a majority of people agree on the "right thing to do," this can motivate a majority vote in favor of the policy. In classical utilitarianism, the device of sympathy creates the moral obligation that ensures such policies are forthcoming.

Unlike the twentieth-century version of "possible" compensation (discussed later in this chapter), classical utilitarians employed a compensation principle in which compensation was actually paid. When Mill listed the important functions of government in his *Principles of Political Economy*, he used the Act of Emancipation as a paradigm for political reform. We quote an extensive paragraph:

> But while much of the revenue is wasted under the mere pretence of public service, so much of the most important business of government is left undone, that whatever can be rescued from useless expenditure is urgently required for useful. Whether the object be education; a more efficient and accessible administration of justice; *reforms of any kind which, like the Slave Emancipation, require compensation to individual interests*; or what is as important as any of these, the entertainment of a sufficient staff of able and educated public servants, to conduct in a better than the present awkward manner the business of legislation and administration; every one of these things implies considerable expense, and many of them have again and again been prevented by the reluctance which existed to apply to Parliament for an increased grant of public money, though (besides that the existing means would probably be sufficient if applied to the proper purposes) the cost would be repaid, often a hundredfold, in mere pecuniary advantage to the community generally. If so great an addition were made to the public dislike of taxation as might be the consequence of confining it to the direct form, the classes who profit by the misapplication of public money might probably succeed in saving that by which they profit, at the expense of that which would only be useful to the public. (*Principles*, V.6§2; emphasis added)[21]

The Act of Emancipation was a complicated political trade (Drescher

---

20. Jevons objected to Mill's attempts to allow pleasures to vary qualitatively (Peart 1995b); he maintained that all pleasure was reducible to utility and concluded that Mill was "intellectually unfitted to decide what was utilitarian and what was not" (Jevons 1879, 523).

21. Mill considered the possibility that emancipation would not be self-financing in monetary terms because the newly freed slaves might choose happiness in leisure (*Principles*, I.7§7). We

2002). The final bargain is well-known: the West Indian planters received a grant of £20 million and a protective tariff on sugar. The slaves were freed after a seven-year transition (called an "apprenticeship").

It is apparent that Mill employs the same self-financing argument for some government activities that neoclassical economists follow (see "From Classical to Neoclassical Compensation," this chapter)—"the cost would be repaid, often a hundredfold, in mere pecuniary advantage to the community generally." But he does not restrict reform to self-financing situations. In some cases, he advocates reform knowing that material output declines. Here, it is the rewards to taxpayers in the form of sympathy that make up the monetary shortfalls. Three major questions of institutional reform made the basis for discussion at the time: emancipation; Irish self-government and land reform; and women's rights.[22] The question was whether such reforms were self-financing in monetary terms or whether they were to be "financed" in other terms.

If sympathy can be extended to persons farther away from us, the policy analyst has reason to believe that majority-rule politics will entail more than simple monetary transfers. Instead, reform might result in something more akin to an exchange in which the voter gains from the process of reform. The important question is therefore whether Mill held that the sympathetic gradient is flattened in the course of a democratic competition. He did. In *Utilitarianism* Mill claimed that education and "a complete web of corroborative association" serve to extend sympathy.[23]

Mill explicates how competition in the political process extends the

---

have argued elsewhere (Peart and Levy 2003) that the passage on emancipation is important for one of Mill's developmental themes—how a person learns to optimize.

22. Mill considered the inability of women to control their bodies against the wishes of their husbands and to own physical property independent of their husbands as "the primitive state of slavery lasting on" ([1869] 1970, 7). Since the losers in such a reform would be so numerous—the entire male population—and held so much power over women, Mill predicted that current arrangements were "certain to outlast all other forms of unjust authority." "In struggles for political emancipation, everybody knows how often its champions are bought off by bribes, or daunted by terrors. In the case of women, each individual of the subject-class is in a chronic state of bribery and intimidation combined" (Mill [1869] 1970, 13, 12).

23. "Not only does all strengthening of social ties, and all healthy growth of society, give to each individual a stronger personal interest in practically consulting the welfare of others; it also

sympathetic principle in his essay on the second volume of Alexis de
Tocqueville's *Democracy in America*. The development of one's ability
to foresee the personal consequences of one's own actions is said to
resemble foreseeing the effects of one's action on others. (Mill [1840]
1961, xxi)[24]

Political discussions engage the interests of citizens in the well-
being of others and so they provide a sympathetic education. While
politicians wish to deceive the voters, a competition among politicians
even educates voters in the ways of deceit.[25] Mill suggests that the result
of this education is the belief—by rich and poor—that income differences are fair. A competitive economy and a competitive political
process are Mill's explanation for why there is unlikely to be a tyranny
of the majority in America.

> It is not easy to surmise any inducements of interest, by which, in a
> country like America, the greater number could be led to oppress the
> smaller. When the majority and the minority are spoken of as conflict-

---

leads him to identify his *feelings* more and more with their good, or at least with an even greater
degree of practical consideration for it. He comes, as though instinctively, to be conscious of himself as a being who *of course* pays regard to others. The good of others becomes to him a thing naturally and necessarily to be attended to, like any of the physical conditions of our existence. Now,
whatever amount of this feeling a person has, he is urged by the strongest motives both of interest
and of sympathy to demonstrate it, and to the utmost of his power encourage it in others; and even
if he has none of it himself, he is as greatly interested as any one else that others should have it.
Consequently, the smallest germs of the feeling are laid hold of and nourished by the contagion
of sympathy and the influences of education; and a complete web of corroborative association is
woven round it, by the powerful agency of the external sanctions" (Mill, *Utilitarianism*, 231–32).

24. "In all human affairs, conflicting influences are required, to keep one another alive and
efficient even for their own proper uses; and the exclusive pursuit of one good object, apart from
some other which should accompany it, ends not in excess of one and defect of the other, but in
the decay and loss even of that which has been exclusively cared for. Government by trained
officials cannot do, for a country, the things which can be done by a free government; but it might
be supposed capable of doing some things which free government, of itself, cannot do. We find,
however, than an outside element of freedom is necessary to enable it to do effectually or permanently even its own business" (Mill [1861] 1977, 439–40).

25. "It is incontestable that the people frequently conduct public business very ill; but it is
impossible that the people should take part in public business without extending the circle of
their ideas, and without quitting the ordinary routine of their mental acquirements. The hum-
blest individual who is called upon to co-operate in the government of society acquires a certain
degree of self-respect; and, as he possesses power, minds more enlightened than his own offer him
their services. He is canvassed by a multitude of claimants who need his support; and who, seek-
ing to deceive him in a thousand different ways, instruct him in their deceit. He takes a part in
political undertakings which did not originate in his own conception, but which give him a taste
for other undertakings" (de Tocqueville, quoted in Mill [1840] 1961, xxii).

ing interests, the rich and the poor are generally meant; but where the rich are content with being rich, and do not claim as such any political privileges, their interest and that of the poor are the same;—complete protection to property, and freedom in the disposal of it, are alike important to both. (1840, xxvii–xxviii)[26]

Twenty years later, Mill returned to these themes in *Representative Government.* Mutual sympathy plays a critical role in the argument, being a necessary condition for representative self-government.[27] As a source of moral obligation, sympathy constrains people and forms a barrier to injustice.[28] Mutual sympathy creates the boundaries of successful association.[29] Government must take people "as they are," but some sympathy with others is requisite for representative government.[30] Competition and a sufficient number of disinterested sympathetic individuals to influence the election will prevent factional injus-

---

26. But Mill worried about the possibility of a "false democracy" in America: "The natural tendency of representative government, as of modern civilization, is towards collective mediocrity: and this tendency is increased by all reductions and extensions of the franchise, their effect being to place the principal power in the hands of classes more and more below the highest level of instruction in the community. But though the superior intellects and characters will necessarily be outnumbered, it makes a great difference whether or not they are heard. In a false democracy which, instead of giving representation to all, gives it only to the local majorities, the voice of the instructed minority may have no organs at all in the representative body. It is an admitted fact that . . . the American democracy . . . is constructed on this faulty model" (Mill [1861] 1977, 457). The context is Mill's support for the principle of proportional representation in a discussion that continues to this day.

27. "Among a people without fellow-feeling, especially if they read and speak different languages, the united public opinion, necessary to the working of representative government, cannot exist" (Mill [1861] 1977, 547).

28. "Above all, the grand and only effectual security in the last resort against the despotism of the government, is in that case wanting: the sympathy of the army with the people. The military are the part of every community in whom, from the nature of the case, the distinction between their fellow-countrymen and foreigners is the deepest and strongest. To the rest of the people, foreigners are merely strangers; to the soldier, they are men against whom he may be called, at a week's notice, to fight for life or death. The difference to him is that between friends and foes—we may almost say between fellow-men and another kind of animals: for as respects the enemy, the only law is that of force, and the only mitigation the same as in the case of other animals—that of simple humanity" (Mill [1861] 1977, 547–48).

29. "To render a federation advisable, several conditions are necessary. The first is, that there should be a sufficient amount of mutual sympathy among the populations. The federation binds them always to fight on the same side" (Mill [1861] 1977, 547–48).

30. "Governments must be made for human beings as they are, or as they are capable of speedily becoming: and in any state of cultivation which mankind, or any class among them, have yet attained, or are likely soon to attain, the interests by which they will be led, when they are thinking only of self-interest, will be almost exclusively those which are obvious at first sight, and

tice.[31]

Suppose, with Mill, that representative government does hinge upon sufficient sympathy. Suppose further that Smith and Mill are correct that institutionally maintained hierarchy among moral and intellectual equals is a matter of common disapprobation; that is to say, the majority is willing to contribute some amount to make it go away.[32] Then a majority might well vote to tax themselves for a reform that is not necessarily profitable in monetary terms.[33]

---

which operate on their present condition. It is only a disinterested regard for others, and especially for what comes after them, for the idea of posterity, of their country, or of mankind, whether grounded on sympathy or on a conscientious feeling, which ever directs the minds and purposes of classes or bodies of men towards distant or unobvious interests. And it cannot be maintained that any form of government would be rational, which required as a condition that these exalted principles of action should be the guiding and master motives in the conduct of average human beings. A certain amount of conscience, and of disinterested public spirit, may fairly be calculated on in the citizens of any community ripe for representative government. But it would be ridiculous to expect such a degree of it, combined with such intellectual discernment, as would be proof against any plausible fallacy tending to make that which was for their class interest appear the dictate of justice and of the general good" (Mill [1861] 1977, 445).

31. "The reason why, in any tolerably constituted society, justice and the general interest mostly in the end carry their point, is that the separate and selfish interests of mankind are almost always divided; some are interested in what is wrong, but some, also, have their private interest on the side of what is right: and those who are governed by higher considerations, though too few and weak to prevail against the whole of the others, usually after sufficient discussion and agitation become strong enough to turn the balance in favour of the body of private interests which is on the same side with them. The representative system ought to be so constituted as to maintain this state of things: it ought not to allow any of the various sectional interests to be so powerful as to be capable of prevailing against truth and justice and the other sectional interests combined. There ought always to be such a balance preserved among personal interests as may render any one of them dependent for its successes, on carrying with it at least a large proportion of those who act on higher motives, and more comprehensive and distant views" (Mill [1861] 1977, 447).

32. So long as there was some quid pro quo (Mill [1845] 1967): "The higher and middle classes might and ought to be willing to submit to a very considerable sacrifice of their own means, for improving the condition of the existing generation of labourers, if by this they could hope to provide similar advantages for the generation to come. But why should they be called upon to make these sacrifices, merely that the country may contain a greater number of people, in as great poverty and as great liability to destitution as now?" (375). To the acquisition of the capacity for sympathy, "of apprehending a community of interest between himself and the human society of which he forms a part" (*Utilitarianism*, 248), Mill attributes all reform: "The entire history of social improvement has been a series of transitions, by which one custom or institution after another, from being a supposed primary necessity of social existence, has passed into the rank of a universally stigmatized injustice and tyranny. So it has been with the distinctions of slaves and freemen, nobles and serfs, patricians and plebeians; and so it will be, and in part already is, with the aristocracies of colour, race, and sex" (*Utilitarianism*, 259).

33. "In the comparatively early state of human advancement in which we now live, a person cannot indeed feel that entireness of sympathy with all others, which would make any real dis-

In an improving state of the human mind, the influences are constantly on the increase, which tend to generate in each individual a feeling of unity with all the rest; which feeling, if perfect, would make him never think of, or desire, any beneficial condition for himself, in the benefits of which they are not included. (Mill, *Utilitarianism*, 232)

The compensation for British emancipation, the cost to the British taxpayer, was relatively small. The cost of the American emancipation was truly staggering. Here is Mill's judgment of what the willingness to pay this amount revealed about American civilization. Just as savages become civilized though immersion in materiality (Peart and Levy 2003), so civilization can be judged by the willingness to pay for one's sympathy.

> I confess I am not charmed with the ideal of life held out by those who think that the normal state of human beings is that of struggling to get on; that the trampling, crushing, elbowing, and treading on each other's heels, which form the existing type of social life, are the most desirable lot of human kind, or anything but the disagreeable symptoms of one of the phases of industrial progress. It may be a necessary stage in the progress of civilization, and those European nations which have hitherto been so fortunate as to be preserved from it, may have it yet to undergo. It is an incident of growth, not a mark of decline, for it is not necessarily destructive of the higher aspirations and the heroic virtues; as America, in her great civil war, has proved to the world, both by her conduct as a people and by numerous splendid individual examples, and as England, it is to be hoped, would also prove, on an equally trying and exciting occasion. (*Principles*, IV.6§5)

Since, for Mill, "improvement" is to be measured not only in a material dimension but also in a dimension of sympathy, the stationary state was one in which much improvement might still occur.

---

cordance in the general direction of their conduct in life impossible; but already a person in whom the social feeling is at all developed, cannot bring himself to think of the rest of his fellow creatures as struggling rivals with him for the means of happiness, whom he must desire to see defeated in their object in order that he may succeed in his" (*Utilitarianism*, 233). In the case of individual liberty—as it pertained especially to women—Mill maintained that individuals presently undervalued the freedom of others (women): "He who would rightly appreciate the worth of personal independence as an element of happiness, should consider the value he himself puts upon it as an ingredient of his own. There is no subject on which there is a greater habitual difference of judgment between a man judging for himself, and the same man judging for other people" ([1869] 1970, 96).

It is scarcely necessary to remark that a stationary condition of capital and population implies no stationary state of human improvement. There would be as much scope as ever for all kinds of mental culture, and moral and social progress; as much room for improving the Art of Living, and much more likelihood of its being improved, when minds ceased to be engrossed by the art of getting on. (Mill, *Principles*, IV.6§9)[34]

FROM CLASSICAL TO NEOCLASSICAL COMPENSATION

We have sketched two features of the classical analysis of well-being: the concern for the majority; and reform as exchange entailing compensation in terms of sympathy or money. Both of these would be overthrown in what became known as the "new welfare economics," founded on a supposition that welfare-enhancing reform must involve possible compensation in monetary (or physical product) terms.[35] Nicholas Kaldor explained in 1939 that for the economist considering how to aggregate well-being across different individuals, questions involving physical gains are uniquely tractable.[36]

In all cases, therefore, where a certain policy leads to an increase in physical productivity, and thus of aggregate real income, the economist's case for the policy is quite unaffected by the question of the comparability of individual satisfactions; since in all such cases it is *possible* to make everyone better off than before, or at any rate to make some people better off without making anybody worse off. (1939, 550; emphasis in original)

---

34. See Mill's earlier evaluation: "At present I expect very little from any plans which aim at improving even the economical state of the people by purely economical or political means. We have come, I think, to a period, when progress, even of a political kind, is coming to a halt, by reason of the low intellectual & moral state of all classes: of the rich as much as of the poorer classes" (Letter to Edward Herford dated 22 January 1850; Mill 1972, 45).

35. For the argument that such pioneering efforts failed adequately to resolve the issue of what constitutes the "social good," see Sen 1991.

36. Arrow (1963, 39–40): "But a deeper objection is that, in a world of more than one commodity, there is no unequivocal meaning to comparing total production in *any* two social states save in terms of some standard of value which makes the different commodities commensurable; and usually such a standard of value must depend on the distribution of income. In other words, there is no meaning to total output independent of distribution." Robbins (1981) points out that Kaldor independently rediscovered the Pareto principle, but Hicks knew Pareto via Viner. We consider the Pareto principle and cardinal utilitarianism at the end of chapter 10.

This position was immediately seconded by J. R. Hicks (1939) and attained textbook form with Scitovsky.

> It will be convenient to express this by saying that we make sure whether the people who would benefit by the change could profitably bribe those harmed into accepting it. (1942, 91)

In the new welfare economics, policy formulation was thus self-financing in the hypothetical sense made clear by Kaldor and Hicks. A policy that maximized mean income guaranteed this self-financing possibility. For a reform to be justified scientifically, there must be enough physical benefits to redistribute.

Today, economists use the mean for welfare evaluation as a proxy for efficiency. We do so without much reflection. For empirical work, per capita income is the standard for international comparisons; "economic growth" is defined using average income. This chapter suggests the approach that uses the mean is relatively new. We examine the transition, which we link to the influence of F. Y. Edgeworth, in chapter 10. We argue there that when F. Y. Edgeworth articulated postclassical utilitarianism, he set out the maximization of average happiness as the utilitarian goal, and he disavowed consideration of sympathy as part of the utilitarian problem. The classical vision of the majority bound by sympathy was replaced in postclassical discussions by a vision that entailed a knowledgeable expert who prescribed policy for the subjects.

Majority-rule utilitarianism has the problem, obvious in retrospect, of the tyranny of the majority. If, as James Mill claims, the social norm is identified with the happiness of the majority then why isn't this happiness enhanced by plundering the minority? Earlier we considered how sympathy, habituated by competitive democratic politics, can prevent such plundering. It is appropriate to emphasize here how important the problem of "tyranny of the majority" is to a utilitarian who counts and seeks the majority. A policy that is consistent with such a utilitarian norm that is unconstrained by sympathy leads to repugnant conclusions, to a violation of our intuitive sense of justice. Perhaps for this reason, as sympathy disappeared from economic analysis (chap. 7, this vol.), it was inevitable that policy analysis based on the majority would fall by the wayside in economics.

APPENDIX 9.1: UTILITARIANISM BY COUNTING

The "greatest Happiness for the greatest Numbers" slogan was first coined by Adam Smith's teacher, Francis Hutcheson. Thereafter began the utilitarian quest for expressing moral claims in terms of maximizing something. From the beginning, controversy has surrounded the question of just what that something was.[37] We quote the two paragraphs where Hutcheson first presented the formula. The challenge is to recover his precise meaning. The passage contains a mixture of clarity and obscurity. The clear part involves counting people who are helped and harmed. What is less clear is how to make adjustments when counting helps and harms does not suffice.

> In comparing the *moral Qualitys* of Actions, in order to regulate our Election among various Actions propos'd, or to find which of them has the greatest *moral Excellency*, we have led by *our moral Sense of Virtue* thus to judge, that in *equal Degrees* of Happiness, expected to proceed from the Action, the *Virtue* is in proportion to the *Number* of Persons to whom the Happiness shall extend: And here the *Dignity*, or *moral Importance* of Persons, may compensate Numbers; and in equal *Numbers*, the *Virtue* is as the *Quantity* of the Happiness, or natural Good; or that the *Virtue* is in a *compound Ratio* of the *Quantity* of Good, and *Number* of Enjoyers: And in the same manner, the *moral Evil*, or *Vice*, is as the *Degree* of Misery, and *Number* of Sufferers; so that, *that Action is best*, which accomplishes the *greatest Happiness* for the *greatest Numbers*; and that, *worst*, which in *like manner*, occasions *Misery*.
>
> Again, when the *Consequences* of Actions are of a *mix'd* Nature, partly *Advantageous*, partly *Pernicious, that Action* is *good*, whose *good* Effects preponderate the *evil*, by being useful to many, and pernicious to few; and *that, evil* which is otherwise. Here also the *moral Importance* of Characters, or *Dignity of Persons* may compensate Numbers; as may also the *Degree* of Happiness or Misery: for to procure an *inconsiderable Good* to many, but an *immense Evil* to few, may be *Evil*; and an *immense Good* to few, may preponderate a *small Evil* to many. (1725, 163–64)

---

37. On the difficulties associated with defining the maximand, see Hollander 1985, 603f.

We are told in the first paragraph that the *"moral Importance* of Persons" can compensate numbers and in the second paragraph that the *"Degree* of Happiness or Misery" may preponderate. But Hutcheson provides no advice about how to adjust for such niceties.

A precise normative claim about the well-being of the majority was put forward in 1768 by another utilitarian, Joseph Priestley.

> It must necessarily be understood, therefore, whether it be expressed or not, that all people live in society for their mutual advantage; or that the good and happiness of the members, that is the majority of the members of any state, is the great standard by which every thing relating to that state must finally be determined. (13)

When Jeremy Bentham was young, he encountered the Priestley text. This is how Bentham remembered the episode much later.

> Between the years 1762 and 1769 came out a pamphlet of Dr. Priestley's written as usual with him *currente calamo* and without any precise method predetermined, but containing at the close of it, it is believed in the very last page, in so many words the phrases *the greatest happiness of the greatest number*, and this was stated in the character of a principle constituting not only a rational foundation of all enactments of legislation and all rules and precepts destined for the direction of human conduct in private life.
> . . . it was from that pamphlet and that page of it that he drew that phrase the words and import of which have by his writings been so widely diffused over the civilised world. At the sight of it he cried out as it were in an inward ecstasy like Archimedes on the discovery of the fundamental principle of hydrostatics, εύρηκα. (Quoted in Shackleton [1972] 1993, 354–55)

The problem with Bentham's account is that Hutcheson's phrase—either with Hutcheson's "for" or Bentham's "of"—does not appear in Priestley's text. The passage quoted here is as close as one finds (Shackleton 1972). This suggests that the encounter with Priestley gave Bentham an *interpretation* of Hutcheson's phrase which had by then perhaps entered the language of the learned.

Table 9.2. presents important examples of policy judgments on the basis of the counting helps and harms in the texts of Adam Smith,

William Paley,[38] David Ricardo, and James Mill. Ricardo is perhaps the greatest economist who worked with the utilitarian norm of happiness. To find whether a policy is justified, one considers how it affects the most numerous class of society, workers. If free trade benefits the majority but harms the minority, we have the answer. James Mill moved from the "greatest happiness of the greatest number" to democratic conclusions precisely because he identified the happiness of the majority with the public interest. Thus, the common identification of nineteenth-century utilitarianism with majority-rule democracy by those who were close to J. S. Mill himself—Spencer (1851, 22), Maurice (1866, 201–2), and Carlyle (1867, 321)—is justified.[39]

In Mill's *Principles* the word *happiness* is rarely used in a simple material context; more frequently, it involves a mixture of material concerns with sympathy for others or for one's future self.[40] The excep-

---

38. The great English theologian William Paley (1743–1805) published *The Moral and Political Philosophy* in 1785.

39. The next generation of political economists were less comfortable working with a norm of happiness. Nassau Senior emphasized that the science of political economy ought to be wealth, services, and commodities subject to exchange ([1836] 1938, 1). The question of welfare or happiness is then outside the scope of political economy as science: "The subject of legislation is not Wealth, but human Welfare" ([1836] 1938, 2). And with typical acid wit he turned the criticism of political economy on its head: "[I]t has often been made a matter of grave complaint against Political Economists, that they confine their attention to Wealth, and disregard all consideration of Happiness or Virtue. It is to be wished that this complaint were better founded; . . . It must be admitted that an author who, having stated that a given conduct is productive of Wealth, should, on that account alone, recommend it, or assume that, on that account alone, it ought to be pursued, would be guilty of the absurdity of implying that Happiness and the possession of Wealth are identical. But his error would consist not in confining his attention to Wealth, but in confounding Wealth with Happiness" (Senior [1836] 1938, 3–4). Mill, too, attempted to distinguish "happiness" from "good" (Peart 1990, 1995b).

40. "The opinion expressed in a former part of this treatise respecting small landed properties and peasant proprietors, may have made the reader anticipate that a wide diffusion of property in land is the resource on which I rely for exempting at least the agricultural labourers from exclusive dependence on labour for hire. Such, however, is not my opinion. I indeed deem that form of agricultural economy to be most groundlessly cried down, and to be greatly preferable, in its aggregate effects on human happiness, to hired labour in any form in which it exists at present; because the prudential check to population acts more directly, and is shown by experience to be more efficacious; and because, in point of security, of independence, of exercise of any other than the animal faculties, the state of a peasant proprietor is far superior to that of an agricultural labourer in this or any other old country. Where the former system already exists, and works on the whole satisfactorily, I should regret, in the present state of human intelligence, to see it abolished in order to make way for the other, under a pedantic notion of agricultural improvement as a thing necessarily the same in every diversity of circumstances. In a backward state of industrial improvement, as in Ireland, I should urge its introduction, in preference to an exclusive system of hired labour; as a more powerful instrument for raising a population from semi-savage listlessness and recklessness, to persevering industry and prudent calculation" (Mill, *Principles*, IV.7§13).

tion is the case of whether one ought to leave one's resources to a few or to many. Mill seems to settle this by counting. It is important to notice that he makes the case partly on the basis of how ordinary people in fact decide to share their wealth—and so the requisite interpersonal comparisons of happiness are made by those about whom Mill writes—a practice consistent with Lionel Robbins's strictures on the role of economists in such matters.[41] Mill points with approbation to the practice of the United States in which bequests often take the form of public works.[42]

We have noted how Edgeworth vigorously opposed egalitarian ideals in many contexts. He blamed the slogan of utilitarianism for the idealization of democracy and equality before the law.

> Bentham's followers . . . may have been led by Bentham's incautious use of the phrase ["Greatest Happiness of the Greatest Number"] into exaggerating the democratic or isocratic tendencies implicit in *Utilitarianism* . . . (1881, 117)

---

41. Robbins (1981, 5): "Of course I do not deny that, in every day life, we do make comparisons between the satisfactions of different people. When the head of a family carves up a turkey, he may take account of his estimate of the satisfaction afforded to different members by different portions." Nicholson made a similar point in the context of objecting to the measurement of utility in terms of money (1894, 343).

42. It is appropriate to note that the text search for the word *happiness* in Mill's *Principles* was conducted on the public website of Liberty Fund, the foundation established by the estate of Pierre Goodrich.

TABLE 9.2. Utilitarian Policy Evaluation

Person	Policy Issue	Judgment
Adam Smith	Is growth good given that not all benefit?	Is this improvement in the circumstances of the lower ranks of the people to be regarded as an advantage or as an inconveniency to the society? The answer seems at first sight abundantly plain. Servants, labourers and workmen of different kinds, make up the far greater part of every great political society. But what improves the circumstances of the greater part can never be regarded as an inconveniency to the whole. No society can surely be flourishing and happy, of which the far greater part of the members are poor and miserable. It is but equity, besides, that they who feed, cloath and lodge the whole body of the people, should have such a share of the produce of their own labour as to be themselves tolerably well fed, cloathed and lodged. ([1776] 1976, 96).
	Natural liberty of the few or well-being of the many?	Those exertions of the natural liberty of a few individuals, which might endanger the security of the whole society, are, and ought to be, restrained by the laws of all governments; of the most free, as well as of the most despotical. The obligation of building party walls, in order to prevent the communication of fire, is a violation of natural liberty, exactly of the same kind with the regulations of the banking trade which are here proposed. ([1776] 1976, 324).
William Paley	Murder of the wicked—short run	There are occasions, in which the hand of the assassin would be very useful. The present possessor of some great estate employs his influence and fortune, to annoy, to corrupt, or oppress all about him. His estate would devolve by his death, to a successor of an opposite character. It is useful, therefore, to dispatch such a one as soon as possible out of the way; as the neighbourhood would exchange thereby a pernicious tyrant for a wise and generous benefactor. It may be useful to rob a miser, and give the money to the poor; as the money, no doubt, would produce more happiness, by being laid out in food and cloathing for a half dozen distressed families, than by continuing locked up in a miser's chest. It may be useful to get possession of a place, a piece of preferment, or of a seat in parliament, by bribery or false swearing; as by means of them we may serve the public more effectually than in our private station. (1786, pp. 61–62).
	Murder of the wicked—long run	You cannot permit one action and forbid another, without shewing a difference betwixit them. Therefore the same sort of actions must be generally permitted or generally forbidden. Where, therefore, the general permission of them would be pernicious, it becomes necessary to lay down and support the rule which generally forbids them.

Thus, to return once more to the case of the assassin. The assassin knocked the rich villain on the head, because he thought him better out of the way than in it. If you allow this excuse in the present instance, you must allow it to all, who act in the same manner, and from the same motive; that is, you must allow every man to kill any one he meets, whom he thinks noxious or useless; which, in the event, would be to commit every man's life and safety to the spleen, fury, and fanaticism of his neighbour—a disposition of affairs which would presently fill the world with misery and confusion; and ere long put an end to the human species. (1786, p. 64).

David Ricardo	Setting of wages	These then are the laws by which wages are regulated, and by which the happiness of far the greatest part of every community is governed. Like all other contracts, wages should be left to the fair and free competition of the market, and should never be controlled by the interference of the legislature. (1817, ch 5 §34)
	Growth in foreign trade and rise in the rate of profits	It is not, therefore, in consequence of the extension of the market that the rate of profit is raised, although such extension may be equally efficacious in increasing the mass of commodities, and may thereby enable us to augment the funds destined for the maintenance of labour, and the materials on which labour may be employed. It is quite as important to the happiness of mankind, that our enjoyments should be increased by the better distribution of labour, by each country producing those commodities for which by its situation, its climate, and its other natural or artificial advantages, it is adapted, and by their exchanging them for the commodities of other countries, as that they should be augmented by a rise in the rate of profits. (1817, ch 7 § 6)
	Restrictions on imports of corn to protect interests of the few	Yet this is the argument of those who would wish us to prohibit the importation of corn, because it will deteriorate or annihilate that part of the capital of the farmer which is for ever sunk in land. They do not see that the end of all commerce is to increase production, and that by increasing production, though you may occasion partial loss, you increase the general happiness. To be consistent, they should endeavour to arrest all improvements in agriculture and manufactures, and all inventions of machinery; for though these contribute to general abundance, and therefore to the general happiness, they never fail, at the moment of their introduction, to deteriorate or annihilate the value of a part of the existing capital of farmers and manufactures. (1817, ch. 19 §13)

Person	Policy Issue	Judgment
	Extra wages to the workers?	But it may be said, that the capitalist's income will not be increased; that the million deducted from the landlord's rent, will be paid in additional wages to labourers! Be it so; this will make no difference in the argument: the situation of the society will be improved, and they will be able to bear the same money burthens with greater facility than before; it will only prove what is still more desirable, that the situation of another class, and by far the most important class in society, is the one which is chiefly benefited by the new distribution. All that they receive more than 9 millions, forms part of the net income of the country, and it cannot be expended without adding to its revenue, its happiness, or its power. ([1817] 2003, ch. 32 §51)
James Mill	Goal of government and rule of the many?	The end of Government has been described in a great variety of expressions. By Locke it was said to be "the public good"; by others it has been described as being "the greatest happiness of the greatest number." These, and equivalent expressions, are just; but they are defective, inasmuch as the particular ideas which they embrace are indistinctly announced; and different conceptions are by means of them raised in different minds, and even in the same mind on different occasions. ([1820] 1978, p. 55)
		There are three modes in which it may be supposed that the powers for the protection of the community are capable of being exercised. The community may undertake the protection of itself, and its members. The powers of protection may be placed in the hands of a few. And, lastly, they may be placed in the hands of an individual. The Many, The Few, The One; These varieties appear to exhaust the subject. ([1820] 1978, p. 58)
		The source of evil is radically different, in the case of Aristocracy, from what it is in that of Democracy.
		The Community cannot have an interest opposite to its interest. To affirm this would be a contradiction in terms. . . . One Community may intend the evil of another; never its own. This is an indubitable proposition and one of great importance. The Community may act wrong from mistake. To suppose that it could from design, would be to suppose that human beings can wish their own misery. (1820, p. 60)
J. S. Mill	Leave property to a few or to many?	"Munificent bequests and donations for public purposes, whether charitable or educational, form a striking feature in the modern history of the United States, and especially of New England. Not only is it common for rich capitalists to leave by will a portion of their fortune towards the endow-

ment of national institutions, but individuals during their lifetime make magnificent grants of money for the same objects. There is here no compulsory law for the equal partition of property among children, as in France, and on the other hand no custom of entail or primogeniture, as in England, so that the affluent feel themselves at liberty to share their wealth between their kindred and the public; it being impossible to found a family, and parents having frequently the happiness of seeing all their children well provided for and independent long before their death. I have seen a list of bequests and donations made during the last thirty years for the benefit of religious, charitable, and literary institutions in the state of Massachusetts alone, and they amounted to no less a sum than six millions of dollars, or more than a million sterling.' — Lyell's *Travels in America*, vol. i. p. 263

Leave property to a few or to many?

In England, whoever leaves anything beyond trifling legacies for public or beneficent objects when he has any near relatives living, does so at the risk of being declared insane by a jury after his death, or at the least, of having the property wasted in a Chancery suit to set aside the will. (*Principles*, Book II. Ch 2 §.5)

I do not conceive that the degree of limitation which this would impose on the right of bequest, would be felt as a burthensome restraint by any testator who estimated a large fortune at its true value, that of the pleasures and advantages that can be purchased with it: on even the most extravagant estimate of which, it must be apparent to every one, that the difference to the happiness of the possessor between a moderate independence and five times as much, is insignificant when weighed against the enjoyment that might be given, and the permanent benefits diffused, by some other disposal of the four-fifths . . . While those enormous fortunes which no one needs for any personal purpose but ostentation or improper power, would become much less numerous, there would be a great multiplication of persons in easy circumstances, with the advantages of leisure, and all the real enjoyments which wealth can give, except those of vanity; a class by whom the services which a nation having leisured classes is entitled to expect from them, either by their direct exertions or by the tone they give to the feelings and tastes of the public, would be rendered in a much more beneficial manner than at present. A large portion also of the accumulations of successful industry would probably be devoted to public uses, either by direct bequests to the State, or by the endowment of institutions; as is already done very largely in the United States, where the ideas and practice in the matter of inheritance seem to be unusually rational and beneficial. (*Principles*, Bk.II, Ch. 2 §19)

X

DARWIN AND THE
DIFFERENTIAL CAPACITY
FOR HAPPINESS
From Cardinal to Ordinal Utility Theory

> Sympathies can become more and more acute, only as fast as the
> amount of human misery to be sympathized with becomes less and less;
> and while this diminution of human misery to be sympathized with,
> itself must be due in part to the increase of sympathy which prompts
> actions to mitigate it, it must be due in the main to the decrease of the
> pressure of population upon the means of subsistence. While the strug-
> gle for existence among men has to be carried on with an intensity like
> that which now exists, the quantity of suffering to be borne by the
> majority must remain great. This struggle for existence must continue to
> be thus intense so long as the rate of multiplication continues greatly in
> excess of the rate of mortality. Only in proportion as the production of
> new individuals ceases to go on so greatly in excess of the disappearance
> of individuals by death, can there be a diminution of the pressure upon
> the means of subsistence, and a diminution of the strain and the
> accompanying pains that arise more or less to all,
> and in a greater degree to the inferior.
> —Herbert Spencer, *Principles of Ethics*

LIONEL ROBBINS REMEMBERS

Just six years after his *Essay on the Nature and Significance of Economic Science* created a stir in economics, with its query about the scientific status of interpersonal utility comparisons (1932, 136–40), Lionel
Robbins remembered how he came to be a "provisional" utilitarian.

> My own attitude to problems of political action has always been one of
> what I might call provisional utilitarianism. . . . I have always felt that, as
> a first approximation in handling questions relating to the lives and
> actions of large masses of people, the approach which counts each man
> as one, and, on that assumption, asks which way lies the greatest happi-

ness, is less likely to lead one astray than any of the absolute systems. I do not believe, and I never have believed, that in fact men are necessarily equal or should always be judged as such. But I do believe that, in most cases, political calculations which do not treat them as if they were equal are morally revolting. (1938, 635)

A. C. Pigou's utilitarian analysis, involving "the delicate balancing of gain and loss," was attractive.[1]

It follows, therefore, that when I came to the study of economics, I had the strongest bias in favour of a utilitarian analysis. The delicate balancing of gain and loss through intricate repercussions of policy which I found in such works as the *Economics of Welfare*, fascinated me; and I was powerfully attracted by the proposition, urged so forcefully by Edwin Cannan and others, that recent developments of the theory of value could be invoked to demonstrate the desirability of the mitigation of inequality. When I look back on that frame of mind, I find it easy to understand the belief of Bentham and his followers that they had found the open sesame to problems of social policy. (1938, 635–36)

Then, doubts set in about the feasibility of such a utilitarian calculus.

But I began to feel that there were profound difficulties in a complete fusion between what Edgeworth called the economic and the hedonistic calculus. I am not clear how these doubts first suggested themselves; but I well remember how they were brought to a head by my reading somewhere—I think in the works of Sir Henry Maine—the story of how an Indian official had attempted to explain to a high-caste Brahmin the sanctions of the Benthamite system. "But that," said the Brahmin, "cannot possibly be right. I am ten times as capable of happiness as that untouchable over there." I had no sympathy with the Brahmin. But I could not escape the conviction that, if I chose to regard men as equally capable of satisfaction and he to regard them as differing according to a hierarchical schedule, the difference between us was not one which could be resolved by the same methods of demonstration as were available in other fields of social judgment. (1938, 636)[2]

---

1. A. C. Pigou was Alfred Marshall's successor at Cambridge. Pigou's views were selected by J. M. Keynes in the *General Theory* to speak for the classical school itself. Robbins (1971, 135) tells us that of all the London school economists only F. A. Hayek was close to Pigou, and that was because of their shared mountain climbing skills! Pigou was perhaps the only economist of great stature of his time without an interest in the history of economics.

2. Robbins appreciated Smith's egalitarianism: "Adam Smith, that discredited *laissez-faire* economist, with his insistence on the original similarity of porters and philosophers . . ." (1928, 401). Robbins returns to this theme on occasion, e.g., Robbins 1963, 74–75.

This chapter provides the context for Robbins's memory of the debate over the transition from cardinal to ordinal utility. It links the debate to the transition from egalitarianism to hierarchy that has been the overarching theme of this book, and to post-Darwinian accounts of variations in the capacity for happiness. We begin by considering the egalitarian utilitarianism of J. S. Mill and Herbert Spencer in which everyone was supposed to count as one. That is their phrase. Second, we compare Spencer's utilitarian goal with Darwin's goal of the "general good." Here, we suggest that Spencer's goal was egalitarian, while that of Darwin entailed biological perfection or hierarchy. We then follow Robbins's suggestion and consider Edgeworth's hedonic calculus in which the notion of hierarchy enters economics. For Edgeworth, agents have differential capacities for happiness. That is *his* phrase, and he tells us that it came to him through Darwin. Throughout, we consider normative aspects of Darwin's work, in particular Darwin's open and sustained challenge to the early utilitarianism of Mill and Spencer.[3]

Darwin's alternative to the greatest happiness, the "general good," distinguished the *happiness* of individuals from their *perfection*. Post-Darwin, individuals might plausibly be able to judge their happiness, but they are presumed to be less able to judge (still less to effect) their perfection.[4] Supposing the scientist, by contrast, *is* able to evaluate such perfection as well as how to achieve it, the "general good" provides the means to judge social states. Such a notion of "general good" makes it clear that Darwin's conception of natural selection was nor-

---

3. "Again and again the statement has been made that 'Darwin was no philosopher.' . . . In fact, Darwin was keenly interested in philosophy and, as we have seen, attempted to follow in his own writings the best advice of the philosophers of science of his day. Admittedly, he never published an essay or volume explicitly devoted to an exposition of his philosophical ideas, but in his scientific works he systematically demolished one after the other of the basic philosophical concepts of his time and replaced them with revolutionary new concepts" (Mayr 1991, 50).

4. "Much in man's conceptual framework is based on the thinking of pre-science or pre-biological science. Terms like 'progress,' 'perfection,' 'equality,' 'rights of the individual,' etc. were coined and conceptually shaped when everybody still believed in the *scala naturae*, in the concept of a *tabula rasa*, and in a biological (= genetic) identity of all individuals. It is sometimes a traumatic experience to try to reconcile ethical and political principles that have become dear to our hearts with the realities of scientific advances. In our Western world we judge medical and technological advances strictly on the basis of whether or not they are good for the individual. We do not ask whether they are good for the gene pool or for the species" (Mayr 1969, 201).

mative:[5] a social state with more perfect people would be judged superior to one with less.[6]

The contrast between the early utilitarianism of Mill and Spencer and the post-Darwinian pursuit of the "general good" comes into play especially when we consider what to do with imperfect people. Should the less-than-perfect be replaced by more perfect people, or do they—as in Spencer's account—count equally with all others? This question was central to F. Y. Edgeworth's fusion of utilitarianism with biology. Edgeworth held that biological fitness mapped to the capacity for pleasure: as people were biologically superior, they possessed a greater capacity for pleasure. He considered the extreme case of agents with such low capacity for pleasure that they have zero or negative total happiness. Their pleasure from consuming goods is offset totally, perhaps more than offset, by their pain at producing goods. This case is central to Edgeworth's eugenic proposals for racial betterment. If such low-pleasure-capacity people were replaced by people with a greater capacity for pleasure, social utility will increase. While no one at the time suggested that *actual* people be replaced, there *was* considerable public discussion of proposals to give people greater or less discretion over the decision to reproduce.[7]

Our argument has four parts. First, we suggest that Robbins's criti-

---

5. Richards (1987, 234–41) discusses the foundational aspects of Darwin's and Mill's views without linking these differences to attacks on the classical economists' egalitarian supposition of equal capacity.

6. Debate over whether Darwin's concept of evolution progresses toward some goal has focused on the *Origin of Species*. Ospovat (1981, 228) writes: "If Darwin's nineteenth-century readers generally assumed that he, like Spencer (or Chambers), was a progressionist, it is easy to understand why. He was. . . . Without ceasing to be a theory of adaptation, natural selection became also a theory of development." Richards (1992, 176–77) debates Stephen Gould and Ernst Mayr's random walk reading of Darwin. The goal-directed aspect of evolution is clearer in Darwin's later writings than the earlier ones. Ruse says (1999, 332): "Of course, we have long known that 'Social Darwinism' played this ideological role, and I discuss it as such in my book. But historians have had a tendency—a tendency which I exemplify—to treat the socio-political system as something aside from the true evolutionary science, something a bit disreputable and down market. What we now realize is that the science itself and the ideology were never that far apart, even in the minds of the most respectable and influential of post-Origin evolutionists." Ruse conjectures that popular evolution was goal-directed to explain the increasingly "progressive" *Origin* over the editions: "*Descent of Man*, published some twelve years later, is a far more popular-oriented book than the *Origin of Species*" (Ruse 1999, 333).

7. We have considered eugenic debates over immigration—the mix of existing people—in chapters 4 and 5. See also the Postscript to this volume.

cism of interpersonal utility comparisons was part and parcel of the earlier debate over the capacity for happiness. Second, we contrast the utilitarianism of Spencer with the "general good" of Darwin. We show, third, that Edgeworth reconciled utilitarianism with Darwinian natural selection by arguing that biological superiority mapped to greater capacity for happiness. Finally, we demonstrate that Pareto optimality blocks Edgeworth's eugenic proposals.

EARLY UTILITARIANISM AND CAPACITY FOR HAPPINESS

We begin with Spencer's 1851 description, in dialogue form, of the utilitarian theorist (the "plebian") in operation. Since everyone possesses an equal capacity for pleasure, Spencer concluded with the utilitarian commonplace "everyone to count for one," and social utility is then measured in terms of the majority.[8] The calculus of social welfare requires only that the utilitarian theorist *count* the number of people affected by the policy in question.

> "And so you think," says the patrician, "that the object of our rule should be 'the greatest happiness to the greatest number.'"
> "Such is our opinion," answers the petitioning plebeian.
> "Well now, let us see what your principle involves. Suppose men to be, as they very commonly are, at variance in their desires on some given point; and suppose that those forming the larger party will receive a certain amount of happiness each, from the adoption of one course, whilst those forming the smaller party will receive the same amount of happiness each, from the adoption of the opposite course: then if 'greatest happiness' is to be our guide, it must follow, must it not, that the larger party ought to have their way?"
> "Certainly."
> "That is to say, if you—the people, are a hundred, whilst we are

---

8. Robbins's older colleague Graham Wallas made this point in his *Life of Francis Place*: "They [Bentham and James Mill] believed themselves to have found a common-sense philosophy, by which ordinary selfish men could be convinced that the interests of each invariably coincided with the interests, if not of all, at any rate, of the majority. . . . Every man, therefore, if he were reasonably well educated in his youth, would throughout the rest of his life aim at 'the greatest happiness of the greatest number'" (Wallas 1898, 89–90). "The other great inspiration of those days came from Graham Wallas" (Robbins 1971, 86). We provided the context for Wallas's majoritarian reading of James Mill in chapter 9.

ninety-nine, your happiness must be preferred, should our wishes clash, and should the individual amounts of gratification at stake on the two sides be equal."

"Exactly; our axiom involves that."

"So then it seems to us, that as, in such a case, you decide between the two parties by numerical majority, you assume that the happiness of a member of the one party, is equally important with that of a member of the other."

"Of course."

"Wherefore, if reduced to its simplest form, your doctrine turns out to be the assertion, that all men have equal claims to happiness; or, applying it personally—that you should have as good a right to happiness as I have."

"No doubt I have." (Spencer 1851, 22)

Spencer's conclusion that utilitarianism involved a simple counting of affected persons drew the later criticism of Edgeworth, who compared the rough-and-ready policy calculations in the *Data of Ethics* with the delicate calculations required by the utilitarian scientist. The scientist must do more than simply count to determine who was in the majority; policy evaluation required the integration of utility functions.[9]

> Mr. Spencer has "tried" the Utilitarianism of Mr. Sidgwick ("Data of Ethics"), and condemned it; but had the procedure been according to the forms of quantitative science the verdict might have been different. "Everyone to count for one" is objected to Utilitarianism, but this equation as interpreted by Mr. Spencer does not enter into Mr. Sidgwick's definition of the Utilitarian End, greatest possible product of number x average happiness, the definition symbolised above. Equality of distinction is no *proprium* of this definition; *au contraire*. Not "everybody to count for one," but "every just perceivable increment of pleasure to count for one," or some such definition of the pleasure unit, is the utilitarian principle of distribution. (Edgeworth 1881, 122)

---

9. The classical economic utilitarians counted people helped and harmed; they did not weight helps and harms (chap. 9, this vol.). This suggests that the norm employed is akin to the median well-being in which one simply counts persons equally affected by policy. Economists today use the mean for utilitarian welfare evaluation as a proxy for efficiency. How did we go from one to the other, apparently without a discussion? Edgeworth's *Mathematical Psychics* played a decisive role in the transition. For Edgeworth and the economists who followed him, all normative questions were reduced to average happiness.

Spencer held that all count equally in the calculus of welfare. More than this, in their own calculus individuals were able to recognize (and count equally) others affected by their actions. Following Adam Smith, Spencer argued that individuals see themselves as connected by sympathy, and that sympathy is the source of moral obligation. Indeed, the fullest evolutionary discussion of sympathy begins with the work of Spencer. Relying explicitly on Smith's *Theory of Moral Sentiments*, Spencer argued that sympathy is the foundation for our perception that others possess rights, and it consequently forms the basis for moral action.

> Seeing, however, that this instinct of personal rights is a purely selfish instinct, leading each man to assert and defend his own liberty of action, there remains the question—Whence comes our perception of the rights of others?
>
> The way to a solution of this difficulty has been opened by Adam Smith in his "Theory of Moral Sentiments." It is the aim of that work to show that the proper regulation of our conduct to one another, is secured by means of a faculty whose function it is to excite in each being the emotions displayed by surrounding ones . . . a faculty, in short, which we commonly call Sympathy. (1851, 96)

For Spencer (as for Smith), justice and beneficence are rooted in sympathy (1851, 98).[10]

Although Spencer and Mill disagreed on the content of utilitarianism as an intellectual enterprise,[11] they fully agreed that everyone

---

10. Edgeworth (1881) discusses sympathy in connection with Spencer's later *Data of Ethics* and focuses on the impact of sympathy on the range of contract (see Fontaine 1997), but he drops the consideration of sympathy from his analysis of social utility.

11. Upon reading *Utilitarianism*, Spencer explained his views in a letter to Mill: "The note in question greatly startled me by implicitly classing me with the Anti-utilitarians. I have never regarded myself as an Anti-utilitarian. My dissent from the doctrine of Utility as commonly understood, concerns not the object to be reached by men, but the method of reaching it. While I admit that happiness is the ultimate end to be contemplated, I do not admit that it should be the proximate end. The Expediency-Philosophy having concluded that happiness is the thing to be achieved, assumes that morality has no other business than empirically to generalize the results of conduct, and to supply for the guidance of conduct nothing more than its empirical generalizations.

"But the view for which I contend is . . . good and bad results cannot be accidental, but must be necessary consequences of the constitution of things; and I conceive it to be the business of moral science to deduce, from the laws of life and the conditions of existence, what kinds of action necessarily tend to produce happiness, and what kinds to produce unhappiness" (1904, 2:88).

counts as one, and both insisted that rights are established through the device of sympathy. Mill fully agreed with Spencer on the importance of sympathy as the mechanism by which people are connected and thus individual rights are established. To explain justice, Mill appealed to an extended sense of sympathy (Mill, *Utilitarianism*, 248).[12] As noted in chapter 7, sympathy forms the basis of the early utilitarian identification of the Greatest Happiness Principle with the Golden Rule of Christianity.[13]

In the 1863 printing of *Utilitarianism*, Mill carefully summarized Spencer's objections to having been classified as an antiutilitarian. Mill changed the wording to clarify that the argument was about anterior principles instead of whether Spencer was a utilitarian or not.

This implication, in the first principle of the utilitarian scheme, of perfect impartiality between persons, is regarded by Mr. Herbert Spencer (in his *Social Statics* . . .) as a disproof of the pretensions of utility to be a sufficient guide to right; since (he says) the principle of utility presupposes the anterior principle, that everybody has an equal right to happiness. It may be more correctly described as supposing that equal amounts of happiness are equally desirable, whether felt by the same or by different persons. This, however, is not a presupposition; not a premise needful to support the principle of utility, but the very principle itself. (*Utilitaranism*, 257–58)[14]

This letter is quoted by Darwin (*Descent*, 101–2): "Our great philosopher, Herbert Spencer, has recently explained his views on the moral sense. He says, 'I believe that the experiences of utility organised and consolidated through all past generations of the human race, have been producing corresponding modifications . . .'" Darwin seems not to have noticed Mill's response although he quotes the 1864 printing *Utilitarianism* (Darwin, *Descent*, 71, note 5).

12. As noted earlier, Mill envisaged a process by which individuals come to sympathize with a widened set of people. See Mill, *Utilitarianism*, 233 (quoted in chap. 9, this vol.).

13. This identification is noted in Spencer 1893, 1:254. The commonality between Christianity and Utilitarianism was discussed in chapter 8. In Darwin's *Descent* (131), the Golden Rule is quoted as part I, chapter IV ends, and then Darwin considers Wallace's argument that sympathy and concern for others stops natural selection in man and the responses by Greg and Galton (chap. 4, this vol.).

14. The textual details are provided in the Toronto edition of *Utilitarianism* (Mill, *Utilitarianism*, 257–58). Spencer seems not to have noticed Mill's response: "[Spencer] regards happiness as the ultimate end of morality; but deems that end only partially attainable by empirical generalizations from the observed results of conduct, and completely attainable only by deducing, from the laws of life and the conditions of existence, what kinds of action necessarily tend to produce happiness, . . . With the exception of the word 'necessarily,' I have no dissent to express from this doctrine; and (omitting that word) I am not aware that any modern advocate of utilitarianism is of a different opinion" (258).

Soon after this, early eugenicists systematically attacked the classical economists' idea of sympathy as they sought to establish that sympathy, unchecked, interfered with the "salutary effects" of the law of natural selection (chap. 4, this vol.).

SPENCER VERSUS DARWIN

If our case concerning sympathy in Spencer is correct, it would seem that he has been miscast as the founder of social Darwinism at least to the extent that Spencer is regarded as endorsing a plan for directed evolution to achieve the perfection of the species. We turn to a comparison of Spencer and Darwin to shed additional light on this reading. Edgeworth finds Mill and Spencer in common opposition to Darwin because they presuppose a homogeneous human capacity for pleasure. Here is Edgeworth's judgment of the difference between Mill and Darwin on human homogeneity and what would soon be called eugenic considerations.

> Should we be affected by the authority of Mill, conveying an impression of what other Benthamites have taught openly, that all men, if not equal, are at least *equipotential,* in virtue of equal educatability? Or not connect this impression with the more transitory parts of Mill's system: a theory of Real Kinds, more Noachian than Darwinian, a theory of knowledge which, by giving all to experience gives nothing to heredity, and, to come nearer the mark, a theory of population, which, as pointed out by Mr. Galton (insisting only on quantity of population) and, taking no account of *difference of quality,* would probably result in the ruin of the race? Shall we resign ourselves to the authority of pre-Darwinian prejudice? Or not draw for ourselves very different consequences from the Darwinian law? Or, rather, adopt the "laws and consequences" of Mr. Galton? (1881, 132)

Contrary to contemporary discussions that give Spencer "credit" for eugenic ideas,[15] Edgeworth traces the line of descent from Darwin through Galton.

---

15. Black (2003, 12): "In the 1850s, agnostic English philosopher Herbert Spencer published *Social Statics,* asserting that man and society, in truth, followed the laws of cold science, not the will of a caring, almighty God. Spencer popularized a powerful new term: 'survival of the fittest.'

On what basis does Edgeworth link Galton and Darwin? Darwin cites both Francis Galton and W. R. Greg (chap. 4, this vol.), and he quotes Greg at some length in *Descent of Man*. As we noted earlier, Darwin proposes to replace the greatest happiness criterion with a focus on the perfection of the race.

The critical issue of importance was how such perfection would occur. Evolution directed by science and scientific authority is central to social Darwinism, as we can see by noting how the word *fitness* changed from a description to a normative usage.[16] The key question to resolve is where Spencer and Darwin fall on this issue of directed evolution.

Spencer

Since there is no account that compares Spencer and Darwin directly, we examine Spencer's 1852 "Population" in juxtaposition to Darwin. The question we wish to answer is how evolution was supposed to occur. Was there, for Spencer, a need for direction of the evolutionary process, or was evolution envisaged as a process by which progress, however conceived, is achieved by sympathetic, self-regulating individuals?

For Spencer, life is costly: giving life imposes a cost on those who presently enjoy life. And when life-giving agents understand this, the course of evolution changes. Spencer's evolution is, then, directed by evolving and sympathetic agents. Since Spencer sees himself as one of these agents, he looks at evolution from inside the process.

He declared that man and society were evolving according to their inherited nature. Through evolution, the 'fittest' would naturally continue to perfect society. And the 'unfit' would naturally become more impoverished, less educated, and ultimately die off as well they should. Indeed, Spencer saw the misery and starvation of the pauper classes as an inevitable decree of a 'far-seeing benevolence,' that is, the laws of nature. He unambiguously insisted, 'The whole effort of nature is to get rid of such, and to make room for better. . . . If they are not sufficiently complete to live, they die, and it is best they should die.' Spencer left no room for doubt, declaring, 'all imperfection must disappear.' As such, he completely denounced charity and instead extolled the purifying elimination of the 'unfit.' The unfit, he argued, were predestined by their nature to an existence of downwardly spiraling degradation."

16. Leonard Darwin explained that for positive purposes "fittest" means that which survives, but "when we come to discuss eugenic reforms, we are apt to attach a somewhat different meaning to the word 'fittest.' The aim of eugenists is to alter human surroundings in such a way as to increase the chance of 'survival' of those types which are held to be most desirable" (1926, 114).

Spencer introduces the "law of maintenance of all races" (1852, 476), which has the property that the preservation of life varies inversely with propagation.

> Now the forces preservative of race are two—ability in each member of the race to preserve itself, and ability to produce other members—power to maintain individual life, and power to propagate the species. These must vary inversely. When, from lowness of organization, the ability to contend with external dangers is small, there must be great fertility to compensate for the consequent mortality; otherwise the race must die out. When, on the contrary, high endowments give much capacity of self-preservation, there needs [be] a correspondently low degree of fertility. (476)

Spencer regards this as axiomatic, and he offers illustrative examples that include yeast fungus, algae, termites, sharks, rodents, elephants, and man (1852, 476–78). He uses this relationship to conceptualize what today's economists would refer to as the "opportunity cost" of giving life.

> Hence the maintenance of the individual and the propagation of the race, being respectively aggregative and separative, *necessarily* vary inversely. Every generative product is a deduction from the parental life; and, as already pointed out, to diminish life is to diminish the ability to preserve life. The portion thrown off is organised matter; vital force has been expended in the organisation of it, and in the assimilation of its component elements; which vital force, had no such portion been made and thrown off, *would have been available for the preservation of the parent.* (1852, 478–79)

Thus, individual maintenance and development take place at the cost of reproduction (1852, 479).

Next, Spencer proposes an inverse relationship between the degree of fertility and the development of the nervous system (1852, 493). He observes that the "human race is in a state of transition" (1852, 496) toward a state of lower fertility and higher development, and he casts about for an explanation. After ruling out additional strength and agility, Spencer speculates that much might come from additional intelligence (1852, 496, 497). He settles finally on the explanation of improved "morality," including "greater power of self-regulation" related to the acquisition of increased sympathetic tendencies.

> Will it be in morality, that is, in greater power of self-regulation? Largely also; perhaps most largely. Normal conduct, or in other words, conduct conducive to the maintenance of perfect and long-continued life, is usually come short of more from defect of will than of knowledge. . . . A further endowment of those feelings which civilization is developing in us—sentiments responding to the requirements of the social state—emotive faculties that find their gratifications in the duties devolving on us—must be acquired before the crimes, excesses, diseases, improvidences, dishonesties, and cruelties, that now so greatly diminish the duration of life, can cease. (1852, 497)

Then he claims that excessive population growth will be sufficient to reduce fertility rates (and improve the development of the nervous system).

> . . . it may be shown why a greater development of the nervous system *must* take place, and why, consequently, there *must* be a diminution of the present excess of fertility; and further, it may be shown that the sole agency needed to work out this change is—the excess of fertility itself. (1852, 498)

This is because excessive population growth induces improved intelligence, including improved "foresight" and prudential restraint.

> Every improvement is at once the product of a higher form of humanity, and demands that higher form of humanity to carry it into practice. The application of science to the arts is simply the bringing to bear greater intelligence for satisfying our wants; and implies continued increase of that intelligence. To get more produce from the acre, the farmer must study chemistry. . . . Difficulty in getting a living is alike the incentive to a higher education of children, and to a more intense and long-continued application in adults. In the mother it induces foresight, economy, and skilful house-keeping; in the father, laborious days and constant self-denial. Nothing but necessity could make men submit to this discipline, and nothing but this discipline could produce a continued progression. (1852, 498–99)

Then Spencer sketches the survival principle applied to humans and quotes events in Ireland as an instance. It is to be noted that

Spencer's social Darwinism is a description of events, and not an endorsement or a policy prescription; although Spencer would later renounce teleology, here description and prescription blur.

> All mankind in turn subject themselves more or less to the discipline described; they either may or may not advance under it; but, in the nature of things, only those who *do* advance under it eventually survive. For, necessarily, families and races whom this increasing difficulty of getting a living which excess of fertility entails, does not stimulate to improvements in production—that is, to greater mental activity—are on the high road to extinction; and must ultimately be supplanted by those whom the pressure does so stimulate. This truth we have recently seen exemplified in Ireland. And here, indeed, without further illustration, it will be seen that premature death, under all its forms, and from all its causes, cannot fail to work in the same direction. For as those prematurely carried off must, in the average of cases, be those in whom the power of self-preservation is the least, it unavoidably follows, that those left behind to continue the race are those in whom the power of self-preservation is the greatest—are the select of their generation. So that, whether the dangers to existence be of the kind produced by excess of fertility, or of any other kind, it is clear, that by the ceaseless exercise of the faculties needed to contend with them, and by the death of all men who fail to contend with them successfully, there is ensured a constant progress towards a higher degree of skill, intelligence, and self-regulation—a better co-ordination of actions—a more complete life. (1852, 499–500)

Importantly for our reading, Spencer holds that "self-regulation" of numbers will bring about progress. When Spencer came to combine his ethical volumes into the 1893 *Principles of Ethics*, he reported a missing chapter (1:317).[17] Here he continues the theme of human development through expanded sympathy, but he worries about

---

17. Spencer discusses how this came to be in his *Autobiography*. He changed his compositional practices so that he adopted the "practice of devoting a 'copy-book' to each chapter, and putting it aside with the intention of using it as a basis for the final dictation. I name this fact because of a certain accidental sequence worth mentioning. One of the 'copy-books' was mislaid; and when I came to the chapter sketched out in it, I had to re-dictate this without reference to what I had before said. Some time after the book was published, I found this missing rough draft. A perusal showed that, besides a different presentation of the argument, it contained some illustrations which the chapter in its finished form did not contain. . . . When preparing the second edition, I therefore decided to append this rough-draft chapter just as it stood" (1904, 2:316).

impediments to the continued expansion of sympathy, in particular, observed "misery."

> Doubtless the moral modification of human nature which has thus to take place hereafter, analogous to that which has taken place heretofore, will be retarded by other causes than this primary cause. Not only is the growth of sympathy held in check by the performance of unsympathetic actions, such as are necessitated by militant activities, but it is held in check by the constant presence of pains and unhappiness, and by the consciousness that these exist even when they are not visible. Those in whom the sympathies have become keen, are of necessity proportionately pained on witnessing sufferings borne by others, not [only] in those cases where they are the causes of sufferings, but where the sufferings are caused in any other way. To those whose fellow feelings were too keenly alive to the miseries of the great mass of their kind—alive not only to such miseries as they saw but to such miseries as they heard of or read of, and to such miseries as they knew must be existing all around, far and near, life would be made intolerable: the sympathetic pains would submerge not only the sympathetic pleasures but the egoistic pleasures. (1893, 1:328–29)

The human response to such overwhelming misery is to deaden sympathy.

> And therefore life is made tolerable, even to the higher among us at the present time, by a certain perpetual searing of the sympathies, which keeps them down at such level of sensitiveness as that there remains a balance of pleasure in life. (1893, 1:329)

The policy consequence is that a reduction of the birthrate will stop the "human misery" that accompanies the "struggle for existence."

> Whence it follows that the sympathies can become more and more acute, only as fast as the amount of human misery to be sympathized with becomes less and less; and while this diminution of human misery to be sympathized with, itself must be due in part to the increase of sympathy which prompts actions to mitigate it, it must be due in the main to the decrease of the pressure of population upon the means of subsistence. While the struggle for existence among men has to be carried on with an intensity like that which now exists, the quantity of suffering to be borne by the majority must remain great. This struggle for existence

must continue to be thus intense so long as the rate of multiplication continues greatly in excess of the rate of mortality. Only in proportion as the production of new individuals ceases to go on so greatly in excess of the disappearance of individuals by death, can there be a diminution of the pressure upon the means of subsistence, and a diminution of the strain and the accompanying pains that arise more or less to all, and in a greater degree to the inferior. (1893, 1:329)

In this statement Spencer explicitly rejects social Darwinism entailing racial development through misery induced by competition for resources and argues to the contrary that individuals who have developed sympathetic tendencies toward one another will come to reduce misery by reducing births.

Darwin

After this lengthy discussion of an unfamiliar text, we remind the reader of the words from the 1859 *Origin of Species* in which Darwin deduces the struggle for existence from the perpetual excess of population. Note first that Darwin *explicitly* denied that human foresight—Malthus's prudential restraint or Spencer's self-regulation—can successfully counteract the struggle for existence.

A Struggle for Existence inevitably follows from the high rate at which all organic beings tend to increase. Every being, which during its natural lifetime produces several eggs or seeds, must suffer destruction during some period of its life, and during some season or occasional year, otherwise, on the principle of geometrical increase, its numbers would quickly become so inordinately great that no country could support the product. Hence, as more individuals are produced than can possibly survive, there must in every case be a Struggle for Existence, either one individual with another of the same species, or with the individuals of distinct species, or with the physical conditions of life. It is the doctrine of Malthus applied with manifold force to the whole animal and vegetable kingdoms; for in this case there can be no artificial increase of food, and no prudential restraint from marriage. (1859, 63)

Darwin's conception of racial perfection becomes evident in the section of *Descent of Man* entitled "Natural Selection as Affecting Civilised Nations" ([1871] 1989, 138–46). He now employs his proposal, made earlier in the text, to replace "happiness" with "general good" in the conception of social progress and to look at humans as breeding to achieve that general good (125).[18] As the chapter continues, Darwin cites the arguments of Greg and Galton, against the Malthusian recommendation to increase human happiness by delaying marriage, because the "poor and reckless" would be unable to refrain from marriage (see chap. 7, "Sympathy in Nineteenth-Century Biology," this vol.).

Darwin returns to this contention when the book concludes. He insists, in addition, that there is a trade-off in the struggle for survival that results from overpopulation.

> The advancement of the welfare of mankind is a most intricate problem: all ought to refrain from marriage who cannot avoid abject poverty for their children; for poverty is not only a great evil, but tends to its own increase by leading to recklessness in marriage. On the other hand, as Mr Galton has remarked, if the prudent avoid marriage, whilst the reckless marry, the inferior members tend to supplant the better members of society. Man, like every other animal, has no doubt advanced to his present high condition through a Struggle for Existence consequent on his rapid multiplication; and if he is to advance still higher, it is to be feared that he must remain subject to a severe struggle. Otherwise he would sink into indolence, and the more gifted men would not be more successful in the battle of life than the less gifted. Hence our natural rate of increase, though leading to many and obvious evils, must not be greatly diminished by any means. (*Descent*, 643)

This paragraph featured prominently in the Bradlaugh-Besant trial of 1877, in which the contending parties were seen by the *Times* as Darwin and Mill. The passage to which Darwin directed Charles Bradlaugh's attention summarizes his disagreement with the greatest happiness principle of utilitarianism.[19] For Darwin, the scientific goal of

---

18. This passage is linked by Gayon (1998, 78) to the "welfare of the community" in *Origin*. Gayon, however, omits Darwin's sentences that make it clear that Darwin proposes something that would be applicable to animals but which might encounter ethical constraints when applied to people.

19. Charles Bradlaugh is one of the most colorful figures in British history. It is hard to do justice to this imposing man, who described himself as an atheist, a republican, and a Malthusian. In one pamphlet, he proposed that Malthus replace Christ in the Trinity. Scholars understand-

making better humans may mean there is a need to sacrifice the well-being of existing humans. Certainly self-direction and selection are not to be trusted. For Spencer, individuals who realize that population growth was excessive would come to acquire foresight and reduce family size. We turn to the Bradlaugh-Besant case next.

BRADLAUGH-BESANT AND RACIAL BETTERMENT

Bradlaugh-Besant was the turning point in the British neo-Malthusian (birth control) movement in which the public dissemination of contraceptive information was consequently decriminalized. At the trial, Annie Besant discussed a letter from Darwin to Bradlaugh. Although he was aware of the hardships associated with a large family, Darwin wrote disapprovingly of voluntary restrictions on childbearing because they attentuated the working of "natural" selection in the development of the race.

> Mr. Darwin thinks rightly, with reference to the lower animals, that the application of "natural" checks upon the natural rate of increase is really for the welfare and progress of the various classes of brutes; and Mr Darwin thinks this "natural" check good for the human species, and in this he is supported to a certain extent by Mr. Herbert Spencer. I will venture to lay before you what I consider to be his strongest statement of that argument, and therefore of any possible objection. Mr. Darwin, writing to us a few days since, pointed our attention to the following extract from his "Descent of Man," p. 618: — "The enhancement [sic] of the welfare of mankind is a most intricate problem; ..." That is Mr. Darwin's position, and putting aside for a moment the awful amount of human misery which it accepts as the necessary condition of progress,

ably tend to focus on those aspects of his career: his unwillingness to take an oath to enter Parliament, the difficulty that Parliament had in physically expelling him (Arnstein 1965), the Bradlaugh case and trial (Manvell 1976). His regular debates with bishops and his involvement with the neo-Malthusian movement have been relatively neglected (Holden and Levy 1993).

Annie Besant's life was also remarkable, from an association with Bradlaugh's Secular Society to become the great advocate of theosophism. She lost custody of her child because of her neo-Malthusian views. Her presentation of the preventative check of Malthus and the positive check of Darwin as alternatives to consider in social issues has perhaps received insufficient attention. This juxtaposition is noted only in passing in Levy 1978.

let us see if the position be defensible. (*Queen v. Charles Bradlaugh and Annie Besant* 1877, 96)[20]

The report of the case of "The Queen v Bradlaugh and Another," as the *Times* so delicately hid the woman's name, recounted the story as a conflict between J. S. Mill and Charles Darwin.[21] In his *Autobiography*, Mill attributed his election defeat to his support of Bradlaugh's election campaign. But there is more than this. The *Times* focused on the question of what is more important: undirected sympathetic connections among individuals versus assisting the law of natural selection to "develop" the race.

The *Times* quoted Annie Besant describing Malthusian prescriptions.

> They suggested the substitution of prudential and scientific checks for these "natural" or positive checks. In other words, they desired to substitute the birth-restraining check for the death-producing check. The only argument against it worthy of a moment's consideration had been suggested by Mr. Darwin. (20 June 1877, 11)[22]

Two paragraphs later, Besant is said to have appealed to Mill, whose idea of the relation of human development and animal existence differs from Darwin's.

> The idea that the preventive check should be applied after marriage and not before might appear new to most men; but the principle was to be found in Mill's *Political Economy*, in which young men were examined at the Universities. For he wrote,
>   "Poverty, like most social evils, exists because men follow their own

---

20. The words omitted from this quotation are from the *Descent of Man*, quoted earlier in our section entitled "Darwin."

21. *Punch* (23 June 1877, 286) under the heading "More Pernicious Literature" remarks: "A SACERDOTAL manual of auricular confession, privately printed and circulating among an association of Anglican Clergyman . . . entitled *The Priest in Absolution*. An obvious analogy to another treatise, at present under prosecution, suggests a better title for it—Fruits of Theology." The Anglo-Catholic menace rates a cartoon on 30 June 1877, whereas Bradlaugh and Besant on 7 July 1877 get this note (206): "FIRST 'FRUITS OF PHILOSOPHY.'—Two hundred pounds' fine and six months' imprisonment."

22. She continues, quoting from Darwin's *Descent*.

brute instincts without consideration. But society is possible because man is not necessarily a brute. Civilization in every one of its aspects is a struggle against animal existence. If it has not brought population under some restraint it is because it has never been tried." . . .

Mr. Mill having strongly urged the necessity for "continence," went on to observe that from the way in which people commonly talked of off-spring as a sort of necessity it might almost be supposed that they allowed themselves to suppose their own volition had nothing to do with it. (11)

The public discussion of the Bradlaugh case recognized Mill as the great voice against an imposed hierarchy, either the old hierarchy following from the "natural" link between marriage and children or the coming hierarchy of racial remaking. This recognition may have been responsible for one of the most remarkable caricatures that we have encountered in the *Cope's* images (fig. 10.1). In the background of the John Wallace *Diva* is a figure that we bring to the thematic foreground. Although it is not so described by Thomson, the figure bears a striking resemblance to John Stuart Mill, seen as Anti-Everything, personified.

EDGEWORTH RECONCILES DARWIN
AND UTILITARIANISM

Evolutionary theory played into debates about social utility in two major ways. First, as we have seen, birth control became tangled up in discussions of racial betterment. Second, the conception of biological "progress" greatly influenced utilitarian thought concerning the specification of social welfare. At issue here was the early utilitarian claim that all should count as one. Edgeworth disagreed with Mill as to whether the claim was, as Mill put it, involved "in the very meaning of utilitarianism" or a conclusion derived from the presupposition of equality (Edgeworth 1877, 55). Impartiality, for Edgeworth, was the logical result of an equality assumption; and in that case, since evolutionary theory showed the assumption to be incorrect, the early utilitarian conclusion must be mistaken.[23]

---

23. "Where, however, there exists a society within a society, who, by an exclusive intercourse *inter se*, are capable (in virtue of a higher nature) of deriving a more exquisite pleasure, than by association with an inferior class, there begins to arise a genuine case of privilege; as in the rela-

Fig. 10.1. John Wallace, "J S Mill as Anti-Everything," detail from *Diva Nicotina* (1879)

More than this, Edgeworth supposed that evolutionary fitness mapped directly to the capacity for pleasure.

(γ) The *third postulate* simplifying the third inquiry is that capacity for pleasure and capacity for work generally speaking go together; that they both rise with evolution. The *quality of population should be the highest possible evolution*—provided . . . For it is probable that the highest in the order of evolution are most *capable of education* and improvement. In the general advance the most advanced should advance most. (1881, 68)

---

tion of men to apes, and perhaps of the civilized to the savage." "With regard to the theory of distribution, there is no indication that, at any rate between classes so nearly in the same order of evolution as the modern Aryan races, a law of distribution other than equality is to be wished. The more highly evolved class is to be privileged when there is a great interval, as there is between man and ape, as there may have been between the ranks and races of the ancient world" (Edgeworth 1877, 65, 78).

The attainment of Darwin's "general good" runs into the problem of people of lesser capacity.

> The *fifth postulate* appropriate to this case is that to substitute in one generation for any number of parents an equal number each superior in capacity (evolution) is beneficial for the next generation. This being granted, either analytically with the aid of Mr. Todhunter's 'Researches' [Note to text: See Appendix 1, p. 93] or by unaided reason, it is deduced that the average issue shall be as large as possible for all sections above a determinate degree of capacity, but zero for all sections below that degree. (1881, 70)

For that possibility, Galton had offered solutions: celibacy or emigration.

> What approach is useful in such cases is to be determined by Mr. Todhunter's principle. [Note to text: *Researches*; below p. 93] Again, mitigations might be provided for the classes not selected. [Note to text: Cf. Galton, "The weak could find a welcome and a refuge in celibate monasteries, &c." also Sully, *Pessimism*, p. 392] . . . Again, *emigration* might supplement total selection; emigration from Utopia to some unprogressive country where the prospect of happiness might be comparatively zero. (1881, 71–72)[24]

Edgeworth then asks: "*What is the fortune of the least favoured class in the Utilitarian community?*" (1881, 72). He starts with an admittedly unrealistic case where the fruits of nature are free, and immediately concludes from the assumption that consumption goods produce happiness that "*the condition of the least favoured class is positive happiness*" (73).

He then considers realistic cases where means are not free gifts of nature and so the utility of goods must be balanced by the disutility of effort. Then, he concludes, "the condition of the least favoured class is

---

24. "Accordingly in the 'koomposh' of an unlimited pauper population, the most favourable disposition might seem to be (abstracted from practical considerations, and *if* the delineation of Wundt be verified within and beyond the region of sensation), might seem perhaps to be, that adhering *ex hypothesi* to the letter of the first problem, we should be guided by the spirit of the second problem, should wish to cut off the redundant numbers with an illusory portion, so as to transfer substantial (equal) portions to a few. There might be, as it were, a mulcting of many brothers to make a few eldest sons" (Edgeworth 1877, 61).

positive, zero, or negative happiness."[25] The case becomes important when "we consider the case of *selection* for the benefit of the next generation" (1881, 73–74).

Then Edgeworth drops finite limits of integration, noting (1881, 74): "where ∞ is a convenient designation for the utmost extent of *variation*—variation in the Darwinian sense." The conclusion is that "it is no means clear that the condition of the least favoured in the second generation is above zero." This leads him to suggest:

> In fact, the happiness of some of the lower classes may be sacrificed to that of the higher classes. And, again, the happiness of part of the second generation may be sacrificed to that of the succeeding generations. (1881, 74)

Edgeworth considers the happiness of the least favoured from three vantage points: politics, political economy, and hedonics. Even if it were "abstractly desirable" from a hedonic point of view to have negative happiness, there may be political constraints.

> It may be admitted, however, that a limit below the zero of happiness, even if abstractly desirable, would not be humanly attainable; whether because discomfort in the lower classes produces political instability (Aristotle, &c.), or because only through the comfort of the lower classes can population be checked from sinking to the starving-point (Mill, &c.). Let politics and political economy fix some limit above zero. If now Hedonics indicate a limit still superior (in point of comfort)—well. But if abstract Hedonics point to a limit *below* that hard and fast line which the consideration of human infirmity impose, what occurs? Simply that population shall press up against that line without pressing it back. (1881, 75)

The difference in capacity for happiness is critical.

> Yet in the minds of many good men among the moderns and the wisest of the ancients, there appears a deeper sentiment in favour of aristocratical privilege—the privilege of man above brute, of civilised above savage, of birth, of talent, and of the male sex. This sentiment of right has a

---

25. ". . . the zero-point of happiness (a concept facilitated by, though not quite identical with, the economical, 'natural minimum of wages')" (Edgeworth 1881, 64).

ground of utilitarianism in supposed differences of *capacity*. Capacity for pleasure is a property of evolution, an essential attribute of civilisation (α). (1881, 77)

Edgeworth concludes that Mill's doctrine of moral equality must be deeply questioned (chap. 7, this vol.).

Pending a scientific hedonimetry, the principle "Every man, and every woman, to count for one," should be very cautiously applied. (1881, 81)[26]

And when Edgeworth confronts Spencer's *Data of Ethics* (the missing chapter was quoted earlier in "Early Utilitaranism and Capacity for Happiness," this chap.), he links Spencer to Mill on the equal capacity doctrine.[27]

The possibility of differences of capacity in the final state of equilibrium does not seem to be entertained by the author. But can we receive this? Can we suppose that the Examination-list of the Future will consist of an all-comprehensive bracket? If capacities for work differ, possibly also capacities for pleasure. If either or both species continue to differ, Utilitarianism, it is submitted, will continue to have a function not contemplated by the Data, unequal distribution. (1881, 123)

FROM EDGEWORTH TO PARETO

The Pareto principle holds that social state A is superior to B when no individual in society prefers B to A and at least one prefers A to B.

---

26. Mill "take[s] for granted that there is no *material* difference (no difference of kind, as Mill says in his "Logic") between human creatures. If, however, utilitarians were really convinced that there existed either now, or (what is more conceivable) in a past stage of the world's evolution, a broad distinction . . . , presumably the establishment of a privileged class would commend itself to utilitarian sense" (Edgeworth 1877, 55).

27. He was correct in doing so. When Spencer put together his *Principles of Ethics*, he was explicit about the specification of equal capacity: "But chiefly the imperfection of ethical systems appropriate to societies characterized by organized inequality, is that sympathy and all those emotions into which sympathy enters, and all that happiness of which sympathy is the root, remain incomplete. Alien natures cannot sympathize in full measure—can sympathize only in respect of those feelings which they have in common. Hence the unlikenesses presupposed between permanently ruling classes and permanently subject classes, negative that highest happiness which a rational ethics takes for its end. Throughout this work, therefore, the tacit assumption will be that the beings spoken of have that substantial unity of nature which characterizes the same variety of man; and the work will not, save incidentally or by contrast, take account of mixed societies, such as that we have established in India, and still less of slave societies" (1893, 1:27–28).

Economists once believed that the Pareto principle, as value-free, escaped Robbins's strictures against Edgeworth's cardinalism.[28] The Pareto principle requires only ranking, and so it seems we can dispense with Edgeworth's cardinal values altogether. A variation of this theme is that the Pareto principle is weak, and as long as we abstract from complicating issues such as envy (unlike Robbins 1981), it is "as-if" value-free. Either contention provided a strong rationale for the development of ordinal utility theory. We show finally that Paretian analysis blocks Edgeworth's cardinality conclusions, so that it is a stronger and more egalitarian norm than is generally presumed.

A compelling justification for the use of the Pareto principle as a policy norm is the claim that it is consistent with many other norms. More than that, the case is made that if one social state is Pareto preferred to another social state, any other plausible social norm will also rank the former above the latter. The norm of interest here is cardinal utilitarianism.

Consider a society with two possible states of affairs: State N, in which there are N people, and State $N - 1$, in which one of the people has been relocated to some other society. We have seen that, for Edgeworth, "some other society" might entail banishment to some unprogressive country; a darker interpretation is one of nonexistence.

Edgeworth's cardinal utilitarianism sums over the utility of people in N and $N - 1$ to determine which entails greater happiness. Consider

---

28. Thus, we have Bator's account of the move to value-free analysis in the body of his text. Here is "classical economics": "The foundations of modern welfare theory are well embedded in the soil of classical economics, and the structure, too, bears the imprint of the line of thought represented by Smith, Ricardo, Mill, and Marshall. But in classical writing prescription and analysis are inseparably intertwined, the underlying philosophy is unabashedly utilitarian, and the central normative concern is with the efficacy of market institutions. In contrast, the development of modern welfare economics can best be understood as an attempt to sort out ethics from science, and allocative efficiency from particular modes of social organization" (Bator 1957, 57). "In the late 1930's, Nicholas Kaldor and J. R. Hicks took up Lionel Robbins's challenge to economists not to mix ethics and science and suggested a series of tests for choosing some input-output configurations over others independently of value. Tibor Scitovsky pointed out an important asymmetry in the Kaldor-Hicks test and Samuelson in the end demonstrated that a 'welfare function' denoting an ethic was needed after all. I. M. D. Little tried, but I think failed, to shake this conclusion. The Pareto conditions are necessary, but never sufficient" (Bator 1957, 57–58). In footnote 11 Bator points out, however: "Pareto-efficiency is not even a necessary condition for a maximum of just any conceivable W-function. The form of our type function reflects a number of ethically loaded restrictions, *e.g.*, that individuals' preference functions are to 'count,' and count positively" (1957, 29). These "ethically loaded restrictions" are, in fact, the Pareto principle.

first Edgeworth's situation in which there exists a person whose net happiness is zero. By hypothesis, Edgeworth holds that happiness depends on an individual's activity so people are not sympathetic with each other. So a society that has 100 people who obtain positive happiness and 1 such person with zero happiness will be characterized by the same aggregate amount of happiness as a society with the 100 people who obtain positive happiness. Edgeworth's cardinal utilitarianism thus gives state N and $N-1$ equal marks.

Now, consider the Pareto principle. Here, we need to ask how the zero-utility individual views the matter. Again, by assumption the other people are indifferent to his fate, so we only need to consider that person. If he prefers living in the society to not living there—something about which Edgeworth does not inquire—then N is Pareto preferred to $N-1$.

Using the Edgeworth example, it is clear that the Pareto and the cardinal rankings are not identical: the fact that N is Pareto preferred to $N-1$ does not guarantee that N is cardinally valued as higher than $N-1$. We have seen that in fact the cardinal ranking of $N-1$ is the same as N.[29]

Thus, cardinal utilitarianism does not simply ratify what the Pareto principle reveals. In particular, the Pareto principle can block eugenic proposals resulting from the claim that there are people without the capacity for happiness. This simple example suggests that there is a significant difference between allowing people to decide whether to invite someone to become a member of the society and having that decision made by a policymaker or a scientist.[30] Ordinary people make such decisions on the basis of family happiness.[31] We have seen previ-

---

29. Perhaps the reader thinks that we can solve the problem by replacing the strong inequality of cardinal utilitarianism with a weak inequality. To see that this is not so, consider another of Edgeworth's examples, in which person N has negative happiness in Society A but still prefers A to B. Here we have N Pareto preferred to $N-1$, while the cardinal measure assigns a lower weight to N than $N-1$.

30. Our postscript affirms this. Robbins's words on immigration (1929, 78) might be read against those of the eugenic theorists for whom immigration control was the sina qua non of eugenic policy (chaps. 4, 5, this vol.).

31. Robbins: "Of course I do not deny that, in every day life, we do make comparisons between the satisfactions of different people. When the head of a family carves up a turkey, he may take account of his estimate of the satisfaction afforded to different members by different portions" (1981, 5).

ously that early utilitarian economists participated in the policy debate over birth control. Robbins's views on this matter were also clear (1972, 21–22). When Robbins discussed the genesis of the birth-control movement from the utilitarian Jeremy Bentham to James Mill and Francis Place, he came down on the side of Spencer as opposed to Darwin.

> It is said, though complete confirmation is lacking, that the young John Stuart Mill spent a night in a police station, having been caught distributing information of this nature. The movement for deliberate control of population pressure, in our day the best hope of saving humanity from the worst effects of the population explosion, thus takes its rise in the heart of the classical system.[32]

We have considered earlier the historical details of the conflict between eugenics, in the days before it had that name, and private family planning. It is not clear that Robbins knew all these details, but we suspect that none of them would have surprised him.[33]

---

32. Robbins (1968, 33). D. H. Robertson, Robbins's debating partner on theoretical issues of interpersonal comparisons and ordinality, had similar neo-Malthusian views: "I find that I wrote eleven years ago: 'There can be no permanent limitation of armaments till there is an international agreement for the limitation of the birth-rate.'" About the later silence of economists on this issue, Robertson wrote: "It would have been more impressive if we had spoken out, from the World of the Unborn, before the decisive turning-point of the birth-rate in the 'seventies. (Perhaps we did our best; perhaps it was we who whispered into the ear of Mill those too long neglected passages in his *Principles*.)" (Robertson 1923, 207). Robertson's views from 1912 read like those of C. K. Ogden (Holden and Levy 2001).

33. We doubt, for instance, that much of the work in this book would have surprised Robbins: "Why study what the ignorant and the pompous have thought the most dismal of sciences?" (1930, 24). "But we are really not obliged to take seriously the social and economic thought of one who could denounce Adam Smith as 'the half-bred and half-witted Scotchman who taught the 'deliberate blasphemy'—'thou shalt hate the Lord thy God, damn His laws and covet thy neighbour's goods.' This is the voice, not of candid reason and persuasion, but of self-induced hysteria. Nor need we pay any more attention to the eulogist of Frederick the Great, the author of the *Nigger Question*, who stood opposite the Rothschild house at Hyde Park Corner gloating on the torturing of the Jews in the Middle Ages. We know the type too well" (Robbins 1968, 172). We disagree with Lord Robbins on the need to take such doctrines with all due seriousness, and outline our reasons in Peart and Levy 2005.

Part IV

THE THEORIST IN
THE MODEL

XI

ANALYTICAL EGALITARIANISM, ANECDOTAL EVIDENCE, AND INFORMATION AGGREGATION VIA PROVERBIAL WISDOM

> Can the multitude possibly tolerate or believe in the reality of the beautiful in itself as opposed to the multiplicity of beautiful things, or can they believe in anything conceived in its essence as opposed to the many particulars?
> —Plato, *Republic*

ANALYTICAL EGALITARIANISM

When Adam Smith attacked the doctrine of innate differences of people, he singled out the "vanity of the philosopher" for his belief that he was somehow superior to the common porter.[1] We have linked the discussion of sameness versus difference to the attacks on the analytical egalitarianism of classical economists. Those attacks focused on the desirability of self-direction versus the need for direction by experts, one's betters. Consequently, the debate over equality versus hierarchy centered on outcomes or policies that emerged from self- versus expert direction. Examples of the sorts of policy concerns that were central in the debate over hierarchy versus egalitarianism include work effort, savings rates, participation in the democratic process, immigration, and sterilization.[2] Each of these concerns requires that we take the facts of the matter, the phenomena under discussion, seriously.

---

1. Recall the passage quoted in full as an epigraph to chapter 1 (Smith, *Wealth of Nations*, I.2§4).

2. Chapters 3, 4, 5, 6, 7, 9, 10, this volume. The "scientific" breeding of people is an example of the debate over the direction of ordinary people by experts that has been taken up by followers of Adam Smith versus Plato (chap. 6, this vol.).

Here, we set aside the specifics of the policy recommendations to consider instead the methodological underpinnings of the debate over analytical egalitarianism versus hierarchy. At the origin of the methodological debate, in the passage from Plato's *Republic*, we quote as epigraph, Socrates says that ordinary people cannot be philosophers because they remain content with many surface phenomena, whereas the philosopher inquires after the one true explanation.[3] Since Plato's time, "surface phenomena" have acquired a new label, "anecdotal evidence," and Plato's "one explanation" might be called a model. The methodological debate has reemerged as a debate about coherent model-based optimization versus heuristics. In this chapter, we compare how individuals acquire and process information relative to their scientific counterparts. We suggest that individuals rely on a heuristic, what we call *proverbial wisdom*, while experts rely on models. We then examine the properties of proverbial wisdom relative to models.

Today, we often think of a model as something precise. And we tend to think of stories and proverbs as imprecise. Consequently, we may believe that models and stories exist in separate and incommensurate realms of discourse. As a preliminary step toward comparing models and proverbs, we therefore propose commensurate idealizations of models and proverbs.

We regard the Platonic principle, that the expert's model is superior to anecdotes of any sort, as a system of analytical hierarchy. In such a view, the expert's knowledge necessarily dominates that of ordinary people.[4] The valuable contribution of rational expectations in public choice has been to show that in important contexts the expert only *weakly* dominates ordinary people. But we propose to go beyond this point of view. We demonstrate that aggregated anecdotal evidence can *improve upon* the expert's model-based estimation if the model is not exactly correct. Thus, neither the expert nor ordinary people domi-

---

3. Plato, *Republic*, 493e.

4. Gigerenzer, Todd, and the ABC Research Group (1999, 28): "The heuristics-and-biases approach views heuristics and unreliable aids that the limited human mind too commonly relies upon despite their inferior decison-making performance, and hence researchers in this tradition seek out cases where heuristics can be blamed for poor reasoning."

nates the other, and so we allow for the possibility of the relationship of exchange.

Our point of view has much in common with the argument by Gigerenzer, Todd, and the ABC Research Group regarding "fast and frugal heuristics" that can in fact improve upon optimization procedures.[5] Unlike them, however, we examine a means by which informal heuristics might work.[6] So, we present a "model" of heuristics. Although we note the irony of our approach, we believe there is merit to considering the expert and ordinary people on the same analytical grounds so that their use of information can be evaluated.

There are five pieces to our argument. We begin with a series of definitions, in order to proceed with a common understanding of our terminology. Next, to motivate the structure of our approach, we consider Smith's wage theory in which he supposes that ordinary people interpret random events ex post as if they were deterministic. Then we consider how people might randomly select an observation and give it a deterministic interpretation. Since they are aware that such a randomly selected observation is not the only one possible, people make decisions on the basis of a process that centers such selected observations.

The technical burden of the argument is then a demonstration that the expert's model does not dominate the information aggregation possibility of ordinary people. Our technical construct—what we call the median of anecdotal evidence—supports the *possibility* of analytical egalitarianism by providing a *theoretical* counterexample to analytical hierarchy. Our evidence consists of the sort of Monte Carlo study employed to study estimation procedures in nonideal circumstances

---

5. Gigerenzer, Todd, and the ABC Research Group (1999, 28): "We see heuristics as the way the human mind can take advantage of the structure of information in the environment to arrive at reasonable decisions, and so we focus on the ways and settings in which simple heuristics lead to accurate and useful inferences."

6. Gigerenzer, Todd, and the ABC Research Group (1999, 22): "This book adopts a different, adaptive view of rational behavior. We do not compare human judgment with the laws of logic or probability, but rather examine how it fares in real-world environments. The function of heuristics is not to be coherent. Rather, their function is to make reasonable, adaptive inferences about the real social and physical world given limited time and knowledge. Hence, we should evaluate the performance of heuristics by criteria that reflect this function."

(Andrews et al. 1972). We summarize the argument, then present the technical details in appendix 11.1.

If devices such as our median of anecdotal evidence are used to make decisions, they are certainly neither so-called nor so-conceived in ordinary language. We later return to Adam Smith and consider his discussion of the role of "proverbs" as exemplars of experience.[7] In our reading of Smith, proverbs summarize experience. As such, they are information-aggregating stories that become rules of morality.[8] Thus, we suggest that what we call *median anecdotal evidence* for technical reasons goes by the name *proverb* or *maxim* or *parable* in the real world.[9] Consequently, we are not surprised that when Gigerenzer, Todd, and the ABC Research Group point to real-world heuristics, their instances are proverbs.[10] We provide some statistical justification for their conjecture about the role of proverbs in information aggregation.[11]

MODELS AND EVIDENCE DEFINED

We start with two concepts, models and evidence. By a *model*, we understand a K-dimension causal specification that tells us how one or

---

7. "The general maxims of morality are formed, like all other general maxims, from experience and induction. We observe in a great variety of particular cases what pleases or displeases our moral faculties, what these approve or disapprove of, and, by induction from this experience, we establish those general rules" (Smith, *Theory of Moral Sentiments*, VII.3§13).

8. The history of proverbial wisdom has been neglected. Smith's contemporary Gotthold Ephraim Lessing analyzed fables and is still discussed in the philosophy of science. "For Lessing, the fable is a genre intended neither for entertainment nor for the communication and direction of emotions but rather for elucidation. . . . The moral of the fable is a general claim, and hence is symbolic. For us to understand it clearly (and also for it to motivate us to act), it must be made visualizable; it must be given a concrete form" (Cartwright 1993, 268).

9. Discussions with Dan Houser have clarified the possibility of employing experimental procedures to recover what kind of a centering procedure, if any, is used in the formation of proverbs.

10. Gigerenzer, Todd, and the ABC Research Group (1999, 31): "Social norms and social imitation can also help us make decisions with limited time and knowledge. Following heuristics such as 'eat what older and experienced conspecifics eat' or 'prefer mates picked by others' can speed up decision making by reducing the need for direct experience and information gathering."

11. Gigerenzer, Todd, and the ABC Research Group (1999, 363): "Simple heuristics can be advantageous for navigating the complexities of social domains, and can be learned in a social manner, through imitation, word of mouth, or cultural heritage. We suspect that social norms, cultural strictures, historical proverbs, and the like can enable fast and frugal social reasoning by obviating cost-benefit calculations and extensive information search."

more variable(s) effect(s) another (Hoover 2001). By *evidence*, we understand N observations or elements of a K-dimension empirical distribution. Recent discussions in economic methodology have drawn attention to the possibility that anecdotes, conceived of as stories based on observations chosen in some unspecified way, and models influence one another in complicated ways. The stories that economists use to explicate the models (McCloskey 1990) may be *required* to make the models operational (Morgan 2001).[12] We fully agree that stories are used in this way, and we would, in fact, expand upon the argument to suggest that *images* are also used to influence the model. However, we put aside these issues initially, in order to compare how an expert and a well-informed ordinary person might come to understand the world. For our purposes, then, it is not necessary to give priority either to a model or to the evidence.[13]

We proceed from our definition of *model* and *evidence* to define an expert as someone who uses *all* the evidence in a transparent manner to estimate a model. Transparency is central to statistical ethics (ASA 2000) because it allows the requisite movement between the private information of the expert model builder and the common knowledge of the model users.[14] Thus, transparency allows discarding of outliers asymmetrically as long as the reader is appropriately notified.

In some respects, the anecdotal evidence used by ordinary people may be the polar extreme of modeling by the expert. Whereas the expert employs all the evidence available, anecdotal evidence is the minimum required to "connect the dots," to tell a simple story.

---

12. Cartwright (1993, 270–71): "Models make the abstract concepts of physics more concrete. They also help to connect theory with the real world. How does this work? Typically, we design our experiments to look as much as possible like the models we have available. Then we know what specific forms our general laws should take. Obviously, one single model will not serve; we expand it by piecing in others. That usually doesn't work with fables, and that is in part why Lessing keeps the characters in his fables so thin and featureless. If he were to fill in extra details, the characters would fall under new, different abstract concepts, which may suggest different behavior from the first and perhaps even contradictory behavior."

13. Thus, we leave aside the important question of whether we collect evidence because a model tells us that these variables are important, or whether the evidence leads us to believe that some variable affects another and should be included in the model.

14. The expert may prefer one outcome over another (Feigenbaum and Levy 1996), but as long as the bias is transparent, the expert does not exploit information asymmetrically.

Whereas the modeler's practice is transparent, the ordinary person may select anecdotal evidence in an unknown fashion.

Supposing that we wish to compare the expert and the ordinary person, it would seem that the case for the wisdom of ordinary people is already lost. As a matter of *definition*, we have just suggested that the acquisition of information by ordinary people does not satisfy the transparency requirement. Put differently, transparency is a scientific requirement, and ordinary people are not scientists.

However, it does not follow that the expert's employment of a causal model results in a superior *processing* of information relative to that of ordinary people because there are many ordinary people who process the information. A similar confusion is characteristic of a common criticism of democracy. Ordinary people are said to bring nothing to the political process other than their many anecdotes, each evidently inferior to the expert's model.[15] The difficulty with this argument has been pointed out by workers in rational expectations politics. While experts have a deeper understanding of the process, ordinary people may use heuristics to act *as if* they understood the model employed by the expert. Although no individual understands the process as well as the expert, if there are many people and their decisions are made through a political process that centers their informed preferences, then their collective decision will mirror that of the expert (Wittman 1995).

The problem we address here, that of *information* aggregation, is similar to the *preference* aggregation problem raised by Buchanan and Tullock in *The Calculus of Consent* (1962). Of all possible voting mechanisms, why it is that majority rule is so widely employed? We suggest that, just as the political process of ordinary people may be idealized using a median voter idea, information may also be aggregated by ordinary people using centralized anecdotal evidence. As a result of

---

15. Similar arguments were made in the nineteenth century to immunize "science" from criticism by ordinary people: for, if ordinary people cannot abstract from surface phenomena, they have no basis (except anecdotes) upon which to criticize the scientist. See the remarks on Jevons in the *Economist*: "[Jevons's] best work is so original and abstract in character, as to go out of the way, and in some respects out of the reach, of the ordinary student" (20 October 1883, 1220). The argument was used to suggest that women were unable to participate in scientific discussions, and as we have noted (chap. 4) James Hunt left the Ethnological Society to protest the admission of women.

this similarity to the voting context, we call our information aggregation idealization a *regression by voting*. We then argue that what Smith and many since have understood as "proverbial wisdom" or "proverbs" summarize experience. In this way, proverbs are observed examples of aggregated information.

We should say a word about how such proverbial wisdom bears upon the substantive debates we have studied previously. Smith cites one of the books of Hebrew scriptures as a collection of proverbial wisdom. One piece of proverbial wisdom—the Bible-based question that the British Evangelicals asked on behalf of enslaved Africans, "Am I not a man and a brother?"—was critical to the antislavery coalition of classical economists and Evangelicals. This proverb was questioned in the mid–nineteenth century by the newly arisen "science" of anthropology under the influence of James Hunt, for whom Negroes were a species apart, outside the rule of law. We point to this episode[16] and the following argument to suggest that *if* proverbial wisdom and "scientific knowledge" give us opposing directions, *then* we ought to take seriously the possibility that the "science" is at fault.

Just as we idealize the information aggregation possibilities available to ordinary people, we idealize the expert as someone who connects model and evidence transparently. Our idealized expert has no interests other than truth and so estimates a model with all the data in the most efficient manner. Real-world experts sometimes fall remarkably short of this idealization. Perhaps the most grotesque example of this is the expert who attempts to persuade people to disregard the evidence of their senses and/or their information.[17] By this we do not mean that the expert explains to people that there are pieces of information that they need to consider. Instead, the expert insists that what people perceive does not "really" exist because it is not consistent with the expert's

---

16. We fully recognize that we have deliberately chosen a piece of anecdotal evidence here. While this goes beyond our purview in this chapter, the images and texts throughout the book suggest that in fact there was much "evidence" of this sort in the public domain during the latter half of the century. We present an additional piece of anecdotal evidence as our Postscript.

17. The argument was sometimes gendered: women being supposed less competent to make inferences than men. Henderson (1994) describes an episode in which the male theorist (Francis Galton) attempted to remove the participation of female onlookers. See note 15 above.

model.[18] One episode will stand for many. "Scientific" anthropologists assured their readers that the intelligent, dark-skinned people they might observe could not be "real Negroes" because in their "science" all Negroes were childlike simpletons (chap. 4, this vol.).

For convenience, we collect our definitions in table 11.1. The words in quotation marks are supposed to apply to the real, or observed, world.

TABLE 11.1. Definitions

Term	Definition
Model	Equation specifying an unknown but supposed fixed K-dimension causal relationship subject to a random disturbance
Evidence	N elements of the K-dimension empirical distribution
"Expert"	Person who estimates a model employing all the evidence transparently
Anecdotal evidence	K elements of the K-dimension empirical distribution which exactly fit the model
"Ordinary person"	Person who selects anecdotal evidence in an unknown fashion
Regression by voting	An idealized process that aggregates information by a procedure akin to majority rule
Median of anecdotal evidence	A competitive equilibrium in a regression by voting procedure
"Proverb"	Observed median of anecdotal evidence

OBSERVING LUCK, IMPUTING GENIUS

Smith's account of gambles in his chapter on the distribution of wages in the *Wealth of Nations* offers insight into how ordinary people interpret random events. In contrast with standard neoclassical theory, Smith argues that ordinary people interpret a winning gamble as one that deserves an additional reward in terms of approbation. As a consequence, it is important not to read neoclassical treatments back into Smith.[19] In a nutshell, Smith tells us that those who succeed are pre-

---

18. It is therefore no coincidence that the great challenge to Platonic realism applied to society comes from George Grote and J. S. Mill (chap. 6, this vol.).

19. Milton Friedman and L. J. Savage (1948) offered economists an alternative to Smith's illusions-based account in which (1) everyone knows the probability associated with gambles; and (2) no one's perception of the importance of an individual changes after the gamble. Levy (1999) suggests that the second aspect of Smith's approach requires more attention than it has received.

sumed to be deserving of success. To use modern terms, he sketches an updating procedure by which random events ex ante become deterministic events ex post. Since this updating by rendering events deterministic is central to our model of information aggregation, we pay careful attention to Smith's discussion of gambling.

He begins with a simple statement of the problem of the risky choice of occupation:

> The probability that any particular person shall ever be qualified for the employment to which he is educated, is very different in different occupations. In the greater part of mechanic trades, success is almost certain; but very uncertain in the liberal professions. Put your son apprentice to a shoemaker, there is little doubt of his learning to make a pair of shoes: But send him to study the law, it is at least twenty to one if ever he makes such proficiency as will enable him to live by the business. (*Wealth of Nations*, I.10§25)

Not only does the probability of success differ across occupations, but people also overestimate the expected value of the gambles.

> In a perfectly fair lottery, those who draw the prizes ought to gain all that is lost by those who draw the blanks. In a profession where twenty fail for one that succeeds, that one ought to gain all that should have been gained by the unsuccessful twenty. The counsellor at law who, perhaps, at near forty years of age, begins to make something by his profession, ought to receive the retribution, not only of his own so tedious and expensive education, but of that of more than twenty others who are never likely to make any thing by it. How extravagant soever the fees of counsellors at law may sometimes appear, their real retribution is never equal to this. Compute in any particular place, what is likely to be annually gained, and what is likely to be annually spent, by all the different workmen in any common trade, such as that of shoemakers or weavers, and you will find that the former sum will generally exceed the latter. But make the same computation with regard to all the counsellors and students of law, in all the different inns of court, and you will find that their annual gains bear but a very small proportion to their annual expence, even though you rate the former as high, and the latter as low, as can well be done. The lottery of the law, therefore, is very far from being a perfectly fair lottery; and that, as well as many other liberal and honourable professions, is, in point of pecuniary gain, evidently under-recompenced. (*Wealth of Nations*, I.10§25)

Two reasons are offered for this. The first is a bias in estimating one's chances.

> Those professions keep their level, however, with other occupations, and, notwithstanding these discouragements, all the most generous and liberal spirits are eager to crowd into them. Two different causes contribute to recommend them. First, the desire of the reputation which attends upon superior excellence in any of them; and, secondly, the natural confidence which every man has more or less, not only in his own abilities, but in his own good fortune. (*Wealth of Nations*, I.10§26)

The second reason is a possibly correct understanding of the approbation from winning.

> To excel in any profession, in which but few arrive at mediocrity, is the most decisive mark of what is called genius or superior talents. The public admiration which attends upon such distinguished abilities, makes always a part of their reward; a greater or smaller in proportion as it is higher or lower in degree. It makes a considerable part of that reward in the profession of physic; a still greater perhaps in that of law; in poetry and philosophy it makes almost the whole. (*Wealth of Nations*, I.10§27)

Behind the fact of approbation that classical economists supposed for their wage theory (Peart and Levy 2003) there is a generating process that moves from an actor's good luck to the spectator's imputation of superior ability: those who succeed are presumed to be deserving of success. Thus, Smith and the classical economists who followed in his footsteps hold that ordinary people do not use models with explicit random components to understand the world. If this is so, then how might ordinary people aggregate information? We offer a simple model of this next.

ANECDOTES AND EXPERTS

Suppose we accept the common disparagement of model-free evidence, as "anecdotal." Anecdotal evidence is regarded as promiscuous empiricism offered without recognition of randomness. The "welfare queen" is not a representative guide to policy; she is a fragment of a story, not a model. "Anecdotes," as the dictionary tells us, are narratives of episodes.[20] We suppose these narratives offer evidence without the beneficent constraint of a model. If Smith is correct, ordinary people interpret such realizations of a random process in deterministic terms.

Here we inquire into the informational properties of anecdotes. We venture out of well-explored ground because we believe that models and anecdotes, when organized coherently, are competing sources of information, and so we propose to model the information aggregation of anecdotal evidence. We suppose that ordinary people aggregate information as if by voting, where the outcome is determined by the median. Then we consider how such information aggregation compares with expert decision making.

The idea we exploit, that voting itself can be viewed as robust estimation (Bassett and Persky 1999), is a continuation of Galton's proposal in two long-forgotten papers published in *Nature* in 1907 (see appendices at end of book) that called for decision making by majority rule as an estimation procedure that recovered the *sample* median. Galton considers one dimension. We will consider many.

To motivate our conceptualization of the difference between a causal model and anecdotal evidence, we use a picture that relates variables X and Y. This picture also can help make intuitively clear why at least one piece of anecdotal evidence can be thought of as faring as well as a causal model (fig. 11.1).

In figure 11.1, the empirical distribution, the observations of the model comprise points $[x_a, y_a]$, $[x_b, y_b]$, $[x_c, y_c]$, which we have labeled **a, b, c.** These three points are, then, three bits of anecdotal evidence, three stories about the relationship between X and Y. The economists' typical causal model relating X to Y is a regression equation that is marked as **OLS.** The regression equation is an abstracting device, passing among the data and encountering none.

Suppose there are three individuals in society, each of whom has encountered in some unknown manner one and only one of the three

---

20. "The narrative of a detached incident, or of a single event, told as being in itself interesting or striking." *Oxford English Dictionary* (1992) entry for *anecdote*.

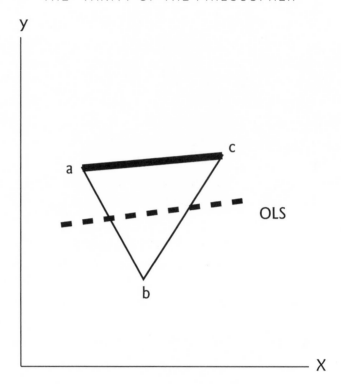

Fig. 11.1.   Fitting a regression

pieces of anecdotal evidence. If we ask each of the three what is the relationship between X and Y, we will obtain three different answers. The slope of **ab** is negative and relatively large in absolute value. The slope of **bc** is positive and relatively large in absolute value. The slope of **ac** is positive and relatively small in absolute value.

Suppose a competitive political process occurs, in which the majority is decisive. Then we can think about the median answer as akin to an equilibrium in "regression by voting." The median of the three slopes here is **ac**.

The picture we have drawn suggests that the slope of **ac** is not all that different from the slope of the expert's regression line. The question that concerns us is whether individuals' anecdotes—aggregated using the majority rule principle—can ever be a better representation of the relationship between X and Y than the expert's regression equation. It turns out that the expert's regression equation will do better under the assumption that the model is always and everywhere true (appendix 11.1). In that case, the expert's model is infallible. Under these circumstances it is efficient to process information subject to the (true) model.

What if the expert's model holds with a high probability, but it occasionally fails? Here, imposing the model on the data might hurt the performance of the expert relative to the aggregated information of regular people (appendix 11.1). Looking at data through a sometimes-broken glass can grossly distort the interpretation of the "evidence."

These are strong, perhaps even counterintuitive, claims. What we have just sketched is the reason why statistical researchers employ "elementary set methods" of regression. The power of model infallibility is bought at a high cost. It is worthy of remark that statistical workers who attempt to find a model that fits the majority of the data might employ such elementary set methods to locate a dependable starting point for their more sensitive procedures.[21]

"UNIVERSAL EXPERIENCE"—PROVERBS IN ADAM SMITH

It is in this context of using elementary set methods as the starting point for traditional estimation methods that we wish to reflect upon what specialists tell us about Adam Smith's epistemology: he has none (Harman 1986). Smith does, however, explain how philosophy begins with proverbial wisdom, and he offers his teaching on public finance only after giving the reader four maxims on taxation.[22] To demonstrate the

---

21. When Rousseeuw and Leroy (1987) revived elementary set methods with the least median of squares, they also proposed a trimmed least squares that begins iteration from this robust solution. Various M-class estimation procedures introduced in Andrews et al. 1972 are sensitive to starting points, and so the sample median is often recommended (e.g., Mosteller and Tukey 1977).

22. Thus, Smith offers his thoughts on taxation as maxims: "Before I enter upon the examination of particular taxes, it is necessary to premise the four following maxims with regard to taxes in general" (*Wealth of Nations*, V.2§25).

importance that Smith attaches to proverbs, we reproduce every occurrence of the word *proverb* in his two books.[23]

In his *Theory of Moral Sentiments* we find that proverbial wisdom — as founded on "universal experience" — is said to come as close
to the truth as possible. Here is Smith's account of the nice properties
of proverbial wisdom:

> The general rules of almost all the virtues, the general rules which deter-
> mine what are the offices of prudence, of charity, of generosity, of grati-
> tude, of friendship, are in many respects loose and inaccurate, admit of
> many exceptions, and require so many modifications, that it is scarce
> possible to regulate our conduct entirely by a regard to them. The com-
> mon proverbial maxims of prudence, being founded in universal expe-
> rience, are perhaps the best general rules which can be given about it.
> To affect, however, a very strict and literal adherence to them would evi-
> dently be the most absurd and ridiculous pedantry. (*Theory of Moral
> Sentiments*, III.I§121)

Smith holds there is a robustness to proverbs, as they discard troublesome outliers.

> Men in the inferior and middling stations of life, besides, can never be
> great enough to be above the law, which must generally overawe them
> into some sort of respect for, at least, the more important rules of justice.
> The success of such people, too, almost always depends upon the favour
> and good opinion of their neighbours and equals; and without a tolera-
> bly regular conduct these can very seldom be obtained. The good old
> proverb, therefore, That honesty is the best policy, holds, in such situa-
> tions, almost always perfectly true. In such situations, therefore, we may
> generally expect a considerable degree of virtue; and, fortunately for the
> good morals of society, these are the situations of by far the greater part
> of mankind. (*Theory of Moral Sentiments*, I.III§32)

Smith's contemporaries would know that *vulgar* is Latin for popular,
which he uses to describe the illusions of the rich.

> The homely and vulgar proverb, that the eye is larger than the belly, never
> was more fully verified than with regard to him. The capacity of his stom-
> ach bears no proportion to the immensity of his desires, and will receive
> no more than that of the meanest peasant. The rest he is obliged to dis-

---

23. "Proverbs" seem to be invariably positive; maxims in Smith's account can be "vile."

tribute among those, who prepare, in the nicest manner, that little which he himself makes use of, among those who fit up the palace in which this little is to be consumed, among those who provide and keep in order all the different baubles and trinkets, which are employed in the oeconomy of greatness; all of whom thus derive from his luxury and caprice, that share of the necessaries of life, which they would in vain have expected from his humanity or his justice. (*Theory of Moral Sentiments*, IV.I§10)

Second, Smith explicates the basis of proverbial wisdom in *Wealth of Nations*. There, he explains how common understanding is formulated as rules or maxims and then written as fables or wise sayings. Then moral philosophy induces systematic treatment. (For the passages in full, see "Competing Views of the Scientist," chap. 7.)

Modern economists who revel in the restatement of proverbial wisdom—"There is no such thing as a free lunch" or "Don't put all your eggs in the same basket"—will find that here too, Smith precedes us.

Money, says the proverb, makes money. When you have got a little, it is often easy to get more. (*Wealth of Nations* I.9§11)

Our ancestors were idle for want of a sufficient encouragement to industry. It is better, says the proverb, to play for nothing than to work for nothing. (*Wealth of Nations*, II.3.§12)

Jack of all trades will never be rich, says the proverb. (*Wealth of Nations*, IV.5.§55)

Light come, light go, says the proverb; and the ordinary tone of expence seems every-where to be regulated, not so much according to the real ability of spending, as to the supposed facility of getting money to spend. (*Wealth of Nations*, IV.7§147)

If the rod be bent too much one way, says the proverb, in order to make it straight you must bend it as much the other. The French philosophers, who have proposed the system which represents agriculture as the sole source of the revenue and wealth of every country, seem to have adopted this proverbial maxim. (*Wealth of Nations*, IV.9§4)

CULTURE AS INFORMATION AGGREGATION

Smith defines "prudential" behavior in terms of proverbs—"The common proverbial maxims of prudence, being founded in universal experience, are perhaps the best general rules which can be given about it." Standard neoclassical economics does not specify where people begin optimization problems; rather, it concentrates on how individuals adjust optimally from where they are. Suppose that what is called prudential behavior is, in fact, how people begin to optimize. This suggests that Smith's insight into prudential behavior as based on proverbs might be an important addition to neoclassical economics as a way into the vexing problem of multiple equilibria. Since we know how to find proverbs—they are still called *proverbs* in ordinary language—we have some hope of coming to an understanding of the starting point problem in consumer choice.[24]

Some of Smith's proverbs confirm the received wisdom of neoclassical economics. "Better to play for nothing than work for nothing" is one. But he also offers proverbs that conflict with the results of neoclassical economic theory. This offers a way of testing Smith's insight via experimental economics.[25]

The question of high-dimensional narration suggests that complex narration may be especially important for the efficient dissemination of information. This thought suggests that stories might be considered to exist in the same plane of information-aggregation existence that prices and models do. When prices, models, and narratives give us the same advice, then we know the answer and proceed to other concerns. When the advice they provide points in different directions, then we might need to ask which one is at fault. What Adam Smith knew, but modern economists have often forgotten, is that proverbial wisdom is a method by which one can test the model.

In keeping with our conviction that stories inform, we close the book with two. One of these, Huck Finn's, is an abstraction. The other, Ali Khan's, is quite concrete.

---

24. A problem with "conventions" is that they are not so called by the ordinary people who presumably use them.

25. These last paragraphs have grown out of discussions with Dan Houser.

APPENDIX 11.1: MODELS AND ANECDOTES

THEORY

We formulate the problem of comparing how ordinary people and experts make decisions in terms of competing methods of estimating regression equations. Both methods are idealizations. First, in the case of experts, we thereby avoid the consideration of the expert's private interest. Second, we represent the procedure of "ordinary people" as akin to the equilibrium condition of preference aggregation in a competitive, majority-rule democracy in which candidates locate their position in policy space so as to maximize their appeal (Downs 1957).[26] In this account, democracy is said to enable voters to aggregate their *desires* through voting. We examine the consequences of aggregating *information* in a similar fashion, although we cannot point to a competitive political process in which such an equilibrium is effected.

The most general question to ask in this comparative spirit is whether the decision function of ordinary people is admissible in this formulation. "Admissible" was first defined for a decision function by Wald (1950) in terms of a unknown distribution F, in the class Ω, and a known risk function $r(,)$. Here is Wald's definition.

> A decision function δ will be said to be admissible if there exists no other decision function δ^* which is uniformly better than δ, i.e., if there exists no decision function δ^* satisfying the following two conditions:
> $r(F,\delta^*) \leq r(F,\delta)$ for all F in Ω, and
> $r(F,\delta^*) < r(F,\delta)$ for at least one element of F of Ω. (Wald 1950, 15)

Admissibility allows us to take into account costs that are consequences of the different rules by noting that $r(,)$ is net of computational costs and the cost of sampling. It requires that we consider all possible alternatives to the one we propose to make sure that one does not dominate it. If we specify the particular alternatives we believe plausible then we can employ the traditional comparison of statistical methods in terms of relative efficiency, that is, by comparing the number of observations,

---

26. The difficulty for median-voter equilibrium in high-dimension preference aggregation (Plott 1967) will reappear later in our information aggregation account.

N_1, one procedure requires to match the precision of another procedure at a given N_2.[27] The efficiency question is the same in statistics as it is in economics: given the same input, what gives the highest output? The efficiency approach assumes, as is plausible in many important contexts, that the cost of observation and computation is invariant to the decision function itself.

Focusing on efficiency issues while keeping that of admissibility in the background, we will abstract from one advantage that goes to ordinary people. There are a lot of us. To conduct the argument in efficiency terms, we allow the experts' regression to have the same sample size (N) as the ordinary people regression. Since the standard errors of the regression techniques, in ideal cases, obey the $\sqrt{N}$ law, the reader can recompute these standard errors. Thus, in our experiments there are N = 5,000 observations seen by experts and 2 or 3 observations seen by each of 5,000 ordinary people. But what if the expert only sees 50 while our 5,000 ordinary people still have their limited ability? Obviously the standard errors of the expert's regression (in ideal cases) will fall by a factor of $\sqrt{100}$. In table 11.2, column 1, the ideal condition for the expert finds the standard error of the voters is twice the expert's. But what would this matter for the question of admissibility of ordinary people's decision making if, by taking account of the superior numbers of the ordinary people, we could inflate the standard error of the expert's model by a factor of 10?[28]

We propose to make one mathematical concept the foundation of our account, the device which is central to recent nonparametric thinking in statistics: an empirical probability distribution $\hat{F}$ which puts mass $1/n$ at each point $x_1, x_2 \ldots x_n$ (Efron 1979, 1981). Each point in the distribution may then be considered either as an observation or as an anecdote in a story. A model of these observations that satisfies the obligation of transparency is an estimate of location applied to all N (Andrews et al. 1972). The plural of anecdote—so runs the joke—is data.

---

27. Here is a textbook description of efficiency for a sample median relative to a mean at normality: "it means that in the normal case the median would require about $n = 157$ observations to achieve the accuracy that the mean achieves with $n = 100$" (Lehmann 1983, 360).

28. Robin Hanson is thanked for this paragraph.

A transparent model might or might not be an anecdote. The mean of the empirical distribution is generally not an observation. The most obvious example where a model is an anecdote is a median of the empirical distribution when N is odd.[29] The anecdotality of other order statistics is obvious. There is of course more to models than estimates of location. Consequently, we turn to consider regression estimation.

We define [ab], [bc], and [ac] in figure 11.1 as "anecdotal evidence," elements of a multidimensional empirical distribution. So defined, anecdotal evidence is collapsed (degenerate) regression. The problem with anecdotal evidence is that compared to the causal model, ordinary least squares or **OLS,** which gives a unique description of the relationship between X and Y, one can pick any of the combinations of anecdotes in a nontransparent fashion to obtain a wide range of relationships. Although OLS will not in general satisfy the anecdotal property, "elementary set methods" will (Farebrother 1997).

We consider the properties of centered anecdotal evidence—here [ac]—which we define as the median of anecdotal evidence (MAE). Such estimators as what we are calling the MAE have (1) desirable properties when the estimating model is mis-specified and (2) serve as a dependable starting point for an iterative procedure. One intuitively appealing method of determining this relationship is simply to find the slopes connecting [a, b], [b, c], and [a, c] and take an average of the three. Such was the first method of computing a regression in the 1750s by Roger Boscovich (Farebrother 1997).

We propose that [a, b], [b, c], and [a, c] are from the set of possible anecdotes from which ordinary people may draw. Each of these is a little story about X and Y; none of these involves an explicit recognition of randomness, and so each might appeal to those who view the world as a deterministic narrative rather than a causal model with a random component.[30] The only randomness will be that different people will

---

29. When N is even, selecting one of Stigler's (1999) "co-medians" at random would allow the median of the empirical distribution to satisfy the anecdotal property.

30. Though there were some exceptions that became increasingly important throughout the century (Peart 1995a), the prevailing view among nineteenth-century political economists and anthropologists was deterministic; see Hacking 1975.

have different stories to tell. Our method of information aggregation will be to select the median.

Representing experts is straightforward. Instead of taking phenomena at surface value the expert posits a causal model, an ordering relationship with fixed α and β.

$$y_i = \alpha + \beta x_i + \varepsilon_i$$

for which all $i = 1$. N of the empirical observations are subject. This too is illustrated in figure 11.1 as the most popular of the standard regression techniques, ordinary least squares. Only when the reliability of the expert's ability to intuit an ordering relationship has been called into question have elementary set methods been revived (Rousseeuw and Leroy 1987).

In terms of figure 11.1 we allow the ordinary person access to a randomly selected pair of points—[a, b], [b, c], or [a, c]—from which a slope can be deduced. The resulting slope will be the opinion of the voter on the informational issue.[31] When we generalize beyond the simple regression we allow the voter access to a randomly selected k-tuple from which the appropriate slopes can be determined. The political decision will be made on the basis of the median of the voter's opinion. In terms of the statistical literature the resulting technique is known as the median of pairwise slopes as extended beyond the context of simple regression with a random-selection algorithm.[32] This differs from Boscovich's 1750s approach mainly by the use of median instead of a subjectively trimmed mean and a random selection process instead of an exhaustive combinatorial approach.

---

31. What if—as will happen—the randomly selected pair of points is [a, a], [b, b], or [c, c]? In the first version of the simulation, we did not allow this to happen by checking the rank condition before we did the computations. The results reported later allow the singular or near singular results to be counted in the computations for the median. This results in slightly higher standard errors. Our current procedure raised a technical detail. Our implementation of *Shazam* (Whistler et al. 2001) computes the sample median by linear programming. Consequently, one must take care to skip over the occasional "Not a Number" returned by the compiler, an unnecessary step in a computation of the median by sorting. The same caution would be needed if the computations of the median were by a reweighted mean. Mosteller and Tukey (1977) discuss LAD computations in terms of a reweighted OLS regression.

32. Rousseeuw and Leroy (1987) systematically discuss the median of pairwise slopes in terms of the contribution of Henri Theil and later workers.

What properties might we expect of this procedure? Bias? Suppose that the expert's causal model is true—subject to a random disturbance, there is some simple linear relationship connecting the pairs (*k*-tuples). In that case the randomly selected pair (*k*-tuple) is an ordinary least squares equation with sample size K. Making the assumptions that (1) the median of the true errors is 0 and (2) these errors are independent of the right-hand side variables, least squares is a median-unbiased estimator (Levy 1992b). If the estimated slope is b_i then the median expectation $M(b_i) = \beta$, so the mean-expectation is $E(M(b_i)) = \beta$. Thus the process of information aggregation that we model as an election procedure with the decision made by the median voter will be unbiased.

Under what conditions is an elementary set method more efficient than the standard regression? Here we propose to think about the class of elementary set methods as an estimation procedure without the benefit of the standard regression causal model. The "causal model" has a particularly interesting status in standard regression theory: it is supposed to hold with probability of 1—the finite that we actually observe and the infinite that we might potentially observe. This allows us to think about the model as a constraint added to a maximum likelihood method. Since it is a constraint with probability 1, it can be imposed *without* reducing the joint probability; indeed, in a world of finite precision, a probability 1 constraint can *increase* the likelihood (Levy 1988a).

Thus, *when the model holds*, we cannot reduce the joint probability by imposing it even if we had a maximum likelihood method of elementary sets. As we do not have such a method at our disposal, imposing the constraint and employing standard regression methods that are maximum likelihood will generally result in a more efficient procedure.[33] Even if we had a method at our disposal—such a technique would presumably induce the model from the data instead of having the model imposed upon the data—it must be bounded by finite com-

---

33. The passage from "maximum likelihood" to "asymptotic efficient" is more troublesome than one might like to believe (Lehmann 1983, 403–27). Here is his review of the historical confusions: "Fisher's work was followed by a euphoric belief in the universal consistency and asymptotic efficiency of maximum likelihood estimators, at least in the iid case. The true situation was sorted out only gradually" (Lehmann 1983, 482).

putational capability that is less good than the probability 1 insight. Thus, we have reason to believe that a maximum likelihood elementary set method will be less precise than a standard maximum likelihood approach when the causal model has probability 1 status. In this case we have reason to believe that an elementary set method would be inefficient, since adding a model constraint cannot reduce the joint probability.

Although figure 11.1 supposes as a familiar illustration that the expert's method of estimating the causal model is ordinary least squares, the statement in the previous paragraph does not. There is no good reason to believe that least squares and its linear weighting of all elements of the empirical distribution would be the technique that would dominate an elementary set method. Indeed, least absolute deviations (LAD) at a heavy-tailed distribution might be arbitrarily more efficient than least squares.[34] Indeed, even if we suppose the causal model has probability 1 but allow the tail mass to get thicker we know that the efficiency of OLS falls relative to LAD and MAE. Our simulations consider the error distribution at the extremes of the t-distribution, normal to Cauchy. When the model holds, MAE will never become as efficient as LAD; LAD is an admissible alternative to maximum likelihood at a Cauchy that takes into account the probability 1 status of the model.[35]

But what if the probability 1 claim is simple vanity, and the causal model holds only frequently? The constraint that helped with the causal model was that probability 1 will hurt when it falls below this. We test this conjecture later.

MONTE CARLO EVIDENCE

Here we employ Galton's idea that we can move between estimation and an idealized election, and so we present the argument as if we held

---

34. Steve Stigler is thanked for emphasizing this point.

35. Andrews et al. (1972) compare the maximum likelihood estimate of location of a Cauchy with the median and find very little gain in precision to repay the computational complexity. The text presumes we can move from location to regression context.

an election to fit a regression. We consider a polity with 5,000 voters who form policy opinions by picking data points at random from 5,000 observations and computing pairwise slopes. Thus, each of the 5,000 voters in the first case is allowed to observe precisely 2 points. The decision is made by the median. This "regression by voting" is compared with two standard regression techniques instantiating causal models that our idealized experts might employ. The experts are allowed to observe all $N = 5,000$. The experts have at their disposal two techniques. First is the maximum likelihood procedure where the errors are independent normal, OLS. The second is LAD, not quite maximum likelihood when the errors are independent Cauchy. Each experiment is replicated 10,000 times. All computations are carried out in Shazam 9.0 (Whistler et al. 2001). The basis of the comparison between "expert as estimator" and "ordinary people as estimators" is the mean of the estimating procedure and the standard error of the estimates. We have turned the debate between friends of Plato and friends of Adam Smith (discussed at the start of this chapter) into a standard Monte Carlo study. We will have something to say about the bias of this procedure at the end of this section.

We study three conditions. In the first, the experts are exactly right: there is a causal model, and the errors are normally distributed. In the second, the experts are perhaps right: there is a causal model, and the errors are distributed Cauchy.[36] In the third case, the experts are very frequently right. The causal model holds 95 percent of the time, but 5 percent of the time the signs of the regression coefficients switch. And by happenstance when this 5 percent occurs, the population from which the right-hand side is drawn changes from a standard normal to a normal with a variance of 100. This third condition is that characterized by influential observations, the favorite drilling ground for those who would revive elementary set methods. The voting results in table 11.2 are taken by the median of pairwise slopes. The results are in accord with predictions when the causal model is true: voting is unbi-

---

36. The normality assumption in the context considered is inconsistent with the possibility of extending the model by exploratory data analysis (Levy 1999/2000). Other error distributions allow EDA.

ased and less efficient than the expert techniques (columns 1-1 and 1-2). When the model fails 5 percent of the time and these observations are influential, voting is the least biased and most efficient technique (column 1-3). This is the appeal of elementary set methods.[37]

TABLE 11.2.   Expert and Ordinary People, Simple Regression N = 5,000; Replications = 10,000

Truth	$p = 1: y = 1 + 2x + \varepsilon$ $\varepsilon \sim$ Normal	$p = 1: y = 1 + 2x + \varepsilon$ $\varepsilon \sim$ Cauchy	$p = .95: y = 1 + 2x + \varepsilon$ $p = .05: y = -1 - 2x + \varepsilon$ $\varepsilon \sim$ Normal
Expert belief OLS estimate β	$y = \alpha + \beta X + \varepsilon$ Mean = 2.00 Std. Dev. = 0.014	$y = \alpha + \beta X + \varepsilon$ Mean = 1.35 Std. Dev. = 72.2	$y = \alpha + \beta X + \varepsilon$ Mean = −1.36 Std. Dev. = 0.063
LAD estimate β	Mean = 2.00 Std. Dev. = 0.018	Mean = 2.00 Std. Dev. = 0.022	Mean = 1.38 Std. Dev. = 0.075
Voter belief Voting on β MAE	$y = \alpha + \beta X$ Mean = 2.00 Std. Dev. = 0.027	$y = \alpha + \beta X$ Mean = 2.00 Std. Dev. = 0.047	$y = \alpha + \beta X$ Mean = 1.84 Std. Dev. = 0.031
Experiment	1-1	1-2	1-3

The case of simple regression is just that—simple. The causal model, such as it is, is hardly something requiring deep reflection, so perhaps it is plausible that proverbial wisdom might encompass the idea that two variables are related. What about high-dimension problems where multiple regression techniques are required?

We now leave the simple regression context and consider multiple regression estimation. In table 11.3 we present the crux of the matter: a multivariable situation where both X and Z impact Y. We allow the

TABLE 11-3. Simple Regression in a Multivariate Context N = 5,000; Replications = 10,000

Truth	$Y = 1 + 2X + 3Z + \varepsilon$ X, Z independent	$Y = 1 + 2X + 3Z + \varepsilon$ X, Z correlated
Voter belief Voting on β MAE	$y = \alpha + \beta X$ Mean = 2.00 Std. Dev. = 0.08	$y = \alpha + \beta X$ Mean = 3.50 Std. Dev. = 0.047
Voter belief Voting on γ MAE	$y = \alpha + \gamma z$ Mean = 3.00 Std. Dev. = 0.06	$y = \alpha + \gamma z$ Mean = 5.00 Std. Dev. = 0.06
Experiment	2-1	2-3

---

37. Contrary to the suggestions in Rousseeuw and Leroy (1987), we find that LAD does not break down nearly as badly as OLS.

ordinary people insight into either X or Z but not both. In the first situation (column 2-1), X and Z are independent; in column 2-2, the variables are correlated, in particular $Z = .5X + .5Q$ where both X and Q are standard normal. ε is a standard normal in both cases.

What kind of proverbs might deal with higher dimensionality? Perhaps proverbial wisdom is embodied in parables, in stories, and what the causal modeler would call a dimension is handled by a character in a narration. We leave this for further study.

Returning to our competition (table 11.4), we allow ordinary people to pick a random 3-tuple and solve the equation. To give the expert more of a chance, we cut the probability of contamination in half (column 3-3). The results are easily predictable from table 11.2. Additional Monte Carlo simulations comparing combinations of cases—ignorant voters and arrogant modelers—give predictably mixed results.

TABLE 11.4.   Expert and Ordinary People, Multiple Regression N = 5,000; Replications = 10,000

Truth	$p = 1: y = 1 + 2x + 3z + \varepsilon$ $\varepsilon \sim$ Normal	$p = 1: y = 1 + 2x + 3z + \varepsilon$ $\varepsilon \sim$ Cauchy	$p = .975: y = 1 + 2x + 3z + \varepsilon$ $p = .025: y = -1 - 2x - 3z + \varepsilon$ $\varepsilon \sim$ Normal
Expert belief	$y = \alpha + \beta X + \gamma Z + \varepsilon$	$y = \alpha + \beta X + \gamma Z + \varepsilon$	$y = \alpha + \beta X + \gamma Z + \varepsilon$
OLS estimate β	Mean = 2.00	Mean = 7.93	Mean = −0.86
	Std. Dev. = 0.014	Std. Dev. = 492.6	Std. Dev. = 0.169
OLS estimate γ	Mean = 3.00	Mean = 2.41	Mean = −1.29
	Std. Dev. = 0.014	Std. Dev. = 292.6	Std. Dev. = 0.210
LAD estimate β	Mean = 2.00	Mean = 2.00	Mean = 1.85
	Std. Dev. = 0.018	Std. Dev. = 0.022	Std. Dev. = 0.035
LAD estimate γ	Mean = 3.00	Mean = 3.00	Mean = 2.78
	Std. Dev. = 0.018	Std. Dev. = 0.022	Std. Dev. = 0.036
Voter belief	$y = \alpha + \beta X + \gamma Z$	$y = \alpha + \beta X + \gamma Z$	$y = \alpha + \beta X + \gamma Z$
Voting on β MAE	Mean = 2.00	Mean = 2.00	Mean = 1.96
	Std. Dev. = 0.027	Std. Dev. = 0.052	Std. Dev. = 0.029
Voting on γ MAE	Mean = 3.00	Mean = 3.00	Mean = 2.94
	Std. Dev. = 0.027	Std. Dev. = 0.052	Std. Dev. = 0.029
Experiment	3-1	3-2	3-3

It is perhaps necessary to emphasize that our construction assumes that anecdotal evidence is randomly selected. It is easy to see what sort of bias can occur if the polity were, for one reason or another, to select among a few anecdotes as, for example, when a large number of people obtain their information about other races from the same visualization. Propaganda is presumably the selection, if not fabrication, of such anecdotes.

We note in conclusion that the technical context in which our theorized proverbs are more efficient than causal models is that of a random regime shift with influential observations. We have been concerned with explaining the *majority* of the data. Instead, however, one could recover a fit of the *minority* of data. Difference between majority and minority experience may explain the existence of "paired proverbs," proverbial advice that points in opposite directions (Simpson 1982, x). Indeed, the condition under which one might expect proverbial evidence to be efficient is precisely where one expected "paired proverbs."

We have interpreted Adam Smith's "universal experience" as "majority experience." The importance of this distinction is stressed by Charles Babbage in the opening words of *The Exposition of 1851*. We quote the passage at length, as it speaks to the many themes for which we are arguing:

> One of the most frequent sources of mistaken views in economical science, arises from confounding the nature of *universal* with that of *general principles*.
> *Universal principles*, such as the fact that every number ending with the figure five is itself divisible by five, rarely occur except in the exact sciences. Universal principles are those which do not admit of a single exception.
> *General principles* are those which are much more frequently obeyed than violated. Thus it is generally true that *men will be governed by what they believe to be their interest*. Yet it is certainly true that many individuals will at times be governed by their passions, others by their caprice, others by entirely benevolent motives: but all these classes together, form so small a portion of mankind, that it would be unsafe in any enquiry to neglect the great principle of self-interest. Notwithstanding, however, all the exceptions we may meet with, it is impossible to take any just views of society without the admission of general principles, and on such grounds they will be used in these pages. (Babbage 1851, 1)

"General principles" that "are much more frequently obeyed than violated" suggests an approach to estimation by counting instances.

Part V

CONCLUSION

XII

SYMPATHY AND THE PAST
Our "Stock in Dead People"
Reconsidered

After supper she got out her book and learned me about Moses and the
Bulrushers; and I was in a sweat to find out all about him; but by-and-by
she let it out that Moses had been dead a considerable long time; so
then I didn't care no more about him; because I don't take no
stock in dead people.
— Mark Twain, *Huckleberry Finn*

Our obligation to treat those distant from us as moral equals has been
a major theme of this book. We have argued that the classical economists' device of sympathy provides the source of moral obligation that
enables individuals to move from self- to group interests. To the extent
that we sympathize with others, we become willing to offer them something in return for something else. We have also argued that these
"things" may include material wealth, resources, or approbation, what
we might refer to today as respect.

We finish this book with two related claims. First, as sympathy may
extend to those who are currently far away from us, it may also extend
to those of the past. Second, there are benefits to be gained from
extending sympathy to those in the distant past. Therefore, we hold
that we are under obligation to the past as a matter of reciprocity. As we
offer this scholarship for reflection and correction, so too we reflect on
the works of scholars of the past, both learning and offering suggestions
for correction.

We make these claims knowing that sympathizing with those of the
distant past is not easy. They are, after all, mostly dead people, and as
Huckleberry Finn put it, "After supper she got out her book and
learned me about Moses and the Bulrushers; and I was in a sweat to

find out all about him; but by-and-by she let it out that Moses had been dead a considerable long time; so then I didn't care no more about him; because I don't take no stock in dead people" (1885, 626). Many economists echo Huck's sentiments, finding the past too lifeless for sympathy, filled with only dead and fruitless ideas.

Like the presumption that the "expert" knows best, this may be the final and most widespread form of hierarchy that persists today.[1] Today, we fail to sympathize with the past, because it is unfamiliar, and, *besides*, we need not give it attention because, today, we have outperformed the past. Our analysis reflects our superior capacity. This is nothing more than Smith's "vanity of the philosopher" applied across time.

We have made this claim repeatedly, that *direction* of sympathy was a key issue in the debates we study. And we have, we hope, made it clear that on this issue we follow the classical economists who held that sympathetic judgments were to be made by individuals, rather than directed by their "betters." We do not wish to contradict ourselves here, by suggesting that "we" know best how sympathy should be directed. But we have identified ourselves with the moral imperative of the Golden Rule. Our point here is simply that today we violate the principles of equality and reciprocity that Smith (and we authors) hold to when we dismiss the thinking and lives of the past without reflection. If we presuppose the past has nothing to teach us, and we do not share Galton's ability to simultaneously present his presuppositions and the counterexample, we are unlikely to find anything worthwhile in the past. And then we fail to learn.[2] We noted in chapter 6 that firewalls do not maintain themselves. One purpose of this book is to help maintain a firewall in the space of ideas by discussing the consequences which have followed from the assumption that surface differences among people reveal underlying differences among persons.

What is to be gained by extending sympathy to those in the past?

---

1. In fact, the presumption that we know best, today, is a form of the presumption that the expert knows best. Today, *we* are the experts, relative to the past.

2. We have made the case in more detail, that knowledge of the past is a public good, in Peart and Levy 2005.

While there are no material resources we can transfer to them, those who offer up respect for the past can learn surprising, sometimes useful insights. We began this project fully disagreeing with the arguments favoring hierarchy in Carlyle and others. Yet only through the course of working out the logic of the position of classical economists did we come to realize that analytical egalitarianism extends to the position of the "expert" relative to the subject, and then come to appreciate the full significance of the device of sympathy in their system.

In disagreement, as well, we learn. We are grateful to Carlyle for his instruction that the utilitarians with whom he dined proposed to make social decisions by counting heads. Our differences with the "science" of eugenics and our obligation to Galton's teaching that one can move smoothly from sampling theory to political theory ought to be equally transparent. We have fewer obligations to those we have found to have bent their doctrine in service of their desires, but even as we recognized such practices, we were led to consider the incentives faced by the "expert" and the subject more deeply.

This book has also presented evidence that the utilitarian economists of the past analyzed the social world through majoritarian devices. We have shown that such devices are rarely used today. The question that arises, of course, is Why? If there had been a discussion in which the comparative advantages of these traditional estimators of location—the median and the average—had been debated, then we would have nothing to contribute with our history but history. But such a discussion didn't take place. And once the profession moved from one estimator to the next, the memory of the older form of utilitarianism was lost.

The only text we have found that compares the merits of counting people and weighting benefits is Edgeworth's *Mathematical Psychics*. And, as we have seen, Edgeworth dismissed counting people as "unscientific," a pre-Darwinian prejudice, and proceeded to develop an alternative. Because we have lost the context of this debate, we now read it as a contest in which technical economics won over the nontechnical classical economists' methods. We entirely miss the context, examined earlier, in which the "science" Edgeworth relied on is the science of natural selection. In our account, such "science" was turned into a form of theology in which the voice of Providence purportedly trumped human happiness. Here, we are not concerned with Edgeworth's arguments. We have said enough on that already. Instead, our point is that a literature that follows Edgeworth without awareness of the alternatives, or perhaps even the consequences, is at best uninformed.

The past is distant from us. We can't touch or experience it directly. We have to imagine it, and, as Adam Smith suggested, we have to learn how to imagine. We suspect it is no coincidence that by the time his story ends Huck has learned to judge distance better. He learns how to sympathize and discovers that an escaped slave can be fully human.[3] And he comes to learn that if the choice is between personal interest and the obligations of reciprocity,[4] J. S. Mill had it right.

---

3. "And got to thinking over our trip down the river; and I see Jim before me, all the time, in the day and in the night-time, sometimes moonlight, sometimes storms, and we a floating along, talking, and singing, and laughing. But somehow I couldn't seem to strike no places to harden me against him, but only the other kind. I'd see him standing my watch on top of his'n, stead of calling me, so I could go on sleeping; and see him how glad he was when I come back out of the fog; and when I come to him again in the swamp, up there where the feud was; and such-like times; and would always call me honey, and pet me, and do everything he could think of for me, and how good he always was; and at last I struck the time I saved him by telling the men we had small-pox aboard, and he was so grateful, and said I was the best friend old Jim ever had in the world, and the *only* one he's got now" (Twain, 1885, 834).

4. "So I was full of trouble, full as I could be; and didn't know what to do. At last I had an idea; and I says, I'll go and write the letter—and *then* see if I can pray. Why, it was astonishing, the way I felt as light as a feather right straight off, and my troubles all gone. So I got a piece of paper and a pencil, all glad and excited, and set down and wrote:

Miss Watson, your runaway nigger Jim is down here two mile below Pikesville and Mr. Phelps has got him and he will give him up for the reward if you send.
          HUCK FINN.

"I felt good and all washed clean of sin for the first time I had ever felt so in my life, and I knowed I could pray now. But I didn't do it straight off, but laid the paper down and set there thinking—thinking how good it was all this happened so, and how near I come to being lost and going to hell. And went on thinking . . . .

"It was a close place. I took it up, and held it in my hand. I was a trembling, because I'd got to decide, forever, betwixt two things, and I knowed it. I studied a minute, sort of holding my breath, and then says to myself:

"'All right, then, I'll *go* to hell'—and tore it up.

"It was awful thoughts, and awful words, but they was said. And I let them stay said; and never thought no more about reforming. I shoved the whole thing out of my head; and said I would take up wickedness again, which was in my line, being brung up to it, and the other warn't" (1885, 834–35).

"If, instead of the 'glad tidings' that there exists a Being in whom all the excellences which the highest human mind can conceive, exists in a degree inconceivable to us, I am informed that the world is ruled by a being whose attributes are infinite, but what they are we cannot learn, nor what the principles of his government, except that 'the highest human morality which we are capable of conceiving' does not sanction them; convince me of it, and I will bear my fate as I may. But when I am told that I must believe this, and at the same time call this being by the names which express and affirm the highest theological morality, I say in plain terms that I will not. Whatever power such a being may have over me, there is one thing which he shall not do: he shall not compel me to worship him. I will call no being good, who is not what I mean when I apply that epithet to my fellow-creatures; and if such a being can sentence me to hell for not so calling him, to hell I will go" (1865, 103).

POSTSCRIPT:
A LETTER FROM M. ALI KHAN

Three days after the copyedited manuscript arrived from our publishers, we received this email from our friend and colleague, Ali Khan. With his kind permission, we include Ali's message here. We find his story to be a powerful reminder of our theme, announced in the *preface* to this volume: "difference" is rarely unsigned, and generally signifies "inferiority" or some such negative characteristic.

Dear Colleagues,

    . . . I write to report to you a somewhat unpleasant episode on a recent trip to [. . .].

The occasion was a Conference on Globalization . . .

However, before my lecture, there was a presentation by an Inspector [. . .] from Homeland Security who began by saying that his Department had given 13 million dollars to [the university] and 18 million to [another university], and whereas academics were "generally cooperative," he was not getting as much cooperation from them as he would like. He exhorted us to "integrate into the system—integrate with the good people." And then he recounted three "heroic" episodes of how his colleagues had subdued recalcitrant academics bringing in samples without licences. And he explained what defending this country really means—"they could not afford to make a single mistake".

After the Inspector's talk, [the next speaker] explained the importance of diversity and that of foreign students to the universities in the US—it was not simply a matter of losing tuition revenue. The Inspector's reply was that whereas he understood this, he was "concerned about those foreign students who do not go back and stay here—it is they we have to watch." The fact that the next talk was being given by someone originally (and perhaps identifiably) from Pakistan, and that he was to be introduced by someone originally from Iran and that the Dean of the Center to whom he (or rather his Department) had given 13 million dollars, was originally from South Korea, did not bother him in the least.

I opened my talk with my hand raised and with the statement that I was one of those who did not go back, that my head was reeling with what I had heard, that I would discard the official CV and begin with a biodata for him alone to put his mind at rest, that I had not "jumped" at the offer of US citizenship and had reflected for several years before accepting it, that I had lived more than three fifth's of my life in this country, that I was teaching two courses on integration this semester (though not of the kind that he would understand), that I had married a fellow graduate student from Lebanon etc. etc. Since I discarded my notes and spoke extemporaneously, I do not remember what I said other than the talk revolved on Hayek and on Inspector [. . .] himself, in particular on Hayek's 1944 chapter titled "Security and Freedom", that it was very well received, and that with all the laughs, it all seemed good fun. After the talk, the Vice-President of the University came up, and very warmly told me how much she had enjoyed my talk. But I could not reconcile her statements with the fact that she had also been nodding and smiling at [the Inspector's] heroic (though I suspect one-sided) narratives. But several others who came up and thanked me were obviously sincere, and made me feel at home.

The last talk was given by Professor [. . .], a dry midwesterner, who then followed my format, and began by talking of how he "also fell in love with a Brazilian—his wife of forty years" and about his three children (one of them adopted), and what each of them were doing, and how the US University system was one of the country's great treasures etc. etc.

However, the next morning the fun seemed to have gone out of it—I was scared, and also somewhat angry that however interpreted, I had been gratuitously put in a position that called on me to defend myself and my attachment to this country—perhaps not gratuitously but certainly on the basis of national origin, and perhaps not that alone. But I suspect this is also what diversity is all about.

Best, Ali

APPENDICES: GALTON'S TWO PAPERS ON VOTING AS ROBUST ESTIMATION

1. INTRODUCTION

Why has it taken so long for theorists of politics to see the relationship between voting and estimation?[1] This good question was asked by Bassett and Persky (1999: 299) when they took the concept of robustness from statistical theory and applied it usefully to voting procedures.[2] Their problem is even more complicated than they propose. The relationship between voting and robust estimation was explained carefully in two 1907 contributions to *Nature* by Galton.

It is easy to believe that important contributions can be overlooked when their author is outside the research community or they are published in obscure journals.[3] But two 1907 articles by Galton in *Nature*?[4] How is it possible for a contribution to be more centrally located in a discussion? Karl Pearson who describes them carefully suggests that Galton published them in *Nature* for "immediate attention . . . at the cost of later oblivion."[5] Is the difficulty here that Galton is simply sixty years ahead of the statistical literature?[6] He evidently uses a technique—an influence curve—which would not become commonplace until the 1970s to make his case against the sample mean and in favor of the sample median.[7]

We have benefitted from conversation and correspondence with Gib Bassett, Roger Congleton, Stephen Stigler and thank them and James Buchanan for their enthusiastic support. Nicola Tynan found several errors.

2. WHY A MEDIAN?

Galton considers a group deciding upon an amount where instead of *preferences*, each member is supposed to possess an *estimate of* the true amount. What estimate is appropriate for the group? Surely not the sample mean:

> That conclusion is clearly *not* the *average of* all the estimates, which would give a voting power to "cranks" in proportion to their crankiness. One absurdly large or small estimate would leave a greater impress on the result than one of reasonable amount, and the more an estimate diverges from the bulk of the rest, the more influence would it exert.[8]

In modern terms, even though the sample mean has ideal properties at normality because it has an unbounded influence curve—the influence of "cranks"—is "in proportion to their crankiness"—it is far too dangerous to employ for serious purposes, i.e., those questions involving real money. Consider on the contrary the nice properties of the sample median. Majority rule is the median estimate:

> I wish to point out that the estimate to which least objection can be raised is the *middlemost* estimate, the number of votes that it is too high being exactly balanced by the number of votes that it is too low. Every other estimate is condemned by a majority of voters as being either too high or too low, the middlemost alone escaping this condemnation.

In the next contribution Galton introduces a device which Stigler (1977) would make famous: judging the properties of an estimator by how it works with real data. While Stigler worked within an austere context—estimators' ability to recover the true parameters of the physical world from experimental data—Galton used a rather homey example—how the median guess of 787 contestants paying a 6d entrance fee recovered the weight of an ox. The median guess was 0.8% high. Galton finds the distribution of guesses strikingly abnormal.

In his later *Memories* (1908: 281) this founder of eugenics admits to an egalitarian conclusion arising from these papers:

> The result seems more creditable to the trustworthiness of a democratic judgment than might have been expected. But the proportion of the vot-

ers who were practised in judging weights undoubtedly surpassed that of the voters in ordinary elections who are versed in politics.[9]

I endeavoured in the memoirs just mentioned, to show the appropriateness of utilising the *Median* vote in Councils and in Juries, whenever they have to consider money questions. Each juryman has his own view of what the sum should be. I will suppose each of them to be written down. The best interpretation of their collective view is to my mind *certainly not* the average, because the wider the deviation of an individual member from the average, of the rest, the more largely would it effect the result. In short, unwisdom is given greater weight than wisdom. In all cases in which one vote is supposed to have one value, the median value *must* be the truest representative of the whole, because any other value would be negatived if put to the vote.

3. "IMMEDIATE ATTENTION"

Galton was 85 when he wrote these papers. Suppose that Pearson was right about the consequence of publishing in *Nature* and further supposing that Galton himself recognized the consequence, what would require immediate attention? First, the title "Vox Populi" recalls Galton's Carlylean doctrine of the foolishness of majority rule democracy. This is Galton from 1872:

> I propose, in these pages, to discuss a curious and apparently anomalous group of base moral instincts and intellectual deficiencies, to trace their analogies in the world of brutes, and to examine the conditions, through which they have been evolved. I speak of the slavish aptitudes, from the leaders of men, and the heroes and the prophets, are exempt, but which are irrepressible elements in the disposition of average men. I refer to the natural tendency of the vast majority of our race to shrink from the responsibility of standing and acting alone, to their exaltation of the *vox populi*, even when they know it to be the utterance of a mob of nobodies, into the *vox Dei*, to their willing servitude to tradition, authority and custom. (Quoted in Pearson [1924: 72]).

The immediate context seems to be Galton's reflection upon just how eugenic policy might be made in a nonhierarchical society:

> Society would be very dull if every man resembled the highly estimable Marcus Aurelius or Adam Bede. The aim of eugenics is to represent

each class or sect by its best specimens; that done, to leave them to work out their common civilization in their own way.

A considerable list of qualities can easily be compiled that nearly everyone except "cranks" would take into account when picking out the best specimens of his class.[10]

Is that which required "immediate attention" a recantation of Galton's former views? If so it is harder to think of a more wonderful display of intellectual integrity.

Without further ado, Galton from 1907.

Notes

1. The median voter theory proposed in Downs (1957) is supposed to apply a *distribution* of voters. The median is a parameter—the population median—not an estimate of a parameter. A search via JSTOR on Downs and median voter and Galton yield nothing.

2. The reader of Bassett and Persky (1999) might get the impression that they wrote in knowledge of Levy 1989. They did not. Their results were completely independent.

3. Stigler (1973) appeals to these facts to explain plausibly why Newcomb's and Daniell's contributions to robust estimation were neglected.

4. Galton (1908: 280–81) gives an account of these contributions in non-technical terms.

5. Pearson (1924, 400): *"The Median.* There are a number of short papers by Galton which are, perhaps, most suitably dealt with in this chapter. A good many of them appeared in the pages of *Nature,* a ready means of attracting immediate attention, but too often at the cost of later oblivion. Several of these papers concern really important points, which have, since their publication, been again and again overlooked." An 1890 *Nature* article "Dice for Statistical Experiments" is reprinted by Stigler (1999, 152–55) along with extensive commentary.

6. Stigler (1999, 151): "Francis Galton (1822–1911) was such a fertile source of statistical ideas over his long life that it should not cause surprise that he contributed to simulation as well."

7. Influence curves play a critical role in the motivation of Andrews et al. (1972).

8. What perhaps compounds the difficulties of seeing the point is that Galton has somehow obtained a reputation of not deviating from the assumption of normality. Porter (1986, 139): "Galton remained one of the most loyal partisans of the error law throughout his life. Even though he was among the first to propose an alternative distribution, the so-called log-normal, in conjunction with a certain class of data, that formula involved no rejection of the conventional error law." Porter does not respond to pre-emptive counterexamples to this claim for such contexts as would justify the use of sample median,

Stigler (1973, 875–76). Galton (1889: 409) uses the fact of outliers to argue against use of the range as an estimator of scale—"The difference between the extreme ends of a marshaled series is no proper measure of the variety of the men who compose it. However few may be the objects in the series, it is always possible that a giant or a dwarf, so to speak, may be included among them. The presence of either would mislead as to the range of variety likely to be found in another equally numerous sample taken from the same group." His argument in favor of the *median deviation*, instead of the mean deviation, is found on the following page. This seems clear recognition of the importance of outliers in selecting a sensible estimator of scale.

     9. Might one—without the slightest disrespect—point out that there will also be more voters in elections than in ox judgment? Robin Hanson helped here in another context.

     10. Galton (1904: 2). This is the only paper in JSTOR written by Galton which contains the word "crank." The search was conducted May 26, 2000.

References

Andrews, D. F., Bickel, P. J., Hampel, F. R., Huber, P. J., Rogers, W. H. and Tukey, J. W. (1972). *Robust estimates of location*. Princeton: Princeton University Press.

Bassett, G. Jr. and Persky, R. (1999). Robust voting. *Public Choice* 99: 299–310.

Downs, A. (1957). *An economic theory of democracy*. New York: Harper & Row.

Galton, F. (1889). Address delivered at the anniversary meeting of the Anthropological Institute of Great Britain and Ireland, January 22nd, 1889. *Journal of the Anthropological Institute of Great Britain and Ireland* 18: 401–419.

Galton, F. (1904). Eugenics: Its definition, scope, and aims. *American Journal of Sociology* 10: 1–25.

Galton, F. (1907a). One vote, one value. *Nature* 75: 414.

Galton, F. (1907b). *Vox Populi. Nature* 75: 450–451.

Galton, F. (1908). *Memories of my life*. London: Methuen & Co.

Levy, D. M. (1989). The statistical basis of Athenian-American constitutional theory. *Journal of Legal Studies* 18: 79–103.

Pearson, K. (1924) *The life, labours and letters of Francis Galton*. Cambridge: Cambridge University Press.

Porter, T. M. (1986). *The rise of statistical thinking; 1820–1900*. Princeton: Princeton University Press.

Stigler, S.M. (1973). Simon Newcomb, Percy Daniell, and the history of robust estimation 1885–1920. *Journal of the American Statistical Association* 68: 872–79.

Stigler, S.M. (1977). Do robust estimators work with real data? *Annals of Statistics* 5: 1055–98.

Stigler, S.M. (1999). *Statistics on the table: The history of statistical concepts and methods*. Cambridge: Harvard University Press.

One vote, one value

A certain class of problems do not as yet appear to be solved according to scientific rules, though they are of much importance and of frequent recurrence. Two examples will suffice. (1) A jury has to assess damages. (2) The council of a society has to fix on a sum of money, suitable for some particular purpose. Each voter, whether of the jury or of the council, has equal authority with each of his colleagues. How can the right conclusion be reached, considering that there may be as many different estimates as there are members? That conclusion is clearly *not* the *average* of all the estimates, which would give a voting power to "cranks" in proportion to their crankiness. One absurdly large or small estimate would leave a greater impress on the result than one of reasonable amount, and the more an estimate diverges from the bulk of the rest, the more influence would it exert. I wish to point out that the estimate to which least objection can be raised is the *middlemost* estimate, the number of votes that it is too high being exactly balanced by the number of votes that it is too low. Every other estimate is condemned by a majority of voters as being either too high or too low, the middlemost alone escaping this condemnation. The number of voters may be odd or even. If odd, there is one middlemost value: thus in 11 votes the middlemost is the 6th; in 99 votes the middlemost is the 50th. If the number of voters be even, there are two middlemost values, the mean of which must be taken; thus in 12 votes the middlemost lies between the 6th and the 7th; in 100 votes between the 50th and the 51st. Generally, in $2n - 1$ votes the middlemost is the nth; in $2n$ votes it lies between the nth and the $(n + 1)$th.

I suggest that the process for a jury on their retirement should be (1) to discuss and interchange views; (2) for each juryman to write his own independent estimate on a separate slip of paper; (3) for the foreman to arrange the slips in the order of the values written on them; (4) to take the average of the 6th and 7th as the verdict, which might be finally approved as a substantive proposition. Similarly as regards the resolutions of councils, having regard to the above ($2n - 1$) and $2n$ remarks.

—Francis Galton

Vox populi

In these democratic days, any investigation into the trustworthiness and peculiarities of popular judgments is of interest. The material about to be discussed refers to a small matter, but is much to the point.

A weight-judging competition was carried on at the annual show of the West of England Fat Stock and Poultry Exhibition recently held at Plymouth. A fat ox having been selected, competitors bought stamped and numbered cards, for 6d., each, on which to inscribe their respective names, addresses, and estimates of what the ox would weigh after it had been slaughtered and "dressed." Those who guessed most successfully received prizes. About 800 tickets were issued, which were kindly lent me for examination after they had fulfilled their immediate purpose. These afforded excellent material. The judgments were unbiassed by passion and uninfluenced by oratory and the like. The sixpenny fee deterred practical joking, and the hope of a prize and the joy of competition promoted each competitor to do his best. The competitors included butchers and farmers, some of whom were highly expert in judging the weight of cattle; others were probably guided by such information as they might pick up, and by their own fancies. The average competitor was probably as well fitted for making a just estimate of the dressed weight of the ox, as an average voter is of judging the merits of most political issues on which he votes, and the variety among the voters to judge justly was probably much the same in either case.

After weeding thirteen cards out of the collection, as being defective or illegible, there remained 787 for discussion. I arrayed [see Table 1] them in order of the magnitudes of the estimates, and converted the cwt., quartors, and lbs. in which they were made, into lbs., under which form they will be treated.

According to the democratic principle of "one vote one value," the middlemost estimate expresses the vox populi, every other estimate being condemned as too low or too high by a majority of the voters (for fuller explanation see "One vote, one value," Nature, February 28, p. 414). Now the middlemost estimate is 1207 lb., and the weight of the dressed ox proved to be 1198 lb.; so the vox populi was in this case 9 lb., or o.8 percent, of the whole weight too high. The distribution of the estimates about their middlemost value was of the usual type, so far that they clustered closely in its neighborhood and because rapidly more sparse as the distance from it increased [Diagram 1 found on p. 281]. But they were not scattered symmetrically. One quarter of them deviated more than 45 lb. above the middlemost (3.7 percent.), and another quarter deviated more than 29 lb., below it (2.4 percent.), therefore the range of the two middle quarters, that is, of the middlemost half, lay within those limits. It would be an equal chance that the estimate written on any card picked at random out of the collection lay within or without those limits. In other words, the "probable error" of a single observation may be reckoned as ½ (45+29), or 37 lb. (3.1 percent). Taking this for the p.e. of the normal curve that is best adapted for comparison with the observed values, the results are obtained

TABLE 1.   Distribution of the estimates of the dressed weight of a particular living ox, made by 787 different persons

		Centiles		
Degree of the length of array 0°–100°	Estimates in lbs.	Observed deviates from 1207 lbs.	Normal p.e. = 37	Excess of observed over normal
°5	1074	−133	−90	+43
10	1109	−98	−70	+28
15	1126	−81	−57	+24
20	1148	−59	−46	+13
q_1 25	1162	−45	−37	+8
30	1174	−33	−29	+4
35	1181	−26	−21	+5
40	1188	−19	−14	+5
45	1197	−10	−7	+3
m 50	1207	0	0	0
55	1214	+7	+7	0
60	1219	+12	+14	−2
65	1225	+18	+21	−3
70	1230	+23	+29	−6
q_3 75	1236	+29	+37	−8
80	1243	+36	+46	−10
85	1254	+47	+57	−10
90	1267	+52	+70	−18
95	1293	+86	+90	−4

q_1, q_3, the first and third quartiles, stand at 25° and 75° respectively.
m, the median or middlemost value stands at 50°.
The dressed weight proved to be 1198 lbs.

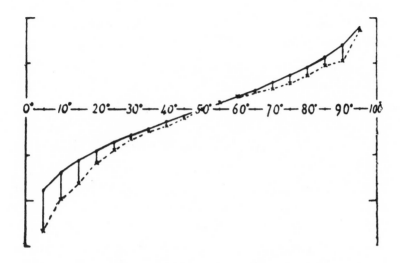

Diagram 1. From the tabular values.
The continuous line is the normal curve with p.e. = 37.
The broken line is drawn from the observations.
The lines connecting them show the differences between the observed and the normal.

which appear in above table, and graphically in the diagram [see Diagram 1].

The abnormality of the distribution of the estimates now becomes manifest, and is of this kind. The competitors may be imagined to have erred *normally* in the first instance, and then to have magnified all errors that were negative and to have minified all those that were positive. The lower half of the "observed" curve agrees for a large part of its range with a normal curve having the p.e. = 45, and the upper half with one having its p.e. = 29. I have not sufficient knowledge of the mental methods followed by those who judge weights to offer a useful opinion as to the cause of this curious anomaly. It is partly a psychological question, in answering which the various psychophysical investigations of Fechner and others would have to be taken into account. Also the anomaly may be partly due to the use of a *small* variety of different methods, or formulae, so that the estimates are not homogeneous in that respect.

It appears then, in this particular instance, that the *vox populi* is correct to within 1 percent of the real value, and that the individual estimates are abnormally distributed in such a way that it is an equal chance whether one of them, selected at random, falls within or without the limits of −3.7 percent. and +2.4 percent of their middlemost value.

This result is, I think, more creditable to the trustworthiness of a democratic judgment than might have been expected.

The authorities of the more important cattle shows might do service to statistics if they made a practice of preserving the sets of cards of this description, that they may obtain on future occasions, and loaned them under proper restrictions, as these have been, for statistical discussion. The fact of the cards being numbered makes it possible to ascertain whether any given set is complete.

—Francis Galton

BIBLIOGRAPHY

Archives
Fraser Collection. Papers of John Fraser. University of Liverpool Library.

Periodicals
The Anti-Slavery Reporter, under the Sanction of the British and Foreign Anti-Slavery Society. London.
The Critical Review or, Annals of Literature. 3d ser. Ed. Richard Fellowes. London.
Punch, London.
Smoke Room Booklets. Cope's Tobacco Plant. Liverpool.

References
Aldrich, Mark. 1975. "Capital Theory and Racism: From Laissez-Faire to the Eugenics Movement in the Career of Irving Fisher." *Review of Radical Political Economics* 7:33–42.
Allen, Robert Loring. 1993. *Irving Fisher: A Biography.* Cambridge, Mass., and Oxford, UK: Blackwell.
American Statistical Association. 2000. "Ethical Guidelines for Statistical Practice." Alexandria, VA: American Statistical Association.
Andrews, D. F., P. J. Bickel, F. R. Hampel, P. J. Huber, W. H. Rogers, and J. W. Tukey. 1972. *Robust Estimates of Location.* Princeton: Princeton University Press.
"Anthropological News: Death of the Best Man in England." 1870. *Anthropological Review* 8:97.
"Anthropology at the British Association." 1863. *Anthropological Review* 1:379–89.
Appletons'. 1873. "Caricature in Politics." *Appletons'* 9, no. 22 (June): 748–50.
Appletons'. 1878. "Ruskin's 'Fors Clavigera.'" *Appletons'* 5, no. 1 (July): 58–65.
Appletons'. 1879. "The Literature of the Victorian Reign." *Appletons'* 6, no. 36 (June): 511–13.
Arnstein, Walter L. [1965] 1983. *The Bradlaugh Case: Atheism, Sex, and Politics among the Later Victorians.* Columbia: University of Missouri Press.

Arrow, Kenneth J. 1963. *Social Choice and Individual Values.* 2d ed. New Haven: Yale University Press.

Arrow, Kenneth J. 1972. "The Theory of Discrimination." In *Discrimination in Labor Markets,* ed. Orley Ashenfelter and Albert Rees, 3–33. Princeton: Princeton University Press.

Arrow, Kenneth J. 1977. "Extended Sympathy and the Possibility of Social Choice." *American Economic Review* 67 (February): 219–25.

Babbage, Charles. [1851] 1989. *The Exposition of 1851.* Volume 10 of *The Works of Charles Babbage.* Ed. Martin Campbell-Kelly. New York: New York University Press.

Bagehot, Walter. 1876. "The Postulates of English Political Economy." *Fortnightly Review,* o.s., 21 (n.s., 15), 1:215–42.

Bagehot, Walter. 1880. *Economic Studies.* Ed. Richard Holt Hutton. London: Longmans, Green.

Bagehot, Walter. 1885. *The Postulates of English Political Economy.* Introduction by Alfred Marshall. Student's edition. New York and London: G. P. Putnam's Sons.

Banton, Michael. 1977. *The Idea of Race.* London: Tavistock.

Barkin, Kenneth. 1969. "Adolf Wagner and German Industrial Development." *Journal of Modern History* 41 (June): 144–59.

Barrington, Mrs. Russell, ed. 1933. *The Love-letters of Walter Bagehot and Eliza Wilson, Written from 10 November, 1857 to 23 April, 1858.* London: Faber and Faber.

Bassett, Gilbert, Jr., and Joseph Persky. 1999. "Robust Voting." *Public Choice* 99:299–310.

Bateman, Bradley W. 2003. "Race, Intellectual History, and American Economics: A Prolegomenon to the Past." *History of Political Economy* 35 (winter): 713–30.

Bator, Francis. 1957. "The Simple Analytics of Welfare Maximization." *American Economic Review* 47 (March): 22–59.

Becker, Gary S. 1960. "An Economic Analysis of Fertility." In *Demographic and Economic Change in Developed Countries.* Universities-National Bureau Conference Series II. Princeton, N.J.: Princeton University Press.

Becker, Gary S., and H. Greg Lewis. 1973. "On the Interaction between the Quantity and Quality of Children." *Journal of Political Economy* 81:S279–88.

Beddoe, John. 1870. "Anthropology and Politics: Kelts and Saxons." *Anthropological Review* 8:211–13.

Bennett, Charles H., and Robert B. Brough. 1860. *Shadow and Substance.* London: W. Kent.

Black, Duncan. 1958. *Theory of Committees and Elections.* Cambridge: Cambridge University Press.

Black, Edwin. 2003. *War against the Weak: Eugenics and America's Campaign to Create a Master Race.* New York: Four Walls Eight Windows.

Blake, Carter. 1870. Discussion of John Beddoe, "On the Kelts of Ireland." *Journal of the Anthropological Society of London*, vol. 8. London: Longmans, Green. clxxxii–clxxxiii.

Blyden, Edward Wilmot. 1876. "Christianity and the Negro Race. — By a Negro." *Fraser's Magazine*, n.s., 13:554–68.

Blyden, Edward Wilmot. 1888. *Christianity, Islam, and the Negro Race*. 2d ed. London: W. B. Whittingham.

Blyden, Edward Wilmot. 1976. *Selected Works of Dr. Edward Wilmot Blyden*. Ed. Willie A. Givens. Robertsport, Liberia: Tubman Center of African Culture.

Blyden, Edward Wilmot. 1978. *Selected Letters of Edward Wilmot Blyden*. Ed. Hollis R. Lynch. Millwood, N.Y.: KTO Press.

Brown, Ford K. 1961. *Fathers of the Victorians: The Age of Wilberforce*. Cambridge: Cambridge University Press.

Buchanan, J. M., and G. Tullock. 1962. *The Calculus of Consent: Logical Foundations of Constitutional Democracy*. Ann Arbor: University of Michigan Press.

Cairnes, J. E. 1862. *The Slave Power*. London: Parker, Son, and Bourn.

Cairnes, J. E. 1863. *Who Are the Canters?* London: Published for the London Ladies' Emancipation Society by Emily Faithfull.

Cairnes, [J. E.]. 1865. "The Negro Suffrage." *Macmillan's Magazine* 12:334–43.

Carlson, Elof Axel. 2001. *The Unfit: A History of a Bad Idea*. Cold Spring Harbor, N.Y.: Cold Spring Harbor Laboratory Press.

Carlyle, Thomas. [1844] 1965. *Past and Present*. Ed. Richard D. Altick. Boston: Houghton Mifflin.

[Carlyle, Thomas]. "Negro Question." 1849. "Occasional Discourse on the Negro Question." *Fraser's Magazine for Town and Country* 40:670–79.

Carlyle, Thomas. 1850. *Latter-Day Pamphlets*. London: Chapman and Hall.

Carlyle, Thomas. 1867. *Shooting Niagara: And After?* London: Chapman and Hall.

Cartwright, Nancy. 1993. "How We Relate Theory to Observation." In *World Changes: Thomas Kuhn and the Nature of Science*, ed. Paul Horwich. Cambridge, Mass.: A Bradford Book, MIT Press.

Cherry, Robert. 1976. "Racial Thought and the Early Economics Profession." *Review of Social Economy* 34, no. 2:147–62. Reprinted in *Economics and Discrimination*, ed. William Darity Jr., 17–32. Brookfield, Vt.: Edward Elgar, 1995.

Christianson, Scott. 2003. "Bad Seed or Bad Science: The Story of the Notorious Jukes Family." *New York Times*, 8 February, B9–B11.

Clark, William. 1901. "Kingsley's Water Babies." *Kindergarten Review* 12:115–18.

Colander, David. 2001. *The Lost Art of Economics: Essays on Economics and the Economics Profession*. Cheltenham, UK: Edward Elgar.

Colander, David, Robert E. Prasch, and Falguni A. Sheth, eds. 2004. *Race, Liberalism, and Economics*. Ann Arbor: University of Michigan Press.

Coleman, William Oliver. 2002. *Economics and Its Enemies: Two Centuries of Anti-Economics*. London: Palgrave Macmillan.

Collard, David. 1996. "Pigou and Future Generations: A Cambridge Tradition." *Cambridge Journal of Economics* 20 (September): 585–97.

Commons, J. R. 1916. *Races and Immigration in America*. New York: Macmillan.

Cooper, Brian. 1994. "What Does Adolphe Quetelet Have to Do with Classical Political Economy." Paper presented at History of Economics Society meeting.

[*Cope's Key*]. 1878. *The Plenipotent Key to Cope's Correct Card of the Peerless Pilgrimage to Saint Nicotine of the Holy Herb: &c*. Liverpool: Cope's Tobacco Plant.

Cot, Annie. 2003. "Irving Fisher and the 'Science' of Heredity." Eastern Economic Association. New York.

Curtis, L. P., Jr. 1968. *Anglo-Saxons and Celts*. Bridgeport: Conference on British Studies at the University of Bridgeport.

Curtis, L. P., Jr. 1997. *Apes and Angels: The Irishman in Victorian Caricature*. Rev. ed. Washington: Smithsonian Institution Press.

D'Arcy, William. 1947. *The Fenian Movement in the United States, 1858–1886*. Washington, D.C.: Catholic University of America Press.

Darity, William, Jr. 1995. "Introduction." *Economics and Discrimination*. Ed. William Darity Jr. Brookfield, Vt.: Edward Elgar.

Darwin, Charles. [1859] 1964. *On the Origin of Species by Means of Natural Selection, or the Preservation of Favoured Races in the Struggle for Life*. Introduction by Ernst Mayr. Cambridge, Mass.: Harvard University Press.

Darwin, Charles. *Descent*. [1871] 1989. *The Descent of Man, and Selection in Relation to Sex*. Vols. 21–22 of *The Works of Charles Darwin*, ed. Paul H. Barrett and R. B. Freeman. New York: New York University Press.

[Darwin, Erasmus]. 1791. *The Botanic Garden: A Poem in Two Parts*. London: J. Johnson.

Darwin, Erasmus. [1803] 1978. *The Golden Age. The Temple of Nature or, The Origin of Society*. New York and London: Garland.

Darwin, Leonard. 1916a. "On the Statistical Studies Needed after the War in Connection with Eugenics." *Journal of the Royal Statistical Society* 79, no. 2 (March): 159–88.

Darwin, Leonard. 1916b. "Quality Not Quantity." *Eugenics Review* (April): 297–321.

Darwin, Leonard. 1919. "Eugenics in Relation to Economics and Statistics." *Journal of the Royal Statistical Society* 82, no. 1 (January): 1–27, with discussion by E. W. Macbride, 30–31.

Darwin, Leonard. 1921. "The Aims and Methods of Eugenical Societies." *Science* 54 (7 October): 313–23.

Darwin, Leonard. 1926. *The Need for Eugenic Reform*. London: John Murray.

Denman, Lord. 1853. *Uncle Tom's Cabin, Bleak House, Slavery and Slave Trade*. 2d ed. London. Longman, Brown, Green, and Longmans.

Desmond, Adrian. 1994. *Huxley: The Devil's Disciple*. London: M. Joseph.

Dickens, Charles. [1852–53] 1977. *Bleak House*. Ed. George Ford and Sylvère Monod. New York. W. W. Norton.

Dictionary of National Biography on CD-ROM. DNB. 1997. Version 1.1. Oxford: Oxford University Press.

Dimand, Robert. 2003. "Fisher, Rae, Senior and the Shadow of the 'Other': Eugenics and Racial Differences in Capital Theory." Eastern Economic Association. New York.

Dobb, Maurice. 1933. "Economic Theory and the Problems of a Socialist Economy." *Economic Journal* 43 (December): 588–98.

Downs, Anthony. 1957. *Economic Theory of Democracy*. New York: Harper and Row.

Drescher, Seymour. 2002. *The Mighty Experiment: Free Labor versus Slavery in British Emancipation*. Oxford: Oxford University Press.

Duff, M. E. Grant. 1881. "Address of the President of Section F, Economics Science and Statistics, of the British Association." *Journal of the Statistical Society of London* 44 (December): 649–59.

Economist. 1883. "Business Notes." 41, no. 2095 (20 October): 1220.

"Economic Science and the British Association." 1877. *Journal of the Statistical Society of London* 40:468–76.

Edgeworth, F. Y. 1877. *New and Old Methods of Ethics, or "Physical Ethics" and "Methods of Ethics."* Oxford: James Parker.

Edgeworth, F. Y. 1881. *Mathematical Psychics*. London: C. Kegan Paul.

Efron, B. 1979. "Bootstrap Methods: Another Look at the Jackknife." *Annals of Statistics* 7:1–26.

Eggen, J. B. 1926. "The Fallacy of Eugenics." *Social Forces* 5 (September): 104–9.

Evans, Merran, Nicholas Hastings, and Brian Peacock. 1993. *Statistical Distributions*. 2d ed. New York: John Wiley and Sons.

[F. S.]. 1926. "Annals of Eugenics." *Journal of the Royal Statistical Society* 89:147–51.

Farebrother, R. W. 1997. "Notes on the History of Elementary Set Methods." In L_1-*Statistical Procedures and Related Topics*, vol. 31, ed. Yadolah Dodge. Institute of Mathematical Statistics Lecture Notes—Monograph Series.

Farrant, Andrew. 2004. "Frank Knight, Worst-Case Theorizing, and Economic Planning: Socialism as Monopoly Politics." *History of Political Economy* 36, no. 4:497–504.

Feigenbaum, Susan, and David M. Levy. 1996. "The Technological Obsolescence of Scientific Fraud." *Rationality and Society* 8:261–76.

Fellowes, Robert. 1801. *Religion without Cant: Or, A Preservative Against*

Lukewarmness and Intolerance; Fanaticism, Superstition, and Impiety. London: J. White.

Fellowes, Robert. 1804. *The Guide to Immortality; or, Memoirs of the Life and Doctrine of Christ, by the Four Evangelists; Digested into one Continued Narrative, According to the Order or time and Place laid Down by Archbishop Newcome; in the Words of the Established Version, with Improvements; and Illustrated with Notes, Moral, Theological and Explanatory; Tending to Delineate the True Character and Genius of Christianity.* London: John White.

Fellowes, Robert. 1807. *A Body of Theology, Principally Practical, in a Series of Lectures.* London: J. Mawman.

[Fellowes, Robert = Philalethes]. 1817. The *History of Ceylon, from the Earliest Period to the Year MDCCCXV; with Characteristic Details of the Religion, Laws, & Manners of the People and a Collection of their Moral Maxims & Ancient Proverbs.* London: John Mawman.

Fetter, Frank A. 1916. *Modern Economic Problems.* New York: Century.

Fetter, Frank A., William B. Bailey, Henry C. Polter, Emily Balch, I. M. Rubinow, C. W. A. Veditz, and Walter E. Willcox. 1907. "Western Civilization and Birth-Rate.-Discussion." *Publications of the American Economic Association,* 3d ser., 8:90–93.

Fisher, Irving. 1907. *The Rate of Interest.* New York: Macmillan.

Fisher, Irving. [1910] 1913. *Elementary Principles of Economics.* New York: Macmillan.

Fisher, Irving. [1909] 1976. *National Vitality, Its Wastes and Conservation.* New York: Arno.

Fisher, Irving. [1930] 1986. *The Theory of Interest.* Fairfield, N.J.: Augustus M. Kelley.

Fontaine, Phillippe. 1997. "Identification and Economic Behavior: Sympathy and Empathy in Historical Perspective." *Economics and Philosophy* 13:261–80.

Friedman, Milton, and L. J. Savage. 1948. "The Utility Analysis of Choices Involving Risk." *Journal of Political Economy* 56:270–304.

Froude, James Anthony. 1885. *Thomas Carlyle: A History of His Life in London, 1834–1881.* New York: Harper and Brothers.

Frye, Northrop. 1963. *The Educated Imagination.* Toronto: Canadian Broadcasting Corporation.

Galbraith, John Kenneth. 1958. *The Affluent Society.* Boston: Houghton Mifflin.

Galton, Francis. 1865. "Hereditary Talent and Character." *Macmillan's Magazine* 12 (June and August): 157–66; 318–27.

Galton, Francis. 1877. "Economic Science and the British Association." *Journal of the Statistical Society of London* 40:468–76.

Galton, Francis. 1885. "Photographic Composites." *Photographic News* 29:243–45.

Galton, Francis. 1892a. *Finger Prints*. London: Macmillan.

Galton, Francis. 1892b. *Hereditary Genius: An Inquiry into its Nature and Consequence*. 2d ed. London: Macmillan.

Galton, Francis. 1904. "Eugenics: Its Definition, Scope, and Aims." *American Journal of Sociology* 10 (July): 1–6.

Galton, Francis. 1907a. "One Vote, One Value." *Nature* 75:414.

Galton, Francis. 1907b. "*Vox Populi*." *Nature* 75:450–51.

Galton, Francis. *Human Faculty*. 1907c. *Inquiries into Human Faculty and Its Development*. 2d ed. London: J. M. Dent.

Galton, Francis. 1908. *Memories of My Life*. London: Methuen.

"Galton's *Human Faculty*." 1883. *Science* 2 (July 20): 79–82.

Gayon, Jean. 1998. *Darwinism's Struggle for Survival: Heredity and the Hypothesis of Natural Selection*. Translated by Matthew Cobb. Cambridge: Cambridge University Press.

George, David. 2001. *Preference Pollution: How Markets Create the Desires We Dislike*. Ann Arbor: University of Michigan Press.

Gibbard, Alan, and Hal R. Varian. 1978. "Economic Models." *Journal of Philosophy* 75:664–77.

Gigerenzer, Gerd, Peter M. Todd, and the ABC Research Group. 1999. *Simple Heuristics That Make Us Smart*. New York: Oxford University Press.

Gilray, James. 1796. *Philanthropic Consolations after the Loss of the Slave-Bill*. Colored etching. Library of Congress Prints and Photographs. PC 1 - 8793 (B size)

Greene, William Chase. 1953. "Platonism and Its Critics." *Harvard Studies in Classical Philology* 61:39–71.

[Greg, W. R.]. "Failure." 1868. "On the Failure of 'Natural Selection' in the Case of Man." *Fraser's Magazine for Town and Country* 78 (September): 353–62.

[Greg, W. R.]. "Realities." 1869a. "Realities of Irish Life." *Quarterly Review* 126:61–80.

Greg, W. R. 1869b. *Why Are Women Redundant?* London: Trübner.

Greg, W. R. 1875. *Enigmas of Life*. Boston: James R. Osgood.

Greg, W. R. 1876. *Mistaken Aims and Attainable Ideals of the Artizan Class*. London: Trübner.

Grose, Francis. [1785] 1968. *A Classical Dictionary of the Vulgar Language*. Menston, England: Scolar.

Grote, George. 1865. *Plato, and the Other Companions of Sokrates*. London: John Murray.

Haakonssen, Knud. 2002. "Introduction." In Adam Smith, *Theory of Moral Sentiments*. Cambridge: Cambridge University Press.

Hacking, Ian. 1975. *The Emergence of Probability: A Philosophical Study of Early Ideas About Probability, Induction, and Statistical Inference*. London: Cambridge University Press.

Hankins, F. H. 1923. "Individual Differences and Democratic Theory." *Political Science Quarterly* 38 (3): 388–412.

Hansen, Bent Sigurd. 1993. "Something Rotten in the State of Denmark: Eugenics and the Ascent of the Welfare State." In *Eugenics and the Welfare State: Sterlization Policy in Denmark, Sweden, Norway, and Finland*, ed. Gunnar Broberg and Nils Roll-Hansen. East Lansing: Michigan State University Press.

Harman, Gilbert. 1986. *Moral Agent and Impartial Spectator*. Lawrence: University of Kansas.

Harris, Abram. 1942. "Sombart and German (National) Socialism." *Journal of Political Economy* 50 (December): 805–35.

Harris, Styron. 1981. *Charles Kingsley: A Reference Guide*. Boston: G. K. Hall.

Hayek, F. A. 1961. "The Non-Sequitur of the 'Dependence Effect.'" *Southern Economic Journal* 27:346–48.

Henderson, James P. 1994. "The Place of Economics in the Hierarchy of the Sciences: Section F From Whewell to Edgeworth." In *Natural Images in Economic Thought: "Markets Read in Tooth and Claw,"* ed. Philip Mirowski, 484–535. Cambridge, New York, and Melbourne: Cambridge University Press.

Hicks, J. R. 1939. "The Foundations of Welfare Economics." *Economic Journal* 49:696–712.

Hill, Alicia, Richard Whately, and Samuel Hinds. 1852. "American Slavery and *Uncle Tom's Cabin*." *North British Review* 18:235–58.

Hilton, Boyd. 1988. *The Age of Atonement: The Influence of Evangelicalism on Social and Economic Thought, 1795–1865*. Oxford: Clarendon Press.

History of Political Economy. 1972. "Papers on the Marginal Revolution in Economics." *History of Political Economy* 4, no. 2.

Hogben, Lancelot. 1931. "The Foundations of Social Biology." *Economica*, no. 31 (February): 4–24.

Hogben, Lancelot. 1998. *Scientific Humanist: An Unauthorized Autobiography*. Ed. Adrien and Anne Hogben. Suffolk, UK: Merlin Press.

Holden, Christine, and David M. Levy. 1993. "Birth Control and the Amelioration Controversy." *History of Political Economy* 25:285–313.

Holden, Christine, and David M. Levy. 2001. "From Emotionalized Language to Basic English: The Career of C. K. Ogden and/as 'Adelyne More.'" *Historical Reflections /Réflexions Historiques* 27:79–105.

Hollander, Samuel. 1985. *The Economics of John Stuart Mill*. Oxford: Basil Blackwell.

Hollander, Samuel. 1997. *The Economics of Thomas Robert Malthus*. Toronto: University of Toronto Press.

Holmes, S. J. 1926. "Annals of Eugenics: A Journal for the Scientific Study of Racial Problems." *Science*, n.s., 63:232–33.

Holmes, S. J. 1939. "The Opposition to Eugenics." *Science*, n.s., 89 (o.s., 2312):351–57.

Hoover, K. D. 2001. *Causality in Macroeconomics.* Cambridge: Cambridge University Press.

Houser, Daniel. 2004. "Ethics and Experimental Economics." Public Choice Working Paper.

Howse, Ernest Marshall. 1952. *Saints in Politics: The "Clapham Sect" and the Growth of Freedom.* London: Allen and Unwin.

Hume, David. [1739–40] 1978. *A Treatise of Human Nature.* Ed. L. A. Selby-Bigge. Revised by P. H. Nidditch. 2d ed. Oxford: Clarendon Press.

[Hunt, James]. 1863a. "Kingsley's *Water Babies.*" *Anthropological Review* 1:472–76.

Hunt, James. "Negro's Place." [1863b] 1864. "The Negro's Place in Nature: A Paper read before the London Anthropological Society." New York: Van Eurie, Horton, and Co.

[Hunt, James]. 1866a. "On the Negro Revolt in Jamaica." *Popular Magazine of Anthropology* 1 (January): 14–20.

[Hunt, James]. 1866b. "Race in Legislation and Political Economy." *Anthropological Review* 4 (April): 113–35.

Hutcheson, Francis. [1725] 1971. *An Inquiry into the Original of our Ideas of Beauty and Virtue.* Hildesheim: Georg Olms.

Hutchison, T. W. 1953. *Review of Economic Doctrines, 1870–1929.* Oxford: Clarendon.

Huxley, T. H. 1870. "Professor Huxley on Political Ethnology." *Anthropological Review* 8:197–204.

Huxley, T. H. [1894] 1934. "Evolution and Ethics Prolegomena." In *Readings from Huxley*, 2d ed., Clarissa Rinaker, 65–100. New York: Harcourt, Brace.

Ingram, J. K. 1878. "Address of the President of Section F of the British Association." *Journal of the Royal Statistical Society* 41 (August): 602–29.

Jacobs, Joseph. 1885. "The Jewish Type, and Galton's Composite Photographs." *Photographic News* 29:268–69.

Jenkin, F. 1887. *Papers, Literary, Scientific, &c.* London and New York: Longmans, Green.

Jevons, W. S. 1869. "A Deduction from Darwin's Theory." *Nature* 1 (December 30): 231–32.

Jevons, W. S. 1870. "Opening Address of the President of Section F (Economic Science and Statistics), of the British Association for the Advancement of Science." *Journal of the Royal Statistical Society of London* 33, no. 3 (September): 309–26.

Jevons, W. S. [1871] 1911. *The Theory of Political Economy.* 4th ed. London: Macmillan.

Jevons, W. S. [1876] 1905. "The Future of Political Economy." In *Principles of Economics: A Fragment of a Treatise on the Industrial Mechanism of Society and Other Papers*, 187–206. New York: A. M. Kelley.

Jevons, W. S. [1876] 1965. "Amusements of the People." Reprinted in *Methods of Social Reform*, 1–27. London: Macmillan, [1883] 1965.

Jevons, William Stanley. 1879. "John Stuart Mill's Philosophy Tested. iv. Utilitarianism." *Contemporary Review* 36 (November): 521–38.

Jevons, W. S. [1883] 1965. *Methods of Social Reform*. London. Macmillan.

Jevons, W. S. [1884] 1964. *Investigations in Currency and Finance*. Ed. H. S. Foxwell. London: Macmillan.

Jevons, W. S. 1972–81. *Papers and Correspondence of William Stanley Jevons*. Ed. R. D. C. Black. London: Macmillan.

Kaldor, Nicholas. 1939. "Welfare Propositions of Economics and Interpersonal Comparisons of Utility." *Economic Journal* 49:549–52.

Keith, Arthur. 1917. "Presidential Address. How Can the Institute Best Serve the Needs of Anthropology?" *Journal of the Royal Anthropological Institute of Great Britain and Ireland* 47:12–30.

Keith, Arthur. 1920. "Galton's Place among Anthropologists." *Eugenics Review* 12 (April): 14–28.

Keynes, J. M. 1937. "Some Economic Consequences of a Declining Population." *Eugenics Review* 291 (April 1937–January 1938): 13–17.

[Keynes, John Maynard = K]. (1943) "Obituary: Leonard Darwin." *Economic Journal* 53 (December): 438–48.

Kiernan, J. L. 1864. *Ireland and America, versus England, from a Fenian Point of View*. Detroit: George W. Pattison.

King, Martin Luther. 1963. *Martin Luther King, Jr. Papers Project*. http://www.stanford.edu/group/King/

[Kingsley, Charles]. 1850. *Alton Locke, Tailor and Poet: An Autobiography*. New York: Harper and Brothers.

Kingsley, Charles. 1855. *Glaucus*. Cambridge: Macmillan.

Kingsley, Charles. 1862–63. "The Water-Babies: A Fairy Tale for a Land-Baby." *Macmillan's Magazine* 6–7 (August 1862–January 1863).

Kingsley, Charles. 1863 *The Water-Babies: A Fairy Tale for a Land-Baby*. London and Cambridge: Macmillan.

Kingsley, Charles [1863] n.d. *The Water-Babies: A Fairy Tale for a Land-Baby*. New edition, New York: Macmillan.

Kingsley, Charles. [1863] 1885. *The Water-Babies: A Fairy Tale for a Land-Baby*. Illustrated by Linley Sambourne. London: Macmillan.

Kingsley, Charles. 1864. *The Roman and the Teuton: A Series of Lectures Delivered Before the University of Cambridge*. Cambridge and London: Macmillan.

Kingsley, Charles. [1871] 1874. "The Natural Theology of the Future." In *Westminster Sermons, with a Preface*. London: Macmillan.

Klein, Judy L. 1997. *Statistical Visions in Time: A History of Time Series Analysis, 1662–1938*. Cambridge: Cambridge University Press.

Knight, Frank H. 1931. "Professor Fisher's Interest Theory: A Case in Point." *Journal of Political Economy* 39:176–212.

Koot, G. M. 1975. "T. E. C. Leslie, Irish Social Reform, and the Origins of the English Historical School of Economics." *History of Political Economy* 7, no. 3: 312–36.

Leaves of Grass Imprints. 1860. *American and European Criticisms on "Leaves of Grass."* Boston: Thayer and Eldridge.

Lehmann, E. L. 1983. *Theory of Point Estimation.* 2d ed. New York: John Wiley.

Leonard, Thomas C. 2003a. "How Progressive Were the Progressives? Eugenics and Progressive-Era Economy." Eastern Economic Association. New York.

Leonard, Thomas C. 2003b. "'More Merciful and Not Less Effective': Eugenics and American Economics in the Progressive Era." *History of Political Economy* 35 (winter): 687–712.

Lerner, A. P. 1934. "Economic Theory and Socialist Economy." *Review of Economic Studies* 2 (October): 51–61.

Leslie, T. E. C. 1873. "Economic Science and Statistics." *Athenaeum* (27 September). Reprinted in *W. S. Jevons: Critical Responses*, ed. Sandra J. Peart, 4:165–70. London: Routledge, 2004.

Leslie, T. E. C. 1879. "Political Economy and Sociology." *Fortnightly Review* 32 (January): 25–46. Reprinted in *W. S. Jevons: Critical Responses*, ed. Sandra J. Peart, 4:215–35. London: Routledge, 2004.

Levinson, Ronald B. [1953] 1970. *In Defense of Plato.* New York: Russell and Russell.

Levitt, Theodore. 1976. "Alfred Marshall: Victorian Relevance for Modern Economics." *Quarterly Journal of Economics* 90, no. 3 (August): 425–43.

Levy, David M. 1978. "Some Normative Aspects of the Malthusian Controversy." *History of Political Economy* 10 (summer): 271–85.

Levy, David M. 1988a. "Increasing the Likelihood Value by Adding Constraints." *Economics Letters* 28:57–61.

Levy, David M. 1988b. "The Market for Fame and Fortune." *History of Political Economy* 20:615–25.

Levy, David M. 1990. "The Bias in Centrally Planned Prices." *Public Choice* 67:213–36.

Levy, David M. 1992a. *Economic Ideas of Ordinary People: From Preferences to Trade.* London: Routledge.

Levy, David M. 1992b. "Public Capital and International Labor Productivity: Tests Based on Median-Unbiased Estimation." *Economics Letters* 39:365–68.

Levy, David M. 1995. "The Partial Spectator in the *Wealth of Nations*: A Robust Utilitarianism." *European Journal of the History of Economic Thought* 2:299–326.

Levy, David M. 1999a. "Katallactic Rationality: Language, Approbation, and Exchange." *American Journal of Economics and Sociology* 58:729–47.

Levy, David M. 1999b. "Malthusianism and Christianity: The Invisibility of a Successful Radical." *Historical Reflections/Réflexions Historiques* 25:61–93.

Levy, David M. 1999/2000. "Non-normality and Exploratory Data Analysis: Problem and Solution." *Econometric Theory* 15:427–28; 16:296–97.

Levy, David M. 2001. *How the Dismal Science Got Its Name: Classical Economics and the Ur-Text of Racial Politics.* Ann Arbor: University of Michigan Press.

Levy, David M., and Sandra J. Peart. 2001–2. "Secret History of the Dismal Science." www.econlib.org.

Levy, David M., and Sandra J. Peart. 2002. "Francis Galton's Two Papers on Voting as Robust Estimation." *Public Choice* 113:357–65.

Levy, David M., and Sandra J. Peart. 2004. "Sympathy and Approbation in Hume and Smith: A Solution to the Other Rational Species Problem." *Economics and Philosophy* 20: 331–49.

Levy, David M., and Sandra J. Peart. 2004a. Contributions. *Dictionary of British Economics.* Ed. Donald Rutherford. London: Thoemmes/Continuum.

Levy, David M., Sandra J. Peart, and Andrew Farrant. 2005. "The Spatial Politics of F. A. Hayek's Road to Serfdom." *European Journal of Political Economy.*

Lindgren, J. Ralph. 1973. *The Social Philosophy of Adam Smith.* The Hague: Martinus Nijhoff.

Lipkes, Jeff. 1999. *Politics, Religion, and Classical Political Economy in Britain: John Stuart Mill and His Followers.* New York: St. Martin's.

Lively, Jack, and John Rees. 1978. *Utilitarian Logic and Politics.* Oxford: Clarendon Press.

Lloyd, W. F. [1837] 1968. *Lectures on Population, Value, Poor Laws, and Rent.* New York: Augustus M. Kelley.

Lorimer, Douglas. 1978. *Colour, Class, and the Victorians.* Leicester: Leicester University Press.

Loury, Glenn C. 2002. *The Anatomy of Racial Inequality.* Cambridge: Harvard University Press.

Lynch, Hollis R. 1965. "Edward W. Blyden: Pioneer West African Nationalist." *Journal of African History* 6:373–88.

MacKenzie, Donald. 1975. "Eugenics in Britain." *Social Studies of Science* 6 (September): 499–532.

Macleod, Helen. 1986. "Charles Kingsley and 'The Water Babies.'" *Book and Magazine Collector* 23:36–43.

Macsyma 2.3 for Windows. 1998. Arlington, Mass.: Macsyma, Inc.

Malthus, T. R. [1798] 2002. *An Essay on the Principle of Population.* www.econlib.org.

Malthus, T. R. [1803] 1989. *An Essay on the Principle of Population.* Ed. Patricia James. Cambridge: Cambridge University Press.

Manvell, Roger. 1976. *The Trial of Annie Besant and Charles Bradlaugh*. New York: Horizon Press.

Marshall, Alfred. 1884. "The Housing of the London Poor." *Contemporary Review* 45 (February): 224–31.

Marshall, Alfred. [1890] 1930. *Principles of Economics*. 8th ed. London: Macmillan.

Marshall, Alfred. 1925. *Memorial of Alfred Marshall*. Ed. A. C. Pigou. London: Macmillan.

Martineau, Harriet. 1834. *Illustrations of Political Economy*. London: Charles Fox.

Maurice, F. D. [1866] 1970. *The Workman and the Franchise*. New York: Augustus M. Kelley.

Maxwell, W. H. 1845. *History of the Irish Rebellion in 1798; with Memoirs of the Union, and Emmett's Insurrection in 1803*. London: Baily, Brothers, Cornill.

Mayr, Ernst. 1963. "The Biology, Genetics, and Evolution of Man." *Quarterly Review of Biology* 38 (September): 243–45.

Mayr, Ernst. 1964. "Introduction." In Charles Darwin, *On the Origin of Species by Means of Natural Selection, or the Preservation of Favoured Races in the Struggle for Life*, vii–xxvii. Cambridge, Mass.: Harvard University Press.

Mayr, Ernst. 1969. "Footnotes on the Philosophy of Biology." *Philosophy of Science* 36 (June): 197–202.

Mayr, Ernst. 1991. *One Long Argument: Charles Darwin and the Genesis of Modern Evolutionary Thought*. Cambridge, Mass.: Harvard University Press.

Mayr, Ernst. 2000. Review of *Darwin's Spectre: Evolutionary Biology in the Modern World*. *Isis* 91 (June): 373–74.

McCloskey, D. N. 1990. "Storytelling in Economics." In *Economics and Hermeneutics*, ed. D. Lavoie, 61–75. London: Routledge.

McDougall, William. 1907. "A Practicable Eugenic Solution." *Sociological Papers* 3:55–89.

McPhail, Edward. 2003. "Chesterton and Eugenics." Paper presented at the History of Economics Society annual meeting, Davis, California.

Mill, James. [1820] 1978. "Essay on Government." In *Utilitarian Logic and Politics*, ed. Jack Lively and John Rees, 53–96. Oxford: Clarendon Press.

Mill, John Stuart. *Essays*. [1836] 1967. "On the Definition of Political Economy; and on the Method of Investigation Proper to It." *Essays on Economics and Society*. Vol. 4 of *Collected Works of John Stuart Mill*, ed. John M. Robson, 309–39. Toronto: University of Toronto Press.

Mill, J. S. [1840] 1961. "Introduction." In Alexis de Tocqueville, *Democracy in America*, trans. Henry Reeve, 2:v–xlix. New York: Schocken.

Mill, J. S. *Logic*. [1843] 1973. *A System of Logic Ratiocinative and Inductive*.

Vols. 7–8 of *Collected Works of John Stuart Mill*, ed. John M. Robson. Toronto: University of Toronto Press.

Mill, J. S. [1845] 1967. *The Claims of Labour*. Vol. 4 of *Collected Works of John Stuart Mill*, ed. John M. Robson, 363–89. Toronto: University of Toronto Press.

Mill, J. S. *Principles*. [1848] 1965. *The Principles of Political Economy with Some of Their Applications to Social Philosophy*. Vols. 2 and 3 of *Collected Works of John Stuart Mill*, ed. John M. Robson. Toronto: University of Toronto Press.

Mill, J. S. [1848] 2002. *The Principles of Political Economy with Some of Their Applications to Social Philosophy*. www.econlib.org.

[Mill, John Stuart]. 1850. "The Negro Question." *Fraser's Magazine for Town and Country* 41:25–31.

[Mill, John Stuart]. 1851. "Newman's Political Economy." Vol. 5 of *Collected Works of John Stuart Mill*, ed. John M. Robson, 441–62. Toronto: University of Toronto Press.

Mill, John Stuart. [1861] *Utilitarianism* 1969. Vol. 10 of *Collected Works of John Stuart Mill*, ed. John M. Robson, 203–59. Toronto: University of Toronto Press.

Mill, J. S. [1861] 1977. *Considerations on Representative Government*. Vol. 19 of *Collected Works of John Stuart Mill*, ed. John M. Robson, 371–577. Toronto: University of Toronto Press.

Mill, J. S. [1865] 1979. *An Examination of the Philosophy of Sir William Hamilton*. Vol. 9 of *Collected Works of John Stuart Mill*, ed. John M. Robson. Toronto: University of Toronto Press.

Mill, John Stuart. [1866] 1978. "Grote's Plato." *Essays on Philosophy and the Classics*. Vol. 11 of *Collected Works of John Stuart Mill*, ed. John M. Robson, 375–440. Toronto: University of Toronto Press.

Mill, John Stuart. [1869] 1970. *The Subjection of Women*. Cambridge: MIT Press.

Mill, J. S. 1972. *The Later Letters, 1849 to 1873*. Vol. 14 of *Collected Works of John Stuart Mill*, ed. John M. Robson. Toronto: University of Toronto Press.

Mirowski, Phillip. 1989. *More Heat Than Light*. Cambridge: Cambridge University Press.

Mirowski, Phillip. 1994. *Natural Images in Economic Thought: "Markets Read in Tooth and Claw."* Cambridge: Cambridge University Press.

Monro, D. H. 1953. *Godwin's Moral Philosophy*. London: Oxford University Press.

More, Hannah. 1840. *The Works of Hannah More*. New York: Harper and Brothers.

Morgan, M. S. 2001. "Models Stories and the Economic World." *Journal of Economic Methodology* 8:361–84.

Morgan, Mary S., and Margaret Morrison. 1999. "Models as Mediating Instruments." In *Models as Mediators: Perspectives on Natural and Social Science*, ed. Mary S. Morgan and Margaret Morrison 10–37. Cambridge: Cambridge University Press.

[Morley, John]. 1866. "Cant and Counter-Cant." *Macmillan's Magazine* 13:75–80.

Mosteller, Frederick, and J. W. Tukey. 1977. *Data Analysis and Regression.* Reading, Mass.: Addison-Wesley.

Mozley, J. R. 1872. "Mr. John Stuart Mill and His School." *Quarterly Review* 133 (July): 77–118.

Muldoon, James. 1975. "The Indian as Irishman." *Essex Institute Historical Collections* 111:267–89.

Myres, John L. 1944. "A Century of Our Work." *Man* (January–February): 1–9.

Newman, Francis W. 1879. "Negro Slavery under English Rule." *Fraser's Magazine*, o.s., 99 (January): 88–106.

Nicholson, J. Shield. 1894. "The Measurement of Utility by Money." *Economic Journal* 4:342–47.

Ospovat, Don. 1981. *The Development of Darwin's Theory: Natural History, Natural Theology, and Natural Selection, 1838–1859.* Cambridge: Cambridge University Press.

The Oxford English Dictionary on Compact Disc. 1992. 2d ed. Oxford: Oxford University Press.

Packe, Michael St. John. 1954. *The Life of John Stuart Mill.* New York: Macmillan.

Paley, William. 1786. *The Principles of Moral and Political Philosophy.* 2d ed. London: R. Faulder.

Pearson, Karl. 1901. *National Life from the Standpoint of Science.* London: Adam and Charles Black.

Pearson, Karl. 1924. *The Life, Letters, and Labours of Francis Galton.* Vol. 2: *Researches of Middle Life.* Cambridge: Cambridge University Press.

Pearson, Karl. 1930. *The Life, Letters, and Labours of Francis Galton.* Vol. 3A: *Correlation, Personal Identification and Eugenics.* Cambridge: Cambridge University Press.

Pearson, Karl. 1936. "Method of Moments and Method of Maximum Likelihood." *Biometrika* 28:34–59.

Pearson, Karl, and Ethel M. Elderton. 1925. "Foreword." *Annals of Eugenics* 1:1–4.

Pearson, Karl, and Margaret Moul. 1925. "The Problem of Alien Immigration into Great Britain, Illustrated by an Examination of Russian and Polish Jewish Children." *Annals of Eugenics* 1:5–55, 56–127.

Peart, Sandra J. 1990. "Jevons's Applications of Utilitarian Theory to Policy Analysis." *Utilitas* 2 (2): 281–302.

Peart, Sandra J. 1995a. "'Disturbing Causes,' 'Noxious Errors,' and the The-

ory-Practice Distinction in the Economics of J. S. Mill and W. S. Jevons."
Canadian Journal of Economics 28:1194–1211.

Peart, Sandra J. 1995b. "Measurement in Utility Calculations: The Utilitarian Perspective." In *Measurement, Quantification, and Economic Analysis: Numeracy in Economics,* ed. Ingrid H. Rima, 63–86. London: Routledge.

Peart, Sandra J. 2000. "Irrationality and Intertemporal Choice in Early Neoclassical Thought." *Canadian Journal of Economics* 33:175–88.

Peart, Sandra J. 2001a. "'Facts Carefully Marshalled' in the Empirical Studies of William Stanley Jevons." In *The Age of Measurement,* annual supplement to vol. 33 of *History of Political Economy,* ed. Judy L. Klein and Mary S. Morgan, 252–76. Durham: Duke University Press.

Peart, Sandra J. 2001b. "Theory, Application, and the Canon: The Case of Mill and Jevons." In *Reflections on the Classical Canon in Economics: Essays in Honor of Samuel Hollander,* ed. Evelyn L. Forget and Sandra J. Peart, 356–78. London: Routledge.

Peart, Sandra J. 2004. "Introduction." *W. S. Jevons: Critical Responses.* Ed. Sandra J. Peart, 1:1–26. 4 vols. London: Routledge.

Peart, Sandra J. 2005. "'Pray Clear the Way, There, for These-ah-Persons': The Status of Women in Classical Political Economy." *Research in the History of Economic Thought and Methodology.*

Peart, Sandra J., and David M. Levy. 2003. "Post-Ricardian British Economics, 1830–1870." In *A Companion to the History of Economic Thought,* ed. Warren Samuels, Jeff Biddle, and John Davis, 130–44. Malden, Mass.: Blackwell.

Peart, Sandra J., and David M. Levy. 2004. "'Not an Average Human Being': How Economics Succumbed to Racial Accounts of Economic Man." In *Race, Liberalism, and Economics,* ed. David Colander, Robert Prasch, and Falguni Sheth, 123–44. Ann Arbor: University of Michigan Press.

Peart, Sandra J., and David M. Levy. 2005. "Valuing (and Teaching) the Past." *Journal of Economic Education* 36 (spring): 171–84.

Persky, Joseph. 1990. "Retrospectives: A Dismal Romantic." *Journal of Economic Perspectives* 4:165–72.

Peters-Fransen, Ingrid. 2001. "The Canon in the History of the Adam Smith Problem." In *Reflections on the Classical Canon in Economics: Essays in Honor of Samuel Hollander,* ed. Evelyn L. Forget and Sandra Peart, 168–84. London: Routledge.

Phelps, Edwin S. 1972. "The Statistical Theory of Racism and Sexism." *American Economic Review* 62:659–61.

Pigou, A. C. 1907. "Social Improvement and Modern Biology." *Economic Journal* 17 (3): 358–69.

Pigou, A. C. 1920. *The Economics of Welfare.* 3d ed. London: Macmillan.

Pike, L. Owen. 1870. "Race in Politics: The 'Celt' and the 'Saxon'." *Anthropological Review* 8:213–15.

Plato. [1937] 1982. *The Republic*. Trans. Paul Shorey. Cambridge, Mass.: Loeb Classical Library.

Plott, Charles R. 1967. "A Notion of Equilibrium and Its Possibility under Majority Rule." *American Economic Review* 57:787–806.

Poliakov, Léon. 1974. *The Aryan Myth: A History of Racist and Nationalist Ideas in Europe*. Translated by Edmund Howard. London: Chatto-Heinemann.

Popper, Karl R. *Open Society* [1945] 1962. *The Open Society and Its Enemies*. 4th ed. New York and Evanston: Harper Torchbooks.

Popper, Karl R. 1974. *Autobiography of Karl Popper*. In *The Philosophy of Karl Popper*, ed. Paul Arthur Schilpp. LaSalle, Ill.: Open Court.

Porter, Theodore M. 1986. *The Rise of Statistical Thinking*. Princeton: Princeton University Press.

Potter, Humphry Tristram. [1800?] *A New Dictionary of All the Cant and Flash Languages, Both Ancient and Modern; Used by Gipsies, Beggars, Swindlers, Shoplifters, Peterers, Starrers, Footpads, Highwaymen, Sharpers, and Every Class of Offenders, From a Lully Prigger to a High Tober Gloak. Carefully Arranged and Selected from the Most Approved Authors, and from the Manuscripts of Jonathan Wild, Baxter, and Others*. London: Printed by W. Mackintosh, and sold by J. Downes.

Prasch, Thomas. 1989. "Which God for Africa: The Islamic-Christian Missionary Debate in Late-Victorian England." *Victorian Studies* 33:51–73.

Priestley, Joseph. [1768] 1993. *Essay on the First Principles of Government*. In Joseph Priestley, *Political Writings*, ed. Peter N. Miller. Cambridge: Cambridge University Press.

Proctor, Robert N. 1991. "Eugenics among the Social Sciences." In *The Estate of Social Knowledge*, ed. JoAnne Brown and David K. van Keuren, 175–208. Baltimore: Johns Hopkins University Press.

The Queen v. Charles Bradlaugh and Annie Besant. 18 June 1877. London: Freethought Publishing Company.

Rainger, Ronald. 1978. "Race, Politics, and Science: The Anthropological Society of London in the 1860s." *Victorian Studies* 22:51–70.

Reade, W. Winwood. 1864. *Savage Africa: Being the Narrative of a Tour in Equatorial, Southwestern, and Northwestern Africa; with Notes on the Habits of the Gorilla; on the Existence of Unicorns and Tailed men; on the Slave-Trade; on the Origin, Character, and Capabilities of the Negro, and on the Future Civilization of Western Africa*. New York: Harper and Brothers.

Reid, B. Archdall. 1906. "The Biological Foundations of Sociology." Paper read 24 October 1905, to the Sociological Society, with comments by C. W. Saleeby, H. Ashby, and H. Bernard. *Sociological Papers* 3:3–51.

Reid, Margaret. 1973. "Comment." *Journal of Political Economy* 81:S165–67.

Reid, Thomas. 1788. *Essays on the Active Powers of Man*. Edinburgh: John Bell.

Ricardo, David. [1817] 2003. *On the Principles of Political Economy and Taxation*. www.econlib.org.

Richards, Robert J. 1987. *Darwin and the Emergence of Evolutionary Theories of Mind and Behavior*. Chicago: University of Chicago Press.

Richards, Robert J. 1992. *The Meaning of Evolution: The Morphological Construction and Ideological Reconstruction of Darwin's Theory*. Chicago: University of Chicago Press.

Robbins, Lionel. 1928. "The Representative Firm." *Economic Journal* 38 (September): 387–404.

Robbins, Lionel. 1929. "Notes on Some Probable Consequences of the Advent of a Stationary Population in Great Britain." *Economica*, no. 25 (April): 71–82.

Robbins, Lionel. 1930. "The Present Position of Economic Science." *Economica*, no. 28 (March): 14–24.

Robbins, Lionel. [1932] 1935. *An Essay on the Nature and Significance of Economic Science*. 2d ed., revised and extended. London: Macmillan.

Robbins, Lionel. 1938. "Interpersonal Comparisons of Utility: A Comment." *Economic Journal* 48 (December): 635–41.

Robbins, Lionel. 1939a. *The Economic Basis of Class Conflict and Other Essays in Political Economy*. London: Macmillan.

Robbins, Lionel. [1939b] 1968. *The Economic Causes of War*. New York: Howard Fertig.

Robbins, Lionel. 1952. *The Theory of Economic Policy in English Classical Political Economy*. London: Macmillan.

Robbins, Lionel. 1963. *Politics and Economics: Papers in Political Economy*. New York: St. Martin's Press.

Robbins, Lionel. 1968. *The Theory of Economic Development in the History of Economic Thought*. London: Macmillan.

Robbins, Lionel. 1971. *Autobiography of an Economist*. London: Macmillan.

Robbins, Lionel. 1972. *Technology and Social Welfare*. Joseph Wunsch Lecture. Haifa, Israel Institute of Technology.

Robbins, Lionel. 1981. "Economics and Political Economy." *American Economic Review* 71 (May): 1–10.

Robertson, D. H. 1923. "A Word for the Devil." *Economica*, no. 9 (November): 203–8.

Rousseeuw, Peter J., and Annick M. Leroy. 1987. *Robust Regression and Outlier Detection*. New York: John Wiley and Sons.

Rubinstein, Ariel. 2000. *Economics and Language*. Cambridge: Cambridge University Press.

Ruse, Michael. 1985. "Admayration." *Quarterly Review of Biology* 60 (January): 183–92.

Ruse, Michael. 1999. "Afterwords: Two Decades Later." In *The Darwin Revolution: Science Red in Tooth and Claw*. 2d ed. Chicago: University of Chicago.

Ruskin, John. [1851–53] 1921–27. *The Stones of Venice*. London: J. M. Dent and Sons.

Ruskin, John. [1860] 1905. "'Unto This Last.'" In *The Works of John Ruskin*, ed. E. T. Cook and Alexander Wedderburn, 17:1–114. London: George Allen.

Ruskin, John. [1883] 1908. *The Art of England*. In *The Works of John Ruskin*, ed. E. T. Cook and Alexander Wedderburn, 33:255–408. London: George Allen.

Ruskin, John. 1893. *Ruskin on Himself and Things in General*. Ed. William Lewin. Illustration by J[ohn] W[allace]. *Cope's Smoke Room Booklet* 13. Liverpool.

Rutherford, Malcolm. 2003. "American Institutional Economics in the Interwar Period." In *A Companion to the History of Economic Thought*, ed. Warren J. Samuels, Jeff E. Biddle, and John B. Davis, 360–76. Malden, Mass.: Blackwell.

Ryle, Gilbert. 1947. Review of *The Open Society and Its Enemies*. *Mind* 56 (April): 167–72.

Samuelson, Paul A. 1943. "Further Comments on Welfare Economics." *American Economic Review* 33:605.

Savage, Leonard J. 1972. *Foundations of Statistics*. 2d rev. ed. New York: Dover.

Schiller, F. C. S. 1914. Review of A. G. Poper, *Ancient Eugenics*. *Eugenics Review* 6:62–63.

Schiller, F. C. S. [1932] 1984. *Social Decay and Eugenical Reform*. New York: Garland.

Schiller, F. C. S. 1934. *Must Philosophers Disagree? And Other Essays in Popular Philosophy*. London: Macmillan.

Schliesser, Eric. 2003. "The Obituary of a Vain Philosopher: Smith's Reflections on Hume's Life." *Hume Studies* 29, no. 2 (November):327–62.

Schochet, Gordon. 2001. "The Political Economy of Rights: Francis Hutcheson and Adam Smith." Eighteenth-Century Scottish Studies Society. Arlington.

Schumpeter, J. A. 1954. *A History of Economic Analysis*. New York: Oxford University Press.

Schumpeter, Joseph A. 2002. "New Translations from *Theorie der wirtschaftlichen Entwicklung*." Translated by Markus C. Becker and Thorbjørn Knudsen. *American Journal of Economics and Sociology* 61:405–37.

Scitovsky, T. 1942. "A Reconsideration of the Theory of Tariffs." *Review of Economic Studies* 9:89–110.

Sebastiani, Silvia. 2001. "Race and Nations in Eighteenth-Century Scotland: Kames, Dunbar, and Pinkerton." Eighteenth-Century Scottish Studies Society. Arlington.

Semmel, Bernard. 1962. *The Governor Eyre Controversy*. London: Macgibbon and Kee.

Sen, A. K. 1991. "Welfare, Preference, and Freedom." *Journal of Econometrics* 50 (1–2): 15–29.

Senior, Nassau W. [1836] 1938. *An Outline of the Science of Political Economy.* London: G. Allen and Unwin.

Senior, Nassau W. 1860. "Opening Address of Nassau W. Senior, Esq., as President of Section F (Economic Science and Statistics), at the Meeting of the British Association, at Oxford, 28th June, 1860." *Journal of the Statistical Society of London* 23:357–61.

Shackleton, R. [1972] 1993. "The Greatest Happiness of the Greatest Number: The History of Bentham's Phrase." In *Jeremy Bentham: Critical Assessments*, ed. Bhikhu Parekh, 353–67. London: Routledge.

Shatto, Susan. 1988. *The Companion to* Bleak House. London: Unwin Hyman.

Shearmur, Jeremy. 2003. "Re: Viner on the Open Society." E-mail to the authors.

Shorey, Paul. [1903] 1960. *The Unity of Plato's Thought.* Chicago: University of Chicago Press.

Shorey, Paul. 1933. *What Plato Said.* Chicago: University of Chicago Press.

Simpson, J. A. 1982. *Concise Oxford Dictionary of Proverbs.* Oxford: Oxford University Press.

Sisson, Edward O. 1940. "Human Nature and the Present Crisis." *Philosophical Review* 49, no. 2:142–62.

Smith, Adam. *Theory of Moral Sentiments.* [1759] 2002. *Theory of Moral Sentiments.* www.econlib.org.

Smith, Adam. WN. [1776] 1976. *An Inquiry into the Nature and Causes of the Wealth of Nations.* Ed. W. B. Todd. Oxford: Clarendon Press.

Smith, Adam. *Wealth of Nations.* [1776] 2002. *An Inquiry into the Nature and Causes of the Wealth of Nations.* www.econlib.org.

Smith, Adam. 1977. *The Correspondence of Adam Smith.* Ed. Ernest Campbell Mossner and Ian Simpson Ross. Oxford: Clarendon.

Smith, Adam. 1978. *Lectures on Jurisprudence.* Ed. R. L. Meek, D. D. Raphael, and P. G. Stein. Oxford: Clarendon.

Smith, John Maynard. 1982. *Evolution and the Theory of Games.* Cambridge: Cambridge University Press.

Soloway, Richard A. 1995. *Demography and Degeneration: Eugenics and the Declining Birthrate in Twentieth-Century Britain.* Chapel Hill: University of North Carolina.

Sombart, Werner. 1951. *The Jews and Modern Capitalism.* Translated by M. Epstein. Introduction by Bert F. Hoselitz. Glencoe, Ill.: Free Press.

Southern Literary Messenger. 1863. "London Punch." *Southern Literary Messenger* 37, no. 12 (December): 711–18.

Spencer, Frank. 1986. *Ecce Homo: An Annotated Bibliographic History of Physical Anthropology.* New York: Greenwood.

Spencer, Frank. 1990. *Piltdown: A Scientific Forgery.* London: Natural History Museum Publications.

Spencer, Herbert. 1851. *Social Statics: or, the Conditions Essential to Human Happiness Specified, and the First of them Developed.* London: John Chapman.

[Spencer, Herbert]. 1852. "A Theory of Population, Deduced from the General Law of Animal Fertility." *Westminster Review* 1, n.s. (January and April): 468–501.

Spencer, Herbert. [1893] 1978. *The Principles of Ethics.* Indianapolis: Liberty Fund.

Spencer, Herbert. 1904. *An Autobiography.* London: Williams and Norgate.

Spengler, J. J. 1955. "Marshall on the Population Question. Part II." *Population Studies* 91:55–66.

Spengler, J. J. 1966. "The Economist and the Population Question." *American Economic Review* 56 (March): 1–24.

Squiers, Carol. 2001. *Perfecting Mankind: Eugenics and Photography.* New York: International Center of Photography.

Stepan, Nancy. 1982. *The Idea of Race in Science.* Hamden, Ct.: Archon.

Stephen, L. 1900. *The English Utilitarians.* London: Duckworth and Co.

Stigler, George J. 1941. *Production and Distribution Theories.* New York: Macmillan.

Stigler, George J. 1965. *Essays in the History of Economics.* Chicago: University of Chicago Press.

Stigler, George J., and Gary S. Becker. 1977. "De Gustibus Non Est Disputandum." *American Economic Review* 67:76–90.

Stigler, Stephen M. 1986. *The History of Statistics: The Measurement of Uncertainty before 1900.* Cambridge, Mass.: Belknap Press of Harvard University Press.

Stigler, Stephen M. 1999. *Statistics on the Table: The History of Statistical Concepts and Methods.* Cambridge, Mass.: Harvard University Press.

Stocking, George W., Jr. 1971. "What's in a Name? The Origins of the Royal Anthropological Institute, 1837–71." *Man* 6 (September): 369–90.

Stone, Richard. 1980. "Political Economy, Economics, and Beyond." *Economic Journal* 90:719–36.

Sugden, Robert. 2002. "Beyond Sympathy and Empathy: Adam Smith's Concept of Fellow-Feeling." *Economics and Philosophy* 18:63–87.

Thomson, J. Arthur. 1906. "The Sociological Appeal to Biology." Paper read 14 March to the Sociological Society. *Sociological Papers* 3:157–94.

Thorndike, Lynn. 1923–58. *A History of Magic and Experimental Science.* New York: Columbia University Press.

Toye, John. 2000. *Keynes on Population.* Oxford: Oxford University Press.

Twain, Mark. [1885] 1982. *Adventures of Huckleberry Finn.* In *Mississippi Writings,* 611–912. New York: Library of America.

Vaughn, Karen I. 1994. *Austrian Economics in America: The Migration of a Tradition.* Cambridge: Cambridge University Press.

Viner, Jacob. 1963. "The Economist in History." *American Economic Review* 53 (May): 1–22.

Von Mises, Ludwig. 1949. *Human Action.* London: William Hodge.

Wald, Abraham. [1950] 1971. *Statistical Decision Functions.* Bronx: Chelsea.

Walker, D. P. 1975. *Spiritual and Demonic Magic.* Notre Dame: University of Notre Dame Press.

Walker, Francis A. [1881] 1995. "The Colored Race in the United States." *Forum* 2:501–9. Reprinted in *Economics and Discrimination,* ed. William Darity Jr., 33–41. Brookfield, Vt.: Edward Elgar.

Wallace, A. R. 1864. "The Origin of Human Races and the Antiquity of Man Deduced from the Theory of 'Natural Selection.'" *Journal of the Anthropology Society* 2:clviii–cixx.

[Wallace, John]. 1878a. *Peerless Pilgrimage to Saint Nicotine of the Holy Herb.* Painting. David M. Levy private collection.

[Wallace, John]. 1878b. *Peerless Pilgrimage to Saint Nicotine of the Holy Herb.* Poster. On exhibition at the Fraser Collection, University of Liverpool Library.

[Wallace, John]. 1879. *In Pursuit of Diva Nicotina.* On exhibition at the Fraser Collection, University of Liverpool Library.

Wallas, Graham. 1898. *The Life of Francis Place, 1771–1854.* London: Longmans, Green.

Webb, Sidney. 1910. "Eugenics and the Poor Law: The Minority Report." *Eugenics Review* 2:3 (November): 233–41.

Weekley, Ernest. 1921. *An Etymological Dictionary of Modern English.* London: John Murray.

Wells, H. G. 1904. "Discussion of Galton 'Eugenics: Its Definition, Scope, and Aims.'" *American Journal of Sociology* 10 (July): 10–11.

Wells, H. G. 1931. "Introductory Remarks." *Economica,* no. 31 (February): 1–4.

Whately, Richard. 1831. *Introductory Lectures on Political Economy.* London: B. Fellowes.

Whately, Richard. [1832] 2002. *Introductory Lectures on Political Economy.* 2d ed. www.econlib.org.

Whately, Richard. 1833. *Easy Lessons on Money Matters; For the Use of Young People.* London: J. W. Parker.

Whistler, Diana, Kenneth J. White, S. Donna Wong, and David Bates. 2001. *Shazam Version 9.0 User's Reference Manual.* Vancouver: Northwest Econometrics.

White, Michael V. 1994. "Bridging the Natural and the Social: Science and Character in Jevons's Political Economy." *Economic Inquiry* 32 (July): 429–44.

Whitman, Walt. 1982. *Complete Poetry and Collected Prose.* New York: Library of America.

Wilberforce, Robert Isaac, and Samuel Wilberforce. 1840. *The Correspondence of William Wilberforce*. London: John Murray.

Wilberforce, William. [1797] 1854. *A Practical View of the Prevailing Religious System of Professed Christians in the Higher and Middle Classes in the Country; Contrasted with Real Christianity*. London: Bohn.

Winch, Donald. 1972. "Marginalism and the Boundaries of Economic Science." *History of Political Economy* 4 (2): 325–43.

Wittman, Donald A. 1995. *The Myth of Democratic Failure*. Chicago: University of Chicago Press.

Wood, Marcus. 2000. *Blind Memory: Visual Representations of Slavery in England and America, 1750–1865*. London: Routledge.

Young, Robert J. C. 1995. *Colonial Desire: Hybridity in Theory, Culture, and Race*. London: Routledge.

Zlotnick, Susan. 2004. "Contextualizing David Levy's 'How the Dismal Science Got Its Name'; or Revisiting the Victorian Context of David Levy's History of Race and Economics," with a response by David Levy and Sandra Peart. In *Race, Liberalism, and Economics*, ed. David Colander, Robert Prasch, and Falguni Sheth, 85–99, 73–81. Ann Arbor: University of Michigan Press.

NAME INDEX

SUBJECT INDEX

abstract economic man, 5, 7, 9–11,
  39–40, 86; as different from idiosyncratic man, 60
actors and agents, economic, xi,
  11–13, 32
"Adam Smith Problem," 141n. *See
  also* sympathy
Æsop, fables of, 129n
affection, as habitual sympathy, 135,
  137
alcoholism. *See* racial "inferior(ity)"
Alton Locke (Kingsley), 139
"Am I Not a Man and a Brother?"
  16, 42, 145, 243; Wedgewood
  image, 16, 188–89
analytical egalitarianism, xiv–xv,
  3–6, 10, 15–16, 109, 125n, 237–39
analytical hierarchicalism, xiv–xv, 4,
  15–16, 238. *See also* eugenics
anecdotes. *See* proverbs and anecdotes
Annals of Eugenics (Pearson), 93–98
Anthropological Review (Hunt), 33,
  41, 42n, 60, 68, 71n, 143, 177
Anthropological Society of London,
  32n, 35n, 46–47, 52, 59, 60–61, 67,
  155
anthropologists, nineteenth-century:
  attack on Mill, 154–55, 156 (Hunt);
  view of Africans, 172–74
anthropology, nineteenth-century,
  xi–xii, 10, 12, 32, 52, 165–66, 244;

on human development, 171;
  opposition to, 177–79; racial views,
  131
antislavery movement, 16–17, 155,
  163–67, 174–75; paternalistic opposition to, 173
Anti-Slavery Reporter, 174–75
approbation, xiii, 7, 12, 21, 22, 131–33,
  137, 244–46. *See also* compensation
Austrian school of economics, 4n, 12,
  85
Autobiography (Mill), 225

behavior, self-directed, 10, 13
biological improvement, 143; and
  perfection, 130–31, 148, 210; and
  self-interest, 147. *See also* "general
  good"
biologists, nineteenth-century, xi–xii,
  xiv, 4n, 22, 146
birth control, 5, 24, 78n, 82, 115n,
  211–20, 224, 226, 233, 237n
birth-control movement. *See*
  neo-Malthusian movement
birth rates, 78–79, 81n, 223n
Bleak House (Dickens), 22, 139–40,
  188
Bradlaugh-Besant case, 151,
  223–26
breeding, human. *See* human breeding

315